The Chinese Postmodern

The Chinese Postmodern

Trauma and Irony in Chinese Avant-Garde Fiction

Xiaobin Yang

Ann Arbor
The University of Michigan Press

Copyright © by the University of Michigan 2002
All rights reserved
Published in the United States of America by
The University of Michigan Press
Manufactured in the United States of America
⊚ Printed on acid-free paper

2005   2004   2003   2002   4   3   2   1

No part of this publication may be reproduced,
stored in a retrieval system, or transmitted in any form
or by any means, electronic, mechanical, or otherwise,
without the written permission of the publisher.

A CIP catalog record for this book is available from the British Library.

Library of Congress Cataloging-in-Publication Data

Yang, Xiaobin, 1963–
    The Chinese postmodern: trauma and irony in chinese avant-garde
fiction / Xiaobin Yang.
        p.   cm.
    Includes bibliographical references and index.
    ISBN 0-472-11241-4 (alk. paper)
    1. Postmodernism (Literature)—China.   2. Chinese fiction—20th
century—History and criticism.   I. Title.
PN98.P67   Y35   2002
895.1'3509113—dc21   2001006517

Contents

Preface   vii

INTRODUCTION   The Absolute and the Problematic in Twentieth-Century Chinese Narrative

1. Modernity: The Historical Subject and the Representational Subject   3
2. The Modern Paradigm Destabilized and Displaced   23

PART I   Trauma, *Nachträglichkeit,* and the Unrepresentable: Conjuring up the Psychic/Historical Past

3. Trauma and Historical Violence in Communist China   47
4. Yu Hua: The Past Remembered or the Present Dismembered   56
5. Can Xue: Ever-Haunting Nightmares   74

PART II   Irony as Verbal Catachresis: Schizophrenia in the Master Discourse

6. Irony and an Alternative Reading of Maoist Discourse   95
7. Xu Xiaohe: Laughter from Despair   111
8. Can Xue: Discursive Dystopias   129

PART III Irony as Structural Parody:
Deconstructing the Grand Narrative

9. Narratorial Parabasis and *Mise-en-Abyme*:
   Ma Yuan as a Model   153

10. Ge Fei: Indeterminate History and Memory   168

11. Yu Hua: Perplexed Narration and the Subject   188

12. Mo Yan's *The Republic of Wine:* An Extravaganza
    of Decadence   207

    POSTSCRIPT Answering the Question:
    What Is the Postmodern/Post–Mao-Deng?   230

    Notes   247

    Glossary   263

    Bibliography   269

    Index   281

Preface

The conceptualization of this work harks back to the early days when I was working at the Institute of Literature, Shanghai Academy of Social Sciences. Modern Chinese literature had not been my major interest before my graduation from college. The advent of Ma Yuan, Can Xue, Han Shaogong, Mo Yan, and Xu Xiaohe around the mid-1980s changed my view of contemporary Chinese literature. I wrote something on Ma Yuan (the first to apply postmodern theory to Chinese literary criticism, according to a fairly comprehensive bibliography of Chinese postmodernism [see Zhang Guoyi 323]) and then the rest of the cohort, in the last few years of the 1980s, with the help of some postmodern theories (Fredric Jameson, Terry Eagleton, and Ihab Hassan, among others) I was exploring at the time. I subsequently took up a book project on Theodor Adorno, Walter Benjamin, and Herbert Marcuse, whose theories have had tremendous influence on this work. My essay on Ma Yuan and postmodernism was commended by Howard Goldblatt, who encouraged me to study with him in 1989 at the University of Colorado, Boulder, where naturally I was fascinated by Mo Yan, as well as everything that stylizes Goldblatt's cultural world: Jessye Norman's Richard Strauss, Philip Kaufman's Milan Kundera, and, of course, his own Xiao Hong.

The theoretical framework of this book was developed from the two graduate seminars I attended at Yale. The decisive event was Jean-François Lyotard's seminar on Freud and Kant in spring 1992. I remember visiting his office one day near the end of the semester for a discussion of the final project, which for some reason I mistakenly thought would not necessarily be a research paper. While waiting outside of his office at Whitney Humanities Center, I was told by a fellow student sitting next to me that Lyotard did in fact expect a paper, which was to be discussed in a moment but about which I had no clue at all. My paper topic—the Chinese avant-garde, historical trauma, and Maoist discourse—was then (forced to be) conceived within the next fifteen or twenty minutes after that student went in, and I was already quite confident when it was my turn. Lyotard supported this topic at the time, and, a month later, I received an A+ for the paper from him. I should also mention Kevin Newmark, whose seminar on the concept of irony was illuminating in terms of theoretical scope and depth. He looked surprised when I, hardly an eloquent participant in class discussion, finally turned in a substantial, though sometimes theoretically "far-fetching" (as he puts it), paper addressing contemporary Chinese literature and the vision of irony by incorporating Adorno's philosophy of "negative dialectics."

As a result of the unfortunate death of Marston Anderson, my advisor at Yale, I, officially still a Yalie, traveled in the early years of the 1990s on weekly basis from New Haven to Columbia University, New York, to work with David Der-Wei Wang, whose incomparably extensive and profound understanding of Chinese literature always attracted my admiration. This book would not be as well rounded without the insightful, and often challenging, advice from David Wang. The chapter on Mo Yan is revised from my paper for Professor Wang's seminar on Chinese decadence.

I would like to extend my gratitude to Kang-i Sun Chang, who guided my academic career in every caring way possible during my years at Yale; to Geoffrey Hartman, whose teachings and conversations (about the Holocaust, in particular) and whose remarks on my earliest manuscript greatly inspired my intellectual imagination; to Yomi Braester, who kindly read an early version of the whole manuscript and made many helpful suggestions; and to Ted Huters, Arif Dirlik, and Xudong Zhang for their comments on one or more portions of this manuscript that were published individually. Two anonymous readers provided valuable comments for the revision of the manuscript. Ingrid Erickson at the University of Michigan Press always offered great help in the whole process.

My thanks also go to the writers, who are not just the subject of this book. The mutual visitations and correspondences with Can Xue, Mo Yan, and Yu Hua over the past few years were often fruitful. My dialogue with Ge Fei, aired by Shanghai Education TV Station in summer 1995, was indeed an educational experience for me. And above all, my perennial friendship with Xu Xiaohe is conducive to closer understandings of his intellectual vision, despite the fact that Zhao Wumian, his nom de plume as a historicocultural critic, is now perhaps more popular than Xu Xiaohe the fiction writer.

I also wish to acknowledge the generous support for this project in different stages from Whiting Fellowship, Pacific Cultural Foundation, John F. Enders Fellowship, Henry Hart Rice Fellowship, and Cheng-Lee Fellowship.

Some chapters have been published previously in different versions. I am thankful to the publishers for granting me permission to use revisions of the following articles: "Maoist Discourse, Trauma, and Chinese Avant-Garde Literature," from *American Imago* 51, no. 2 (autumn 1994); "*The Republic of Wine:* An Extravaganza of Decline," from *Positions: East Asian Cultures Critique* 6, no. 1 (spring 1998); "Answering the Question: What Is Chinese Postmodernism/Post–Mao-Dengism?" from *Chinese Literature in the Second Half of a Modern Century: A Critical Survey* (Indianapolis: Indiana University Press, 2000); "Whence and Whither the Postmodern/Post–Mao-Deng: Historical Subjectivity and Literary Subjectivity in Modern China," in *Postmodernism and China* (Durham: Duke University Press, 2000).

Introduction

The Absolute and the Problematic in Twentieth-Century Chinese Narrative

Chapter 1

Modernity

The Historical Subject and the Representational Subject

The mid-1980s will be remembered as one of the crucial moments of Chinese literary history. "The year 1985," claims Zhao Yiheng (Henry Y.-H. Zhao), "marks a turning point in the development of modern Chinese fiction" ("New Waves" 9).[1] Whether it is a "turning point" once and for all is yet to be fully examined, but to mainland Chinese literature[2] the mid-1980s witnessed the emergence of an alternative cultural/literary paradigm. The dominant literary paradigm in the twentieth century that culminated in the Cultural Revolution was challenged by the so-called avant-garde[3] writing, whose "postmodernity" began a mutiny within the literary discourse of modernity. Avantgarde fiction formed a subversive current that contested the whole paradigm of literary modernity. The self-deconstructive specter that had haunted the entire history of modern Chinese fiction stepped to the foreground.

The Imperative of Grand History and the Mission of Literature

The idea of Chinese modernity, like its Western counterpart, is based on the theory of historical progress in social and intellectual spheres. The fiascoes of the Qing Empire in the wars during the nineteenth century prompted many Chinese to believe that the only way to rescue the nation from decline was through modernization. To modernize China thus meant to propel the Chinese society toward a new, that is, socially, technologically, and economically more advanced, phase. Chinese intellectuals in the twentieth century were excited by this idea that would hopefully salvage the decrepit nation from chaos and backwardness to establish a unified, industrialized state. Here, ironically, the May Fourth intellectuals did not escape the overshadowing tradition of Confucianism, which they relentlessly denounced. Confucianism was modified to stipulate that it was the intellectual's social responsibility to introduce modernity into China. The Confucian moral demand for self-cultivation and social responsibility—embodied in the maxim "inwardly a sage and outwardly a king" (*neisheng waiwang*)—remained in the Chinese intellectual discourse of modernity to uphold superior subjectivity and to serve nationality at the same time.[4] Modernity, best expressed in the Enlightenment discourse (which was later boiled down to Marxism by the communists), came to be the redemptive force to push the nation forward on the globally progressive track of history, whether named socialism, communism, industrialism, commercialism, or transnational capitalism. The intellectual thus must voice the most urgent need of his nation at the time and identify his own subject with the grand historical, national Subject. An imaginary superior, omniscient subject became the ultimate impetus for the writer-as-intellectual to play a role that would convey messages of great historical consequence.

Having said this, however, we must also attend to the fact that the predominant trend of modernity in twentieth-century China was at the same time antimodern. Chinese modernity, as Wang Hui formulates, was a "modernity against modernity" (50). To be more precise, the idea/ideal of modernity was conceived as a way to resist the Western power of modernity and to establish a new nation comparable to the old Chinese Empire in terms of economic and cultural productivity. To examine the blending of premodernity (including the Confucian legacy) in the concept of modernity is to reveal the impurity or even the intrinsic discrepancy within the Chinese conception that nevertheless gives rise to a unique formation of modernity that equally, if not more strongly, requires an absolute historical Subject.

The grand historical Subject, accordingly, can be understood as neither an intellectual created on the principle of purely Cartesian epistemology nor a revolutionary born for the sake of Marxist praxis. It is a hybrid of both *and*, more important, of a modern messenger of the consummation of human history and a premodern sage anticipating the Grand Ultimate (*taiji*). Bemused by the equally significant role in its previous/premodern life, the modern Subject, not unlike Confucius, who struggled to revive a declining dynasty, often took social responsibility for the nation, now in the name of the grand, teleological world history.

Since the beginning of the twentieth century the paradigm of modern Chinese literature has been saturated with the idea of grand history, which postulates a predestined teleological order of historical progress. Historical telos became the primary idea, appealing strongly to the Chinese intellectuals who, from the end of the last century on, were obsessed with the idea of rejuvenating the declining nation. C. T. Hsia's famous characterization of modern Chinese fiction as an "obsession with China" may well be phrased more specifically as "obsession with the redemption of China."5

Writing, an intellectual practice that aims at social (r)evolution or national liberation, is thus obligated to expose unmistakably the oppressive/reactionary and advance the emancipatory/progressive. This was the fundamental idea expressed, explicitly or implicitly, in the canonical literary works of modern Chinese literature, including not only Ba Jin's rebellious *Jia* (Family, 1931) and Guo Moruo's idealistic *Nüshen* (Goddesses, 1921) but also Yu Dafu's sentimental "Chenlun" (Sinking, 1921) and Wen Yiduo's symbolistic *Hongzhu* (Red candle, 1923). Despite the different aesthetic tendencies and political implications, all these works brought out social evils or existential agonies to be condemned and thus hints at their final disappearance. Most typical of all is perhaps Yu Dafu, whose type may include Lu Yin, Bing Xin, and the major Creation Society (*Chuangzao she*) writers in the May Fourth era. Yu's "autobiographical" account of personal experiences conveyed the message of collective emancipation, and his concern about individual destiny expressed the universal concept of national strength.

One of the works carefully contrived on the basis of a "teleological plan" and an "anticipation of the inevitable self-realization of History" is Mao Dun's monumental novel *Ziye* (Midnight, 1932), in which the "capitalist Shanghai will fall, only to beget the new paradise" (D. Wang, *Fictional Realism* 13, 64). In modern Chinese literature, as Theodore Huters observes,

> [The] concept of the modern [. . .] functioned as the major premise lying behind such subsidiary intellectual formulation as democracy, science, self-liberation, and revolution. Literature was

regarded primarily as the vehicle by which one or more of these new and liberating ideas would be brought to China. ("Ideologies" 150–51)

Back at the turn of the last century, Liang Qichao, a major advocate of political reform, proposed that, "if one intends to renovate the people of a nation, one must first renovate its fiction" (74). This culturo-political agenda, stated from the perspective of a social reformist, presaged what would become the primary principle and the widely accepted, though sometimes tacit, standard of modern Chinese literature during the ensuing seven to eight decades: the practical, or at least cognitive, function of literature. Statements by such writers from disparate factions as Guo Moruo, Mao Dun, or even Xu Zhimo prove that their ideas of literature were all associated with social (r)evolution.

To the early Creation Society writers, especially Guo Moruo and Cheng Fangwu, the endorsement of the self-expressiveness of literature, which appears to be a claim to the autonomy of art, certainly has implications to serve the grand agenda of the emancipation of human nature. In his essay "Shengming de wenxue" (Literature of life, 1920), for example, Guo Moruo proposed a so-called literature of life, which is both individual and universal, because life is both autonomous and common (4). His romantic passion, never purely individualistic, took up a more revolutionary stance soon after. He alleged in 1923: "Every real revolutionary movement is an art movement. . . . Every sincere artist who intends social reform is an authentic revolutionary" (17).

It is not surprising, then, that the foremost Creation Society writers grew so hastily from radical romantic individualists to radical leftists only a few years later. When the Creation Society began to advocate "revolutionary literature," the Crescent Society (Xinyue she), often considered a conservative literary coterie, offered an alternative way of literature that is, ironically, by no means antagonistic to the May Fourth cultural paradigm. In the quasi-manifesto of the Crescent Society (the piece harshly castigated by the Creation Society) Xu Zhimo, trained in an Anglo-American tradition rather than influenced by the Soviet Russian ideology, was equally concerned about the destiny of the nation and no less captivated by the discourse of the "reform of human life," even though his tone had not reached as high a revolutionary pitch as the Creation Society. Despite his famous indictment that "thoughts are suffering from the rape by isms!" (*shiji* 182), written in the previous year, Xu Zhimo also envisioned a "creative idealism," which would be embodied in the practice of the awakening of the people and the struggle against the "insult and violation to human dignity and health" ("'Xinyue' de taidu" 10). The example of the Crescent Society demonstrates that even the admittedly most "aesthetic" literary proposal contains a socially practical intention, and thus the voice for the true autonomy of aesthetic value in literature is kept to a minimum. Mao Dun, the most ardent advocate of realistic, or even naturalistic, objectivity, was also fully convinced that "the task of literature is to imbue the accurate representation of real human life with the goal of guiding human life to a more beautiful and better future" (*quanji* 18:539). In his article "Wenxuezhe de xin shiming" (The new mission of writers, 1925), although he was more concerned about "the pain and need of modern mankind," Mao Dun, not unlike Guo Moruo, clearly proposed that "the current mission of the writers is to grasp the spirit of the revolutionary movements of the oppressed nations and classes" in order to "call for a greater and fierier revolutionary movement!" (541).

It has been noted that, although they explicitly opposed the traditional, orthodox doctrine of writing, *wenyizaidao* (literature is to convey principles), the May Fourth iconoclasts engaged even more eagerly than their cultural opponents in a literary movement to cherish literary didacticism. "New literature movement," as Marston Anderson observes, strengthened, rather than weakened, the Chinese literary convention (which the May Fourth intellectuals vehemently attacked) that requires literature to convey principles (20–26). While only the content of the principles (*dao*) was changed, the presumption that the literary text is subjugated to the truth (subjective or objective) remained intact. In other words, the instrumentalization of literature lay in the belief that the function of language, literary language in particular, is to signify as precisely as possible the subjective intention of the author or the objective historical facts (while what is objective is yet to be determined by the subject). The ultimate aim of literature became to transmit the meaning of the work (the signified) through literary language (the signifier) contrived by the author. In "*Zhongguo xinwenxue daxi zongxu*" (General introduction to the *Grand Anthology of Chinese New Literature,* 1935) Cai Yuanpei asked: "Why does transforming ideas have to be associated with literature? Because literature is the *instrument* to transmit ideas" (9; my emph.). In fact, as early as 1925, Mao Dun already proposed that writers "make efforts in the propaganda of proletarian culture" (*quanji* 23:541) and thus replaced traditional didacticism with modern propagandism.

During such an era of sociocultural change, it seems justifiable that the Chinese intellectuals attended more to the practical function of literature than to its aesthetic value. The conception of instrumentalization of literature was not only legitimate to Cai Yuanpei and Mao Dun, who seemed more concerned about the social significance in literature, but also essential to Hu Shi, one of the pioneers of vernacular literature devoting himself primarily to the reform of literary language. In the original preface to his *Changshi ji* (Experiments, 1920), the first collection of *baihua* (vernacular) poems in the history of Chinese literature, Hu Shi stated that only vernacular Chinese can be "used as a *vehicle* of new ideas and new mentalities" (174; my emph.). Whether understood as Cai Yuanpei's concept of "instrument" or Hu Shi's concept of "vehicle," literature was not considered as autonomous as the May Fourth intellectuals took it to be.

Insofar as their undertaking to liquidate traditional Chinese literature was not thoroughly carried out, such theoretical statements in the May Fourth period paved the way for the paradigm of modern Chinese fiction. The authorial intervention in classical Chinese narratives (mainly historiographical narratives) foreshadows the narrative subjectivity in modern Chinese fiction, though it does not mean to create a subjective position to serve the logic of historical modernity.[6] The mode of subjective narration in Chinese tradition was not simply retained but transformed into a rationalizing mechanism to serve history. Modern Chinese fiction endeavors more to convey emancipatory messages than traditional fiction to convey moral messages (which are inserted, often in poetic form, within or at the end of the narrative).

Traditionally, fiction was considered a secondary literary genre to the Chinese literati. Without a fully developed narrative theory, the classical paradigm of Chinese literary aesthetics centers on poetic theory and poetic commentary. What is favored in Chinese poetics is literary nuance and ambiguity on the basis of the withdrawal of a definitive subject from the text. Narrative fiction, especially the vernacular fiction after the Song Dynasty, seems to be a literary genre more accessible to the public and more effective in producing didacticism than poetry. This is why Liang Qichao designated fiction alone to be a means to renovate the nation. This is also why the traditional mode of subjective narration was inherited in modern Chinese fiction.

As we peruse the history of Chinese literature, the subjective intention to "convey the principles" is a far more dominant tendency in the paradigm of modern Chinese literature than in that of traditional Chinese literature, especially because poetry outweighed fiction in Chinese literature until the twentieth century. In classical Chinese poetics neither the Confucian standard that required the practical function to "elevate, observe, congregate, and expostulate" (*xing guan qun yuan*) nor the Confucian maxim "poetry speaks of will" (*shi yan zhi*) that endorsed the authorial intention had a more profound aesthetic influence than the Taoist shibboleth "The way that can be spoken of / Is not the constant way; / The name that can be named / Is not the constant name." Even Confucius himself, as recorded in the *Yijing* (I Ching, or Book of Changes), paid much attention to the insufficiency of language. He admitted that "language cannot exhaust meaning" (*yanbujinyi*) and proposed to approach the truth by replacing language with images and diagrams.

Yan Yu's "Canglang shihua" (Canglang's remarks on poetry), one of the seminal works on Chinese ars poetica, favored a kind of poetic language metaphorized as "an antelope hanging by its horns, leaving no traces to be followed" (688). From this point Yan Yu rejected the principle that poetry conveys ideas: "Poetry has its special source, which has nothing to do with knowledge; poetry has its special gusto, which has nothing to do with conceptions" (688). Like most literary critics in traditional China, Yan Yu concentrated on the technical and rhetorical aspects of poetic writing. He warned against direct or explicit expression that secondary poets usually adopt: "Avoid straight words, avoid shallow meanings, avoid exposed veins, avoid evanescent flavors" (694). This poetic tradition, which originated in Sikong Tu's *Shipin* (Poetic categories) and developed in Wang Shizhen's conception of *shenyun* (spiritual diapason), was epitomized in Wang Guowei's theory of *jingjie*, or *jing*, the scene (from Sanskrit *visaya*, referring to a cosmic domain that incarnates spirituality), which Wang divided into "the scene with self" and "the scene without self" (1). Greatly influenced by Schopenhauer's philosophical attempt to purge the self with desire, Wang Guowei regarded, though implicitly, "the scene without self," which suggested a forgetting of the self or a questioning of the authenticity of the subjective projection, as superior to "the scene with self." In both cases, nevertheless, *jing/jingjie* referred to an objective realm empathized with subjectivity without being directly modified by emotional or intentional diction. As other traditional literary theories and criticisms in China, Wang Guowei's dealt extensively with stylistic, technical, and rhetorical problems when discussing poetic expression. Likewise, *Wenxin diaolong* (The literary mind carving dragons), the most systematic work of literary theory in premodern China, discussed ethical principles of writing only in a few preliminary chapters and elaborated emphatically upon the problems of genres, forms, styles, techniques, etc. Even ethical principles were expressed in aesthetic terms: Shen Deqian's concept of *gediao* (tune), for example, rendered more formalistic and metrical instructions than metaphysical and ethical criterion in complying with the Confucian cultural ideal. His poetic standard, *wenrou dunhou* (gentle and candid), was also to be understood more in a stylistic sense than in a moral sense.

In fact, the retreat or concealment of an authorial/authoritative subject and the emphasis on stylistic technique are among the unique characteristics of classical Chinese aesthetics, including not only poetics, but also theories of narrative, painting, and calligraphy. Traditional narrative criticism, especially that of the literati fiction, was greatly influenced by Chinese poetics. In his Marginalia to the *Honglou meng* (The story of the stone) Zhiyanzhai applauded the poetic "word refining" (*lianzi*) in fictional writing: "It is known to everyone that there is a method of 'word refining' in poetry. Unexpectedly, its excellence has been much achieved in *The Story of the Stone*" (Cao, *Gengchen* 265). Taken from an example of a specific description of Jia Baoyu's action, word refining in such masterworks as *The Story of the Stone* suggested not the author's intention to characterize but, rather, his technique for obtaining the effect of characterization within description per se. Zhiyanzhai's suggestion of the poetic feature in *The Story of the Stone* prevailed in his commentaries. For example, he used elsewhere the statement by Yan Yu, "an antelope hanging by its horns, leaving no traces to be followed," to praise Cao Xueqin's subtle or elusive narrative style without simple and direct authorial tendency (Cao, *Gengchen* 420). Parallel to word refining, "plain drawing" (*baimiao*) was another descriptive technique in the traditional Chinese novel favored by such critics as Jin Shengtan, the commentator of the *Shuihu* (The water margins), and Zhang Zhupo, the commentator of the *Jin ping mei* (The plum in the golden vase). Plain drawing avoided the subjective intervention in narration and endorsed "pure" objectivity.

The May Fourth intellectuals probably considered the sophistication of subjective expression in Chinese poetics a sign of a lack of subjectivity. They embraced omnipotent subjectivity in literary writing according to the Enlightenment discourse, which sanctions the use of unconstrained human power to achieve emancipation. As Lu Xun acknowledged: "As for why I wrote fiction, I still uphold the principle of 'enlightenment,' which I upheld more than a decade ago. I think it must 'serve life' and furthermore reform life. . . . Thus my subjects were often taken from the wretched people in this sick society; my aim was to expose the disease so as to draw attention to its cure" (*quanji* 4:512). The aim to "serve life," on the one hand, inherits the Confucian legacy of helping with social improvement and, on the other hand, accepts the Enlightenment idea that establishes a superior subjective position in literary writing and social practice. Here Marston Anderson observes, "[Realism's] high estimation of the critical observer's stance is anchored in the Enlightenment faith in the capacity of human beings to free themselves from superstition and prejudice through the exercise of their faculty of reason" (11). In this sense the theme of cultural Enlightenment that haunted the intellectuals and writers in the May Fourth period may well be taken from both its external appearance, i.e., the historical messages, and its internal mechanism, i.e., the representational mode of writing. In other words, the *historical subject* (one who possesses a consciousness of the mission to serve, or even lead, the progress of history) must be realized in the formation of the *representational subject* (one who possesses a consciousness of the task of writing as a direct rendering of historical truth). Historical subjectivity (from which the political discourse derives) and representational subjectivity (from which the literary canon develops) consist of the two major aspects of the discourse of Chinese modernity.

Anderson has convincingly demonstrated that Chinese realism, the canonical paradigm of modern Chinese fiction, was intended to engage literature in social reality to form the didactic schema of the intellectual enlightenment (27–37). Replacing traditional didacticism with modern didacticism signals the failure of any "scientific," ideology-free ideal of realism, partly because the epistemological basis of realism, which exists on the assumption that language can rationally reflect or represent reality, is itself ideological. Representational realism insists on the reconciliation of consciousness and reality, of the perception and the perceived, and of the subjective and the objective. But, as Adorno says: "By appearing as art, that which insists that it is realistic injects meaning into reality, which such art is pledged to copy without illusion. In the face of reality this is a priori ideological. Today the impossibility of realism is not to be concluded on inner aesthetic grounds but equally on the basis of the historical constellation of art and reality" (*Aesthetic* 322). I would like to argue that Chinese realism, too, depends on authorial manipulation in order to "inject meaning into reality."

The project of Enlightenment endows the modern Chinese literary paradigm not only with historical subjectivity, which establishes a teleological order of social progress, but also with representational subjectivity, which assumes an infinite capacity to interpret human and social existence. If to represent is to historicize, the authorial voice contains the paradigmatic essence of modern Chinese fiction. The historical subject is unfolded by the power of the representational subject as a means to transmit the homogeneous formation of history.

Lu Xun's intention to "cure" people exemplifies modern Chinese writers' desire to identify themselves with the superior, or supreme, historical subject (metaphorized as a "doctor" to deliver the people from the spiritual pain). Such a superior subject enables the authorial voice to transcend merely objective reality and to speak in an omnipotent way. It is clearly the superior representational subject that was obligated to play the role of the historical subject. The author is empowered with a voice that conforms to the rational logic or imperative of the grand history, of which the main theme is, at least potentially, a progressive history from oppression/repression to emancipation.

The discourse of emancipation—social or individual—was realized and thus embodied in the literary practice insofar as the author possessed the mighty power to textualize and historicize the objective world. This literary paradigm requires a lucid picture represented to the reader so that the meaning can be clearly perceived and easily digested. Through the "avenue of direct communication" and based on belief in a "new language [that] would provide the unmediated voice," "the author is constantly embodying his or her most closely held views" (Huters, "Introduction" 7–8). The subjective tendency exists not only in those works directly associated with pathetic, romantic subjectivity (such as Guo Moruo's poems or Yu Dafu's short stories) but also in those works presumably categorized as realistic (such as Mao Dun's, Lao She's, and Ba Jin's novels). Such a narrative paradigm is, manifestly or covertly, *susceptible to narratorial intervention or manipulation.*

Diegetic Determination in Modern Chinese Fiction

> *Intolerance of ambiguity is the mark of an authoritarian personality.*
> —THEODOR W. ADORNO

Representational subjectivity in the formation of literary modernity was initiated in the late Qing "novels of exposure." In Li Baojia's *Guanchang xianxing ji* (The exposure of the official world, 1905) and Wu Woyao's *Ershi nian mudu zhi guai xianzhuang* (The strange circumstances witnessed over the last twenty years, 1905) authorial responsibility for historical change and progress relied heavily on subjective intervention.[7] Even Liu E, who did not make direct commentaries, infused subjective sentiments and attitudes in his narration. Jaroslav Průšek observes that in *Lao Can youji* (The travels of Lao Can, 1906) Liu E was inclined to "look at things with his own eyes, express his own views and feelings, and put his own experience into his book. The artificial barrier which exists between an author and a completely fictitious character, in novels where the hero has no connection at all with the author, has disappeared" (*Lyrical* 119). Though arbitrarily believing that the distance between the author and his or her character would be "artificial" and thus applauding the "natural" identification of the author with his or her protagonist, Průšek discovers one of the most significant phenomena among modern Chinese narrative. As we shall see, the author not only manipulates his or her characters but, more covertly, his or her narratorial voice as well.

In modern Chinese fiction mimesis is replaced by diegesis, a narrative style that stresses telling in the authorial voice instead of showing without subjective involvement, even though many writers (Mao Dun in particular) desire mimesis in theory.[8] Most typical of all, the diegetic characterization that prevails in modern Chinese fiction impatiently abolishes narrative objectivity and offers direct comments to express the author's subjective attitudes. Mao Dun, for example, in the first chapter of his novel *Hong* (Rainbow, 1929), characterizes his heroine Mei in a diegetic mode:

> She is an extraordinary girl, she is a rainbow-like character, but her original wish is far beyond this, and far more unsatisfied, she is marching forward like a soldier only because the time is different! Her characteristic is "marching forward!" Her only ambition is to conquer the environment and destiny! Her only goal over the past few years was to repress her strong femininity and even stronger maternity! (3)

It would be mistaken to assume that the diegetic tendency results from the fact that Mao Dun was one of the major literary critics at that time and particularly inclined to make direct judgments. In fact, the Chinese tradition of storytelling is a significant factor in the narrative stance of modern fiction, although a traditional Chinese storyteller usually limits his role within the showing of the external appearances.[9] Lao She, a writer influenced equally by Anglo-American realism and Chinese narrative tradition, is not immune from the paradigm of omniscient diegesis. Průšek acutely point out that "Lao She starts from Dickens' novel, in which the author-narrator constantly intervenes in the narration in the same way as the Chinese story-tellers" (*Lyrical* 61). But such intervention extends beyond external characterization. In the first chapter of his novel *Luotuo Xiangzi* (Camel Xiangzi, 1936) we find a passage (similar to Mao Dun's) intended to characterize the protagonist, Xiangzi:

> He was almost like a tree; sturdy, silent and yet alive. He had his own plans and some insight, but he did not enjoy conversation. [Xiangzi] was a peasant; his speech was not as glib as the city fellows'. Assuming that cleverness of speech comes from innate ability, what was innate with him was an unwillingness to talk. (*Luotuo* 7–8 / *Rickshaw* 5–6)

In his popular novel *Family* Ba Jin, by exploiting the characters' own utterances to express the authorial discourses (either about their own roles or about social history), more blatantly implants subjective intention into his narration. Here are some of his characters' words:

"Juehui ... is a humanitarian" (*Jia* 10 / *Family* 15; trans. modified); "Qin is certainly a brave girl" (21/25; trans. modified); "I have to fight too. My condition is even worse than yours" (18/22); "Sichuan has entirely too many feudal moralists, and their influence is very strong" (11/16; trans. modified); "I know that a high price must be paid for any reform to be put through, that many sacrifices must be made" (20/24; trans. modified). All the voices, then, are subsumed under, or subdued under, a single voice of the author in a homogeneous way.

In many cases the subjective intervention may not be in the form of a direct narratorial statement. The narrator's voice might be hidden in the seemingly smooth and realistic representation. One of the most illustrative cases is the excess use of modifiers intended to define what is represented, particularly, those that habitually condition the characters' actions. Tag clauses, for instance, are prevalent in modern Chinese fiction, with "Someone says in a certain way" probably the most preferred syntax; it does not read as an objective account but, rather, clearly guides the reader by categorizing the character's mood or otherwise defining the nature of the episode. The most obvious examples can be drawn, again, from Ba Jin's *Family*, in which such tag clauses are spread throughout: "the more he talked the more excited he became"; "he said in an agitated voice"; "Qin ... said in a trembling voice" (*Jia* 18 / *Family* 22; trans. modified); "the more she talked the more excited Qin became" (20/24; trans. modified).[10] Clearly, a work in which the representational subject is endowed with authoritative power relies much less on imagination, reduces ambiguity, and imposes determinacy. Ironically, from the excessive self-references we perceive boredom with, as well as the hyperbole and absurdity of, the discourses uttered by the representational subject.

Examples can also be taken from Mao Dun's *Midnight*, which begins with stereotypical characterizations. To describe that "the purplish-faced man asked in a loud and arrogant voice" suggests nothing more than the arrogance of that person. This is clear by the next sentence, in which the person is defined directly as "a 'bigwig' accustomed to ordering people about." Right after that, when another character is needed to show a toadyish manner, Mao Dun calls on a person who "stepped forward hastily with his creased smile, and humbly answered" (*Ziye* 4 / *Midnight* 10). Here, obviously, covert subjective intervention enables the reader to catch the simplistic categorizations of the characters (bossy and slavish, in this case) intended by the author/narrator. Průšek argues that Mao Dun, as a writer "striving after maximum objectivity employs a form which . . . was peculiar to his purely subjectively inclined contemporaries" (*Lyrical* 130). Mao Dun's subjective style of writing is by no means restricted, however, to his representations of the mental activities of his characters, as Průšek has found. Průšek is far from correct, therefore, in alleging that in his works Mao Dun avoids expressing his own emotions and viewpoints by "[excluding] the author's person from the narration" and narrating with "the function of *a photographic lens in a camera or of an accurately recording instrument*" (123–24). In fact, Mao Dun typifies the intentional, though sometimes concealed, subjectivity inherent in the paradigm of modern Chinese fiction, in contrast to the Kantian aesthetic standard of "purposiveness without purpose."[11]

The representational subject is expected to bring forth *the historical subject with whom the modern Chinese intellectual aspires to be identified*. Even when an unqualified intellectual is represented, the self-critical impetus establishes a distance between the inept intellectual and the superior author/narrator. We may find that the transcendent subject overshadows such self-reflective narratives as Lu Xun's "Zhufu" (The New Year sacrifice) and Ding Ling's "Shafei nüshi de riji" (Miss Sophie's diary). In the last entry of "Miss Sophie's Diary," for example, the first-person voice shifts abruptly to a third-person one that, calling her own name, observes herself from the viewpoint of a critical subject distanced from the narrator, "I": "All her life Sophie has been too passionate and too sincere about wanting people to understand her and share her feelings. That's why she's been submerged in bitter disappointment for so long" (61). In this way the author disentangles herself from the indefinable flux of experiences and feelings and achieves a superior status that transcends the corporeal but ambiguous female character.

The intellectual "I" in Lu Xun's "The New Year Sacrifice" has been viewed as a self-critical or self-doubting subject who is unable to redeem a lower-class woman (Xianglin's wife) from distress and misfortune. Marston Anderson has astutely noted that Lu Xun exposes the protagonist's "intellectual poverty and, more profoundly, his moral cowardice" (89). The stuttering, uncertain voice of the intellectual character epitomizes the ineffectiveness of enlightenment discourse and the incompetence of a grand historical subject. Nevertheless, on the diegetic level, which reveals the author's attitude, the inept subject is exactly what the confident narrator attempts to critique and negate by establishing a critical distance between them. If we clearly distinguish the narrator from the "I" (the character), we would not miss the narrator's voice that characterizes the "I"'s responses to Xianglin's wife with such words as *falteringly* and *faltered* (*quanji* 2:6 / *Selected Works* 1:171) and describes the "I"'s feeling with such phrases as "preying on my mind" (6/170), "taking fright" (7/171), "feeling thoroughly disconcerted" (7/172), and "remained uneasy" (8/173).

By representing an inferior or unsuccessful historical subject, by distancing itself not only from the character to be redeemed but also from the character who fails to perform redemption (the "I"), the author/narrator secures its *own* status as *the* modern historical subject. In other words, although the intellectual "I" in the story fails to achieve his subjective superiority, Lu Xun ultimately establishes another voice (through the narrator) that formulates a transcendental subject elevated from all the imperfect, "quasi-modern" historical roles. The self-critical perspective yields, ultimately, to another arbitrary voice. It is this invisible but omnipresent historical subject that occupies a position superior not only to the intellectual but also to the lower-class, secondary-gender object of observation (and, it is hoped, of redemption). This is evidenced by the condescending voice in the depiction of Xianglin's wife: "Her shallow, dark-tinged face that looked as if it had been carved out of wood was fearfully wasted and had lost the grief-stricken expression it had borne before" (6/170). This is a picture that calls not merely for pity but also, more significantly, for a desire to deliver the piteous object from that state by the self-elevated historical subject, who is, in this case, not represented by the character but by the narrator.

"Authoritarian narration," Theodore Huters argues, "has [been a] central feature of modern Chinese literature" ("Lives" 271). Omniscient narration and omnipotent expression were increasingly prevalent throughout the history of modern Chinese fiction until the heyday of the Cultural Revolution, for the desire to transmit ideas, or ideologies, became increasingly imperative to the writers who envisioned rapid social progress. Ba Jin's *Family* uses numerous means to impose authorial intention upon the text. If the characters' utterances with highly revolutionary, counterrevolutionary, or vacillating overtones suggest the author's ideological agenda, the overwhelming modifiers that label all the actions of the characters appear to be the most typical use of omniscient narration to transmit ideas. Here Liu Zaifu's theory that "the more a work fails, the more its author can dispose of his characters" (18) is especially pertinent, as long as the author's effort to "dispose of his characters" is understood not only as purposive characterization but also as a purposive attitude of narration.

In communist literature the historical subject and the representational subject function to formulate the absolute imperative of the grand history. Since the major motif of communist literature is the final triumph of the Communist Party, or the Maoist political line, over its enemies, the intended meaning must be represented transparently, without the slightest ambiguity. The authorial tendency is to insert oneself into the text in every detail. Marxist dialectics, which outlines a historical ascension from the struggle between the reactionary and the progressive to the failure of the former and the victory of the latter, serves as the supreme formula and thus the basic structure in communist literature. This can be evidenced by those works from the pre-1949 period, Ding Ling's *Taiyang zhaozai Sangganhe shang* (The sun shines over the Sanggan River, 1948) and Zhou Libo's *Baofeng zhouyu* (The hurricane, 1948), to the Cultural Revolution, the novel *Hongnan zuozhan shi* (The warring history of Hongnan, 1972), Hao Ran's *Jinguang dadao* (The golden road, 1972–74), and the *yangbanxi* (model operas). Historical order can be delineated simply as the victory of the correct party line over its opponents. Communist literature, marking the apogee of historical and representational subjectivity, is carefully designed to legitimize the progressiveness of the Communist Party or to present Mao as the secular savior.

In terms of the representational mode, then, Hao Ran's novels, *Yanyang tian* (Bright sunny sky, 1964–66) and *The Golden Road*, are intimately tied to the canonical novels written in the first half of the century. It is the same narrative omniscience that allows Hao Ran to characterize his communist hero Xiao Changchun in a plain, direct, and functional way: he is "very active and capable of working, especially selfless; the commune members, particularly young people, all uphold him" (*Yanyang tian* 1:18). Indeed, the ideological messages cannot be transmitted effectively in a genuinely "realistic" (if it existed) or impartial narrative: subjective operations are necessary to map out the grand historical project. Such pseudorealism culminates in the novel *The Warring History of Hongnan*, a collective product of propaganda for popularizing Maoist ideologies and policies. The novel demonstrates the paradigm of omniscient narration to the extent that it makes a fifteen-page direct remark—occupying almost all of chapter 25—on the ideas and thoughts of Hong Leisheng, the hero of the novel (Shanghaixian 518–32). Such overt and excessive subjectivity is on the verge of obsolescence, since the superfluous comments on the authorial intentions, on the ideas expressed in the work, and even on how the work is being written, expose—though unwittingly—the potential of self-referentiality, which signals the crisis of narrative consistency. It is simultaneously the zenith and the abyss of representational subjectivity.

The Historical Subject Reconfirmed in "New-Era Literature"

In "new-era literature" (*xinshiqi wenxue*), as Zhang Yiwu argues, "from Wang Meng's 'Hudie' [The butterfly, 1980] to Zhang Wei's *Guchuan* [The old boat, 1986], the justice of History and the power of Time are affirmed, reinforced and ascertained over and over again" ("Lixiangzhuyi" 109). The use of the term *new era* after the death of Mao Zedong in 1976 (which marked the end of the Cultural Revolution) indicated an attempt to open up a new possibility for the nation, which desperately desired to overcome the painful memories of its recent past (a decade of social disturbances and disasters). It seems that, when a dark age comes to an end, literature must perform its social function to help eradicate the bad past and welcome a good future. In his influential 1979 essay "Duiyu wenxue chuangzuo de yige huigu he zhanwang" (A retrospect and prospect of literary production) Feng Mu, a literary critic and "liberal" cultural official, stated optimistically:

> Preceded by the great May Fourth mass movement and starting from the elimination of the vile Gang of Four, our literary production has, along with our socialistic enterprise, entered a new era. . . . Our literary and artistic soldiers and people hail and fight together, get rid of layers of shackles around our bodies together and plunge into a new movement of mental emancipation together, cure the scars on our bodies together, sweep away the obstacles on our path of progress together, and then march bravely together toward the magnificent goal of establishing our country into a strong, modernized socialistic country! (3)

Feng Mu went on to applaud the earliest product of new-era literature—that is, "scar literature" (*shanghen wenxue*), named after Lu Xinhua's 1978 short story "Shanghen" (The scar). Taking the example of "The Scar," he insisted on the practical value of scar literature because it "reflects the gravity of people's trauma and appeals for [*sic*] the importance of curing the wound," even though it may "not be aesthetically mature and perfect" (Feng 6). In the same essay Feng Mu paid special attention to literary works published in 1979 that mark the rise of "new-era literature," such as Jiang Zilong's "Qiao changzhang shangren ji" (Manager Qiao assumes office) and Lu Yanzhou's "Tianyunshan chuanqi" (The legend of Tianyun Mountain).

Taking a closer look at these works, we find that new-era literature consists of two additional categories, labeled by later critics as "retrospective literature" (*fansi wenxue*) and "reform literature" (*gaige wenxue*). Both, as we shall see, are designed to provide a drama of historical dialectics through which the unjust is to be expelled by the just. Perceiving the simplistic tendency in scar literature, which connects social tragedies to a specific historical era (the Cultural Revolution), retrospective literature attempts to open up a broader historical scope that spans the entire period of the People's Republic. Lu Yanzhou's novella "The Legend of Tianyun Mountain," for example, invokes the Anti-Rightist Campaign, during which Luo Qun, the protagonist, suffers from both emotional and political misfortunes. His struggle with the orthodox party leader, Wu Yao, who had persecuted him during the political movements and married his fiancée, abated but then resumed following the Cultural Revolution, when the political situation showed promising signs for those "misjudged Rightists." In the end, after being officially rehabilitated, Luo Qun is appointed to a high position, and Wu Yao, his rival in both political and romantic arenas, is finally sent to the brainwashing party school.[12] Narrated by Song Wei, Luo Qun's former love and Wu Yao's wife, the just and unjust historical forces at play are revealed by the narrator, who justifies the historical cause by confessing her own personal errors. Her authoritative voice thus creates stereotypical characterizations. As a negative character, Wu Yao is denigrated as "shouting aloud without allowing my retort" (Lu Yanzhou 99), "foaming at the mouth," "having a fierce-looking face" (100), and "knocking me down, cursing crudely and yelling hysterically" (114). Accordingly, Luo Qun, a heroic victim, is depicted as having "flaming ardor and energetic personality which made me overwhelmed with admiration" (26) and still showing "stalwart physique and sculpturesque face" twenty years later (120).

If "The Legend of Tianyun Mountain" is a representative work of retrospective literature, Jiang Zilong's "Manager Qiao Assumes Office" is a typical piece of reform literature, which directly supports the party policy of economic reform. The basic plot of the novella is built around the continual conflicts between Manager Qiao and his visible or invisible opponents in business administration. It is implied, of course, that the difficulties left by the preceding social chaos will eventually be swept away by reformers such as Manager Qiao. Manager Qiao is created as a representative historical subject who has "deep-set intense eyes" that sometimes "swept the meeting room like lightning" (Jiang *daibiaozuo* 40–41 / "Manager" 57; trans. modified), and he is "vigorous and bold, with the courage to practice and experiment" (72 / [omitted in "Manager"]).

The mode of characterization of these two novellas is reminiscent of that in communist literature; the heroes exemplify the charismatic redeemer in the aftermath of the Cultural Revolution. They suffer from past historical mistreatment and/or are striving to disentangle the difficulties created by the conservative/reactionary forces. On the basis of the Hegelian-Marxist dialectics, historical teleology is the fundamental message conveyed in new-era literature to endorse the political agenda in Deng's era. The historically just is always positively incarnated in the charismatic figure. Toward the end of "Manager Qiao Assumes Office," however, the description of the immoderate toughness of Manager Qiao virtually impairs the subjective purpose of representation: "He anxiously paced up and down the room, the muscle of his left cheek continuously twitching. Suddenly, something cracked in his mouth: a lower molar tooth split. He said nothing, but spat out the dropped half of the tooth" (83/84; trans. modified). This is quite a ludicrous scene, foreshadowing Mo Yan's characterization of the bandit-hero, who would be a figure with defiant and self-disruptive charisma within the gallery of modern Chinese heroes.

What we need to realize, when examining works of retrospective and reform literature, is that the narrator as the absolute subject of representation is not solely a phenomenon of mainstream literature, which supports the official political agenda. Writers typically regarded as dissidents, such as Liu Binyan, Wang Ruowang, and Bai Hua, also retain the narrative paradigm in their works.[13] Communist literature was, in fact, "dissident" before 1949. Its explicit political stance prompted all politically oriented works to show their clear authorial tendency.

In Liu Binyan's reportage, for example, the conflict between communists (or the oppressed people) and their opponents in communist literature is turned into a conflict between real communists, such as Chen Shizhong and Ni Yuxian in "Di'erzhong zhongcheng" (A second kind of loyalty), and pseudocommunists, including Wang Shouxin in "Renyao zhijian" (People or monsters). Throughout the whole piece the crucial terms used to characterize Wang Shouxin are *arrogant* and *oppressive* (38); she is described as a "crude, shallow housewife" (49) and indeed portrays a wicked person to represent the hero-villain pattern of history. Nonetheless, Liu Binyan uses such phrases as "with generosity and concern" (38) and "straight talking and industrious," which are clearly intended to be read ironically, to describe Wang (50). While relying on an authoritative narrative voice, at one point Liu Binyan goes so far as to incorporate contending statements into his own narrative (a device later widely used by Can Xue), such as giving "many different accounts of Wang Shouxin's character," all of which "were true": she is described as "straightforward one moment and phony the next" (Liu 30). Ironic moments such as these will appear in a truly pluralistic and self-critical manner with the rise of the avant-garde.

Chapter 2

The Modern Paradigm Destabilized and Displaced

In modern Chinese fiction, realism as the literary paradigm is susceptible to its own disintegration, deviation, or transformation in every detail. The absolute and homogeneous subjectivity of representation, then, cannot always come through the text in a transparent way and is frequently confronted with the dangers of being heterogenized. Avant-garde fiction, to a certain extent, is an uncovering or rereading of the heterogeneities expelled toward the margins, or suppressed under the surface, of the paradigmatic history of modern Chinese fiction. The connotation of uncovering, or rereading, occurs on at least two levels. First, we locate the noncanonical writers and their works, or the uncanonized works of the paradigmatic writers, that have been relegated so far to oblivion due to the insufficiency of their historical/representational subjectivity. And, second, we reexamine the canonized, paradigmatic works in order to see their vulnerability to self-deconstruction of historical/representational subjectivity. Both paths show the instability of the modern literary paradigm and foreshadow the advent of the avant-garde.

Self-Disruptive Hazards Inherent in the Project of Literary Modernity

The representational paradigm of modern Chinese narrative was, in the first place, challenged by such minor, or marginalized, writers as Fei Ming, Shi Zhecun, Li Jianwu, Huang Pengji, and Li Tuozhi, some of whom are still not recognized to this day. In many of their works, the unified concern for an ultimate, absolute subjectivity dissolved into ambiguous, decentered narration in one way or another. At the same time, it is discernible that the crises of historical and representational subjectivity appears in the marginalized works of major writers, which have been expelled from the literary canon due to the intrinsic problematics of the grand historical narrative.

In the case of Mao Dun's trilogy *Shi* (Eclipse, 1930) the "anxiety about the eclipse of time as progress" (D. Wang, *Fictional Realism* 36) determines its destiny of being depreciated by the canon based on a teleological, if not mythical, history. This is not to say, however, that Mao Dun's belief in teleological history is unsettled. On the contrary, the title *Eclipse,* interpreted by Mao Dun himself, "signifies that the failure of the 1927 Great Revolution was temporary and the victory of the revolution would be positive; it was like the eclipse of the orbs, after which light will appear" (*Shi* 444). Such an abstract idea of historical dialectics, however, only allows Mao Dun to focus on the most chaotic features of the historical present from which, ironically, we can hardly perceive anything dialectically positive. This is the conflict between Mao Dun's grand historical idea that necessitates a visible telos and his representational imperative that demands a truthful illustration and thorough critique of the depravity and decadence of reality. Mao Dun's theoretical realism/naturalism was unsuccessful in that his mode of representing the pattern of history is by no means "objective" but, rather, typically subjective. Personal subjectivity, then, is irreconcilable with the collective subjectivity, or the rupture of historical subjectivity is exposed wherever representational technique persists in the historical circumstances that cannot be regularized. Mao Dun's failure to seize the grand historical prospect—the structural incompleteness and rupture in his works, for example—opens up the possibility of discerning the inherent incongruity within the realist work and the Enlightenment project.

Among the three novellas in *Eclipse, Dongyao* (Vacillation, 1928) is perhaps most remarkable for its ambiguous representation of the historically progressive and retrogressive forces. According to Mao Dun's own exposition in his 1979 "*Dongyao* Fawenban xu" (Preface to the French translation of *Vacillation*), *Vacillation* "reflects the intensity and complexity of the struggle between revolution and counterrevolution during the 1927 Great Revolution, as well as the eventual decline of capitulators and appeasers." In other words, it is a work intended to represent the critical historical moment from which a dialectical movement of history can be detected: the "struggle" between the historically antithetical parties and the "decline" of the historically backward factions are to be overcome and negated by a new era. Mao Dun's historical agenda, however, is seriously troubled in this work. A half-century after the appearance of this work, Mao Dun confesses that it "has its flaws, for the clear-headed and correct forces in the revolutionary camp are not amply described . . . and the author's intention did not have the actual effect." It is most intriguing that in the same article Mao Dun's own judgment of this novella is somewhat inconsistent. On the one hand, he admits that the reason it is flawed "lies in that the author's analysis and recognition of the situation were erroneous and incomplete at that time." On the other hand, he alleges that "the characters in *Vacillation* are much more complex [than those in the other two] and closer to the actual circumstances" (*Shi* 445). It seems that, as Mao Dun implies, the proper representation of "the circumstances" (*shiji qingkuang*) cannot shed light on "the situation" (*xingshi*), insofar as the phrase *shiji qingkuang* refers merely to experienced reality, whereas *xingshi* has to be understood in relation to a broader sociohistorical context and within the sphere of grand history. Ironically, the closer the representation in *Vacillation* appears "to the actual circumstances," the more "erroneous and incomplete" "the author's analysis and recognition of the situation" are.

Indeed, the failure of Mao Dun's "intention" to describe "the clear-headed and correct forces in the revolutionary camp" is caused by his perception of the chaotic "actual circumstances," which impairs his conception of the historical "situation" that could be rendered in the narrative. A rational representation, which could perhaps clearly define the *situation* and the characters in it, cannot gain control over the unexpectedly increased "complex[ity]" of the *actual circumstances*. It is precisely the complexity, then, that questions the grand historical subject by bringing narrative "vacillation" into characterization and emplotment. Fang Luolan, who is supposed to exemplify a historically progressive force in *Vacillation*, is unfittingly involved in an extramarital affair, however, and unable to fulfill his historical duty to avoid the disastrous riot. His historical role, formulated to signify the *situation*, is thus watered down by the *actual circumstances* affecting his private role.

The most remarkable passage in *Vacillation* can be found at the ending, when Mrs. Fang is surrounded by ruins following the counterrevolutionary riot and unable to get over the psychic shock. The grotesque cruelty of Mao Dun's narrative vision, at some point, approaches avant-garde aesthetics (in Yu Hua, e.g.), though the text still employs narratorial intervention to help define what is represented.[1] Nonetheless, when Mao Dun spares authorial/narratorial subjectivity, he touches the indefinable and inextricable nightmare that one perceives in the historical ruins:

> When Mrs. Fang raised her head again, the first thing that came into her sight was the little spider which, dangling in the air a minute ago, was now much lower and almost touched her nose. While she was watching, the little insect was getting larger and larger until it was as large as a person. Mrs. Fang clearly saw the fat body hanging on a wavering thread, struggling in fright and in vain; she also saw the creased face of the spider gasp bitterly and numbly. In a moment, the face transformed into numerous faces, fluttering in the air. There suddenly grew many bloody, naked, headless corpses with fat breasts, and the transformed bitter faces flew onto the bleeding necks, heaving the same low and scary sighs. (263)

In this passage the narratorial voice is overwhelmed by the horrid images in the character's psychic domain—her unspeakable fright—and does not represent her mind in a "realistic," rational way that might categorize her as "disillusioned" or "desperate." The Kafkaesque insect that appropriates a human shape, though not self-transformed, acts as a mirror to reflect back the unsettled, shattered image of the viewing subject. The narrative intended to establish a rational development of history thus ends with an unreasonable scene of mental and representational disorder, which undermines the validity of the grand history. The goal of representing tragedy in history has been disseminated into indefinable psychic images devoid of determined historical meaning. Here Mao Dun's exploration of the abnormal psyche foreshadowed the surrealistic imagery in Can Xue's short stories—for example, "Guling zhi qiu" (The autumn of Guling, 1933), another of his stories in which narrative silence indicates the crisis of the historical/representational subject[2]—and is comparable to the avant-garde narrative collage in the works of Ma Yuan and Ge Fei.

Like Mao Dun's *Eclipse*, which was intended to represent the sublimity of revolution, communist literature was replete with scenes and images of barbarity and chaos over which the narrative subject was hardly able to take control. The behavioral and narrative transgression can be seen as another legacy of avant-garde fiction, which, in this sense, is at once attached to and detached from the spirit of rebellion inherent in Chinese cultural and literary modernity. Barbarity and chaos, in whatever historical context, were rationally conceived to be either revolutionary or counterrevolutionary forces and represented as integral to the grand historical logic of the narrative. Mao Zedong, from his earlier acclaim for the "unruly" peasant movement, which he praised as "a little terror" (*Selected Works* 1:27, 1:39), to his later reemphasizing that "to rebel is justified" ("Gei Qinghua," 87), greatly inspired the writers of his time to be attracted to images of blood and fire.

More often than not, however, the rationality on which bloody representations are based goes awry when the very acts of barbarity fail to imply anything about historical justice. In Liang Bin's *Hongqi pu* (Keep the red flag flying), for example, when Jiang Tao "threw a handful of coppers at one of the thugs, who fell down with blooding gushing from his head" and, together with his comrade, "taking to their heels they ran west as fast as they could" (400), it is portrayed as a heroic deed. While certainly not the cruelest scene in the communist novel, this episode merely registers a ruffian act that, being inherited in part from classic novels such as *The Water Margins* and *Xiyou ji* (The journey to the West), more or less caricatures the serious struggle between the two social classes.

More examples can be drawn from war novels (set in the Civil Wars or Sino-Japanese War), which typically show the savageness of the enemy, the misery of the people, and the sacrifice of martyrs. These representations attempt to justify the Communist army's battles against the Japanese or the Nationalist army, which are the focus of the narrative.

Du Pengcheng's *Baowei Yan'an* (Defend Yanan) is, in this sense, rich in descriptions of bloody battlefields and brutal carnage. The novel lays out (through recollection) a scene of annihilation by the anti-Communist forces, which creates the emotional background of the heroic figure: "The enemy caught Dayong's mother and . . . set fire to her hair, but she didn't breathe a word. Her corpse hung from the big tree outside of the village for seven days!" (136; trans. slightly modified). Only on the basis of wrath can actions of violence done to the enemy be justified. Thus, the description of a rescuer from among the communist guerillas butchering an enemy soldier represents arbitrary, apathetic cruelty (which will be seen decades later in Yu Hua's fiction, though without ideological leanings): "A big sword flashed in the air, then slashed down and cleaved the sentry in two" (125). By contrast, representations of the death of martyrs in the novel are intended to intensify sublime heroism by directly displaying their bloodshed. Here is a (stereo)typical hagiographic, and at the same time repulsive, picture: "with every shout, every move, blood gushed from his chest wound" (348). The gory effects in these passages enhance the sublimity of revolution, on the one hand, and expose sheer horror within a potentially, or ultimately, utopian scenario, on the other. Both to glorify heroic death and to desensitize "justifiable" murder, historical rationality is obfuscated by descriptions of excessive barbarity from the subjective narrative voice. The unrestrained representation of barbarity paved the way for post–Cultural Revolution generation writers—Yu Hua, Mo Yan, and Can Xue, in particular—who more decisively call into question the grand subject that aspires, but fails, to rationalize historical brutality.

In this regard Lu Xun's case may be most striking in terms of the instability of the superior subjectivity. If Mao Dun's *Vacillation* exemplifies those works that remained uncanonized due to their malfunctioning historical/representational subjectivity, Lu Xun's "Kuangren riji" (A madman's diary, 1918) typifies canonized works whose self-deconstructive potential has been suppressed by the paradigmatic zeitgeist. "A Madman's Diary" is certainly among the greatest influences on the avant-garde narratives of Can Xue, Mo Yan, Xu Xiaohe, and Yu Hua. Nevertheless, unlike the schizophrenic narration in avant-garde fiction, the narration of "A Madman's Diary" can be categorized as paranoid,[3] the Madman depicted as an orator who breaks the silence of premodern history by decrying the brutality and apathy of the existing society. His reading of the classical Chinese texts and culture reveals cannibalistic tendencies beneath a benign surface. The Madman represents a rebel against the devouring society who sends out an echoless appeal for salvation.

Since his "birth" the Madman, denouncing his cannibalistic society and calling for redemption, has been read as a transcendental historical subject with whom the author, as well as the reader, is naturally identified.[4] As Leo Ou-fan Lee points out, "the Madman's voice may be regarded as an artistic version of Lu Xun's inner voice" (*Voices* 53). The Madman, as the narrator, is a persona behind which the vehement denunciator is Lu Xun, the author. Indeed, the first-person narrative, with its highly idiosyncratic voice, suggests a positive evaluation of individual power in its contest with the collective society, which is presented as a cannibalistic, oppressive inferno. This individual subjectivity, as opposed to the individual-devouring collectivity, is presumably derived from Nietzsche, who called for the *Übermensch* in order to transcend social repression. Such an *Übermensch* appears in the 125th aphorism in *Die Fröhliche Wissenschaft* (The gay science) exactly as a Madman, through whose voice Nietzsche announces the murder of God by human beings. Like Nietzsche, who had tremendous influence on him, Lu Xun persisted in seeking truth in the voice of the individual, and the means he chose to resist the systematically suppressive status quo was precisely what Nietzsche chose for his character and what he himself finally reached: madness.

Not only does Lu Xun's singular form of Madman indicate an individual peculiarity (unlike Xu Xiaohe's use of plural "madmen," which displays a collective lunacy, as we shall see), but *kuangren*, Lu Xun's original term for *Madman,* clearly implies eccentricity. *Madman* is in fact not a perfect equivalent to *kuangren* in Chinese, for the connotations of the word *kuang* also include *unruly, unrestrained, wild,* and even *arrogant*. It is notable that the concept of *kuang*, referring to a madman, alludes to an anecdote by Confucius in *Lunyu* (Analects): when Confucius traveled to Chu (a state in the south), Jieyu, the so-called *kuang* sang a "Phoenix Song" to laugh at Confucius' political expectations. In his authoritative exegesis of *Analects* Zhu Xi remarks, "Jieyu, the man of Chu, feigned madness and secluded himself from society" (184). Accordingly, the word *kuangren* in Chinese does not refer to a real madman but to a type of unruly person who attempts to resist the order of society with intentional mad behavior.[5] Jieyu's image as a *kuangren* is later evoked by Li Bai (Li Po) in his poem "Lushan yaoji Lu Shiyu Xuzhou" (A song of Lu Mountain: To censor Lu Xuzhou): "I am the madman [*kuangren*] of the Ch'u country / Singing a mad song disputing Confucius" (63). Here Li Bai, by calling himself *kuangren,* again posed a challenge to Confucius, the name representing the dominant paradigm of traditional Chinese culture. Lu Xun's earliest use of *kuangren* can be found in his 1907 essay "Moluo shili shuo" (On the power of Mára poetry), in which he designates the admirable romantic poet

Percy Bysshe Shelley a *kuangren:* "The poet's mind sprouted the omen of rebellion quite early; later he wrote narratives, gave his remuneration to eight friends and then left, bearing the name of madman" (*quanji* 1:83).

In "A Madman's Diary," no matter how absurd it appears, madness has been interpreted as something that conveys individual and historical *truth,* something saner than social "rationality." Lu Xun's Madman seems to represent the iconoclasts of the May Fourth epoch, a time that envisioned the creation of a promising future by destroying the existing system. The paranoid (as he is called in the prologue of the story) who searches continuously for a universal understanding of everything around him and thus "submits history to a new totalization," David Wang argues (*Fictional Realism* 9), embodies the intellectual zeitgeist of Lu Xun's time. Here, however, individuality is both a nonconformist factor that breaches the old coherent system and yet another new conformist power that strives to represent the grand history. A more caustic critique of Lu Xun's conception of the Madman is waged by Wu Xiaoming in his article "Wangxiang, zilian, youyu yu xianshen" (Paranoia, narcissism, melancholia, and self-sacrifice), who claims:

> The horrifying collective madness [of the Cultural Revolution] and the devouring of the individuals are not irrelevant to *the discourse of the modern* initiated in the May Fourth era. From Lu Xun's paranoia to Mao Zedong's megalomania, from the May Fourth New Culture Movement to the Great Cultural Revolution, the link between is probably—from the textual perspective—the principle of narcissism and the logic of subjectivity. The Cultural Revolution is probably not a counteraction to the May Fourth, but rather its logical culmination. There is probably no unbridgeable gap between the paranoia of the "I" and that of the "We." (189; my emph).

It might be an overstatement to say that the Cultural Revolution was an absolutely "logical culmination" of the May Fourth Movement, but drawing a connection between the two cultural paradigms prompts us to see how intellectual modernity (cultural "enlightenment") develops into political modernity (cultural "revolution"). Indeed, what connects the May Fourth Movement and the Cultural Revolution is none other than the idea of modernity: the grand narrative of historical teleology is based on the belief in the emancipation of the human being—the unbounded, supreme subject.

Lu Xun's paranoid narration, however, sets in motion the forces that disrupt subjective totalization. This is evident in a hitherto neglected article by Lu Xun, "Ji 'Yang Shuda jun' de xilai" (An account of the abrupt visit of "Mr. Yang Shuda" [hereafter "Account"]), a piece once again intended to depict feigned madness. In "A Madman's Diary" the one who feigns madness is not the Madman-narrator but Lu Xun the author. What is different in "Account" is that Lu Xun viewed the feigned madman not as a critical subject but, rather, as someone dispatched by an antagonistic faction to intimidate him. The essay is an "account" (but we shall see the subjective distortion in the representational account) of an incident that happened to Lu Xun on November 13, 1924. A student of Beijing University, self-introduced as the famous professor Yang Shuda, came to see Lu Xun and tried to extort money from him, using insane words and actions. The young visitor mentioned in particular the contribution fees that Lu Xun and his fellow writers (including Zhou Zuoren, Lu Xun's brother) were supposed to receive from the same journal. After "critical" scrutiny, Lu Xun "discerned" that the student was feigning his madness and, with indecent wile, trying to coerce him to stop writing (Lu Xun, *quanji* 7:41–47).[6] This essay, however, published in the second issue of the weekly *Yusi* (Thread-of-talk) on November 24, 1924, was not the whole story. A week later (December 1, 1924), in the third issue, there appeared another short article by Lu Xun, "Guanyu Yang jun xilai shijian de bianzheng" (A rectification apropos of the event of Mr. Yang's visit [hereinafter "Rectification"]) and a short letter by Lu Xun to Sun Fuyuan (editor of *Thread-of-Talk*), along with an article by Li Yu'an (one of Lu Xun's students), all explaining the details of the event. In "Rectification" Lu Xun admitted that, according to other students' statements, the visitor "was truly insane" and that he "was susceptible to suspicion too much"; "the fact is the fact . . . I only wish that he gets well soon" (49–50).

From these two articles we can see that, indeed, Lu Xun was inclined to interpret madness as feigned behavior. His obsession with rationality made him virtually disregard any real mental disorder, for all his points of view (or even the points of view he surmised other people would have) conformed to the narrator's stance in "A Madman's Diary," a *rational* stance of feigning madness. When realizing that it was real insanity, Lu Xun could only wish a return to health for the student, that is, a return to the track of reason. Nevertheless, in his letter to Sun Fuyuan, Lu Xun asserted in a self-critical tone: "the account [in "Account"] could remain there: this is an unexpected exposure of mutual suspicions in reality between people—at least between him and me" (49–50). Lu Xun's self-critique in this passage is illuminating: by identifying himself with the madman, Lu Xun uncovers the fact that a written work with overconfident rationality potentially contains immense irrationality. Obviously, as the real insanity of the student named Yang is revealed, any reading of "Account" reveals Lu Xun's own paranoid mode of narration.

The narrative mode of "Account" that exposes Lu Xun's paranoid mind is not much different from the narrative mode of "A Madman's Diary." (And his own diary on November 13, 1924, becomes truly "a madman's diary.") The paranoid oversensitivity to an external threat fits the specific type of psychosis named in the preface to "A Madman's Diary," "persecution mania," a type of paranoia. More significantly, then, the intrinsic affinity between "Account" and "A Madman's Diary" lies not simply in the shared madness of the Madman and the psychotic student, Yang. The affinity between the two narratives is shown in the *identical* paranoid symptoms of the two narrators: the Madman (as Lu Xun's persona in "A Madman's Diary") and Lu Xun (the real person in "Account").

This is how Lu Xun, with a highly subjective voice, describes the visitor in "Account": "Sure enough, he began to act, that is, quivered the corners his eyes and mouth so as to show monstrosity and madness; but each time it was so laborious that his face finally calmed down before the tenth quiver" (*quanji* 7:44). Now consider how Lu Xun's Madman narrates: "Sure enough! My elder brother came slowly out, leading an old man. There was a murderous gleam in his eyes, and fearing that I would see it, he lowered his head, stealing side glances at me from behind his glasses" (*quanji* 1:425 / *Selected Works* 1:43). The stylistic similarities between the voice of the Madman and that of Lu Xun himself (in "Account") is more than clear. And thus the feigned Madman, who mirrors Lu Xun's real paranoia, exposes the illusion of rationality. The paranoid voices of narration in both "Account" and "A Madman's Diary" ultimately undermine their own attempts to rationalize. Their pitfalls lie in the excessive confidence placed in cognitive subjectivity and the omniscient capacity to represent objectivity. Unfortunately, in such a situation omniscience slips into ignorance, just as with the predicament that Lu Xun ran into in "Account." It is not unreasonable, then, to attempt an alternative reading of "A Madman's Diary" as a story staging a supreme, and indeed paranoiac, historical subject endowed with the discourse of modernity, which, nonetheless, fails to maintain its legitimacy.

It is truly ironic that this harbinger of modernity, who was considered to have led the Chinese to "step into the *modern* from the middle age" (Zhang Dinghuang 33; my emph.), is mentally abnormal. After all, for Lu Xun, why choose a *Mad*man? Is the traditional kind of feigned madness exempt from his critique of premodern China? Or has Lu Xun, at least unconsciously, planted self-disruptive seeds by equating the discourse of modernity with the discourse of madness? The representational mechanism suggests the untruth of the Madman's narrative, which canonical reading tends to ignore. For example, the "seven or eight others who discussed me in a whisper" and "were afraid of my seeing them" (423/40) are obviously talking furtively about his madness, but the Madman interprets their behavior as preparing for murder; likewise, when the doctor says, "To be eaten at once!" (426/44), he is most likely referring to taking medicine, but the narrator, again, interprets the words as a message about eating him; the narrator's suspicion of the Zhaos' dog as an "accomplice" is even more unreliable. The examples are too many to enumerate. The canonized reading of the text, therefore, is perfectly reversible: in "A Madman's Diary" it is more than obvious that all the Madman-narrator's interpretations of the external occurrences are paranoid *misinterpretations*, and the whole narrative can well be revealed as full of misrepresentations.

Such an apparent fact, as apparent as the misinterpretation that Lu Xun the narrator gives in his "Account," has hitherto escaped (and to some extent been forced to escape) critical and scholarly observations of the story (just as the nakedness of the emperor evades everyone's disclosure, including his own). Lu Xun himself pronounces the epistemological function of "A Madman's Diary," but one can see that even his own statements about the story are inconsistent. In his 1918 private letter to Xu Shoushang, one of his friends, Lu Xun talked about the origin of the writing of "A Madman's Diary": "While reading *Comprehensive Mirror for Aid in Government* randomly, I suddenly realized that the Chinese were a cannibalistic nation. Thus I wrote this story. Such a discovery is of great importance, but rarely have people recognized it" (*quanji* 11:353). In his authoritative 1935 introduction to the "Second Volume of Fiction" of *Zhongguo xinwenxue daxi* (The grand anthology of Chinese new literature), however, Lu Xun asserted that "A Madman's Diary" was "intended to expose the evil of the family system and the ethical code" in a way "more indignant and more profound than Gogol's [story by the same title]" (*quanji* 6:239).

Obviously, although he insisted on having had an original intention in writing "A Madman's Diary," Lu Xun could not provide a unified, reliable picture of what it was. Or was there a self-sufficient "original" that precludes other interpretations? It is true that Lu Xun most likely intended to offer a teleological scenario, since in his preface to *Nahan* (Call to arms, 1923) he explicitly indicated that his writing is meant to serve those who reject pessimism and cynicism. Yet it is not impossible to read his Madman differently, even cynically, as it may well be that Lu Xun's equivocal unconscious undermines the message he intends to deliver. The most intriguing question is why the discourse of modernity has to be uttered through insanity, which, though pertinent to the traditional type of eccentric literati, is essentially incompatible with the claimed rationality of that discourse.

In any case the narrative paranoia of the story, the "vertiginous interplay between madness and rationality" (D. Wang, *Fictional Realism* 7), calls into question Lu Xun's own statements, as well as all the critical statements over the past eight decades in China, about the story. In this sense, ironically, the higher representational fidelity is to the state of madness (produced by Lu Xun's realistic technique), the more susceptible the whole story becomes to the dangers of self-deconstruction. Lu Xun's characterization of a paranoid Madman, however rational the term *kuang* suggests, provides the basis for a double, or self-contradictory, meaning. As *the* paradigmatic work of Chinese realism, "A Madman's Diary" can be regarded as the epitome of the paranoiacally subjective and absolutely omniscient paradigm of (mis)representation in the canonical modern Chinese fiction, a symptom that, in fact, self-disruptively undermines its claim to totalization. Such a misrepresentation in modern Chinese fiction, a representation that potentially abolishes its own absoluteness and questions its own adequacy, is exactly what is revealed in Chinese avant-garde narratives. By reading the discourse of modernity as paranoia, avant-garde fiction exposes, in a schizophrenic way, the actual insanity of the totalistic representation in modern Chinese fiction.

The Emergence of the Avant-Garde

In the post-Mao era the first autonomous literary trend to try to dissociate itself from the discourse of modernity was "root-seeking" (*xungen*) literature, advocated by Han Shaogong, Ah Cheng, Li Hangyu, and many others. Root-seeking literature no longer looked to the historical telos but turned back to the premodern and aboriginal so as to rescue the meaning of history from the "pure" past or, at least, the spiritually primitive realm. Nevertheless, (mis)named following the translation of Alex Haley's novel *Roots*, root-seeking literature in essence did not invert the historical logic. Its reevaluation of rational history was not purely nostalgic but, to a great extent, reaffirmed the validity of grand history by guiding the historical development toward an ideal future through the detour of recalling the presumably purer and more vital primitive. This is evidenced especially in Zhang Chengzhi's works, such as "Hei junma" (The black steed, 1982) and "Beifang de he" (Rivers of the north, 1984). Although, strictly speaking, Zhang Chengzhi is not a root-seeking writer, his works (some written before the rise of the root-seeking movement) epitomized the essence of root-seeking by endorsing a lifestyle remote from an urban area to revitalize one's transcendental spirituality. The protagonists in Zhang Chengzhi's work, always struggling for a progressive condition, were again elevated to a high subjective level. The historical subject who rules the whole structure to fit the historical order maintained the same charismatic voice and image as in communist literature. Zhang Chengzhi's symbolism (of the steed, the rivers, etc.), though detached from the representational realism, guides and dominates the entire narrative and signifies unambiguously a different, yet still grand and absolute, Idea. By idealizing the past and the primitive state, Zhang Chengzhi reoriented and reconstructed the concept of modernity.

Confronted with the disillusionment of the discourse of grand history, root-seeking was a nostalgic movement that sought to regain cultural purity that was not historically tarnished. More sophisticated works of root-seeking, such as Ah Cheng's novellas, began to place over history the cultural quintessence that, it was hoped, would protect human beings from external historical pressures. Wang Yisheng's obsession with Chinese chess in "Qiwang" (The chess king, 1984) and Wang Fu's devotion to pure knowledge of Chinese language in "Haizi wang" (The king of children, 1985) are both significant in their cultural resistance to the discourse of grand history at the time. Ah Cheng's works attempt to exhaust historical subjectivity by creating a connection between the void of historical pressure and the vitality of cultural quintessence. In so doing, however, Ah Cheng evades the real conflicts and pains in historical experiences: his quandary lies in the impossibility of having a pure, ahistorical, everlasting culture, which is shown to be an illusion being that it is well assimilated into the powerful discourse of grand history.

In "The Chess King," most obviously, the pure cultural endeavor ends in another struggle for supreme subjectivity: only by winning a competition, that is, by metaphorically undergoing a struggling and triumphant human history, does Wang Yisheng attain his ultimate value of life. The cultural power, therefore, is deprived of its strength to resist historical power and conforms to the same subjective pattern. Even in "The King of Children" the cultural spirit is aloof from reality but still implicated in the authoritative rhetoric. Wang Fu, the boy imbued with the author's ideal, longs for the ability to write (as a way of remaining detached from political turbulence), but his practice of writing about his father (a typical peasant) going into the morning sun is not immune from the grand symbolism. The description of the morning sun as a "white" (rather than red) one only develops the symbolic order without escaping the system of political discourse. This is probably another example of the impossibility of having a primordial, uncontaminated culture detached from social reality. In his story "Shuwang" (The king of trees, 1985) the cultural ideal, embodied in its spiritual affinity with nature, encounters a tragic failure. The novella thus consciously highlights the conflict between the historical and the cultural: this conflict is, in any case, a problem that Ah Cheng finally acknowledges is unresolvable. Like the historical subject, the cultural subject (believing in the purifying and reviving function of Chinese culture) fails to serve successfully as the redeemer of the nation.

In 1985 there appeared the earliest important works of avant-garde fiction—early attempts in post–Cultural Revolution literature to deal with the complexity of the cultural and historical subject—including Han Shaogong's "Ba ba ba" (Pa pa pa); "Guiqulai" (The homecoming), and "Lan gaizi" (The blue cap); Can Xue's "Wushui shang de feizaopao" (Soap bubbles on dirty water), "Shanshang de xiaowu" (Hut on the mountain), and "Gongniu" (The ox); Xu Xiaohe's "Yuanzhang he tade fengzimen" (The madhouse director and his madmen); Ma Yuan's "Gangdisi de youhuo" (The temptation of Gangdisê); and Liu Suola's "Ni biewu xuanze" (You have no other choice).

Han Shaogong's novella "Pa pa pa" is a root-seeking work that confounded root-seeking ideology. If Bingzai, the antihero of "Pa pa pa," can be seen as a national symbol, he is certainly one that fails to capture the vitality of the nation. He becomes an allegorical figure that deconstructs the idea that Han Shaogong himself holds of envisioning "the chance of revival" of the national culture by enlivening "the traditional culture embodied in native soil" as "magma under the earth's crust" ("Wenxue de 'gen'" 4–5). Bingzai is obviously an idiot whose national identity is represented in the simplest swearwords. When the villagers regard him as an incarnated genius loci, disturbances and disasters occur. Distorted due to the tension between the expected and the effected characterization, Bingzai shatters national symbolism into national allegory and transgresses the original goal of root-seeking in a self-disruptive way.[7] The cultural ideal of root-seeking, which crystallizes into such symbolic characters as Wang Fu in Ah Cheng's "The King of Children," is disrupted in "Pa pa pa." What the idiotic character symbolizes is no longer the revivable national spirit but an enigma encoded with indecipherable messages that contain more problems than simple promises. The subjective intention of Han Shaogong that conceives a grand national symbolism is disoriented.

Compared to such works as Lu Xun's "Guxiang" (My old home, 1921) or Yu Dafu's "Huanxiang ji" (Reminiscences on returning home, 1923) and "Huanxiang houji" (Sequel to reminiscences on returning home, 1923), Han Shaogong's short story "The Homecoming" confronts more squarely the disorder of historical and personal experiences. The "I," Huang Zhixian, is agitated with déjà vu in a strange place and actually identified by the villagers with their old acquaintance, Four-Eyed Ma, whom he has never known or heard of. He, as the story goes, involuntarily begins to play the role of Four-Eyed Ma so as to meet the expectations of the people around him and finally is so identified with the role he plays that, awkwardly, his true identity has become suspicious even to himself. If Lu Xun's and Yu Dafu's "homes" intensify their feeling of alienation as well as their subjective superiority in coping with this alienation, Han Shaogong's home, imposed upon the "I," drives him to a situation in which his personal identity becomes incoherent and thus imperils his subjective integrity. At the end of "The Homecoming," when he is befuddled upon hearing someone call him Huang Zhixian, the narrator says, "I'm tired, I'll never be able to get out of the enormous I" (Han *Youhuo* 18). It is precisely this inextricable "I" that has been infinitely alienated, unable to come to a reliable home, even the metaphorical home of narration. This "enormous I," a formerly omnipotent one, becomes a confining and incomprehensible self with dubious subjectivity.

The avant-garde novellas and short stories published in 1985 are generally regarded as the beginning of the challenge to the canonical paradigm of modern Chinese fiction. In fact, some of the avant-garde works published in 1985 or later were written much earlier. By the end of 1983 Can Xue had completed one of the major works of Chinese avant-garde fiction, *Huangni jie* (Yellow mud street), which was not published until 1986. This novella can well be taken as a parody of communist fiction as well as of the overarching paradigm of modern Chinese fiction. In *Yellow Mud Street* grand history runs aground when the Maoist concept of class struggle does not develop into a triumphant, or at least tragic, climax but degenerates into boundless disturbances of discourses, which Can Xue renders as the incomprehensible essence of historical experiences. This incomprehensibility, then, is what Can Xue smuggles into representation, which should have brought along subjective confidence in attaining truth.[8] Lu Xun's totalizing paranoia is ruthlessly uncovered as disordered schizophrenia, in which no absolute or determinant statement can be maintained. Can Xue's narrative is self-refutable in every detail: every utterance of the narrator or character is to be read as unsound. But the unsoundness of history and historical discourses may well be the implication of this novella.

Narrative self-suspicion forms one of the most significant characteristics of avant-garde fiction, since the representational subject is no longer an omniscient power in control of the "narrativized" history. It needs to be emphasized that, in most cases, narrative indeterminacy that disrupts and undermines representational integrity usually takes place in minor, negligible spaces. In Xu Xiaohe's "The Madhouse Director and His Madmen," for instance, the narrative style frequently offers self-discrediting possibilities. For instance, after Old Wei is drowned in the Weigong Pond, it is discovered that his surname is actually not Wei but Tan, and thus he should be called Old Tan (*Yuanzhang* [1987] 152). Another trivial example is that, in the complaint letter against the noisy sawmill, the residents add three exclamation marks on their petition, yet "Granny Zhou said they did four" (154). If the entire narrative is grounded in such vacillations about the "facts," we are forced to realize that the reliability of the narrative is no longer stable but only contingent.

Narrative indeterminacy is best demonstrated in Ma Yuan's fiction as structural uncertainty. "The Temptation of Gangdisê," which brought him instant fame in 1985–86, introduced the incompleteness, or fracturing, of the narrative whole by displaying an incoherent narrative voice and omitting indispensable clues. In Ma Yuan's stories, since everything is accidental and nothing is predestined, narrative development becomes divergent and erratic without being able to be rearranged into a clear progression. While the root-seeking movement proposes to elicit national vitality from inland cultures, Ma Yuan's fiction finds its geographical background in Tibet, a region of ambiguous national attributes. The mystic and inextricable Tibetan culture is absorbed in Ma Yuan's narrative style to challenge the dominant logic of modernity.

The so-called post–Ma Yuan writers (a term mainland Chinese critics coined to pay homage to Ma Yuan's innovation), such as Yu Hua, Ge Fei, Sun Ganlu, and Bei Cun, emerged around 1986–87, carrying through the formalistic venture that Ma Yuan had initiated. Ge Fei's early short stories, such as "Xianjing" (The pitfalls, 1987), "Hese niaoqun" (A flock of brown birds, 1987), and "Meiyou ren kanjian cao shengzhang" (No one sees the grasses grow, 1987), relate subjective experiences in an elusive way not to apotheosize but to displace the subjective voice. His ethereal mode of narration corresponds to the enigmatic happenings in memory and manifests their incomprehensible contradictions. The narrator of "The Pitfalls," for example, is a decrepit man, who claims at the very beginning that his "story is like a long-deserted ruin" and feels that as if he "had only experienced the beginnings and ends plus some fragmentary scraps of those events" (*Mizhou* 11). He is further reminded of "the trivial matters that are not related closely to the story, such as the decayed debris, the coffee-colored river, as well as those somewhat pleasing landscapes of various seasons." Even these, however, "perhaps did not happen at all" (11–12). These statements indicate the fundamental feature of Ge Fei's narrative, which is not a series of integrated, consistent events but, rather, a pile of "ruins" that, as Walter Benjamin speculates, are wrecked historical fragments in a putrefied or petrified form.

In his preface to the Taiwanese edition of *Diren* (The enemy, 1990), his first novel, Ge Fei acknowledges that he is "shrouded by a shadow from long ago, which spanned my whole childhood and left indelible traces in my memory." He further suggests that he "adopts a textual structure that roughly resembles the external experiences (memory)," because "to restore the personal experiences in fiction is inconceivable" (*Diren* 7). The memory trace, for Ge Fei, cannot detail past events but only touches upon their margins, which are still unascertainable to some extent. In his more widely read pieces, such as "Mizhou" (The lost boat, 1987) and "Danian" (New year, 1988), Ge Fei reveals the fissure of the grand history by injecting fluxional and disintegrative human desire into the overpowering pattern of history. His "Qinghuang" (Green-yellow, 1988) consists of various narrators' exposés of the same topic related to a past event that is being displaced and shattered to the extent that the original focus of investigation is diluted through the process of narrative friction and only reemerges randomly in an unbecoming way. "Green-Yellow" can well be seen as a narrative about narration, an allegory about a single narrative being disrupted by multiple narrative voices.

Narrative self-deconstruction in avant-garde fiction calls realism (especially its claim to the capacity of representing true reality) into question. In his 1989 essay "Xuwei de zuopin" (The deceptive works) Yu Hua elaborates on his ideas of writing. He admits that, when he wrote his most influential works, such as "Yijiubaliu nian" (Nineteen eighty-six, 1986) and "Xianshi yizhong" (One kind of reality, 1987), he "could not dodge the chaos given by the real world," in the face of which "the order becomes a decoration" (*zuopinji* 2:280). What "the real world" means to Yu Hua, therefore, is no longer an orderly, rationalized picture of the "objective" world. He carefully maintains his concept of "truth" as "mental essence" (277), which is precisely what necessitates the indeterminacy of objective reality. We are thus compelled to ponder: is there something that can be mentally essentialized as truth? In another passage Yu Hua's dilemmatic expression can be highlighted:

> When I suggest that life is unreal but only mentality is real, it would unavoidably be understood that I am escaping the real life. The word "escape" (*taoli*) in Chinese implies a flurry of panic. Another understanding is a deepening of the above one: I am emphasizing the perception of the world by oneself. I admit the rationality of this statement, but what I would like to emphasize now is that one's ultimate goal of the perception of the world is the disappearance of oneself. One can experience the boundlessness of the world only by entering the broad mental realm. I do not deny that one can dissolve oneself in daily life, but then he/she would be melted in the masses and in the commonsense. Such a self-dissolution results quite probably in the loss of individuality. (281)

In this passage Yu Hua attempts to reject two possible (mis)understandings of his viewpoint. First, he avoids the understanding that he is escaping reality because the implication of the loss of subjective control would annoy him. Second, he argues that the perception of the objective world will lead to the dissolution of the subject. On a surface level it seems clear that Yu Hua is proposing a pure realm of subjective mentality that does not even have to do with objective reality. Yu Hua's theorization of "psychological time," or "mental chronology," however, precipitates the tranformation of his own concept of truth, or essence, into an aporia:

> In one's mental realm, all the values provided by commonsense are on the verge of collapse, all the old things will obtain new meanings. There, the fixed meaning of time will be annulled. The events ten years ago can be arranged after those five years ago and followed by those six years ago. The same events, recalled in another time-space, will be rearranged to display new connotations. The order of time alters casually in tranquillity. The boundary of life and death also begins to blur. (281–82)

Clearly, there is nothing conceived by Yu Hua that is not susceptible to "the perception of the world," which, he warns, will lead to "the disappearance of oneself." In a sense, then, the disappearance of oneself is precisely what Yu Hua is envisioning, not alarmingly but affirmatively as long as *oneself* is read as the traditional whole, absolute subject. That is to say, as Yu Hua posits, personal experiences do lead to the disarray of experiences, and subjective truth only lies in the disintegration of subjectivity. This paradox inherent in Yu Hua's theory epitomizes the problematic narratives of Chinese avant-garde fiction.

In the face of the disintegration of modern subjectivity, Yu Hua advocates the "mode of selfless narration": "I like the narrative approach commonly characterized as telling about others, and try to avoid the approach of telling about oneself" (283). Here, against the authorial control of the narrative, Yu Hua, again, calls for the disappearance of the authorial/authoritative subject. In opposition to the narrative paradigm that dominates modern Chinese fiction, Yu Hua grapples with the problem of covert authorial/narratorial intervention. "If you understand an emotion that surfaces from deep inside," he says, "you would find that such determinate words as pain, fear and joy are not real expressions of the internal emotion but merely simplifying reductions." Paradoxically, the mental essence, an essence of psychic complexity, cannot be essentialized. Thus, Yu Hua proposes an "indeterminate language" "in order to seek the most real and credible expression" (284).

The epistemological paradox, therefore, highlights the paradox of avant-garde writing. One the one hand, Yu Hua claims that "the indeterminate language does not indicate helplessness as one faces the world or a quibble as one is at a nonplus." On the other hand, he admits that "language feels powerless to give ultimate judgments from time to time in front of the diversity and complexity of things." In other words, he wishes to maintain the subjective power to grasp reality, on the one hand, and is fully aware of the limitation, or the inherent destiny, of such power, on the other. Yu Hua illustrates the technical distinctions of narration of avant-garde fiction, that is, to "seek a mode of expression that simultaneously manifests multiple possibilities and multiple levels and is able to grammatically juxtapose, displace or transpose without being restrained by the established grammatical order." In the conclusion of the essay Yu Hua declares that "the distinction between the indeterminate narrative language and the determinate common language lies in the fact that the former stresses the perception of the world and the latter the judgment of it" (284). "The perception of the world" rests, of course, in both the self-consciousness and the self-disintegration of the authorial subject.

In Yu Hua's fiction the limitations of representability result from the traumatic pathos and the unrealizable desire of coping with excessive fear or violence. In "Nineteen Eighty-Six," one of his earliest works, Yu Hua does not simply indict the evil of the Cultural Revolution but reveals the repetitiveness and the incomprehensibility of the evil. Not only does the protagonist of the novella reach the climax of his madness ten years after the end of the Cultural Revolution, but the representation of madness, on the level of narratorial voice, also appears insane. Diegesis as disguised authorial intervention is intolerably parodied when direct characterization is imposed upon the self-mutilation that the mad protagonist follows.

At times Yu Hua's narrator uses the descriptions "contentedly" (*zuopinji* 1:159 / *The Past* 154), "smiling complacently" (162 / [trans. omitted]), "with evident satisfaction," and "satisfied" (164, 170/160, 168) to reveal the protagonist's feeling as he mutilates himself. These expressions reinforce the struggle between the desire to represent and the incapacity to represent adequately by misappropriating rhetorical devices to the extreme of narrative perversion. In the scene in which "he" cuts off his own nose, the nose "dangled loose from his face like a swing" (162/158; trans. modified). The sound of the madman sawing his own leg is described as "like he were polishing a pair of pretty leather shoes" (163/159; trans. modified). Others' comments, as in Ba Jin's novels, reemerge *via the narrator's voice* but only to aggravate narrative discord:

> They cheerfully ate and chatted. . . . The madman cutting his own flesh surprised them over and over again, and then laughed heartily. . . . They felt this sort of thing so interesting and, since interesting things happened from time to time around town, they discussed them from time to time. . . . Then they walked over to the window, stepped out to the balcony. They saw the moon so bright, and felt the air so gentle and sweet. (173/171–72; trans. modified)

In Yu Hua's writing the omniscient narrator is a displaced, irrational narratorial subject. Then, if the madness of the protagonist indicts the violence of history, *the madness of the authorial/narratorial subject* (the discord between narration and content) indicates the subversion against absolute representation and denies the illusion that the reality we are confronted with can be comprehended and redeemed in a rational and complete way (such an illusion is precisely what new-era literature attempts to provide).

In regard to the limitation of subjectivity Yu Hua insists that a writer must "often counter oneself" and that "an artist [should] come from ignorance and go back to ignorance" (*zuopinji* 2:290). In his short stories "One Kind of Reality," "Nantao jieshu" (The inescapable fate, 1988), and "Gudian aiqing" (A classical romance, 1988) he adopts a narrative mode that withholds any authorial involvement. Some critics regard the absence of subjective engagement as comparable to the ideal of pure objectivity that Alain Robbe-Grillet proposed.[9] Since Yu Hua's narrative apathy is so incongruous with the violent and sanguinary content of narrative, however, the absence of subjectivity in his work can only be seen as a deprivation of subjective power, as a lament of the ineptitude of subjectivity in face of the evil of history and humanity. It also differs from the "neorealism" (*xinxieshizhuyi*) of the early 1990s, which, at least in theory, claims the identification of narrative with the "original pattern" of "raw" reality.

The rejection of integrated subjectivity does not suggest a carnival of the disappearance of subjectivity but, rather, shows a predicament arising from the elimination of subjective capacity. What Yu Hua shows here is the inevitable repression and censorship of subjectivity *within* the process of self-presence. Repression occasions the evacuation of subjectivity, and censorship can be seen in the narrative contradictions, disjunctions, lacunae, and paradoxes. These characteristics are clearly detectable in Yu Hua's "Siyue sanri shijian" (The April Third incident, 1987), "Wangshi yu xingfa" (The past and the punishments, 1989), and "Ciwen xian'gei shaonü Yang Liu" (A story dedicated to the girl Willow, 1989), all of which can be read as narratives that are unraveled into more intricate knots.

Modern Chinese fiction from Lu Xun to the generation of Can Xue and Yu Hua unfolds a process from a totalizing, self-sufficient subjectivity doomed to break down into a subjectivity self-exposed as split or displaced. Modernity, whose homogeneous cultural power has upheld the political totalitarianism in communist China, is challenged by the literary practice that questions its absolute mode of discourse. Thus arises the postmodernity of the Chinese avant-garde: a cultural/literary mode that results from the disastrous modern to point to a historical wound.

Part I

Trauma, *Nachträglichkeit,* and the Unrepresentable

Conjuring up the
Psychic/Historical Past

Chapter 3

Trauma and Historical Violence in Communist China

In the core of what is to be expressed is dread. Dread is neither forgettable nor erasable by means of reason or logic. In a certain sense, it is both history and reality.
—GE FEI, "INTRODUCTION" TO *DIREN*

The traumatized, we might say, carry an impossible history within them, or they become themselves the symptom of a history that they cannot entirely possess.
—CATHY CARUTH, "INTRODUCTION" TO TONI MORRISON, *BELOVED*

The paradigm of modern Chinese fiction hinges on the omnipotent subject of narration to transmit the ultimate truth about external or internal reality. In avant-garde fiction, as the presumption that the subject can cope rationally with the object is confronted with crisis, narrative irrationality is activated to defy such omnipotent subjectivity. A narrative no longer offers a lucid, integrative, and easily comprehensible picture or event but, rather, registers distorted, displaced, excessive, or deficient fragments. In a sense it is not reality but the impossibility of reality that is being constantly pursued and examined in avant-garde fiction.

In avant-garde fiction the representational subject no longer functions as a superior and omniscient one. Rather, it shows its own inadequacy, insufficiency, and disintegration. The disintegration of subjectivity results from the fact that individual experiences have been traumatized by historical violence. By *historical violence* I refer not only to the intermittent social calamities in communist China but also to the official discourse that serves as temptation and threat. Trauma can be perceived as the psychic origin of the breakdown of representational subjectivity, the very basis of literary modernity. It is no accident that the Chinese avant-garde writers—from the those born in the 1950s, Can Xue (b. 1953) and Ma Yuan (b. 1953), to the youngest, Ge Fei (b. 1964)—all belong to the generation that grew up or spent their adolescence during the age of numerous communist political movements, from the Anti-Rightist Movement to the Cultural Revolution. Their individual lives are each marked by intense, ideologically imposed duress. This duress, as a psychic assault, turns out to be the trauma that each of them seeks to trace. As the literary critic Chen Xiaoming remarks:

> To this generation, the colossal historical phantom of the Cultural Revolution lurking in the depth of memory adequately animates their preoccupation with boundless illusions: endless verbal games, irresistible desires of expression, unreasonable violent actions, random escapes without returns or homes, and indifferent deaths. . . . The tendency of so-called postmodernism . . . is a kind of historical narrative in the face of reality and "cultural memory." (*Wubian* 31)

Here Chen Xiaoming keenly characterizes the Cultural Revolution as a "colossal phantom" and its psychic effects "illusions" to indicate the tremendous, haunting, and *immemorial* shock of the experience. Traumatized and incapacitated by historical violence, the representation of the experience is deprived of rational subjectivity and no longer claims to convey the absolute truth.

Trauma, as Freud suggests, is "an experience which within a short period of time presents the mind with an increase of stimulus too powerful to be dealt with or worked off in the normal way, and this must result in permanent disturbances of the manner in which the energy operates" (16:275). The intensity of the stimulus disallows the possibility of immediate response and implants into the deep unconscious the psychic agitation, which lies dormant until years later, when relevant circumstances occur to reactivate the traumatic affect. In other words, trauma is a psychic affect that, not perceived instantly or directly, only inhabits the unconscious as deferred and unrepresentable experience.

This is what Freud calls *Nachträglichkeit* (deferred action, or aftereffect): "a memory is repressed which has only become a trauma by *deferred action*" (1:356).

In the light of Freudian theory, which is not confined to the study of personal life or pure sexuality, a broader perspective can be induced to interpret the culturo-historical status of contemporary China.[1] It is *Nachträglichkeit* of the deeply ingrained trauma that correlates the previously experienced historical violence with the current act of writing of Chinese avant-garde fiction. There are at least two aspects that relate Freud's theory of trauma with our analysis of the Chinese avant-garde. First, it was a belated recurrence of a traumatic experience. The impetus to grapple in Chinese avant-garde fiction with the past traumatic experience did not begin to surface during or immediately after the Mao era but was activated, *as a deferred action*, many years after the end of the Cultural Revolution, the so-called "tremendous catastrophe" (*haojie*). In the mid- and late 1980s the recurrent historical violence during the Deng regime—such as periodic suppressions of democratic movements and persecutions of dissident intellectuals—reanimated the traumatic memory trace engendered during the Mao regime. Representation of reality is thus constantly agitated by the dark unconscious undercurrent, which decisively dissolves the subjective rationality. The second, and more important, trauma in Chinese avant-garde fiction remains beyond memory. Illustrating the difficulties of writing history, Chinese avant-garde fiction revises the modern paradigm of direct, unmediated representation by representing obscure, distorted, or inconsistent pictures, ambiguous perceptions, and uncertain feelings about reality.

Trauma, as Freud interprets it, is related to the "scene of seduction," or the "primal scene." Referring to the experience of or witness to sexual violence that appears to be at once hideous and captivating, the primal scene as the origin of psychic shock is incomprehensible to the prepubescent mind and causes an ambivalent attitude toward it. The historical violence that the Chinese avant-gardists have experienced, too, has the duality of being hideous and captivating. It not only exerted pains through political persecution but also offered alluring prospects through ideological demagogy. The Cultural Revolution, as well as other political campaigns during which large-scale persecutions prevailed, cannot be seen as simply social catastrophes. The Cultural Revolution was also a carnival, though very likely a sinister one, which brought enormous exhilaration and reverie. Such an incomprehensible past was, in Chen Xiaoming's words, both a "political catastrophe" and a "final celebration of culture," in which "the ferocious and awkward actions [that] all had poetic significance of historical signs—they became fragments after the death of culture, not only pieced into a despairing situation of the doomsday, but also indicating an enchanting golden age" (*Wubian* 30). This is the very basis for us to approach the affective ambivalence and the rhetorical ambiguity of Chinese avant-garde narrative.

Chinese avant-garde fiction is a profound textual adventure that reexperiences the inextricable relationship between the hideous atrocities of the past and the captivating discourse that justifies historical violence and invalidates the comprehensibility of the whole situation. A number of Chinese scholars have discussed the overpowering sway of "Maoyu" or "Mao huayu" (Maoist discourse)[2] in the daily life of communist China. The haunting apparition of political totalitarianism in the realm of language and expression has cast an immense shadow on the Chinese avant-garde. Maoist discourse, the master discourse, and the fundamental form of ideological manipulation in China,[3] especially during the Cultural Revolution, is exactly what avant-garde narrative attempts to examine. Li Jie, a perceptive critic, optimistically believes that, "once the system of Maoist discourse is deconstructed, Mao's historical image, as well as the history he symbolizes, will come to an end" (102). Emphasizing the ideological and discursive aspects of historical violence is not meant to downplay the intensity of the trauma that this violence has caused at psychic depths. On the contrary, it is the "discursivity" of historical violence that intensifies the traumatic experience, which cannot be easily worked out in a rational and comprehensible way but must be "worked through" by way of a detoured and distorted process.

Maoist discourse itself, indeed, possessed a peculiar attraction and, at the same time, exerted intense violence, which paralleled the visible atrocities, to every individual. The unmerciful political persecution of "class enemies" in the name of "proletarian dictatorship" caused physical and mental suffering, on the one hand, and formed part of the essential content of Maoist discourse, which affirms the historical necessity of violence in the teleological scenario, on the other. As a totalitarian discipline, Maoist discourse wielded its outrageous weapon against everything and everyone beyond its control: the principle of "class struggle" was utilized as an arbitrary law to liquidate all other transgressive, heterodox genres. At the same time, it generously offered a rosy landscape of communist utopia in which altruism was said to be the only rule of the existing society. Only by producing such a discourse could the party apparatus ravish individual mentality from those who were presented with the discourse. Li Jie, aware of this doubleness of Maoist discourse, singles out passages from *Mao Zhuxi yulu* (Quotations from Chairman Mao), the principal scripture during the Cultural Revolution, and divides them into "le rouge et le noir" ("red and black"). *Red* includes the positive statements and pronouncements, mostly concerning heroes, ideals, and moral paradigms, whereas *black* refers to harsh denunciations of and warnings against class enemies (Li Jie 102).[4] This is a phenomenon that Robert Jay Lifton perceived in Chinese totalitarianism even before the Cultural Revolution. Analyzing the "language of the totalist environment," Lifton discovered that the "thought-terminating cliché" contains "either 'god terms,' representative of ultimate good; or 'devil terms,' representative of ultimate evil": "'progress,' 'progressive,' 'liberation,' 'proletarian standpoints' and 'the dialectic of history' fall into the former category; 'capitalist,' 'imperialist,' 'exploiting classes,' and 'bourgeois' (mentality, liberalism, morality, superstition, greed) of course fall into the latter" (429).

These two aspects—red / "god terms" and black / "devil terms"—are intertwined in the single system of Maoist discourse. The aggressive factor of Maoist discourse was intended to be as bewitching as sexual assault, insofar as its style implied simultaneously psychological excitation and release. But the magnificent and seductive visage of Maoist discourse turned out in fact to be tremendous terror, not only as a verbal threat but also as a real historical power that produced homicide, mutilation, and torture. Such a master discourse was thus too colossal to embrace, too "mature" for children or adolescents (which the avant-garde writers were at the time), to comprehend. It should be noted that the original response to this historical violence was not pure repugnance or pain; rather, there was also a great degree of pleasure associated with it, which was induced by the *seeming intimacy* of Maoist discourse. This is analogous to the "scene of seduction" in Freudian theory: an excitation in which the affective shock is too strong, too complex, and too incoherent for the prepubescent child to articulate. Political assault, supported by discursive assault, impregnated trauma into the unconscious. The shock provoked no immediate response and did not manifest itself until many years later.

The historical violence underlying Maoist discourse left in the unconscious a traumatic memory trace, for the shock it caused exceeded the bounds of the psyche's understanding and sensibility. Here the origin of trauma corresponds to the Kantian notion of the sublime, which, as Lyotard interprets it, "bears witness to the fact that an 'excess' has 'touched' the mind, more than it is able to handle." The traumatic affect, accordingly, lies in the aesthetics of the sublime.[5] Lyotard views the sublime "as a combination of pleasure and pain, as the trembling ('on the spot,' at the moment) of a motion both attractive and repulsive at once, as a sort of spasm, according to a dynamic that both inhibits and excites" (*Heidegger* 32).

"If in artworks the subject finds his true happiness in the moment of being convulsed," Adorno writes, "this is a happiness that is counterposed to the subject and thus its instrument is tears, which also express the grief over one's own mortality. Kant sensed something of this in his aesthetic of the sublime, which he excluded from art" (*Aesthetic* 269). The aesthetics of the sublime thus exists in Chinese avant-garde narrative as a deformative act of trauma. There is no adequate representation, however, since the sublime is not only "outside art" but also outside conscious perception. Lyotard, when discussing modern art, points out that the aesthetic of the sublime, adhering to the unconscious, is a "nostalgic one" that "allows the unrepresentable to be put forward only as the missing contents" ("Answering" 81). The "missing contents" of Chinese avant-gardism are the trauma embodied in the anamnesis and anamorphosis (the attributes that Lyotard ascribes to postmodernism) of the anterior violence from the master discourse.

As inadequate representation of the shock experience, the avant-garde narrative aims at an anamnesis of the original violence and disrupts the authoritarian mode of interpreting the past. In other words, the grim aim is intermixed with a nearly ecstatic one of undermining the hegemonic order established by the traces of the original violence. It is in this sense that Bloom suggests: "the terror of the literary Sublime must and can give pleasure" (225). In Can Xue, for example, the chaotic, neurotic narrative rips up the submerged trauma, signals the terror and absurdity of the violence, and erupts as a carnival with barbarous imagery. The original moment, never represented directly and entirely, can only be detected by way of its fragmentation.

By representing the unrepresentable, Chinese avant-garde narratives, such as many of Yu Hua's and Ge Fei's short stories, indicate ruptures of time. Only by *deferring* the past, in the Derridean sense, can memory *differ* from what it contains and then maintain its deconstructive force. "Memory," says Derrida when he touches upon the problem of *Nachträglichkeit* in his essay "Freud and the Scene of Writing," "is not a psychical property among others; it is the very essence of the psyche: resistance, and precisely, thereby, an opening to the effraction of the trace." This "opening," of course, assumes a discrepant and critical distance between the present and the past. Here is the very impetus of writing, of the abrupt, evocative intrusion into history. The evocation of the unconscious is not a process of identifying but, rather, in the form of a compulsion to repeat, an attempt to stress the gap, or to "breach," in Derrida's words, the original: "*Repetition* adds no quantity of present force, no *intensity*; it reproduces the same impression—yet it has the power of breaching" (Derrida, *Writing* 201). The repetition compulsion, as the psychic action of resistance in the unconscious, educes the repressed onto the present surface of the literary work while revealing the irreconcilable fissure. The crisis of representational subjectivity corresponds to the fact that the ultimate truth is a truth of untruth, a truth without a determinant, invariant pattern. Avant-garde fiction shows the temporally deferred/anachronized and spatially differed/distorted mode of representation.

The idea of *Nachträglichkeit* thus conceived implies not only the incongruity between subject (the conscious self) and object (the perceived real) but also that within the subject per se. It marks the disintegration of one's identity. The representation of the deep structure of psyche is accordingly unrealizable (since the shock is not affected until the second blow when the shock is not there) and the split, or wound, is incurable. The "depth" of literary work, in this respect, is manifested within the operation of misrepresentation. In a sense a simple representation of the trauma becomes an accomplice to the violence because of its lack of distance, because of its transparent formation, which is equivalent to the pattern of political power presenting the false whole. The failure of "scar literature" results from its inclination toward displaying psychic agony against the setting of social misery without mediation. Its literary form is captured in the same system of discourse it aims to oppose. It points to the same telos of the grand narrative that Maoist discourse offers.

"It would be false," suggests Lyotard, "to imagine that the cure could end on a reconciliation of consciousness with the unconscious" (*Inhuman* 33). The incurable aftereffect of trauma is dispersed or disseminated in the present as a disfigured repetition. Traumatizing assault (physical and discursive) can only be explored with an impaired subjective voice that, through misrepresentation, subverts the existing order of the master discourse. This departure from positive, totalistic comprehension of reality can be understood as "negation" in both Freudian (psychic) and Adornian (historical) senses. Based on Freud's conception that "negation is a way of taking cognizance of what is repressed" or "with the help of the symbol of negation, thinking frees itself from the restrictions of repression" (19:235–39), Harold Bloom elucidates the affinity between negation and the mode of the "literary Sublime":

> [In the literary Sublime] the poet, while expressing previously repressed thought, desire, or emotions, is able to continue to defend himself against his own created image by disavowing it, a defense of *un-naming* it rather than *naming* it. Freud's word "Verneinung" means both a grammatical negation and a psychical disavowal or denial. . . . Freud joins himself to the tradition of the Sublime . . . by showing us that negation allows poetry to free itself from the aphasias and hysterias of repression, *without* however freeing the poets themselves from the unhappier human consequences of repression. Negation is of *no* therapeutic value for the individual, but it *can* liberate him into the linguistic freedom of poetry and thought. (224–25)

Obviously, it is positive representation that would ironically fall into "the aphasias and hysterias of repression," inasmuch as it could never reach the shock, which is insensible and unidentifiable on the level of consciousness. At this point Adorno's political understanding of aesthetic negativity is compatible with Freud's and Bloom's formulations: "Artworks have no truth without determinate negation; . . .The truth content of artworks cannot be immediately identified" (Adorno, *Aesthetic* 129).

What Chinese avant-garde fiction tends to grasp is not the concrete ferocity of historical violence itself but, rather, the brutal, horrid, and maniac affect it deposited beyond consciousness. The unidentifiable is always outside the text as the immemorial, which cannot recur in memory. As Cathy Caruth points out, "The flashback or traumatic reenactment conveys, that is, both *the truth of an event,* and *the truth of its incomprehensibility*" (153). At stake is the violence transformed into psychic fright and threat that are not simply represented as hideous but misrepresented as sinisterly sublime and indeterminate. Remaining obscure in memory, trauma in Chinese avant-garde fiction is phrased through figural or rhetorical deformation. Yu Hua and Can Xue do not simply describe the inhumanity and agony of human life; they also reveal the difficulties of representing inhumane and agonizing scenes in order to evoke and exonerate the immemorial trauma within the unconscious.

Incessantly startled by the traumatic experience of historical violence that culminated in the Cultural Revolution, the Chinese avant-gardists in the mid- and late 1980s had anticipated another historical catastrophe, the brutal Tiananmen Incident in 1989, before it really occurred. Their premonition of the impending catastrophe was derived from their sensitivity to trauma. The consecutive assaults of historical violence created mental ruins in the unconscious in advance of the new disaster.

Chapter 4

Yu Hua

The Past Remembered or the Present Dismembered

Yu Hua's early career as a dentist may be comparable to Lu Xun's early devotion to medicine. Lu Xun's rational literary project to "cure" the national malady, however, is dismissed by Yu Hua, whose connection with his dentist career might be seen as a stylistic one: the callousness required in the dentist work can be detected in Yu Hua's narrative aesthetics. In fact, the rational basis of the physiologically related science repels Yu Hua for the lack of imagination: "[in medical science] it would be impossible to imagine the heart inside the thigh or confuse teeth with toes" (*zuopinji* 3:385), as Yu Hua puts it in a short autobiographical essay. If, for Lu Xun, the aim to write is to replace the rational physical therapy with the rational mental therapy, for Yu Hua, the cognitive or representational rationality of the medical/dental science is in conflict with his personal propensity toward the obscure, the ambiguous and the inconceivable. Unlike Lu Xun, Yu Hua writes in opposition to his early career by turning inward to the complexity of personal experience to save the unrecognizable and the implausible, which Lu Xun, despite his theoretical rationality, could not really resist the temptation to explore, especially in his *Yecao* (Wild grass, 1927).[1]

The Return of the Historical Apparition

Yu Hua's "Nineteen Eighty-Six"[2] is one of the few works of Chinese avant-garde fiction clearly set against the background of the Cultural Revolution. Unlike those works of "scar literature" or "retrospect literature," which usually focus on the misfortunes of people during a specific period that has been, or will be, surpassed, "Nineteen Eighty-Six" reads not as much an "objective" representation of the past as a subjective struggle with traumatic experience from the past (in a narrative of the present). In "Nineteen Eighty-Six" the narrator's voice no longer maintains a realistic "objectivity" established by the rational subject, namely, the conscious author. On the contrary, the rationality of the narrative subject is faced with crisis, since it is the traumatic experience caused by the historical violence, which the narrative subject attempts to articulate, that shapes the impaired subjectivity of articulation.

Much of "Nineteen Eighty-Six" relates a madman's self-mutilation as a belated reaction to the political persecution during the Cultural Revolution. In the prologue, Yu Hua introduces the historical background of the story. Over a decade ago, during the climax of the Cultural Revolution, a high school history teacher disappeared, leaving his wife and daughter. His wife buried her memory until one day, in the recycling station, she accidentally saw a sheet of paper with notes on the outline of history of Chinese penology written by her supposedly "late" husband. Then, the narrative switches back to what happened during the Cultural Revolution. His notes that contain references to the most barbaric punishments in the feudalistic times were considered a proof of his guilt and he was thus coerced to write confession in his ruined office. He witnessed his colleague hanging himself in the office and people jumping down from the blazing building. Frightened, he lost his sanity and tried to escape from a black exit that was actually his own shadow on the wall. Watching the raging flames, he "laughed fiercely" with "extreme excitement" and "full zest" (*zuopinji* 1:147).

Back to the present, since her agitation in the recycling station, his wife has been hearing his shuffling footsteps all the time, the sound reminiscent of what she heard when he was taken away from home by the Red Guards nearly two decades ago. The climax of the catastrophe does not occur until the present. There is no sentimental scene of reunion, which can be seen in many works of similar topic. Only his daughter, with hair bows and braids reminiscent of his wife (when he first saw her), runs into him, now a madman loitering on the street, without knowing they are related. The madman reappears, as a fictional character, a decade after the end of the Cultural Revolution and, as a figure in the literary history, seven decades after the birth of his modern archetype—that is, the Madman of Lu Xun.[3]

It is essential to note the fact that, in addition to the madness of the protagonist, there occurs the madness of narration, for the traumatic experiences provoke the neurotic symptoms in both the protagonist and the author/narrator of the story. Narrative madness becomes a sign of traumatized subjectivity that is deprived of its integrative ability of articulation. If Lu Xun inverts the existing logic of sanity and insanity and speaks in feigned madness, Yu Hua, too, identifies the narrator's voice with the madman's. Madness in Yu Hua, however, is devoid of rational foundation and no longer represented as a formation of the discourse of the modern that, as Lu Xun intends, soberly accuses the oppression of the premodern. Rather, it is a deformation of the discourses of both the modern (Maoist discourse about historical violence) and the premodern (traditional Chinese penological conceptions). It neither adopts a transcendental attitude toward them nor converts them into a new form of discourse.

"Lacking the redeeming qualities found in Lu Xun's works" (Ban Wang 257), Yu Hua's narrative of madness must be seen as a distrust of the simple rejection of the past. In his essay "The Deceptive Works" Yu Hua claims that the "logic of memory" can "reconstruct the world" (*zuopinji* 2:286). The past, for him, is part of the destiny of the present. "The experience of the past," he suggests, "exists for the things in its future because it can generate new meanings only through the guidance of the future things." He thus elucidates:

> Although the events I narrate all occur in the state of the past, the narrative process can only be conducted on the level of the present. ... All the recollections and predictions are contents of the present.

> ... Since the experience of the past and the things in the future exist simultaneously in the present, the present is indeterminate and capricious. (282–83)

What is perceivable, for Yu Hua, is only the synchroneity of the past (from which unconscious affects are transmitted), the future (which is foreshadowed by persistent unconscious affect), and the present (which emerges as the activation of unconscious affect). The nullification of historical progress, in Yu Hua's own words, rests on "a kind of truth in personal mentality," since "my mental world does not contain any chaos because it does not even have a conception of temporality. Things which happened a long time ago exist along with those which happened yesterday" ("Wo de zhenshi" 107–8). This anachronism, too, becomes the psychic basis for the madman, whose present behavior seems to occur without a ten-year distance from his past. The indelible, traumatic past, existing in the unconscious, is reanimated in a more fierce way in the present.

The lack of progress signals the lack of distance between the past (which is to be negated) and the present (which is the force of negation). Thus, the present narrative is no longer an action of exhausting the traumatic experience but an evocation of and a struggle against its grip. In "Nineteen Eighty-Six" the indelibility of the past lies in the recurring psychic agitation not only of the mad protagonist but, more significantly, of the narrator. In other words, the narrator cannot distance himself from the character, as they both suffer from the traumatic past. The correspondence between the narrator's point of view and the madman's is a sign of the decline of the rational representational subject. The narration itself becomes an "irrational" one, rather than a rational *representation of* irrationality or a rational discourse camouflaged by irrational utterances. The narrator virtually identifies himself with the character and perceives in an equally irrational way without translating it into rational discourse:

> He saw a person lying somewhere around his feet. The man's feet somehow seemed connected to his own. He raised his foot and tried to kick away the prostrate foot. But that foot unexpectedly recoiled almost before he had even lifted his leg to strike. When he put his foot down, the other foot shifted back to its original position next to his own. He couldn't help getting excited and lifted his

own foot once more. He found that the foot on the ground had once again evaded his own at the same time and he felt that his rival was alarmed. Holding his foot motionless in the air until he saw that his rival's foot was also poised motionless in the air, he suddenly pounced, landing full force on the waist of that person. He heard a solid thump and looked down. The prone figure seemed unhurt and his feet still linked to his own. . . . Seeing the prone figure shift into a crouch underfoot, he was walking with more alertness. The person didn't flee but was sliding his body along the ground toward the pond. Coming closer, he saw the person's head drop into the pond, followed by his torso and his limbs. Standing at the edge of the pond and watching that fellow float on the surface of the water without sinking, he bent to pick up a big stone and threw it toward him. He turned away in satisfaction only after seeing the person shattered into pieces. A burst of golden sunbeam suddenly pierced his eyes and made him giddy and dazzled. He didn't close his eyes but looked up instead. Then he saw an effulgent head spurting blood. (*zuopinji* 1:151 / *The Past* 144; trans. modified)

The narrator's voice is preoccupied with the same susceptibility to threat as a madman's when it uses "he saw" as its own point of view without rationalizing it from a superior position. If Lu Xun's discourse of paranoia forms an intended indictment (though ostensibly insane and thus unreliable, for all practical purposes) against real oppression, Yu Hua adopts a parodied discourse of paranoia that points nowhere except to an agitation within the self. The source of threat, ironically, becomes the madman's own shadow, the objectified self, which can never be eliminated and is destined to adhere to himself, no matter how vehemently he tries to destroy it. This shadow can well be interpreted as a symbol of the dark, traumatic experience in the unconscious that cannot be obliterated.

The subsequent events in the novella indicate that the self, indeed, becomes the target of the counterattack against the traumatic past. Both being irrational ways of penetrating the inextricable, Yu Hua's narration of self-mutilation and the madman's action of self-mutilation are equally perverse in their allegorical disfiguring of bodily existence. Trauma in Yu Hua's personal past is transformed into the present mode of perplexed writing, which deals with equally perplexed, abnormal actions. The narrator's insane voice hardly does justice to the pain of torture: "He looked as if he were joyously blowing on a harmonica at the moment when he was sawing his nose" (161/157; trans. modified).

Created by beautiful discourse, the tension between behavioral cruelty and rhetorical zest evokes the obscurity and ambiguity of traumatic experience. The whole narrative of "Nineteen Eighty-Six" is set in the lyrical atmosphere of a "vigorous and gleeful" spring, when "the sound of melting snow was like a harmony plucked from the rays of the sun" (148–49/141; trans. modified) and girls "garbed themselves beautifully [and left] the house in search of the hero of the novel, enveloped in the aroma of their own perfume" (149–50/142; trans. modified). The hair bows of the madman's daughter, which make "his chest [feel] tight and strange" (153/146) but do not remind him of anything clear, are another inauspicious sign that past historical experience will be recreated. She wears hair bows and shops for dresses in the "Spring Commodity Fair," an appropriate symbol of Deng's age. But does this mark the end of Maoism? Here, again, Yu Hua metaphorically challenges historical teleology, which would not tolerate the recurrence of the image of hair bows, which, in Yu Hua's narrative, leads to further catastrophes.

To evoke the immemorial is thus to deal with the recurrent or reactivated traumatic affect in the present. The tragedy of the madman is a biting accusation against historical violence, not because it directly and clearly reflects the evil of the past but because it reveals the untraceability of the shocking past. Such a past permanently occupies the deep psyche and induces only deferred reactions to traumatic experience. At the same time, it is notable that the narrator shares the catastrophic destiny of the protagonist, insofar as the author's own trauma has been transformed into the deformative, irrational phrasing of the experience of violence.

The most shocking part in "Nineteen Eighty-Six," as I mentioned in the introduction, is its narrative admixture of torture and rapture in the repetitive expressions of being "(self-)satisfied" or "smiling complacently" (159–70), which refers to the scenes of self-mutilation. Georges Bataille, in the last chapter (entitled "Chinese Torture," a topic that preoccupies Yu Hua) of his book *Les larmes d'Eros* (The tears of eros), comments on a series of photos of a convict's limbs being amputated and his breast removed in 1905 Beijing, in public (he had murdered the Mongolian prince). The horrifying scene of the traditional Chinese physical punishment called *lingchi*[4] (slowly cutting a person into pieces) is conceived by Bataille as "the most anguishing of worlds accessible to us through images captured on film." It is not the pure atrocity and pain, however, but "the ecstatic appearance of the victim's expression ... due at least in part to the opium" administered to the condemned person "to prolong the torture" that "augments what is most anguishing about this photograph" (205). Like Bataille, who cannot help "being obsessed by this image of pain, at once ecstatic (?) and intolerable" (206), Yu Hua focuses on the double sensation in barbarity: the atrocious and the beautiful. If the ecstasy of the tortured person in Bataille's photos is influenced by opium, what Yu Hua explores is another kind of anesthetized effect, not pharmacologically but psychically generated, which dislocates the boundaries of pain and delight. This double sensation, again, embodies the aesthetics of the sublime, the quintessence of avant-gardism, upon which Lyotard has elaborated.

The Impossible Journey to the Past

In "The Past and the Punishments" Yu Hua examines the aesthetics of sinister sublime in an involute allegory. Inspired by Kafka's story "The Penal Colony," "The Past and the Punishments" is Yu Hua's most penetrating work. It is both a narrative that traces the personal traumatic unconscious and an allegory that pursues the anachronism of the disastrous history. At the beginning of this story the stranger receives a telegram containing only two words, "return quickly." This seems to be the penologist's call for remembering past crimes or punishments. Through the journey of time the stranger has settled the five dates of the crimes but fails to reach the one he has chosen (March 5, 1965) and misses the other four. He only encounters their metaphor, the penologist, who is the operator of the crimes, which, being synonymous with punishments, were performed on those four dates. The stranger arrives at the town named Smoke (where the penologist resides), a name that suggests the obscurity that he is involved in. He becomes aware that it would be impossible for him to reach any of the five dates in his past, because the other four always divert his journey.

Most of the story is devoted to the penologist's insinuation and prefiguration of his performances throughout the mixed-up temporality of the past, the present, and the future. The penologist, a character specializing in physical punishments, may be interpreted as a symbolic executor of historical violence who has nevertheless concealed the real crimes, which only vaguely agitate the stranger. Theoretically, the penologist affirms the persistence of the past. He reminds the stranger: "Actually, we always live in the past. The past is forever. The present and the future are just little tricks the past plays on us" (*zuopinji* 1:34/117). "You are not cut off from your past," says the penologist. "You've always been deeply immersed in your past. You may feel alienated from the past from time to time, but that's merely an illusion, a superficial phenomenon, which only means that you're really that much closer" (35/117; trans. modified). When the stranger implies that he is the obstruction between him and his past, the penologist declares, "I am your past" (35/118). Obviously, the penologist, as a historical incarnation who is confident of his own totality, reintroduces the stranger to past experience but, precisely because of his barbarity and arbitrariness, deprives the stranger of the capability of identifying the memory of past punishments.

When the penologist elucidates his enterprise, "the most outstanding part of human wisdom" (36/119; trans. modified), the stranger detects that there is only one kind of punishment missing, namely, the gallows. From the blank space of historical discourse he is suddenly assured of the fact that someone connected to him hanged himself on the very date he has been searching for. The penologist, requested by the stranger to provide details on the gallows, refuses to do so but, by metaphorizing the relation between time and atrocity, elaborates upon the other four historical dates, which were subject to four traditional Chinese punishments—dismemberment (with five carriages), castration, waist slitting, and head smashing:

> He had drawn and quartered January 9, 1958, tearing it into so many pieces that it had drifted through the air like a flurry of snowflakes. He had castrated December 1, 1967, cutting off its ponderous testicles so that there hadn't been a drop of sunshine on December 1, 1967, and the moonlight that evening had been as dense as overgrown weeds. Nor had August 7, 1960, been able to escape its fate, for he had used a rust-dappled saw blade to cut through its waist. But the most unforgettable was September 20, 1971. He had dug a trench in the ground, in which he had buried September 20, 1971, so that only the head was still exposed. Owing

to the pressure exerted on the body by the surrounding earth, the blood of September 20, 1971, had surged up into the head. The penologist had proceeded to crack open its skull, from which a column of blood had immediately spurted forth. The fountain of September 20, 1971, had been incomparably brilliant. (37/120–21; trans. modified)

The stranger is thus reminded of the terror of historical violence, not realistically but tropologically, yet the concrete truth of the past is still possessed and concealed by the penologist. The only thing that the stranger can obtain is the fragmented imagery of the atrocity, or the reactivated, shuddering traumatic affect, which derives from the ruins of disastrous history. "Through the incessant rephrasing and the historical crevice of metaphors," the critic Dai Jinhua remarks, "Yu Hua obstructs the way of root-seeking and proclaims the futility of historical reflection and the death of history *per se*" (33).

If the penologist's rhetoric of describing the crimes demonstrates the atrocious violence of history beyond rational articulation, his second version about these crimes shows exactly the aesthetic discourse that history adopts on the other side of its Janus face. The penologist suggests that the stranger, during the experiment of torture, be chopped apart at the waist and sees not only blood from his own body spreading on the glass but also his memory being refreshed agreeably—that is, with aesthetic pleasure:

> While you are breathing your last, you will catch sight of the first dewdrop of the morning of January 19, 1958. You will see this dewdrop gazing at you from an inconspicuous green leaf. You will see a bank of clouds at noon of December 1, 1967. Owing to the radiation of the sun, the clouds will glow in brilliant colors. You will see a mountain road on the arrival of the dusk of August 7, 1960, when the sunset clouds will lie on the road and warmly wait for you. You will see two fireflies in the moonlight on the night of September 20, 1971, dancing like a pair of distant tears. (39/122–23; trans. modified)

In order to regain the memory of the event on March 5, 1965, through another blow, the stranger agrees. The execution of the punishment, however, turns out to be a fiasco because the penologist's hands are too weak and tremulous to conduct it in a pure and perfect way. Again, to maintain the lyrical power of evil, the penologist highlights the aesthetic value of his barbarous crime, just as he did before when describing the scattering body parts and gushing blood as a "flurry of snowflakes" and a "brilliant" "fountain" (37/120–21). Now the penologist would simply not conduct the execution without an ideal aesthetic value.

Despite the disappointment of the stranger, the penologist envisions the ultimate and conclusive punishment for himself. He imagines himself to be sentenced to death, as a punishment for torturing his family members. He will be standing on a high platform in a square where thousands of people are gathering to arraign his crimes. The soldiers will be aiming at him with the pistols from different directions. It will last for ten hours, during which he has to tolerate all the intolerable feelings before death. This is truly the moment when the aesthetics of the sublime reaches its climax. The tragedy of sacrifice in which the penologist plays the major role is to be conceived as part of a grand narrative, indicated by the conception of "penological science." The death of history, however, whether symbolic or practical, fails to show its grandiosity. Because the penologist's scheme neglects a fatal bullet that should shoot him, his effort to die by his imaginary supreme punishment turns out to be such an extremely messy struggle that he eventually hangs himself instead, in a way that he originally despised as a deteriorated form of the gallows.

Thus, allegorically, rational history destroys itself out of its impulse to reach the aesthetic perfection of reason, "the perfection to which the punishment is inclined" expressed in the penologist's "self-confident narrative" (*zuopinji* 1:43). The result, as we have seen, becomes aesthetically inferior insofar as punishment or torture can only lead to violence and perversity, rather than perfection, no matter how rational it is. In the end, when the stranger is disappointed with the loss of his memory along with the death of the penologist, he unexpectedly sees a suicidal note by the penologist with the date of his death, March 5, 1965, which is exactly the date he has sought. Finally, the stranger seems to have returned to his traumatic past, whose authenticity is, however, problematic to the stranger as well as the reader. It remains unknown whether this is the allegorical recurrence of the stranger's past experience or merely another trick that "rational" history plays in a repetitive way. The paradox lies in the fact that the likely return to the past appears at the same time as the death of what contains the past and thus prevents the stranger from returning to the past. Yu Hua leaves a perpetual enigma in his allegorical struggle with the traumatic experience of historical violence. Ultimately, this is a symptom of the limitation of narrative: a narrative that no longer claims absolute determinacy, which leads not to a single destination but to various possible destinations.

Indefinable Disasters and Inhumanities

To trace the memory of historical violence, for Yu Hua, is to trace the problematics of the memory traumatized by shocking violence. In his novella "One Kind of Reality" trauma effects a kind of indifferent narration, a narration apathetic to atrocious and cruel actions. The plot of this novella is unusually simple. At the beginning Shangang's son, Pipi, accidentally causes the death of his younger cousin, Shanfeng's son. After Shanfeng takes revenge on Pipi by kicking him to death, Shangang employs unusual wile, enticing a dog to lick and tickle Shanfeng's soles until he cannot stop laughing and breathes his last. In the end Shangang is executed, and his organs are removed in the course of the autopsy. What is remarkable in this novella is that all the inhuman scenes are described in an unnaturally detached narrative tone, which is entirely lacking in subjective involvement. The most striking aspect here, therefore, is not the intentional or unintentional killings between brothers, cousins, uncle, and nephew or between executioner and felon but the impassive voice of narration that sharply contrasts with the atrocious content. The symptom of this kind of narration seems to be the impossibility of proper phrasing caused by the affective disorder of the narrator.

Like many of his other works, Yu Hua's "One Kind of Reality" has a multilayered construction. First, the representation of cold-blooded murders among family members demolishes, in an extreme way, the conventional Chinese cultural idea that envisions an ultimate harmony of family as a grand symbol of ideal society. Second, unlike the canonical novels that deal with the decomposition of a big family, such as Ba Jin's *Family,* Wang Xiyan's *Guwu* (The old house, 1946), or Lu Ling's *Caizhu de ernümen* (Children of the rich, 1948), "One Kind of Reality" does not resort to a hidden historical agenda to transform the destruction of the old into the emergence of the new. Atrocities are shown as either mechanical acts of revenge or mechanical processes of legal routine. Without aiming at a further positive end, representation of the internally destructive family becomes a narrative drifting between evil and nothingness. In addition, the seemingly ignorant voice of narration intensifies the indefinability of subjective pathos. By showing a barbarous world that appears normal and ordinary, Yu Hua alludes to a traumatized and incapacitated subject both alert and numb to the shocking violence. The final chapter of the novella details the autopsy of Shangang, whose still fresh organs are to be used in transplantation. Neither tragic nor comic, the process of autopsy unfolds in such an awkwardly indifferent way that even the "normal" subjective voice is lost in (mis)representation:

> The woman doctor carries Shangang's skin over to one corner of the Ping-Pong table and, smoothing out the various pieces of the skin, begins to scrape them one by one. Using her dissecting knife like a scouring brush, she scrubs at the fat cells lining the skin. The sound made by each stroke of her knife is like the disconsolate whine of a car wheel trapped in sand. . . . By now the woman doctor has finished scraping the pieces of skin, and, after folding them like a suit, she leaves as well. (*zuopinji* 2:43–44 / "One Kind" 65–66; trans. modified)

Without a purposive critical reflection upon the brutality, the perverse tone of narration here implies a questionable narrative subject. Rather than create a critical distance, the narrative subject exposes vulnerability from within, for there is in reality no superior subject who can be immune, or completely detached, from despair. Yu Hua's tale provides a picture that is opposite that of the ideal harmony of familial prosperity, even though, ironically, Shangang's testicles are transplanted to someone else who later begets Shangang's offspring, beyond the expectation of Shanfeng's wife, who turns him in.

The inextricable snare of mutual injuries, defacements, and murders also structures Yu Hua's novella "The Inescapable Fate," in which people bring violence to their own spouses and friends in unreasonable ways. The story starts with the arrival of Dongshan (East Mountain), whose passionate appearance to his love, Luzhu (Dewdrop), is concurrently an exposure to Luzhu's father, the old doctor. To prevent Dongshan from abandoning her after their marriage, Luzhu accepts the "dowry," a bottle of nitric acid, which her father has prepared for her. Then, several threads of the story spread out from the wedding of Dongshan and Luzhu in the bridal chamber, in which many of their friends are gathering. Guangfo (Massive Buddha) and Caidie (Colorful Butterfly), aroused by the sound of lovemaking in Dongshan and Luzhu's bedroom, go out of the house together but find a boy following them with a flashlight. Guangfo kicks and tramples the boy until he is dead. Inside Shazi (Sand) furtively cuts off a girl's plait from behind (this habit changes into cutting up girls' pants on another occasion). The misfortunes continue after the wedding. During the night Luzhu pours the nitric acid on Dongshan's face. Dongshan later kills Luzhu but drinks the liquid provided by the old doctor, which causes his permanent impotence. A few days later Senlin is arrested for his misconduct and, before his release, betrays Shazi, who is subsequently arrested. Caidie jumps to death from a high building, not because Guangfo receives a death sentence but because her face-lifting operation turns out to be a total disaster.

Yu Hua discloses the darkest human desire that disrupts the socioethical order: love and marriage are not far from mutual injury; friendship means nothing more than mutual betrayal. This would not be surprising if one is familiar with the recent history of contemporary China. Murder and mutilation, such as defacement, cutting others' plaits, or scissoring women's pants, were an essential part of social life under the Communist regime, particularly during the Cultural Revolution, though in the name of revolution and justice. Here the evils are deprived of their sociohistorical backdrop and allegorized at the core of human behavior. In other words, social disaster is shown as an uncontrollable psychic impulse or mechanism. This is, however, by no means a depoliticization of the disaster; rather, it is the absence of the political that indicates the original lack of ability to articulate the disaster. This lack implies the traumatic affect whose real origin is unidentifiable. The unidentifiability of the origin of trauma opens up an obscure view toward the experience of atrocity. Psychic desire and impulse appear to be the tangible but indirect figuration of history, whose turbulence is not merely externally but also internally active. Luzhu's defacement of Dongshan is justified as an action to prevent him from abandoning her in the future. The "moral" rationality of violence is established as a ground for psychic irrationality, but the logic of behavior is so tenuous that the lofty concept of rationality has to fall into the irrational abyss.

Once again, in this novella, what piques us is not only the devastation of traditional ethical ideals such as marriage and friendship but the mode of narration that appears to be inadequate to articulate the shocking violence. Perverse lyricism permeates only to evince the psychic incapability of phrasing or to imply the ambivalence derived from the traumatic experience of the assaults:

> Dongshan walked out first. He smiled *like a rotten apple,* but he looked like a bridegroom anyway. His bride followed him, her face glittering *like a twenty-watt bulb.* (*zuopinji* 1:188; my emph.)

> Blood flew out *hilariously* from the corner of the boy's mouth. It had the color of mud. Guangfo looked at his chest for a little while and thought it wouldn't be bad to listen to the cracking sound of his ribs. (191; my emph.)

Prevailing in the narrative, such improper similes or modifications reject immediate, simple comprehension of the represented events. By evoking the historical violence in the memory trace, Yu Hua unveils the ferocious, bloody scene underlying moralistic and just discourse. The narrative uneasiness in Yu Hua is a symptom of affective complexity and obscurity, inasmuch as the natural articulation of shocking experience has been incapacitated by historical violence. The (an)aesthetics of agony lies in the perverse apathy to the atrocities.

The serene or lyrical tone in Yu Hua's narrative about dismembering human bodies corresponds to the serious, standard genre of Maoist discourse, whose rationality is in constant conflict with bloody reality. In other words, the bloody characteristics of Yu Hua's stories are not produced as a remembering function that implies the cruelty of political persecution or the destructiveness of Maoist discourse. Rather, their irrational form, or form of deformation, abolishes the rational order (e.g., the dichotomies of just/unjust, proletarian/bourgeois, revolutionary/reactionary, etc.) that the master discourse appropriates to exert historical violence. In this sense Yu Hua's narrative is a particular way of evoking the complexity of historical trauma as the primary repression, whether the violence is related to the Cultural Revolution (in "Nineteen Eighty-Six" the protagonist is a mental victim of the Cultural Revolution) or not ("One Kind of Reality" and "The Inescapable

Fate" are unrelated to any historical background). The real past and the disasters, for Yu Hua, are irretrievable. This is why, even though many of his titles contain the word *shi*—"event(s)" or "incident(s)"—such as "Ouran shijian" (Occasional incidents, 1989), "Siyue sanri shijian" (The April Third incident), "Shishi ruyan" (World like mist, 1988), "Wangshi yu xingfa" (The past and the punishments), these events/incidents are essentially unidentifiable, intangible, and ungraspable.

"World like Mist" is a narrative in which the linear, consecutive history is illegible. Disturbed by various deaths, the progress of the narrative is disrupted, although none of the shocking scenes is displayed visibly. What exists *now* is only the aftermath represented as deformative figures. As Dai Jinhua acutely observes, in "World like Mist" "there is never an eyewitness to death itself; death is invisible and insensible yet ascertainable to both the narrator and the characters in the narrative. The narrative of death always shows a deferral of narration and an obstruction to the narrated object" (28). For Yu Hua the impossibility of approaching the traumatic origin is the only way to speak of that trauma. Or, put another way, trauma is not represented as objective but internalized as part of the subjectivity, as the deformation and disjunction of narrative that evince the traumatized memory.

It is impossible to summarize the plot of "World like Mist," in which fragmented incidents that happen to the neighbors on a street are dispersed and interwoven into an intricate collage. Besides the fortune-teller, the driver, the midwife, among several others, most of the characters are only identified by numbers (7, 4, 3, 2, and 6). The ninety-year-old fortune-teller plays a crucial role in this story. He has gained longevity from the deaths of his four children and from absorbing spirit from girls' vaginal secretions. He uses the method again with 4, a little girl, who in the end drowns herself. The fortune-teller promises 3, an old woman, that he will adopt the child she is conceiving, a child who resulted from her incest with her seventeen-year-old grandson. He also tells 7 to get rid of his son in order to recover from his illness. He tells the driver to stop his truck whenever he sees a woman in gray. The driver buys a gray coat from the woman he accidentally passes by and runs over it with the truck. She dies in bed wearing her coat with the trace of truck wheel, and her funeral and her son's wedding are held on the same day. The driver feels insulted by 2 at the wedding and kills himself by cutting his own throat. There is a person called 6, who has sold his six daughters and, when trying to sell his sixteen-year-old youngest daughter to someone who assaults her in her dream every night, insists on a high price. The dead driver comes to 2's dream asking for help with his marriage, and 2 buys the drowned corpse of 6's daughter to arrange a "posthumous wedding" for the driver and 6's daughter. The midwife, the driver's mother, helps deliver a baby in a strange place, which becomes a graveyard that she later revisits,[5] and her body gradually withers.

These episodes are pieced together along with various minor but equally surreal occurrences, some with causal connections and others without. Yu Hua presents a jumbled picture of inexplicable events with an emphasis on their ultimate obscurity. The narrative leaves numerous mysteries about deaths and focuses on dispersed and fragmentary feelings of danger. Moments of real accidents are not represented logically: history is here constituted by chasms that cannot be filled. The death of 6's daughter, for example, is presumably related to the man appearing in her dream, but the connection is not directly established. The background of the incident is much more perceptible than the incident itself. The ferocious feature of the man in her dream, the startling sound of his knock at the door, and the bargain on the price of bartering her all develop into a perilous situation that leads to her death on the riverbank, while the real cause is left unknown.

In another episode the driver's suicide is a result of "humiliation," which is at first not taken negatively and seems even pleasant to him: the driver sees the bride's slender arms glistening, her fingers dancing, and is enthralled with her tender touch. What perplexes him is that the bride gets paid by 2 to scour 2's face in the same tender way over and over again, and his bid to stop her from doing this is beaten by 2's. Here humiliation seems to be inseparable from pleasure, desire, and envy. It is thus an ambivalent psychic disturbance that Yu Hua attempts to explore. The tragedy comes not from simple agony but from a kind of unnamable shock that deprives the driver of the courage to live. To most people the link between what happens to him and his decision to die would seem unreasonable, precisely because the overwhelming incomprehensibility of the shock is far beyond reason.

Comparatively, 4's suicide is clearer to understand, for she was raped by the fortune-teller. What is not so clear is why her father, who takes 4 to the fortune-teller to cure 4's somniloquy, assists the rape. When the fortune-teller proposes therapy to "pull the ghost out from inside her nether parts" (*zuopinji* 2:75 / *The Past* 99), her father is stunned but acquiesces. But:

> This sudden turn of events made 4 feel at a loss. She could only gaze imploringly toward her father. Instead of looking at her, he took up a position behind her. She heard him say something, but before she made out just what it had been, her body was firmly latched around by her father's hands, which made her feel completely powerless. (75/99; trans. modified)

In this passage the "inescapable" sense of hopelessness comes not merely from the absolute power of the attacker but also from the dubious role of the supposed protector, the father. It seems preposterous that a father would accept such a "treatment" in order to stop his daughter's somniloquy. Just like the relationships among relatives and friends in Yu Hua's other works, the relationship between father and daughter is manifested here by inevitable disorder. The similarly treacherous relationship occurs between 6 and his daughters, as he has sold six daughters for profit and bargains for a good price on the corpse of his youngest daughter. The fortune-teller (who is destined to bring his children's deaths), 7 (who gives away his own son for the sake of his recovery of health), and 3 (who does not hesitate to abandon her child), among others, constitute the sinister patterns of kinship in this novella.

The episodes intertwined in Yu Hua's fiction consist of a fragmentary and discontinuous picture without being integrated into a spatial and temporal whole. This disintegration means the infeasibility of a universal reason by which the tragedies could be fully comprehended. Atrocities, deaths, and evil remain enigmatic and cannot be rationalized by any discourse that would have established another historical subject to redeem the disastrous past. Only by not presenting the historical whole, by forgetting in a certain sense, are we allowed to touch profound historical meaning, which is, ironically, the loss of meaning of history. As Dai Jinhua remarks: "In the silence and the fade-out of the discourse, death not only presents itself as unbridgeable textual crevices, but also means an absolute extermination for a 'nation' that has lost its desire and fecundity. [. . .]And the political unconscious, as an enormous discursive taboo, is also presented as a sign of silence, as the unspeakable oblivion and the similar 'real pursuit'" (28–29).

This "real pursuit," originally used by Yu Hua himself in "The Past and the Punishments" (*zuopinji* 1:38) to describe the Stranger's motivation for remembering, should be understood as anamnesis, which never brings out real incidents from the past. It is a lurking memory trace in the unconscious agitated by present happenings. In Yu Hua's fiction trauma is indicated as the suffering from the unidentifiable shock in the past, the inexorable danger and ferocity that have been secretly transmitted to the present from the primary, ambiguous assault. Here Judith Herman's observation of the psychic conflict can best elucidate Yu Hua's narrative style: "The conflict between the will to deny horrible events and the will to proclaim them aloud is the central dialectic of psychological trauma. People who have survived atrocities often tell their stories in a highly emotional, contradictory, and fragmented manner that undermines their credibility and thereby serves the twin imperatives of truth-telling and secrecy" (1).

Yu Hua's ahistorical approach focuses on the present, since the unconscious affect can only be phrased within "the Now" (*Jetztzeit*) in the Benjaminian sense, in which all the past events are dispersed as ruins, discontinuities, or collages in an instant and from which the revolutionary, nihilistic force rockets up. There is no temporal duration in this moment, no rational development of history; everything is conjured up in the Now:

> To articulate the past historically does not mean to recognize it "the way it really was" (Ranke). It means to seize hold of a memory as it flashes up at a moment of danger: Historical materialism wishes to retain that image of the past which unexpectedly appears to man singled out by history at a moment of danger. (Benjamin 257)

The image of the past, in this sense, is not the real image through which the past is remembered but the affective image that occurs "unexpectedly," unintentionally, evoked by the historical occasion of the "second blow," which is understood as a "moment of danger." The past events cannot but be shown as incomprehensible, or, if represented "realistically" (i.e., with subjective confidence), they would be only repetitions of terror. A Derridean *différance* stretches out the distance between the violence during the earlier age and the belated reaction to its violence and disrupts the repressive form of totality.

Chapter 5

Can Xue

Ever-Haunting Nightmares

> *How can you be so confident? . . . On the contrary, there will never be any ending. They're right in my nerves, packed together tightly. They only leak out a little in nightmares.*
> —CAN XUE, OLD FLOATING CLOUD

Once in an interview, when asked by her Japanese translator about the lack of a "horizontal" dimension (linear narrative development) in her works, Can Xue made a statement quite analogous to what Yu Hua states in his "The Deceptive Works":

> That might be related to memory. I regard myself as a person who has lost memory. People who write fiction as a horizontal flow must have memory. Because my situation is the loss of memory, I neither consider nor want to consider things in the past. I always consider only "the present." (Xiao 428)

It is not surprising that Can Xue, like Yu Hua, emphasizes the present as the only temporal concept in her narrative. Yet, while Yu Hua is aware of the constellation of psychic images that contains the past and the future simultaneously in the present, Can Xue's attitude toward memory is first suggestive ("related to") and then negative ("has lost memory"). Therefore, the only way we can read this passage is that her fiction is related to her lost memory, rather than the absolute void of memory.

To mention and then to deny memory indicate the psychic shield in consciousness that resists traumatic experiences from the past. This can also be evidenced by a short memoir Can Xue wrote, "Meili nanfang zhi xiari" (The beautiful summer in the south, 1986), in which she recalls her childhood during a most difficult time in terms of both national and personal histories. The brief preface to the memoir reads:

> In 1957 my father, as head of the "anti-Party clique" at the *New Hunan Daily*, was condemned as an ultrarightist and transferred to Hunan Teachers' College to reform through labor, and my mother was sent to Hengshan Mountain for labor reform. In 1959 the whole family of nine was moved from the newspapers' residential area to a tiny hut of about ten square meters at the foot of Yuelushan Mountain. We lived on an income of less than ten yuan per person. That was the time of nationwide natural disasters. Since my father had neither savings nor help from outside, the whole family struggled along on the verge of death. ("Meili nanfang" 75 / *Dialogues* 1; trans. modified)

This passage is important because, first, it provides us the historical background of Can Xue's life in childhood and, second, it omits, as the whole memoir does, all the *mental* sufferings she must have had during the period her memoir deals with. Can Xue stresses the difficulty of earning a livelihood at the time. Given the fact that her family was exiled out of the central city because her father had been "condemned" as a "class enemy," it is unusual that political persecution per se is not brought up. The whole memoir, mainly describing her grandmother's mystic and shrewd character and her father's optimistic and tenacious disposition, does not provide an atmosphere as abominable as her fictional world. Nonetheless, there are a few indications of mental agitation that, though still not referring to the historical origin, show the disturbed young mind in that specific situation. Pushing the kitchen door open, she "heard a strange noise" of somebody pacing the pitch dark room (75/1). When going to the toilet on the hill (a scene reminiscent of "Hut on the Mountain," one of her best-known stories) at night, she was scared by "a lizard [that] lay there in ambush" the whole time (75/2).

One of the distinctive images in the memoir that recurrently appears in her fiction is bodily swelling. Can Xue was often plagued by a "red swollen lump" caused by pine caterpillars (76/3). Her grandmother's body was depicted as "swollen like an oxygen pillow" (76/4) when she died of dropsy (a disease whose Chinese name literally means "water-swollen disease"). Although not directly related to political reality, the image of swelling itself is to be understood as a symptom that evokes the traumatic affect of widespread suffering at the time. The image of swelling can be detected in many of Can Xue's works. In "Wo zai neige shijie li de shiqing" (The things that happened to me in that world, 1986) "my face was swollen, oozing pus from morning to night" (*Tiantang* 327 / *Dialogues* 92). In "Hut on the Mountain" the narrator tells us, "The back of my head . . . would get numb and swollen" whenever "mother was glaring ferociously" at it (289/48). In "Tianchuang" (The skylight, 1986), "[because] I was steeped in urine, my head was swollen like a ball when I grew up" (310/107). In *Yellow Mud Street* Old Hu San's cheeks would get swollen whenever Old lady Qi chewed (*Tiantang* 99 / *Old Floating Cloud* 103).[1] Swelling signals a bodily reaction to violence that cannot be thoroughly grasped. The images of swelling in these cases can be seen as figural allusions to traumatic experience, since it is always unreasonable or implausible forces that are assumed to underlie it. The external assaults that cause the symptom of swelling are so elusive or far-fetched that they seem to be unreal or surreal.

In Yu Hua's fiction inadequate narration of atrocities alludes to traumatized subjectivity. In Can Xue it is the dense, grotesque imagery of bodily afflictions and incoherent expressions of often seemingly rational thoughts that imply the nebulous, untraceable trace of traumatic memory in the unconscious. She turns Yu Hua's indifferent, inept, and perverse narratorial voice into a hypersensitive tone that reveals the incomprehensibly and unreasonably disturbing reality.

A World of Harassment and Laceration

In some cases, nevertheless, images of uneasiness such as swelling are not a result of an external attack. In Can Xue's novella "Zhong zai zoulang shang de pingguoshu" (Apple tree in the corridor, 1986), again, the image of swelling plays a significant role. Awen kicks in the wall to search for everyone in the house, and his toes swell up ("Zhong zai" 67 / Embroidered 142–43); the doctor/detective falls from the room, which results in his having a blue nose and swollen face (67/143); Awen's mother, who appears to be a young woman to "me," says that her feet "are swollen like carrots" (69/149);[2] the "I"'s legs swell seriously in a morning (70/152); Awen's sister sprains her ankle, which "swelled as big as buckets" (75/166).

These symptoms of swelling, if not occurring spontaneously, result from one's own behavior. The real pain is not always directly tangible, and the culpable causes are not always visible, although this novella indeed manifests an astonishing picture of interpersonal attacks, suspicions, and betrayals that reminds us of historical periods during which there is much sociopolitical chaos. "Apple Tree in the Corridor" consists of different narrators, including Awen (the "I"), his third sister, the detective or doctor (i.e., his sister's fiancé), and Awen's mother. Each of them, in different chapters, is immersed in his or her vagarious observation of the world. Awen's remark in the beginning—"Everything gives the appearance of being true" (61/127)—suggests the unreliability of what he observes, which spreads throughout the narrative. We see, for example, that the mask speaking on the wall turns out to be an old man who picks odds and ends from refuse heaps and later, after his death, is claimed to be a transformation of the detective/doctor. Everyone else in the novella, analogous to this old man, who hangs himself on the lintel of Awen's apartment, behaves too oddly to be comprehensible. Awen's father, who deliberately breaks his leg in order to install a false leg (with which he hopes to look better), is ardently engaged in excursions to the Green Mountain before his death. He is found dead under a chestnut tree with a bag full of dead, rotten, and stinky orioles and doves. What we discern is only the absurdity and futility of his journey or project, a project as worthless as the one that Can Xue's own father—as well as his generation—was undertaking.

Unlike Yu Hua, who reveals the atrocity and cruelty in human nature, Can Xue focuses on the deformity and abjection of her characters. Nonetheless, like Yu Hua, Can Xue never represents a rational, logical story as a direct indictment against political or social injustice. Her multiple and paradoxical subjective voices seem to be struggling in a narrative perplexity without being able to clarify anything. The link between false leg and good appearance, for example, is (dis)connected without rational justification. So is the link between a father's love for nature and his disposition to cherish killed birds. The (dis)connections can best be interpreted from the traumatic experience of the author within the memory of the inexplicable ambiguity of the past, in which depravity might be rationalized into decency. Such an aesthetic of the sublime, which confounds pleasure and pain, is rooted in what cannot be remembered soberly: a kind of dread that is ungraspable within the scope of reason. The unconscious affect derived from past experience recurs but without an integrative frame or formation.

The interpersonal attacks, suspicions, and betrayals in "Apple Tree in the Corridor," too, seem to be detached from their historical background and immune from political influence. But unexpected and unjustifiable interpersonal attacks and betrayals *are* among the prevalent social maladies during the numerous political movements in the second half of the twentieth century.[3] Awen is concerned that he can "never see through" (63/132; trans. modified) his father. His sister's fiancé declares that he is a doctor and inspects the wall of Awen's apartment with his stethoscope. All their thoughts and behavior are absurd, not simply because they do not make sense but because they intend, yet fail, to make sense. What they denote, then, is nothing but the psychic agitation that arises from suspicion and fear, which, however, may have no real object. Every day when it gets dark, Awen begins to seek those people, going from one room to another, but finds that they have all vanished and are hiding. The narrator confesses that, in such a silence, he opens the window and keeps spitting toward the boundless dark. Then he takes out the hammer to hit the wall all night long. Except the invisibility of the object of the search, we are told nothing about why the searching and hiding, the spitting, and the hammering are going on, and the whole scene seems to be pointless. Such a lack of objective, nonetheless, does not deny the reality of psychic agitation but, rather, indicates the elusiveness of reality in the deep psyche due to an immemorial shock.

Thus, we are probably no longer surprised to here the contradictory statements by Awen's mother, who first complains that she sleeps in the trunk and suffered from her son's stepping on her eyeball and then declares that this whole story is but her fabrication. Such hallucinations or realities of (self-)torture constitute the fragmentary or discontinuous unfolding of the narrative. The whole story is made up of a series of incidents that create a lunatic ambiance in which there is no family but only a jungle. For example, Awen's sister is so belligerent that she chases her mother, who talks in the dark to scare people, to smash her with a spade. Every morning she and her fiancé drive Awen away from his apartment and make chaos by throwing everything out. Awen, in turn, holds a toy gun to shoot the shadows on the wall with water, for he suspects that they are going to kill him. On the other hand, Awen's sister also shoots her fiancé with a pistol she usually hides in her pocket and strikes him with an iron hammer. Jean-Paul Sartre's aphorism "Hell is other people" fits perfectly well in this family: there are no allies, only enemies.

The discontinuity and indeterminacy of the disturbances are perhaps the most perplexing factors in this novella. The narrative maintains disconnections between violent actions and their motivations without clarifying them rationally. Not only is the novella constituted by different narrators, but the characters themselves also serve as narrators who are susceptible to suffering from inexplicable suspicion and fear. Can Xue's narration is a reexperience, rather than an explanation, of the inarticulate. The detective (i.e., the doctor or the sister's fiancé), in the chapter narrated by him, admits that he is "forever circling around, never able to approach reality. Once I open my mouth, I discover I'm telling something that I have falsified, instead of *the thing*" (84/192). The emphasized *the thing* is exactly what is omitted in Can Xue's narrative as the immemorial, the unrepresentable. At times the characters themselves suggest such a difficulty of memory or inability to articulate. "I lost my memory," Awen's mother claims, "So the thing cannot be confirmed" (62/129). When he wants to talk about "obstacles in verbal expression," Awen feels that his "mind was working" but his "mouth was motionless" (70/151).

The spatial setting of corridor, the titular image, becomes a jungle full of dangers. It is "horrifying" to Awen's mother (74/162) and the detective (78/175), "hazy and tricky" (79/177) and "disastrous" (68/146) to Awen's sister. Yet nothing has really happened in the corridor. The only real occurrence is that Awen's aunt holds a flashlight in the corridor to dazzle people. The other reference to the corridor occurs in a more whimsical way in Awen's dreams, in which two panthers were raised in the corridor and a fox ran into the clouds from the window of the corridor. The panthers and fox create the barbarous atmosphere in the family. In other words, the family becomes a real jungle, in which, of course, the law of the jungle predominates. The law of the jungle, make no mistake about it, is the core of evolutionary theory, from which historical dialectics has learned that evil is the force that propels the progress of the grand history. Hannah Arendt, in her famous treatise on totalitarianism, points out that the Marxist notion of class struggle involves a historical law of survival, while Darwin's indicates a natural one (Arendt 463–64).

In his dream Awen becomes a troglodyte who escapes from home to dwell in a cave. The perplexing thing is that the home itself does not lack in brutality, and the cave will be decorated (as Awen's aunt suggests) as home so as to become aesthetically refined. This mental impasse he runs into in the dream divulges his feeling of helplessness. The love of nature is indistinguishable from the hunger for barbarity, and the disposition to civilization is indistinguishable from the inclination to artificiality. It is not until the end of the novella that the narrator claims that the apple trees planted in the corridor have grown ripe fruits. This idyllic scene is incomprehensible in relation to the previous descriptions of the corridor, in which only fear and danger are generated. But, again, the jungle is to be seen as beautiful, just like a totalitarian society always shows its gaudy decorations. The real and the impossible, the attractive and the repulsive, all of these are intertwined in the flux of the unconscious.

The whole novella, lacking a linear plot, disseminates the episodes in various narrators' statements of experiences and descriptions of dreams. Realities and illusions can hardly be differentiated from one another, insofar as all the scenes and events are, like the dream works, distorted, replaced, or condensed to the extent that they are only explicable when interpreted as oneiric visions. Contrary to the paradigmatic mode of modern narrative that establishes absolute verity of signification, Can Xue's style suggests the elusiveness of representation. In so doing, Can Xue hints at the origin of narrative distortion: the confident and integral voice is broken down as a result of the historical trauma. This is why, in Can Xue's works, fears and agitations are not generated by real assaults. What Can Xue presents is a traumatized memory that is not allowed to surface from the unconscious. The complete and proper articulation of the truth is thus incapacitated, and the representation of it appears to be distorted and dreamlike. While many works recount the miserable experiences under political persecution and thus maintain the absolute subjectivity as the ultimate safe harbor, Can Xue's narratives, without resting on a dependable authority of voicing the truth, focus on the subjective fragmentation resulting from the historical trauma. It is precisely "in its repeated imposition as both image and amnesia" that trauma, as Cathy Caruth argues, "evoke[s] the difficult truth of a history that is constituted by the very incomprehensibility of its occurrence" (153).

A World of Indifference and Horror

Compared to "Apple Tree in the Corridor," a medley of dreams and hallucinations, *Canglao de fuyun* (Old floating cloud, 1986), another of Can Xue's novellas, has a more tangible plot. The central thread is how Xu Ruhua, in fear of her husband, relatives, and neighbors, confines herself in a room with doors and windows fenced with iron rails, in which her body gradually turns into a hollow shell stuffed with reeds. This novella, too, primarily dwells on abnormal human relationships. Again, while Can Xue does not provide a background of political persecution, she traces the unconscious affect caused by the psychic assault in a specific historical situation. Redolent of the specific historical age, the psychic assault here takes shape in rhetorical aggression, which indicates the antagonistic atmosphere of the society. For example, Xu Ruhua's mother posts a slip of paper to her door, "which said in big characters: *Coveting idleness or daydreaming is bound to lead to deterioration of the will and finally to end in your becoming the garbage of society!*" (*Tiantang* 205 / *Dialogues* 201; trans. modified). Here Can Xue's reference to the phrase *big characters* reminds us of the "big-character poster" (*dazibao*), a form of political attack prevalent in the Cultural Revolution, often an abrupt and far-fetched criticism of one's political standpoint or a sudden revelation of one's private life by a close acquaintance. Idioms such as *coveting idleness* (*haoyiwulao*) and *daydreaming* (*chixinwangxiang*) are fairly common pejorative terms applied to disparage "nonproletarian" inclinations or "reactionary" views.

Even though Xu Ruhua secludes herself in her room to avoid her mother, the latter keeps writing notes, "sometimes wrapping them around a stone and leaving them outside the door, sometimes striking them on the trunk of the mulberry tree. Once she even hid behind the tree and threw the paper-wrapped stone into the room when her daughter opened the door" (205/201). Such a scene of assault can be perceived as an oblique representation of the past experience of historical violence. Xu Ruhua, in the beginning of the story, receives a small wad of paper through the window, presumably thrown by her neighbor Geng Shanwu, which enjoins her not to "spy on others' private lives" (181/180). Here, while Geng Shanwu is suspicious of Xu Ruhua's espial that violates "private lives," his own behavior, in turn, perturbs her. Surreptitious mutual aggression, rather than direct, face-to-face conflicts, constitutes the enigmatic impetus of everyone in this novella. More significantly, what is involved here is an assault with words—or, more precisely, with discourses—that have long belonged to an intangible political power that startles and horrifies Can Xue and her contemporaries.

The psychic shock, nonetheless, does not simply stem from a discursive threat. In *Old Floating Cloud* we see Xu Ruhua and Geng Shanwu, despite their mutual suspicions, having an obscure extramarital liaison in which, however, desire for each other and alarm against each other alternate or even intermix: "they hugged each other in terror, then separated in disgust" (250/243). Here Can Xue explores the ultimate complexity of affection and repulsion. Indeed, under the sway of the historical violence and the master discourse, suffering is inseparable from sensual attraction or emotional attachment. This also holds true for the relationship between Old Kuang (Xu Ruhua's husband) and his mother. The latter, out of love for them, comes to Xu Ruhua and Old Kuang's home frequently with "tall rubber boots" or "an iron club": "As soon as she arrived, she cast her eyes around the room suspiciously, even peering cautiously behind the door" (205/201). In addition, she keeps sending someone to deliver notes with such words as "Be on guard of the spies around you!" and "Push three pebbles under your pillow" and "Never look around, especially toward the left" (199/195–96).

The style of these notes is, more or less, a parody of the propaganda discourse, which is supposed to set rules for the rationalized historical scenario. The austere style of rational instruction still remains, while it hardly makes sense but only produces agitating effects. Old Kuang, characterized as an immature man intimately dependent on his mother, overreacts ambivalently to his situation under her shadow. On the one hand, disturbed by her anxiety about the imminent murder or robbery, he "complained that he could not live in such fear" (198–99/195). On the other hand, he "got so worked up when he received his mother's notes that he itched all over" and "scratched here and there and twisted back and forth in the chair for a long time before he could managed to write a reply." His reply can be something like "[execute] immediately; the former instruction is very effective" (199/196).

Indeed, Old Kuang is an accomplice to his mother when he and his mother, together, "were 'exorcising evil spirits' by waving the iron club" (198/195). The novella remarkably portrays Old Kuang's ambivalent reaction toward his situation, his excitation from the aggressive behavior and discourse, and his position as a victim and an accomplice at one and the same time. His mother, then, has been a colossal phantom under whom Old Kuang cannot but lose his subjective integrity. Later on, as his mother is "undergoing a thorough cleaning of the soul" by "collecting famous quotations," Old Kuang, "took a walk arm in arm with his mother, swollen with arrogance, his heart filled with a curiosity and pride he had never experienced" (230/223–24). This arrogance or pride, after he has helped Xu Ruhua set up the iron bars, degenerates to absolute subordination to his mother. He keeps groaning, "Mama," with a "voice as weak and soft as an infant's," entreating her not to abandon him (261–63/252–53). This psychic alternation of superiority and inferiority designates the unstable subject whose emotional orientations are inextricable. The Oedipus complex does not seem to be the only explanation of Old Kuang's relationship with his mother, since the mother figure here is not so much maternal as witchy (as shown in the scene of wavering club to exorcize spirits). Old Kuang's Oedipus complex, therefore, becomes an attachment to his mother, as a result of his degeneration to infancy, while his mother has already changed to a state in which no motherhood exists.

How can a mother, a symbol of affection and warmth, be described as a termagant? Even the Freudian myth is seemingly inverted here, as in many of Can Xue's works, to indicate the perverse relationship between the son and the mother. Such a mother figure can be compared to what has been called a "'phallic' mother," "mother as master," or "paternal power in disguise" (Lieberman 39–40) in canonical modern Chinese fiction, such as Ye Shengtao's "Yi he ta" (She and he). While Ye presents an ode to the "paternal power in disguise," as an imago of what is to become (a modern metaphor), Can Xue reveals the wayward, oppressive power of the phallic mother. This transition is triggered by communist literature, art, and cinema, in which, as Ban Wang has observed, "the image of woman/mother is often associated with the image of the party" (150). When associated with such concepts as "motherland," the maternal figure is used to represent the loving and caring character of the practically unmerciful political power. In fact, it is the mother, rather than the father, that has been adopted as a mythical symbol in the dominant political discourse in China. One of the typical examples can be found in a "popular" song (under the specific political circumstances, of course), which starts in the following lines: "Let me sing a song for the Party / I compare the Party to mother / Mother only bears my body / The radiance of the Party illuminates my heart" (Lei 9).[4] The mother figure is thus to be regarded as a symbol of amiability, which, however, is harshly incongruous with what it stands for in reality.

This is the essence of Can Xue's nightmarish fiction: the positive images or symbols are transformed into obscurity and ambiguity that exceed subjective comprehensibility. Even visions of natural images are usually deterioration of the cultural mythos. The fall of flowers, usually lamented as a sign of the transience of time or of the departure of youth for the traditional literati, frightens Geng Shanwu, who, like Lin Daiyu in *The Story of the Stone*, buries fallen petals. But the similitude is only superficial. Unlike the sentimental Daiyu, Geng Shanwu defies the lyrical significance of "Daiyu burying flowers" and "[tramps] angrily on one of those arrogant little things and dug a shallow hole with his toe to bury it in the mud" (178/178). By the same token Can Xue's "moonlight" is no longer a beautiful image but something that "spread on the ground like a long shroud" (237/230; trans. modified).

Among all the ominous images in the novellas the sun is probably the most significant one. In the beginning Geng Shanwu "searched his mind for *grand* expressions" to convince himself that "[everything] will be different when the sun is out" and "[it's] a rebirth, a new beginning" (178/178; my emph.). It is the same sun that, despite its symbolic position in the "grand expressions," is an image of horror to the heroine Xu Ruhua, who mentions that "[over] the forest hangs a blood-red sun, horribly red," which makes her "temples throb" (249/242). The red sun, supposedly the principal symbol of the historico-political supremacy exclusively reserved for Mao or the Communist Party (traditionally, of course, for the emperor), appears as the "blood-red sun" that implies violence and savagery. Although it can still symbolize a "rebirth" or "new beginning," the splendid image becomes "horribly red" insofar as the politically loaded function of the sun image brings harm. It is indeed one of the major sources of discursive violence that, along with physical violence, causes trauma. In this sense Can Xue's writing is an unrelenting attempt to return to origins (the original event, symbol, mythos, etc.), which are, however, inevitably perverted in representation because of the perverted experience under their constant impact.

On a symbolic level the sun corresponds to the man figure that brings both splendor and catastrophe: in Xu Ruhua's reverie "there was always a mature man in a tweed overcoat who made touching remarks, generously and tenderly, until her ears hummed. . . . Following all this, there was the coming of the gigantic, irresistible destruction" (254/246). Certainly, if the "mature man" stands for the archetypal figure in the Freudian "scene of seduction," the "touching remarks" (*dongren de huayu*) must be the discourse that charms ("generously and tenderly") and harasses ("her ears hummed") at one and the same time. It is in such a fragmentary, rather than logical, way that destruction unexpectedly occurs in Xu Ruhua's (or Can Xue's) reverie. The ominous vision of destruction is to be taken as disintegrated subjective perception, through which the objective world undergoes distortion and displacement.

The major theme of *Old Floating Cloud* is unmistakably the persistent psychic agitation that haunts each character. At times anxiety becomes the only thing ascertainable to a person, whereas the source and the objective of the anxiety are ungraspable. By the same token not all miseries can be clearly recalled. To Xu Ruhua's mother, for instance, what happened in her traumatic past only comes to her mind as a phantasmagoric vision: "She couldn't forget the incident in which she lost her hair. That wet autumn, the dried leaves in the trees were as red as blood. Black water oozed out of the walls. She was sitting in the rocking chair in a constant state of anxiety . . . " (272–73/261; trans. modified). The original ellipsis leaves the actual details of the incident in an unidentifiable condition, while it is at the same time unforgettable. The "anxiety," in any case, remains in this gap between the unforgettable and the immemorial, or between the discernible and the ungraspable.

The anxieties of Can Xue's characters differ from the paranoid vision of Lu Xun's Madman, insofar as they are not projected on a single, integral event but are randomly and sporadically triggered by unexpected incidents, which are *un*ascertainable to these characters. The novella begins with an episode in which Geng Shanwu wakes up at midnight and shouts, "There's a thief crouching in the corner!"

(178/177), before he realizes that he has actually had a dream. On the other hand, anxieties result not merely from illusions or phantoms. In many instances we at least see the anxiety stem from tangible incidents that are horrible and ridiculous at the same time. Xu Ruhua's father once suspected that her mother ate his flesh when he was sleeping; after one night he saw her suck his leg and found that his whole body was getting more and more skinny. But when he asked, "You, why should you eat my flesh?" she yelled back more fiercely: "Bah! Snob! Schemer! Good heavens!" (241–42/234) The conflict recurs between Old Kuang and Xu Ruhua, who, inheriting her mother's habit, becomes a vampire who bites her husband's shoulder and sucks his blood at night (233–34/226–27). Here, even if cannibalism and vampirism do exist as the sources of anxiety, the representational mode deprives the occurrence of any realistic sense. In other words, it cannot but be read as a nightmarish scene in which cannibalism and vampirism serve as the extreme and allegorical expression of fear in society or family.

The question is disputable to what extent Xu Ruhua, the claustrophile who finally confines herself in a cagelike room, can be identified with Can Xue the author. Can Xue's self-description, in a short essay about her own writing, reveals her personality cognate to Xu Ruhua's: "A person, with inborn odd temperament that displeases other people, is in the fear of being violated by the others all the time and yet looks at the world in a constantly bizarre, caustic way" ("Wo shi zenme" 50). It is also this kind of psychic sensitivity or vulnerability to the external world that causes Xu Ruhua's claustrophilia, although it seems unlikely to be legitimate to claim that a temperament like this is "inborn." In fact, as I have argued, the obsessive anxiety of assault stems from the traumatic experience of real psychic shock. This is why, whenever she falls asleep, Xu Ruhua feels the branches from outside the window whip her face. She asks her husband, Old Kuang, to install iron rails on all the windows and doors, so that "the room will look like an iron cage" because she perhaps "can only sleep in an iron cage" (*Tiantang* 197 / *Dialogues* 194).

Naturally, the image of the iron cage is reminiscent of Lu Xun's famous metaphor, the "iron house," from which he desires (though with hesitation) to awake the sleepers by crying out (see Lu Xun's "Preface to *Call to Arms*," *quanji* 1: 419 / *Selected Works* 1: 37). Can Xue's heroine, on the contrary, willingly stays in the iron house in order to sleep peacefully. The antithesis between the two figures of the two ages is significant. It is precisely the revolution that the May Fourth intellectuals zealously brought to history that has led to the successive catastrophes that, in the name of continuous revolution (according to Mao's political scenario), exert shocking violence against individuals whose traumatic experience now haunts their memory. Xu Ruhua's claustrophilic defense against the harassment from the outside is a consequence of historical violence done using the discourse of emancipation. Such a discourse is developed from the May Fourth discourse of modernity that Lu Xun and his intellectual comrades had in mind.

The novella ends in a miserable scene in which Xu Ruhua has become a dried, hollow woman—redolent of T. S. Eliot's verses "We are the hollow men / We are the stuffed men"—whose body is stuffed with reeds and resonates emptily when she taps on it. The iron cage, now filled with corpses of crickets, a ragged blanket, and a termite-eaten cane chair, appears to be an appropriate site for such a dead, ruinous ending. Xu Ruhua's metamorphosis suggests no enlightened transfiguration but, on the contrary, signifies an existential impasse into which Can Xue is driven by the recurrent and concurrent traumatic experiences. At bottom it is not Xu Ruhua but Can Xue's "objectified self," which is visualized as a depleted person whose corporeality has been exhausted, allegorically, in the growing danger from the outside world. We may go back to the earliest reference to Xu Ruhua's drying body: "Long, long ago, when she was a girl, she had dreamed of becoming a mother. But, when the paper mulberry outside the door came into red berries, something in her body dried up. She often patted her belly and joked, 'In here grows nothing but reed stalks'" (180/179; trans. modified). Indeed, the red berries here indicate a present and external stimulation or excitation that awakens the traumatized memory and diverts the normal growth of a person. Thus, the tragic metamorphosis of Xu Ruhua can well be interpreted from the psychic motivation of Can Xue the author, who imbues the character with her affective peculiarities.

Disfigurement of Psychic Imagery

Metamorphosis, the Kafkaesque prototype of allegory, once appeared in Can Xue's first published work, her 1985 short story "Wushui shang de feizaopao" (Soap bubbles in the dirty water), which starts with the sentence "My mother has melted into a basin of soap bubbles" ("Wushui" 405 / *Dialogues* 31). This beginning, to be read as a brief summary of the story, was unusual to most readers at the time (the mid-1980s) for its disregard of the realistic ground required by rational representational subjectivity. This fact, however, perhaps divulges Can Xue's own inimical, if not matricidal, attitude toward the mother, a figure, again, characterized as a paranoid despot, "an iron woman" (406/33) who keeps yelling, vexing herself, and complaining about her son's "scheme" to maltreat her. Nevertheless, the mother figure would be of less interest if taken merely as an archetype in Can Xue's experience of her family history. In Can Xue the mother does care for the son but in a violent and peremptory way that disturbs rather than "illuminates." In one episode she plans to arrange the marriage between her son and her section chief's daughter, an ugly old virgin, in order to fawn over her boss. But in this story Can Xue attends more to the son's ambivalent, if not inimical, attitude toward his mother.

In the rest of the story the mother keeps blaming her son for his impiety. Such an oppressive voice repetitively causes physical pains of the "I," who virtually becomes the murderer of his mother. Seeing his mother's face generate bubbles and get hollowed as she rubs the tea on it, he, "as if commanded by a *ghost*" (407/34; my emph.), suggests that she take a bath and prepares boiling water in the basin for her. The haunting "ghost" is, obviously, the dark unconscious, the hidden self that he denies. Out of his unconscious wish to do away with his mother, he does not rescue her when he hears her weak, stifled scream before silence comes. He forces open the door to see in the basin only dirty soap bubbles, which, significantly, still stare at him and utter his mother's voice from underneath. Despite his conspicuous matricidal proclivity, there is a subjective ambivalence that prevents the plot from being simple wish fulfillment. The censorship functions here as the ethical principle for the narrator to deny or conceal his satisfaction at seeing his mother's disappearance. This is the conflict between the universal morality—his fear of people accusing him of having a will to murder—and his harsh reaction to the constant harassment from his mother. He even warns his mother to beware of gas poisoning when she moves her bed into the kitchen. His matricidal impulse, though denied, is later revealed as stronger than his moral consciousness about maintaining his normal relationship with his mother.

"Soap Bubbles in the Dirty Water" contains many of the same characteristics as Can Xue's subsequent short stories: psychic aggressions and distortions, narrative ambiguities, descriptive deformations, and expressive predicaments. "Hut on the Mountain," one of her most celebrated short stories, focuses on the subtle fear of the first-person narrator about all sorts of imaginary or potential dangers and threats. The hut on the mountain, in which someone is "banging furiously against the door" and around which are the whipping of north wind and the howling of wolves (*Tiantang* 287–88 / *Dialogues* 47), seems to be an ominous sign with which the "I" is possessed. The person in the hut is a character comparable to Xu Ruhua in *Old Floating Cloud*, in that he stays in a sealed space and is secluded from the public, despite the involuntary isolation this time. Once, after a futile visit to the hut, the "I" sees her own image in the mirror as someone with "purple shades around her eye sockets" (288/48; trans. modified), and the person "squatting inside" the hut "got big purple shades under his eye sockets, too" (290/50; trans. modified). Such a figure can thus be seen as a mental projection, or an imaginary reflection, of the "I." But, even though the visualized person in the hut can be identified with the reflected image in the mirror, such a visualization is enigmatic, as it is eventually revealed that the "I" can no longer find the hut, which may be an illusion or fantasy.

Can Xue's mysterious narration provides a psychic vision that is to be understood as real and at the same time is exposed as unreal. Failure to realize the visionary, however, by no means denotes the unreality of mental pressure but, rather, implies the impracticality of tackling with such a psychic/historical repression in a realistic way. The hut is not merely a symbol of real conditions but an image that allegorizes the psychic (in)comprehensibility of the world. Here Lu Xun's parable of the iron house is again relevant. For Lu Xun the iron house is a clear symbol of the sociohistorical confinement that can be smashed by another historically committed power. Lu Xun is so astute, nonetheless, that he questions the purity of his writing as a historical undertaking by suggesting that it might be even worse if the sleepers are awakened and aware of their own miserable conditions. Can Xue, more skeptically, reduces the problem of confinement into the mental realm of illusion. In other words, Can Xue is caught not in the question of smashing apart the confinement—since the attempt to escape from the hut is rather hopeless—but is voicing and visualizing feelings of anxiety, tension, coercion, and aggression. These feelings, however, cannot be easily conceptualized and then abolished.

The subjective inability to conceptualize is correspondent to the frightful atmosphere in the "I"'s daily life. Such frightfulness results from the inexplicable psychic assaults emerging in the "I"'s fancy. There appears in "Hut on the Mountain" another set of Can Xue's principal images: the pierced or perforated object. For instance, the "I" sees "countless tiny holes poked by fingers in the windowscreens" (287/47), the wolves "poke their heads in through the cracks in the door" (288/48), and the mother's appearance is described as "[poking] in her small dark green face from the edge of the door" (291/51; trans. modified). The perforation of the home is a metaphor of violation, such as the violation of virginity, as an allegorization of the trauma in the unconscious. In any case such scenes cannot be read as deriving faithfully from the personal past. Rather, the intrinsic visions of being pierced that have been evoked here should be understood as a figural resuscitation of the untraceable, traumatized historical experience of psychic assaults from which Can Xue—like all others who underwent the "proletarian dictatorship"—has suffered.

Here, again, Lu Xun's influence is discernible. Just like the narrator of "A Madman's Diary," who is tormented by the suspicion that everyone around him is waiting to eat him, the "I" in "Hut on the Mountain" is also oversensitive to people in the family (a mutually threatening community). Yet again, Can Xue's narrator is haunted by anxiety and fears that do not have as clear an origin and target as the phobia of Lu Xun's Madman. What disturbs the narrator of "Hut on the Mountain" is not a planned murder (as conceived by Lu Xun's Madman), for the real cause of the disturbance is undiscoverable. There is one perceptible incident, however, in which the "I" finds out that her parents have rummaged her drawer and thrown her treasures, the dead moths and dragonflies, onto the floor. Nevertheless, this can hardly be viewed as *the* origin or focus of her anxiety (not to mention that, normally, the intensity of such a shock would not be great enough). Nor is this incident, throughout the whole narrative, the central concern of the "I." It appears to be one of the allegorical episodes that exposes the sensitivity to violation but conceals, or decenters, the original event, which remains unknown. Other than the tangible incidents like this, the "I" is actually agitated by anything perceived or conceived. Her parents' snoring is perceived as shaking the utensils in the kitchen cabinet, mother's stare at the back is felt to cause numbness and swelling on the head, and father's glance is conceived as from a wolf's eyes. It is laid bare that everything bizarre results from the schizophrenic perception—or rather, conception—of the narrative subject, which is drifting through numerous episodes that distract it from any central matter.

Therefore, unlike Lu Xun's Madman, the narrator of "Hut on the Mountain" does not, and cannot, focus on *the* event that she is forced to tackle. This fact is significant because, if the exclusive danger is missing, what is to be confronted becomes the enigma of dangers, which are everywhere and indeterminate. The dangers and threats in "Hut on the Mountain" are reciprocal among people, in the sense that not only is the "I" the victim of the pressure from the others, but the others are also agonized by the disturbances from the "I" or from one another. The "I"'s mother states that she would tremble with fear every time the "I" comes into her room looking for things and she would be driven crazy, as disclosed by the little sister, when she hears the "I" open and shut the drawers. The father has been haunted and afflicted for decades by the suspicion that he might have dropped a pair of scissors into the well and one day, after his failure to get out the scissors, sees the hair on his left temple suddenly turn white. The whole narrative is not a protest against the oppression of the collective on the individual but a formation of the menacing atmosphere in which individuals mutually create unreasonable suffering and obscure threats.

Another widely anthologized story of Can Xue's is "The Ox," in which the central image is an ox whose horn disturbingly *pierces* through the wall of the narrator's bedroom. The narrative montage shows that, when she tries to caress the horn, the "I" touches the back of her husband's head. We can thus assume that the ox is a metamorphic vision of the narrator's husband, Old Guan, whose threat to her is visualized as a phantom image of ox. When she once more detects the resemblance between her husband's head and the ox's horn (she is pricked by his bristly hair when touching his forehead), she also notices his "comic expression of threat" (285/76), as he bares his decayed teeth to her. The "comic expression of threat" here becomes an oxymoron that complicates, or disarranges, the condition of threat, because what is comic lies in the fact that one's torment comes not from a tormenting but from another tormented situation. As another focus in the story, Old Guan's persistent concern about his decayed teeth enables this continuously extended chain of anxieties or torments. Furthermore, at the end of the story one can see Old Guan swing a big hammer to destroy the mirror, in which his own reflection is shown as a savage and anguished ox that perturbs himself. The ox in such a horrible scene is described not as an assailant but itself a sufferer: "A huge beast had fallen into the water and was splashing and writhing in the throes of death. Black smoke was belching from its nose, dark red blood spurted from its mouth" (286/76).

In Can Xue the source and the target of disturbances are maladjusted and interchangeable without clear boundaries. Hence, the narrator is no longer the single voice; the original *one* becomes transmissible to others and thus vulnerable to self-dissemination. As a matter of fact, direct quotations of Old Guan's utterances, which decenter the original narrative voice, occupy a great portion of the story. At the same time, as the presumed central symbol of the narrative, the ox is enigmatic and indeterminate, indicating the subjective limitations of reaching the ultimate truth in representation. The first appearance of the ox many years ago (as the scene of seduction) only shows flashing purple light and its slowly moving rear, which can barely be distinguishable. Once the "I" hears the knock at the door by the ox, she becomes suspicious that it could be just an illusion. The ox is to be conceived only as an elusive danger not comprehensible in the rational sense because, after all, it is merely a presumption that the ox be identified with Old Guan. At least, the ox in this story can be interpreted as a metaphoric archetype of the colossal shock, sexually both seductive and menacing, and thus hardly categorizable. Furthermore, in the specific case here such an archetype is not only ambiguous, as it is aggressive in an equivocal way (both appealing and appalling), but also paradoxical, since it is at once despicable and vulnerable. This double equivocality functions as the ultimate indeterminacy of the traumatic affect prevailing strongly in all Can Xue's works. Here emerges the conception of irony, embodied in the irreconcilable ruptures of the archetypes.

Part II

Irony as Verbal Catachresis

Schizophrenia in the Master Discourse

Chapter 6

Irony and an Alternative Reading of Maoist Discourse

If ontology were possible at all, it would be possible in an ironic sense, as the epitome of negativity.

Language becomes a measure of truth only when we are conscious of the nonidentity of an expression with that which we mean.
—THEODOR W. ADORNO, *NEGATIVE DIALECTICS*

From Psychoanalysis to Rhetorical Analysis

In Can Xue and Yu Hua, as we have seen, the unrepresentable in the unconscious can only be represented in a negative or deflective way; or what is represented is not the original but the negative or deflective function of the original. The original, therefore, is ungraspable, insofar as the excessive intensity of psychic trauma deforms the accurate and lucid mode that might otherwise be able to articulate it. The swerving into obscurity and equivocality shows the impossibility of adequate representation and signification. Irony is a rhetorical characteristic shared by the Chinese avant-garde writers necessitated by an inadequacy of representation, an excess or deficiency of phrasing and structuring. The avant-garde narrative can be defined as constantly displaced signification that exposes discrepancies within the process of representation. From a psychoanalytic point of view we can say that such an activity to represent the unrepresentable is comparable to what is called "compulsive repetition," that is, an acting-out that allows the repressed original to resurface but not in an unmediated way. The fact that it both discharges/releases and resists/withholds signals the doubleness that also characterizes the rhetorical distinction of Chinese avant-garde narrative.

Theodor Reik, one of Freud's disciples, analyzed the case of a young patient who suffered from neurotic obsessions about nobility and menial status, respectively, by means of "obviously overstated, forced, and absurd" ("Grenzland" 300)—and thus ironic—utterances concerning both subjects. Reik discovered that it was a result of the shock the patient had experienced in his childhood when the concept of nobility was introduced to him through education, supported by religious principles such as humility and love, yet conflicted with his aristocratic parents' mean attitude toward the servants, which he had witnessed. Reik thus concluded that, taking the doctrines to an extreme of absurdity, "consciously the obsessive idea has the meaning of being obedient to the parents' teachings; unconsciously it represents resentful mockery of these authorities" (302). In another essay Reik elaborated on the origin of irony from the psychoanalytic theory, though not explicitly treating the original as the source of the shock:

> The creator of irony is for a moment tempted to lapse into an old faith, to give himself again to an overcome illusion. The emergence of the unconscious memory seems to reawaken the grief and the disappointment, as if, together with the illusion, the revolt and the despair that followed the disenchantment were renewed.... In the ironic expression not only are the old illusion and the old disenchantment reawakened from the past, but also the indignation and the bitterness, which are the more deeply felt, the more genuinely and sincerely the old faith was once embraced. (*Secret Self* 166)

This theorization of the function of irony is surprisingly pertinent to the case of the post–Cultural Revolution Chinese avant-garde writers, as long as the notion of the ideological "old faith" is understood as a sharply discordant state that produces not only illusion, from which the "disenchantment" naturally grows, but also trauma, which causes the obscurity and equivocality in the (mis)representation of the original.

Catachresis, which denotes ironic misrepresentation or the misuse of words, phrases, idioms, allusions, and mythic archetypes, is a particular characteristic in post-Mao Chinese avant-garde narrative. While the traumatic experience invalidates rational understanding and representation of reality, irony becomes the primary rhetoric that speaks for the unconscious, evokes the irrationality of representation, and points to the perversion and absurdity of a reality formulated within the discourse. Historical violence as a crucial factor in post-Mao avant-garde fiction presents itself in a style of overstatement or understatement that exposes the gap between the historical real and the grand narrative that has textualized history in its authoritative way. Therefore, it is a historical consequence, not purely an intellectual one, that post-Mao avant-gardism is an inquiry into the (inter)textuality of writing. This, of course, distinguishes its aesthetic dimension from the paradigmatic narrative mode dominant from the May Fourth epoch to the early post-Mao era, which insists, at least theoretically, on a transparent representational relationship between literary text and social reality, a relationship ultimately determined by the authorial/authoritative subject.

To discredit the congruence between signifiers and signifieds is to withdraw the intentional subject, which forcefully connects these two, into its unconscious depth, where no statements can be claimed determinant and no signification remains stable. This kind of metawriting—writing that concerns the writer's status of writing—leads to a self-referential problem that the Chinese avant-garde attempts to cope with. In other words, to articulate is always to undergo and modify what has been articulated and to trace what cannot be articulated. This is the origin of irony, which enables the text to be self-reflexive, involute, and susceptible to conflicts.

Irony as Negative Dialectics: A Theoretical Preamble

The epigraphs by Adorno at the beginning of this chapter suggest the philosophical aporia of modernity. In discerning the impossibility of establishing the ultimate interpretation of the world, Adorno turns the whole project of philosophy into a subjunctive status, that is, into a domain in which the only "sense" we may obtain is one of irony, which is in a constant flux of self-contradiction. From this point we may perceive that what the Chinese avant-gardists share with Adorno is a sensibility for the instability and vulnerability of grand narratives. Writing, therefore, can no longer be conceived simply as a negative phase, from which the old or backward could be driven away and the teleological ideal (the synthetic phase, in the Hegelian sense) could be successfully developed.

For the Chinese avant-garde, then, it is not a one-dimensional task to abolish the oppressive form of reality. Rather, the form of reality cannot be eradicated in toto: in fact, even the literary effort to abolish that form cannot evade its immense shadow, since to write is an activity to participate in reality. The only possible negation is, therefore, an interminable negation within writing itself: a perpetually textual, as well as historical, deconstruction of the logic of discourse. Writing as such is not a textual pilgrimage but a negative play in the infernal chaos of the given sociocultural system. In this sense the standpoint of the Chinese avant-garde can be categorized as the Adornian "negative dialectics," an endless dialectical movement implying that, unlike the Hegelian agenda, "a negated negative is not a positive" (Adorno, *Negative* 393). In such a dissonant history the antagonists can only be grasped as irreconcilable conflicts, negations, and inconsistencies that do not lead to synthesizable or realizable consummation. Here Adorno obstructs the dialectical way to the teleological goal despite an internalized utopian criterion (which remains utopian).

His philosophy of nonidentity can well be characterized as a philosophy of irony, inasmuch as he maintains that an effective way of thinking would be unfeasible unless it takes the form of negativity. In this respect Adorno is greatly indebted to Kierkegaard.[1] Kierkegaard, following Hegel but abandoning the pejorative sense in Hegel, categorizes "irony as infinite absolute negativity" (278). Kierkegaard's early notion of irony as "the negative way, not the truth but the way" (340) implies a history without a teleological ultimate that can be positively seized. Kierkegaard eschews the later existentialists' obsession with the positive purity of authenticity by suggesting that "the ironist must always posit something, but what he posits in this way is nothingness," and thus "[irony] is the infinitely delicate play with nothingness" (286). In his inaugural lecture at the University of Frankfurt, Adorno sums up Kierkegaard's philosophy, as opposed to Heidegger's, in the following passage:

> Kierkegaard's plan is irreparably shattered. No firmly grounded being has been able to reach Kierkegaard's restless, inner-subjective dialectic; the last depth which opened up to it was that of the despair into which subjectivity disintegrated, an objective despair which transformed the design of being within subjectivity into a design of hell. ("The Actuality" 123)

Thus, by emphasizing Kierkegaard's conception of the disintegration of subjectivity, Adorno not only grounds his own theory on the debris of Hegelianism but also invalidates the modern format of affirmative subjectivism in Heidegger.[2] To Adorno the most ironic fact is that the affirmative, totalistic narrative of Enlightenment has been transformed into the modern order of social alienation or even totalitarianism, as he and Horkheimer pronounce in *Dialectic of Enlightenment*.

The irony inherent in modernity is embodied in the crisis of its grand narrative, which claims the ultimate totality but contains intense incompatibility within. The Chinese avant-garde narrative can be categorized as ironic, since it confronts this incompatibility in various rhetorical ways. Here both Freud's psychoanalytic theory of *Verneinung* (negation) and Adorno's philosophical/aesthetic theory of negative dialectics ought to be translated into a rhetorical theory of irony, in order to operate their concrete mechanisms in our analysis. This technical turn is by no means merely an expedient. Rather, only by resorting to the technical device of the form can we approach the experience of the original "thing." Adorno, the defender of the primacy of literary form and technique, suggests, "In dialectics, contrary to popular opinion, the rhetorical element is on the side of content. Dialectics seeks to mediate between random views and unessential accuracy, to master this dilemma by way of the formal, logical dilemma" (*Negative* 56). At stake here is the aporetic and self-questioning characteristic of language that contains not only rhetorical but also politico-historical problematics. Adorno constantly insists on inner dissonance and the fragmentation of a literary form, which for him are the negative forces that transgress the ideology of totality.

This is the starting point from which we can take irony seriously in terms of both aesthetics and politics. As Kierkegaard puts it: "Irony in the eminent sense directs itself not against this or that particular existence but against the whole given actuality of a certain time and situation" (271). Irony, in this sense, is the restless dynamic that finds the discrepancies in the status quo and preserves the irreconcilability of the tension. Only from this point can we understand Chinese avant-garde fiction's alert perception of the intricacy of reality. In this sense irony always means an effort of "metarepresentation" (representing the process of or idea about representation) that unfolds the unrepresentability of reality and the deviations in the performance of representation. Inevitably, this metarepresentation has to do with misrepresentation, that is, catachresis in terms of literary rhetoric.

A Rereading of Maoist Discourse

The unrepresentability of reality is rooted in the fact that reality as such is a formation of conceptions and discourses. To represent a pure, plain, ideology-free reality is impossible and destined to be infected with the dominant discourses that may not be perceived consciously. As we have seen, the paradigmatic modern Chinese literature, inflicted by the burden of modernity, was inclined to turn itself into a product of discourse through the endeavor of narrative intervention (explicitly or implicitly). The author's voice in Ba Jin's novels, as noted in the introduction, aims to categorize the characters in the system of new idea—an ideological system of verisimilar reality—in which characters and their performances are arranged as agents of historical emplotment.

It is not impossible, however, to deconstruct communist literature insofar as a careful reading will reveal the excessiveness of subjective involvement. In Ding Ling's celebrated novel *The Sun Shines over the Sanggan River*, for example, rhetorical devices determine the disposition of the historical forces. At the end of the novel, when the Communists have triumphed over their enemy and the historical drama reaches its zenith, Ding Ling attempts to intensify the festive atmosphere that defines the historical consummation brought by the masses. The jubilant villagers are "sturdy, quick and in high spirits" (*Sun* 359), "all filled with new spirit, brimming over with happiness," "full of self-confidence and satisfaction!" (361). Nevertheless, when such a wild "rejoicing" (358) is described as excessive euphoria, Ding Ling touches upon the absurdity of the historical comedy:

> [All] the grown-ups seemed to have become children again, enjoying this tumult of noise. For the sake of an extreme joy and a meaningful emotion, they got excited and plunged into a seemingly unconscious tumult. (*Taiyang* 311–12 / *Sun* 358; the latter sentence omitted)

As the grand history is deprived of its rigid law, the carnivalesque feature of revolution is shown here as "tumult of noise" or "unconscious tumult." To "become children," too, involuntarily discloses the blindness of the social mentality. The representation of the magnificent is on the verge of the irrational and turns into one of the crucial moments in the modern Chinese literary paradigm that prefigures the ironic inversion of grand historical causes in avant-garde fiction.

Communist literature is permeated with Maoist discourse, which, nevertheless, contains self-disruptive elements. Maoism, an amalgamation of Leninism and traditional Chinese thoughts,[3] is the dominant ideology in contemporary China. It is not my primary intent to trace the cultural context of Maoism in detail here. Yet I must point out the compatibility of practical Leninism and traditional Chinese thought in Maoism, in that they both emphasize the unified, superior nature of the state.

Again, it would be impossible to deal with Chinese avant-garde writing without discussing "Maoist discourse," since Mao, however appealing he might be for the Euro-American Marxists, is nevertheless the "Word Incarnate" of the Chinese master discourse. Althusser's remarkable reading of Mao, for example, has nonetheless neglected Mao's hegemonic implications. Mao's argument in *Maodun lun* (On contradiction) posits a so-called principal aspect of contradiction, as opposed to a secondary aspect of contradiction. Theoretically, the attempt to distinguish the superior/inferior parts within the "dialectical" process indicates a tendency to provide a historical arena, in which both sides are struggling to become the dominant. There is no doubt that Mao had a practical intention in developing his theoretical underpinnings. He insists that the study of abstract theory be associated with concrete situations, especially the "concrete methods [that] are employed in the struggle with its opposite" (*Selected Works* 1:323), in order to transform the status quo. Mao rejoices in the fact that "by means of revolution the proletariat, at one time the ruled, is transformed into the ruler, while the bourgeoisie, the erstwhile ruler, is transformed into the ruled and changes its position to that originally occupied by its opposite" (338–39). His dialectics can never be conceived as an endless "overdetermination," which Althusser understands as a "reflection of the conditions of existence of the contradiction within itself" (206), since it maintains unevenness in dialectical movement that aims at a concrete, absolute political end.[4] Althusser, however, assured of the non-Hegelian implications in Maoism, fails to recognize that unevenness as something that persistently requires an intent to totalize and hegemonize and directly points to the condition in which one "aspect" is absolutely subject to the other. As a matter of fact, Maoism is the theoretical basis of the Chinese version of "class struggle" as an arbitrary discourse that purges diverse voices and leads to successive social catastrophes (among which the Anti-Rightist Movement, the Cultural Revolution, and the 1989 Tiananmen Incident are the most memorable).[5]

Moreover, although Mao asserts the absoluteness of contradiction in the dialectical movement, all the contradictions are, in the final analysis, to be subsumed into a higher level of synthesis, even though this synthesis is considered pregnant with further contradictions that need to be leveled. For Mao dialectics ought to be utilized to reach the teleological end. He clearly declares that some social contradictions, though not all, can be gradually resolved "in the course of the advance from socialism to communism" (*Selected Works* 1:318). It is undeniable that the concrete political totality that the contradictory parts struggle to reach is maintained in Mao's dialectical conception. This political totality is the primary agenda in Mao's thought, which Althusser fails to recognize. Mao's emphasis on absolute contradiction, which Althusser recognizes, is indeed what can be viewed as an ironic potential within, or an unwitting deconstruction of, the totalistic schema of Maoism itself.[6]

A reading of Maoist discourse ought to reveal the discrepancies not only between its constructive magnificence and its destructive cruelty but also between its highly organic activity demanded by its grand narrative and its chaotic absurdity existing in the conflicts. The disruptive elements that Maoist discourse has developed within itself have shown us the implosion of the grand narrative. It is from this point that the concept of irony begins to emerge, not only in the avant-garde texts as a conscious subversion of the domination of the master discourse but also in the texts under the sway of Maoist discourse itself as an involuntary breakdown of its self-declared consistency. From this starting point the only possible reaction to the serious cultural productions of Cultural Revolution becomes laughter.[7] It becomes a necessity, therefore, to trace the self-deconstructive potentiality in Maoist discourse, which is ignorant of this inherent effect of irony and conceives itself a flawless system. The genre of Chinese avant-gardism meets with the destiny of the master discourse, unfolds the rupture or wound from within itself, and shows the severe discrepancy of the ideologized reality.

Maoist discourse exists not only in Mao's own writings but also in official literature, especially in "model operas," a type of artwork created to help inculcate the basic codes of Maoist discourse. I would like to choose *Haigang* (On the docks), one of the five major model operas, for my analysis, because it is one of the few such works set against the background of contemporary society.[8] As other political enterprises of communist literature, *On the Docks* is full of literary clichés in order to be accepted and easily accessible to the public. Qian Shouwei, a class enemy, plots to sabotage the plan of loading the rice meant to aid African countries. He gets the young docker Han Xiaoqiang, who is dissatisfied with his occupation, to quit his job and later shifts the responsibility of the accident to him. His plot is detected by Fang Haizhen, a female party leader, who enlightens Han Xiaoqiang by disclosing Qian's evil intention and action and finally secures the accomplishment of a political task significant to the idea of internationalism (which was nearly synonymous with communism and crucial to the Marxist-Maoist grand narrative as a historical goal).

The play can be read as a dramatized version of Mao's thesis on contradiction, since there are the "principal contradiction" and the "secondary contradictions," another pair of dichotomous concepts of Maoism.[9] The principal contradiction refers primarily to the class struggle, that is, the contradiction between the "positive characters" (*zhengmian renwu*)—Fang Haizhen, Gao Zhiyang, and Ma Hongliang—and the "negative character(s)" (*fanmian renwu*), Qian Shouwei. Then, according to Maoist doctrine, the secondary contradictions between positive characters and "middle characters" (*zhongjian renwu*) (Zhao Zhenshan and especially Han Xiaoqiang) are essentially determined by the principal contradiction and can be resolved as soon as the principal contradiction is revealed and resolved.[10] In addition, the positive characters certainly occupy the principal aspect of contradiction in each set of contradictions and eventually win the victory. Thus, the meaning structure is simple, rigid, and absolute, and it conforms to Mao's demand for the value of political edification.

It is, however, precisely this simplicity—or simplified version of the grand narrative model—that fails to maintain the consistency of discourse in the work. It is apparently unconvincing that Qian Shouwei, a deliberate, unyielding saboteur of the "enterprise of socialism," remained disguised during the long period of fourteen years from 1949 (when he began to cloak himself in the regime of the People's

Republic) to 1963 (the present). Even though it is hinted that during the Korean War period he created an accident and caused severe damage to the plan of "internationalism," for the rest of the time he seems to have forgotten his desire to take vengeance on the existent system to regain his "lost paradise" (Shanghai jingjutuan *Haigang* 50 / "On the Docks" 36; trans. modified). Qian Shouwei is a person whose existence is doomed to be inconsistent, since he has to, at one and the same time, "[pretend] to work diligently" and "[make] trouble behind our backs" (49/35). It is because of this specific role (functioning in the political arena of class struggle) that fails to play perfectly (the artificial fabrication is too obvious) that Qian Shouwei becomes an inconsistent agent inherent in the system. The inevitable textual hiatus embedded in the grand narrative disrupts the claim to the perfect truth.

This is the fatal problem: the rational form of Maoist discourse is the very source of its irrational nature. Since the characters are designed to fit the abstract models, and subject to a grand historical logic without being able to maintain their own personal logic, their actions become entirely uncontrollable and even deranged. The characters can only be considered puppets manipulated by the power of Maoist discourse, and each of them functions only as a mindless part of the whole mechanism. This discord between the rational totality and the irrational components is highly discernible and reminiscent of the reality during the early years of the Cultural Revolution: the Red Guards' irrational actions prove the ruin of the rational feature of the political schema of Maoism. The overwhelming mastery of the master discourse determines the weakest autonomy of the characters. Qian Shouwei has to behave as a nice person for ten years without exposing his real vicious identity. Similarly, as soon as Han Xiaoqiang hears Fang Haizhen's statement—without proof—that Qian Shouwei "is dissatisfied with our social order and hopes to change it" (49/35) and her exposition of the significance of the dockers' job, he immediately confesses "with remorse" that "I've been a fool" (51/36) and "I've been infected by bourgeois ideas" (53/37).

Despite its drama form, the script of *On the Docks* is filled with narrative constituents: numerous descriptions beyond actor's lines are added as guidance to the categorization of the characters, actions, and events. These superfluous verbal mechanisms epitomize the most typical symptom of authorial intervention in Chinese communist literature. Gao Zhiyang is first described as "full of lofty sentiments" (*manhuai haoqing*) (6/1; trans. modified) and later "having an imposing appearance" (*qigai xuan'ang*), "lofty" idioms usually adopted to characterize heroes. Subsequently, Fang Haizhen's words are described as being delivered "heroically" (*haomai de*) (10/4; trans. modified), "resolutely" (23/15; trans. modified), "meaningfully" (*yuzhongxinchang de*) (25/17; 48/34, trans. modified), "sincerely" (26/17), and "confidently" (43/30). Her feeling after reading the communiqué is "excited and fluttered" (24/[trans. omitted]) (*xinchao pengpai*), with self-admitted "boundless passion" (*jiqing wuxian*). By the same token, when he sees the renovated dock under Mao's Big Leap Forward policy (which has proven to be a pompous failure), Ma Hongliang, a retired docker, has to be "in buoyant spirits" (*xinggaocailie*) (12/6; trans. modified) with "tears of joy [springing] to [his] eyes" (*relei yingkuang*) (12/6). Only Qian Shouwei's action is given hints of "pretending anxiety" (8/2), being "threatening" (28/20; trans. modified), "startled" (39/27), or "frightened out of his wits" (41/28; trans. modified). His behavior of "feigning composure" is sharply contrasted by Fang Haizhen's speech delivered "with composure" (39/27).

Such a distinct dichotomy is designed to rationalize the historical arena of class struggle. Rationality, again, frequently slips into the mud of irrationality. The diction depicting the "revolutionary" crowd, likewise, is highly symbolic. They are "full of vigour," "[bold] in spirit, strong in will" (10/5), and "hold their heads high and advance by long strides" (*angshou kuobu*) (10/[trans. omitted]) when reciting "Quotations from Chairman Mao" or sometimes "strike a pose in a daring and energetic manner" (31/21; trans. modified). Apparently, mannerism here is significant in that it implies the empty essence of the pose: when a symbolic gesture is revealed as simply a pose, its symbolizing power is undermined. As a matter of fact, when posed on stage, the realized action indeed appears mannered and ludicrous.

Han Xiaoqiang, a character tempted by Qian Shouwei's description of "bourgeois" life style and finally enlightened by Fang Haizhen, is not ignorant of the master discourse. Significantly, his utterances uncover the proclivity of the master discourse to its own deviation. Han's ideal is to be a seaman: he dreams of his journey with an "ocean liner riding wind and cleaving waves, sailing across the sea and making a tour around the world" (13/7; trans. modified). While the idiom "riding wind and cleaving waves" (*chengfengpolang*) is deeply implicated in the system of the master discourse, Han's fantasy veers off nonetheless to "making a *tour* around the world" (my emph.), a statement that alarms Ma Hongliang immediately for verging on "bourgeois hedonism" and being obviously alien to the grand historical scenario. Although Han's thought is censored from time to time in the rest of the play, the logic that connects internationalistic ambition and individualistic pleasure is untouched and thus remains problematic. Moments like this, therefore, breach the neatly designed scheme of the discourse.

In the play Fang Haizhen is certainly the "leading heroine" (according to the official rules of the model opera) who not only acts in strict conformity with the law of Maoist discourse but also speaks directly—to other characters, to herself, and to the audience—in ideological jargon. Therefore, Fang is produced as a representative to guide the rational progress of the whole play. Her words and behavior are so dependent on the master discourse, however, that it is impossible for her not to digress from the real situation. When she finds that there must be fiberglass in the spilled wheat sack, her ultimate concern is not the danger to human life but, rather, the legitimacy of the political plan, which is based on the dominant master discourse. As she declares:

> And if people swallow it, the fiberglass will stick to their
>   intestines,
> That could be . . . (*Sings*)
> *Very dangerous.*
> *The political effect would be the worst of all,*
> *Worst of all!*
>
> (23/14)

Likewise, for her individual life should be entirely ignored or eliminated. "Searching the warehouse at night" can only be viewed as a collective lunatic act (extremely comparable to the scenes in Xu Xiaohe's and Can Xue's fiction, as we shall see), which indicates an alienated, heteronomous, paranoiac humanity created within the system of Maoist discourse.

Of course, the irrational elements in *On the Docks* are intended to consolidate the rationality of Maoist discourse. The paranoiac feature of the characters shows a constant attempt to level all the contradictions and variances by their senseless efforts. Nevertheless, this collective construction of rationality is destined to break down and becomes absurd because of the irreconcilable discrepancies under the superficial harmony imposed by the power of ideology. Therefore, it is Maoist discourse that provides a self-referential and thus self-disruptive condition, insofar as its operation can only be ensured by its own logic. In other words, Maoist discourse must be viewed as a textual entity based on its own theoretical exposé, which, in turn, confirms its historical necessity. This self-referential formation will eventually invalidate its own power rather than strengthen it.

If Paul de Man's substitution of reading for irony is legitimate (de Man, *Critical Writings* lxxiii), irony in Chinese avant-gardism exists in its rereading of Maoist discourse. It becomes a permanent task to uncover the incompatibility between the rhetorical elements and their function within Maoist discourse, that is, the self-conflicting characteristic of the master discourse. The experience of incompatibility is, of course, a shock experience that violently splits or shatters the integral condition of human consciousness. Chinese avant-garde writers discern the decayed atmosphere of reality permeated with Maoist discourse and burst into desperate laughter through their delirious narrative modes and their unsound characters. They share a propensity to schizophrenia deeply embodied in the paranoia of Maoist discourse.

Here de Man's thesis is more than appropriate to elucidate the function of irony in Chinese avant-garde fiction: "absolute irony is a consciousness of madness, itself the end of all consciousness; it is a consciousness of non-consciousness, a reflection on madness from the inside of madness itself." We must notice, therefore, that irony is not something projected outward (as is social satire). Rather, it is a derision inward, a *"folie lucide"* (de Man 216), a self-awareness of ignorance and folly (as Socrates frequently claims), and thus a paradox of being ludicrous and being aware of the ludicrousness at one and the same time. In a similar way Kierkegaard, whose *The Concept of Irony* pays "constant" attention to Socrates, distinguishes irony from doubt by maintaining irony's alienated subjectivity and its reflection on its own disjunctions and tensions.

De Man's conception of irony in "The Rhetoric of Temporality" is mainly derived from Baudelaire's comment on laughter. He sums up Baudelaire's notion of *dédoublement*: the simultaneous feeling of inferiority and superiority, of being the self and the other:

> The ironic language splits the subject into an empirical self that exists in a state of inauthenticity and a self that exists only in the form of a language that asserts the knowledge of this inauthenticity. This does not, however, make it into an authentic language, for to know inauthenticity is not the same as to be authentic. (214)

The concept of irony here differs from what is understood by New Criticism as the equilibrium of oppositions. I. A. Richards, for example, defines irony as something that "consists in the bringing in of the opposite, the complementary impulses" (250) that organize a balanced whole. By contrast, de Man stresses disproportions and inconsistencies that are not to be integrated but to be displaced/misplaced, that operate concurrently on different levels of consciousness within the text.

In Chinese avant-garde fiction the *dédoublement* of narration consists in the coexistence of the inevitability of the internal proneness to Maoist discourse *and* the acute perception of the absurdity of the discourse. Insofar as Maoist discourse had become the dominant reality underlying social and psychic life, the only way for the Chinese avant-garde writers to react to this situation was through insanity, in which the impossibility of reconciling the split subject is made clear. It is the violent assault by Maoist discourse that imposes the disintegrative experience on the psychic reality and causes the schizophrenic mentality of the post–Cultural Revolution generation. The clashing disparity between the rational Maoist discourse in theory and its irrational atrocity in practice provides the very ground for the ironic quality of avant-garde writing. In spite of the self-deconstructive factors in Maoist discourse, the discourse is not intended to be ironic: it is our reading that reveals the hidden irony of its display. Such reading, rereading, and rewriting are what the avant-garde narrative persists in doing.

The ironic rewriting, or parody, of the Maoist discourse can be seen as a prevailing feature of Chinese avant-garde fiction, in which some formal characteristics of Maoist discourse are retained but situated within different contexts. Parody, by way of appropriating and transfiguring what already preexists, bears the same self-reflexive, self-digressive impulse as irony. If irony is an expression that reveals its own discrepancies, parody means specifically an imitation that unmasks the imitated by unmasking the imitator in the first place. Linda Hutcheon characterizes parody as "one of the major forms of modern self-reflexivity; it is a form of inter-art discourse" (*Theory* 2). In the case of the Chinese avant-garde, parody is not only a form of "inter-art discourse" but "intercultural discourse," in that the targets of parody are not only artworks but also other cultural products, whether politically or commercially conceived.

This is precisely the kind of parody "in modern times" that, as Bakhtin puts scornfully in order to uphold the prime, healthy, and heroic notion of parody in early times, "has grown sickly." Nevertheless, modern parody, including that in Chinese avant-garde fiction, cannot be dismissed as "narrow and unproductive" (71), simply because it is intended not to have a positively productive effect but a *negatively* productive one, generating mishandled or displaced expressions. Parody, therefore, is an inadequate imitation, an imitation that ironically exposes the incapacity to imitate.

In Baudelaire's concept of "the absolute comic" laughter, in which superiority can only be evoked when inferiority in its own is recognized, is distinguished from joy: "Joy is a unity. Laughter is the expression of a double, or contradictory, feeling" (Baudelaire 156). For such Chinese avant-gardists as Can Xue and Xu Xiaohe it is this *dédoublement* that shatters the harmony of subjective expression, because the power of the master discourse is experienced simultaneously as the atrophy of the discourse. Here we are approaching the epistemological core of irony: a haunting aporia, that is, an inevitably self-referential paradox, in which no master discourse (as a joyful, enjoyable "unity") is stable. Insisting on self-discrepancy and self-disruption of narration, irony in Chinese avant-garde fiction is an unmasking of the allegedly integrated historical narrative.

In Chinese avant-garde fiction irony, or the (re)reading of Maoist discourse (as well as the entire modern literary paradigm), is where the concept of postmodernity arises, if we understand Maoist discourse as a typical discourse of the modern. To be postmodern is thus to disclose the inherent irony within the modern. In this sense irony is no longer to be conceived as a split of modern subjectivity, from which another critical, superior subject might be generated. If modernist irony relies on a conscious, manipulative ironist, the Chinese avant-garde's postmodern irony destines the self-disruptive or multiplied voice to never being able to be reduced to a single, determined position. This is a transition, as Linda Hutcheon observes, "from the modernist remains of Romantic Irony, with its affirmation of (at least) the ironizing subject, to the postmodern suspicion of transcendental certitudes of any kind, including of the subject. Postmodern irony also denies the form of dialectic and refuses resolution of any kind in order to retain the doubleness that is its identity" ("Power" 35). The postmodern subject in Chinese avant-garde fiction is doomed to be dispersed as an intertextual(ized) one, that is, to be implicated constantly and endlessly in a labyrinthine web of texts and discourses that have defined Chinese modernity.

Postmodern irony in Chinese avant-gardism is not to be viewed, however, as the superlative literary quality without any danger. Arising out of the disillusionment of the absolute truth of the master discourse prevailing over idealism within social culture in the mid- and late 1980s, it verges on, or at least corresponds to, the widespread social trend of cynicism that reflects the ideological decline in the aftermath of the Cultural Revolution. Narrational self-skepticism is not tantamount to cynicism, but it manifests the typical social mentality of one who has been traumatized by a catastrophic experience. To take caution against the pitfall of cynicism, reading postmodern irony in Chinese avant-garde fiction must reveal its negative, and thus utopian, power, which, nonetheless, persists in the self-involvement in, self-reflection on, and self-critique of the aporetic experience.

There is, in Chinese avant-garde narrative, what Adorno calls the moment of "hope of nonsense," in which "suffering presents itself on such contingent occasions with the absurd promise of happiness" (*Kierkegaard* 94). Adorno's project of negative dialectics can be understood as ceaseless disruptions of the internalized given system, inasmuch as the most powerful resistance consists in a preoccupation of the object as part of the subject, rather than in a distant denunciation. As Adorno puts it, "Dialectics is the self-consciousness of the objective context of delusion; it does not mean to have escaped from that context. Its objective goal is to break out of the context from within" (*Negative* 406). The critical distance should thus be characterized as an intrinsic one: a Derridean *différance,* or an infinite deferral or deviation "from within." It is in this sense that Kierkegaard, in discussing the irony of Socrates, brings up "the infinite negativity *within him,*" since "he becomes estranged from the whole world *to which he belongs*" (221; my emph.). The postmodern irony of Chinese avant-garde narrative exemplifies such an "infinite negativity."

Chapter 7

Xu Xiaohe

Laughter from Despair

The man of our days only finds his truth in the enigma of the madman.
—MICHEL FOUCAULT,
MADNESS AND CIVILIZATION

The profound importance of Xu Xiaohe's fiction has yet to be fully discovered. In his short stories and novellas trivial and absurd actions give way to the pleasure of misrepresentations, in which Maoist discourse is not seriously resisted but, rather, deformed, in order to grasp the miserable and meaningless situation of in the given society or community. The incapacity to represent means that, for Xu Xiaohe, the only way to represent is to entrap oneself in the snare of the existing discourse, which always misleads reality to the preposterous situation in which representation is proved to be a sheer failure.

Formerly a poet occasionally associated with the school of "obscure poetry" (*menglong shi*), Xu Xiaohe turned to fiction in 1983. "Canju" (Endgame, 1983), his first published narrative work, anticipates his affinity with Samuel Beckett, whose suspicion of language and communication in the modern time also marks Xu Xiaohe's literary endeavor. The most distinguishing aspect in Xu Xiaohe's "Endgame" are the "blanks" in narration, that is, the omissions of essentials of the story. As the central concern of the story, the "trophy" (what is contained in the iron box) that the young man finally wins from the old man (who offers it for the endgame challenge) remains unknown to the reader. Such a narrative device would be, after 1985, more widely and attentively used by other avant-garde writers such as Ma Yuan and Ge Fei.

The ludic impulse in Xu Xiaohe's fiction situates his style in the middle point between Ma Yuan / Ge Fei and Can Xue / Yu Hua. His ambivalent attachment to the Cultural Revolution discourse, as we shall see, is more than clear. What differentiates him from Can Xue and Yu Hua, then, is his not only ironic but also farcical illustration of the folly of the masses derived, though obliquely, from the personal and collective experience of pompous and preposterous historical events.

Narrative Irrationality and the Master Discourse

Xu Xiaohe began his "madmen" series in 1985 with the short story "Yuanzhang he tade fengzimen" (The madhouse director and his madmen), from which most of his later works develop (with similar background and characters). Like the other works in the series, this one has no central plot but depicts a special community in which the insane and the sane are indistinguishable. At the beginning the director chases a madman who escapes from the madhouse, while the villagers, like Lu Xun's onlookers, follow the race and cheer on the fleeing madman. This beginning initiates Xu Xiaohe's primary interest in the nonsensical, insofar as we discern that the villagers are no saner than the madmen. At stake is that the nonsensical is shaped in a familiar or even popular way. Over the wall of the madhouse the villagers see how the madmen gather: "Some of them lined up, walked straight ahead and about-faced after bumping the wall. Someone began to sing, with a louder and louder voice. Someone was giving a speech, poking the forehead of another with his finger; and the latter scurried off like a frightened rat. A madwoman picked a huge bunch of oleander flowers, crying out welcome, welcome" (*Yuanzhang* [1987] 147).

This scene is not nonsensical if we are aware of its resemblance to the typical political life in Mao's China, especially during the Cultural Revolution. It is perceivable that the memory trace of the past creeps into the narrative. The "military training" (*junxun,* as a way to strengthen political manipulation and injunction), the "criticism and denunciation meeting" (*pidouhui,* in which class enemies are cursed and humiliated), and the welcome ceremony, usually held in an overexcited atmosphere all resurface here but only as foolish activities without justifications or objectives. In another episode a fugitive madman, resembling an underground revolutionary in communist literature, evades the director's hunt but, when hearing the lad who shelters him deceive the director, giggles and then exposes himself. The director grabs from the madman's hands two steamed stuffed buns given by the lad and throws them right at the lad's face. The archetypal relationships among the roles of hero, sympathizer, and enemy are parodied.

The madhouse is a momentous enterprise for the director, as we see him passionately bring those fugitive madmen back to the madhouse and even solicits those who are not mad to live in the madhouse. Xu Xiaohe is attentive to the narrative tone that reinforces the ironic function of the director's enterprise. When the director "graciously" persuades Daft Su (who later proves himself to be sane by taking a career as an engineer) to the madhouse, Su replies with a heavy slap in his face: "there is written a scarlet print of five fingers on [the director's] gallant face" (153). Near the end of the story, as the village is urbanized, the madhouse has been rebuilt into a school. The former director is reluctant to resign himself to such a conclusion and goes to another village in order to "establish a madhouse that can comprehensively accommodate the madmen of all the villages" (154). It remains unknown whether his project is finally carried out or not, but, when he chases a madman to "demonstrate" his project, he himself stumbles and falls into a pond. The director's grand narrative is again undercut by a ridiculous accident. Thus, the more magnificent the narrative seems, the more flawed the rationality of the director's project becomes. The story ends with a description of the director, for some obscure reason, digging a ditch, from which "we wonder if the tadpoles will swim out when spring comes." The grand narrative eventually gives way to a minor and perhaps nugatory work that, however, is still misunderstood as, within the frame of Maoist discourse, "cadre participating in labor" (155). The grace of the discourse is haunting the narrative but dissociated from genuine historical significance.

Xu Xiaohe's short story "Ren huo hongmao yeren" (Human beings or red-hair bigfoots, 1986) deals allegorically with the problem of discourse and truth by transforming the dominant discourse into an enigmatic and even illusory project. It not only parodies root-seeking literature, which claims to have found the ultimate cultural value and essence in the primitive (in this story neither the bigfoots nor the eyewitnesses to bigfoots are reliable), but also shows how the master discourse rules without realizing its promise to render truth. The whole piece, having only one passage, describes a gathering to seek eyewitnesses who have sighted red-hair bigfoots. The discourse about red-hair bigfoots excites everyone, whose demonstrations of red-hair bigfoots are completely pointless. Such a situation is analogous to the gathering in the numerous mass movements in contemporary China as a typical form of political demagogy and ideological inculcation. No one in this gathering has a personal name—comparable to the nameless crowd in Lu Xun's "Shizhong" (A public example), one of his neglected masterpieces—simply because no one has his or her true identity amid the masses. But the rubric here is *red-hair bigfoot*, which is as tempting as any ideological rubric that has been ardently followed. (Deliberately or not, it is truly a rubric with red color, the dominant symbolic color of communist China, while the Chinese word for "hair" is *mao*.)

Significantly, at the gathering someone claims to have shaken hands with a red-hair bigfoot and takes out a red hair that, however, has become discolored after being circulated. The instability of red demythologizes the grand symbolism and suggests a distrust of the discourse in which everyone is engaged. Nonetheless, the narrative voice is by no means skeptical but remains jubilant. Hearing that someone has shaken hands with a red-hair bigfoot, "people came immediately to surround that hand as if surrounding a flag" (*Yuanzhang* [1987] 116). "Flag," another ideology-laden symbol intimately associated with the red color, is (mis)used here to "symbolize" the hand that has to do with a bigfoot. The predicament is interrupted by another crowd that clamors to designate a lad (who comes to prove himself an eyewitness to red-hair bigfoots) as the descendant of the red-hair bigfoot. After his failed attempt to escape, an old man tells a long story about how the lad's mother met a tiger in the mountain. Before he tells what happened next, the old man suddenly chokes and is about to breathe his last. The lad is thus blamed as the cause of the tragedy and regarded as "not qualified to be the descendant of a red-hair bigfoot." Here we encounter a surreal scene typical in Xu Xiaohe's fiction: the blamed lad says that he is not the one they were talking about, and the previous one has already escaped. But people grasp him and reconfirm his identity, for they believe that red-hair bigfoots cannot "lack successors to carry on (*houjiwuren*)" (117). He is thus asked, as a descendant of red-hair bigfoot, "whom you act worthily of (*duideqi shui*)?" and feels really apologetic (118). The power of discourse is truly overwhelming, even though there is nothing substantial contained but clichés echoing the irreconcilable context. Those idioms are supposed to be contextualized in the propaganda of "revolutionary genealogy": for example, the communist enterprise cannot "lack successors to carry on," or the young generation must "act worthily of" the revolutionary martyrs. Misappropriated, the idioms deteriorate into the topic of bigfoot and thus infringe on narrative coherence.

Thus, the lad volunteers to "carry on" the old man's story with the help of others, who tell him that his mother was not eaten but rescued by a red-hair bigfoot and "only then would there be your today (*caiyou nide jintian*)."[1] Like a stock character in communist literature (e.g., Han Xiaoqiang in *On the Docks*) who is listening to the "proletarian revolutionary edification," the lad "heavily lowers his head" and "thereafter conducts seriously like a descendant of red-hair bigfoot" (118). He is determined to do whatever people ask him to do (as if he were a real red-hair bigfoot), such as climbing a tree and rescuing another lass from a tiger. A lass is chosen to match the lad, but he has gone on a long journey to seek a tiger. People are tired of waiting for him and begin to call the lass red-hair bigfoot. After he comes back with nothing but duck eggs and garlic, the lad is astonished by his stand-in and argues his uniqueness with the lass, while she naturally disputes him and argues for hers. The story ends with a false alarm of the tiger when both the male and female "red-hair bigfoots" disappear, and even the one who claimed to have collected a red hair denies his previous statement by taking out a leaf, instead. The grand enterprise of seeking the red-hair bigfoots or their eyewitnesses seems to have evaporated, because of the irreconcilable chasm between the self-sufficient mode of discourse and the insignificant sense of practice.

The Sublime and the Absurd

Xu Xiaohe's aesthetics of catachresis culminates in his novella "Fengzi he tamende yuanzhang" (The madmen and their madhouse director, 1986), in which irony "is unrelieved *vertige*, dizziness to the point of madness" (de Man 215). On the surface level the whole story describes the madmen's "eastern expedition" (a magnificent name that resonates the historically majestic "Northern Expedition" in the 1920s), a *danse macabre* (dis)organized by the madhouse director. In the preceding short story, "The Madhouse Director and His Madmen," the director fails to establish an ideal madhouse that could "epitomize the madmen in all the villages" (*Yuanzhang* [1987] 154). "The Madmen and Their Madhouse Director" enables the director to fulfill his desire by bringing all the lunatic figures together in the same arena to act out their jubilance, sorrow, regret, anxiety, passion, and anger in a negatively conceived Bakhtinian carnival. Under the rubric *eastern expedition* the whole event does not constitute a linear plot (or even a disconnected plot). In other words, *nothing* substantial really happens.

The story is structured around various, sometimes repetitive actions of the madmen, who become the only vehicle of truth, indicating the ultimate meaninglessness of rationality. On the other hand, the madmen's actions are not meaningless, as long as we can trace the historical context within which they can be read as parody. We see the madmen passionately flit over "an iron barrel, a steel ingot, a wooden box, a four-wheel cart, a water vat, a car wheel, an air-blower, a broom, cobwebs, moss, an avometer" and then to "get around and flit again over retemova na, ssom, sbewboc, moorb a, rewolb-ria na, leehw rac a, tav retaw a, trac leehw-ruof a, xob nedoow a, togni leets a, lerrab nori na" (*Yuanzhang* [1989] 119).[2] This scene seem to be a lexical burlesque of the "revolutionary" expedition, which is shown as a blind and ludicrous journey of simple twisting and reversing among rubbish (material and literal).[3] "Shrugging buttocks swinging to the left and to the right" (102) while crawling forward mocks the military training and exhausts its real significance by featuring caricatured images to decrease the value of the ideology in that activity. Moreover, the director's "putting on a pair of moist undershorts, turning on the light again and spreading a piece of white paper to design the future of the madhouse, which would become more and more beautiful in many years" (128), apparently parodies (by taking away the real positive significance in the context) the narrative topos that depicts the diligent party leaders, who are supposed to guide the way to the teleological future.

"The Madmen and Their Madhouse Director" renders an ironic Maoist discourse in revealing the sharp disjunction between the abstract grand narrative and the concrete lunatic behaviors: throughout the whole story we find nothing but insignificant acts *supported by* the magniloquent expressions. Here is the depiction of Zhang Jin'e's mother joining the marchers of the eastern expedition:

> Carelessly, she was patted by the door in her belly and felt the ripples inside. Her crotch immediately got wet. This rather *strengthened her resolve* (jianding le tade juexin); she bent her body, put a cold rock at her door, then *took a final look* (wang le zuihou yiyan) at her hut, and turned right around to join into the madmen's troops. (106; my emph.)

Although the English translation has inevitably lost some nuance of the original,[4] we can still discern the ironic discrepancy between the discourse of heroism and the trivial, insignificant facts. Similar passages are found almost everywhere in this novella:

> The madmen and the madwomen *joined forces* (huishi) on the bridge, *shaking their hands* (woshou) one after another without words. (131; my emph.)

> The madmen were *in buoyant spirits* (xinggaocailie) and wanted to sing a lot of songs. *With the force of justice* (yizhengciyan), the director's wife did not allow them to sing. They had to stop singing. Humming and murmuring and pretending not to care about anything, they were actually *full of passion* (chongman le jiqing) in their minds. (93; my emph.)

> The madmen *raised their unbending heads* (angqi buqu de toulu) from *woe and indignation* (beichuang youfen). Flurried like ghosts, they *were ready at any moment* (shike zhunbei zhe) to *wet their pants in terror* (pigunniaoliu). (112; my emph.)

While the first passage may be simply viewed as a parody of the official style of historical writing about the Red Army,[5] the second and third passages are worth a detailed analysis. Obviously, to describe the madmen with such ideology-laden phrases as "in buoyant spirits" and "full of passion," "woe and indignation" and "raised their unbending heads,"[6] is highly ironic, inasmuch as these phrases are supposed to be used to portray mentally resolute or physically stubborn heroes. The mixture of tragedy (suggested by those phrases) and ludicrousness (suggested by the actions of the madmen) disables our reliance on the majesty of the master discourse and liberates us from the abstract essence of the grandiose cliché. Narrational liberation by no means leads us, however, to a linguistic utopia in which communication becomes unobstructed ecstasy (as Habermas conceives) but, rather, to a self-awareness of the irresolvable paradox that language must be confronted with. The next sentence in this passage immediately indicates the inhumane abjection ("like ghosts") to undermine the legitimacy of the previous characterization. When the orthodox representation of the valiant revolutionary (such as Fang Haizhen in *On the Docks*, who is "ready at any moment") and that of the craven enemy (such as Qian Shouwei, who "wet[s] their pants in terror") are mixed up, the narrative voice forcibly distorts the ordinary order of the discourse and reinforces unbalance or deviation.

The ironic discrepancy also appears in Xu Xiaohe's other works. For instance, it is both a rhetorical amusement and a psychic fright to take a surreal shower in a public bathhouse (in "The Bathhouse" [*Yushi*, 1986]) or explore the "organic" relationship between beating a dog and the establishment of the factory (in "The Specimen" [*Biaoben*, 1986]). The only "truth" lies in the absoluteness of the master discourse, which is, unfortunately, in discord with reality. Narrative overstatement intensifies the dissonance between the high-flown discourse and the low-down historical reality. Also, parody prompts ironic exhaustion of the prototype (i.e., Maoist discourse), or a deviation from the original power, without completely losing its impact. Therefore, madness in Xu Xiaohe implies an interruption of the hegemonic system in the Foucauldian sense:

> Through madness, a work that seems to drown in the world, to reveal there its non-sense, and to transfigure itself with the features of pathology alone, actually engages within itself the world's time, masters it, and leads it; by the madness which *interrupts* it, a work of art opens a void, a moment of silence, a question without answer, provokes *a breach without reconciliation* where the world is forced to question itself. (Foucault, *Madness* 288; my emph.)

Xu Xiaohe's fiction is not sarcastic, insofar as it is not simply the objective event or person that is ridiculed; rather, it is the subjective narration saturated with the self-contradictory master discourse that induces hollow laughter to burst out. Shattered into the fragmentary game of lunatic and ludic eruptions, Xu Xiaohe's fiction does not maintain a facade of the totality of (hi)story. The disappearance of the linear story in the frame of grand narrative points to a disintegrated reality. The self-skeptical narrative is incompatible with what the grandiloquent Maoist discourse has suggested. Not only are the madmen's actions completely absurd, the *logic* of the occurrences is also irrational. This is best illustrated in the description of the director's "recruitment" of Yanwu Xu:

> The first time we saw him [Yanwu Xu] was a morning with thick fog, when he was singing and walking with a limp along the Black River, his body all wet. Zhang Jin'e's mum, carrying a bucket of vegetables, slipped three times and nearly fell over. The little white dog *only* barked twice to him and *then* (zhi . . . jiu) caught cold and sneezed its heart out. As the director heard and arrived at a rush, he was still singing barefoot in a vast expanse of whiteness. Plaintive one moment and melodious the next, myriads of sentiments. The director pretended to get on the bridge, with smile and smile, then suddenly made a dash and grabbed him. As Yanwu Xu *was just about to* (zhengyao) quibble, Zhang Jin'e's mum had ladled out a complete sandal with a dung scoop from the lower reaches. *Not until then* (zhecai) did he hang his head wordlessly and move into the madhouse. (*Yuanzhang* [1989] 97; my emph.)

Apparently, the conjunctions between clauses and sentences only reinforce the disjunctions between the abstract, discursive logic designated by these conjunctions and the concrete, real illogic of everyone's behavior. To a large extent "The Madmen and Their Madhouse Director" suggests the disorder of human activities that the grand narrative fails to represent in an adequate way. This novella exemplifies almost all aspects of Chinese avant-gardism: anachronism, repetition, wordplay, self-negation, collage, and so on, each disclosing the insanity of history under the sway of the master discourse. In this sense it is both an exhibition and a rejection of madness. As Shoshana Felman remarks, "*To talk about madness* is always, in fact, *to deny it*. . . . [To] represent madness is always, consciously or unconsciously, to play out the *scene* of the denial of *one's own* madness" (252). This is why the concept of irony is germane to Xu Xiaohe's narrative in its display of the rupture of consciousness. Thus, the critical project of Xu Xiaohe's fiction is radically different from the frivolous jesting in Wang Shuo's narrative, in which the orthodox value system is secretly embraced through its compromise with all the dominant principles of society and narration. Unaware of the fundamental dilemma of the posttraumatic experience, Wang Shuo only *represents* the feckless aspect of human behavior in social life, whereas Xu Xiaohe exhausts the possibility of representation by exploring the constant friction between exterior triviality and interior gravity. We see in Xu Xiaohe's fiction the "movement of non-totalizable, ungovernable linguistic play, through which meaning misfires and the text's *statement* is estranged from its *performance*" (Felman 252). This movement consists of a ceaseless game of negation, that is, a desperate dialectic that relentlessly unmasks the hypocrisy of the status quo.

If Lu Xun's short story "A Madman's Diary" is paradigmatic in the May Fourth literature, Xu Xiaohe's "The Madmen and Their Madhouse Director" may well be regarded as paradigmatic in post-Mao avant-garde literature. The connection and the distinction between the two epitomize those between the different but correlative literary canons of the two periods, both faced with a crucial historical transition from an old, disastrous sociocultural mode to a new (yet unforeseeable) one, even though their visions of the future may be utterly different. Their common standpoint is, in any case, to reveal the irrationality of the society ideologically accepted as rational in the existent system of discourse.

The distinction between "A Madman's Diary" and "The Madmen and Their Madhouse Director" is as evident as the affinity between them. Lu Xun's Madman, inverting the "normal" and "civilized" society into an abnormal and savage one, is intended to be a sane spokesman for the repressed history, whereas Xu Xiaohe's madmen only arouse endless snickers among themselves. In Xu, as the discrepancy between language and reality or the profound aporia of subjective expression is manifested, madness cannot be magically transformed into reason but remains a truth of madness or chaos that implodes the totality of the master discourse, which has manipulated social consciousness with its rational power. Xu Xiaohe's divergence from his predecessor is to be seen as a denial of any absolutely positive meaning of history. If the "logic" of madness of Lu Xun's Madman is highly visible, Xu Xiaohe's madmen show merely entropic, chaotic behavior. By disclosing the unconscious secret of Lu Xun's Madman, Xu Xiaohe provides an antinarrative that aims at the impossibility of rendering rational meaning of history through his misrepresentation, or catachresis. Their distinction also rests on the different sociohistorical backgrounds. Behind Lu Xun's Madman is a heroic (however desperate) spirit obsessed with the future (however murky the future would look like). Yet for Xu Xiaohe there is only the tragicomic present without the vision of the progress of history, a traumatized sociopsychic present still afflicted with the overpowering yet unstable master discourse.

Lu Xun is certainly not the only major modern writer who deals with madness. Similarities and disparities about how madness is conceived also exist between Xu Xiaohe and Lu Xun, though in a different fashion, between Xu Xiaohe and other writers such as Mao Dun and Shen Congwen. Mao Dun's short story "Fengzi" (The madman, 1934), for example, interprets madness as an inevitable reaction to the repressive and dehumanizing discourse of reality. Mao Dun's madman, Asi, is a real *fengzi*, rather than a self-conscious *kuangren* (which Lu Xun's designates his); it is through the event of becoming madness that Mao Dun expresses his denunciation of reality. In this story it is the madman who mumbles, "You deserve to be killed!" yet this is no more than an agitated reaction to the real danger:

> Only when walking close to him could I see his sight unsettled and his complexion pallid; he, too, sneaked away from other people like a rat evading a cat, while taking a furtive glance at other peoples' faces, as if everyone would hurt him.
> It was not that he wanted to kill people, but that he feared being murdered by other people, I was afraid. ("Fengzi" 107)

Obviously, Mao Dun's diegetic mode of narration attempts to identify his madman with Lu Xun's by defining the madman, again, as a victim of society, despite his own motive to attack people. Mao Dun's "The Madman" is remarkable for its implicit awareness of the formative power of discourse in reality. Several times in the story, Axiu is described as a gibbering (*jijiguagua de*) tattletale (106, 107, 108). She is certainly a character treated as a conveyor of traditional, oppressive discourse, while her old maid status symbolizes Chinese culture that glorifies asexuality and stifles desire. The narrator's conclusion of the story is significant: the old maid Axiu "remained so garrulous that she would never become mad" (108). In this sense "sanity" is only established on the basis of traditional discourse: by gibbering, that is, by imposing a discursive taboo upon the human psyche, the "sane" system produces madness. Not unlike Lu Xun, then, Mao Dun evokes madness as an accusation of the sane society.

In Shen Congwen the sharp contrast between madmen and society disappears. Madness is treated as a realm that, in one way or another, keeps its distance from sociohistorical reality. Wuming's becoming mad, in "Ahei xiaoshi" (A brief story of Ahei, 1933), is—like Asi in Mao Dun's "The Madman"—also a psychic reaction to the tragedy of love. Madness, as psychic disintegration, is described here as a shattered dream that—through remembrance—implicitly quests for a reintegration in imagination. "Shangui" (The mountain ghost, 1928), on the other hand, is a story about a madman who detaches himself from society. This "unearthly" character not only reminds us of the mythical prototype created by Qu Yuan but also implies a romantic role that embodies the aesthetic quality of life. Undoubtedly, his "silent" (withdrawn from social discourse), "innocent," and "unrestrained" characteristics (*wenji* 2:151) epitomize Shen Congwen's conception of ideal humanity: "He laughs at unseemly occasions and cries casually. He behaves boldly, not afraid of ghosts or beasts. He loves flowers and the moon; he loves to sing and to look at heaven alone" (151). It is remarkable that Shen Congwen's term for *madness*, in both cases, is neither *kuang* nor *feng* but *dian*, a word that hints at obsession or infatuation. The madman's temporary absence from the society must be seen as a failed effort to pursue a higher mode of existence. There exists in his madness, then, "an impossible desire to own what is denied by reality or by realist writing, to unite a world that has been partitioned into these signifiers" (D. Wang, *Fictional Realism* 256). Shen Congwen's mode of madness thus implies a profound "desire" to "reunite," or totalize, the shattered reality, a desire that is universally possessed but unfulfilled by modern Chinese writers and eventually questioned by post-Mao avant-garde writers.

The Grand Project Parodied

In any case Shen Congwen attempts to offer a model in his narrative aiming to essentialize an authentic existence, an ideal that opposes the chaotic social reality, though such a subjective effort has its own obstacles and problems. In Xu Xiaohe, then, the challenge against absolute narration lies in the disclosure of the problematics of the totality or self-sufficiency of the representational subjectivity. A critique of the objective world is based on an self-critique of the narrative subject probing an internal crisis. In his novella "Shuiling de rizi" (The juicy days, 1988) such grand projects as the Maoist "Cultural Revolution" or the Dengist "Economic Reform" are allegorized as an inferior, absurd, collective practice. The surreal and dreamlike scenes in the novella dislocate representational logic and, therefore, examine the disorder of representational subjectivity. Certainly, such a narrative does not display a complete and omnipotent voice of the narrator: narration becomes a suspicious, indeterminate, and self-negating process, in which the subjective, individual basis of the dominant, collective discourse is undermined. In "The Juicy Days" the earliest perception of the big fish originates from the moment when the "I" hears that "someone without identifiable sex was singing from a distance with a twist in the tongue. I thought it was Yanwu Xu." After a few passages the narrator says, "I suddenly remembered the so-called someone from a distance was actually the crooked-horn ox." Immediately after that, it is discovered that this "fatigue-looking, at times affectedly crying" thing now "no longer sounded like a crooked-horn ox but a ready-to-voyage ocean liner" (and "moreover an ocean liner that is voyaging in a wind-riding and waves-cleaving way"). Nonetheless, it finally turns out to be a big fish that, when jumping up, "thought it could reach a new height" (64).

Not only does the narrative indeterminacy expose the subjective deficiency, but the misuse of such clichés as the political metaphor "wind-riding and waves-cleaving" "ocean liner" (*chengfengpolang de julun*)[7] and the propaganda slogan "reach a new height" (*dadao yige xinde gaodu*) draws our attention. It is neither the Maoist "People's Commune" nor the Dengist "Reform and Opening" but a fish more dead than alive that has been associated with such metaphor and slogan. The allegorical implication in this novella, intended or not, derives from the historical situation of Communist China. Mayor Jiaopo Lan (a character corresponding to the madhouse director, who is also occasionally mentioned in this novella), a "great leader" (like Mao) or "general designer" (like Deng) who "planned to construct the road now here, now there" (64), "had conceived everything for us"—a totalized and teleological future is prescribed—though "he thought no one had recognized this point." For the poor "I," "before we got clear whether or not the term 'no one' included us and which point we did not recognize, the fog had started" (63). What we see here is not an indictment against the catastrophe of modernity but, rather, puzzlement in the face of the grand project of modernity.

Xu Xiaohe has not simply destined the bankruptcy of the project of modernity. Rather, in the penultimate chapter, "Jiaopo Lan finally led us to the road he had constructed." The scene in which "people along the road continuously greeted him, Jiaopo Lan nodded to them again and again, and we also had to nod after him" is a stereotypical description of leaders' local visitation. To Xu Xiaohe, however, senselessness becomes the core of catastrophe. A parody of the master trope recurs: "The road in front of us was still long. At least it would require great effort to reach the end before it got dark" (74). The insertion of the phrase *before it got dark* makes the master discourse a little comical, insofar as we know neither what the function of the road really is nor why it is necessary to "reach the end" of the grand road that symbolizes modernity "before it got dark" (rather than "toward dawn," according to the regulations of the master discourse).

In any case, for Jiaopo Lan "this is the outcome of having been engaged in a long-term enterprise." Besides, the completion of the enterprise seems to be the only, absolute goal, in which the lack of real significance is the crux: "It seems nothing has happened, and nothing will happen. People pouted their lips in the manner of fish, chuckled and that was it. Or even worse than the manner of fish." As a note on the project of modernity, this passage implies that Jiaopo Lan's grand enterprise is only connected to the senseless behavior of the people. Only "from close up"—micrologically, rather than from a historical panorama—could we "see the scar on the back of Jiaopo Lan's head." This arouses the memory of the "I" about the event of fish killing, the major plot of the novella: "The fish did not swing away until it was hit by the ladder. Nevertheless, I am still suspicious. It was too long ago, after all. Or even might not have happened at all. Memory is usually wrong, usually a mere illusion. My disease came right from this" (74). The disease here, according to the entire narrative, refers to the madness of the narrator. The irrationality thus originates from the trauma caused by a seemingly rational event: the immemorial truth becomes the displaced event in memory or even illusion, suggested by the unstable narrative mode. Such a trauma triggers the disintegration of subjectivity and deprives it of its capability of articulating the origin of the event. This is why the elusive narration of the whole novella can never exhaust the account of the event of fish killing.

This central event in the narrative is itself nonsensical: commanded by Jiaopo Lan, the townspeople enter the belly of the dissected big fish and cut off the instantly edible intestines and meat. The crux is the equivocal narration, which bases the absurd objective event on subjective absurdity. It needs to be reemphasized that the indeterminacy of Xu Xiaohe's narration, that is, the recurrent misstatements and incessant digressions, can be seen as the most radical challenge in avant-garde literature against narrative totality. The absolute narration in modern Chinese fiction is undermined: no discourse is irreversible, no statement can be immune from suspicion. For instance, "Some people had changed so much that Uncle Shao did not look like Uncle Shao but like Jiaopo Lan. Only after a long time did it become clear that he was indeed Jiaopo Lan." And "the one who puffed a mouthful of wine toward the face of the dog was the real Uncle Shao. It's because his eyeballs were reddish. But later it turned out that Jiaopo Lan's eyeballs were more reddish. That I couldn't care." It seems that every narrative unit may deviate from, or contradict, the previous ones. Narrative stability is thus reduced to the minimum. Such an "unreliable" narration goes to the extreme in the chapter about the tryst of the "I" and Shuangmu Lin:

> I knew I wouldn't be wrong, but I was still wrong. She smiled, and a slice of stone slipped down from her shoulder. It turned out to be a piece of crab shell. No wonder. I asked her if she knew the director. She said of course. But asked me which director. I myself wasn't sure which director. Even to this day I still don't understand why I asked about the director whom I didn't know until many years later. So I suspect that all was but a dream. Shuangmu Lin didn't consider it a dream. Because it is impossible that many people have the same dream. Though it's not entirely impossible either.

As if this passage were not awkward enough, the chapter ends with a more dizzying scene:

> I looked at Shuangmu Lin, yet she was not Shuangmu Lin. She was Aunt Fatty.
> "It's been like this for a long time," she said. (68)

It is this kind of narrative mode, not merely the narrated event, that is to be regarded as the core of the novella. The dreamlike scene is the starting point, rather than the end, of the narrative labyrinth. We must go through the dizzying labyrinth of narration to comprehend the dizzying event. This is the most uncompromising rhetorical politics in Xu Xiaohe's fiction. It interrupts the totalistic mode of not only the political discourse but the subjective discourse in general, because what we are facing is no longer an object to be easily corrected but a predicament of subjectivity that requires constant self-analysis. Certainly, such a predicament is entangled with the blow of the external event from which the subject suffers; otherwise, the narrative would not link the etiology of madness to the event of fish killing. Not only does the "I"'s "disease come right from this," but the other characters also receive a shocking blow in similar situations:

> The big fish moved a little bit, and exhaled leisurely.
> "It's not dead! It's not dead yet!"
> Aibao was stunned, cut a caper and ran away. Yanwu Xu and Guyue Hu popped out their heads from the fish belly, wiped blood off their faces and then drew back in to jolt and churn. Aibao turned deranged from that time. Whenever hearing something unusual he would cut a caper and run away. (69)

Indeed, nothing is more destructive than our own participation in the bloody history. Because of our own participation, history is not tragedy but theater of the absurd. In "The Juicy Days" we can perceive the conflict between the magnificent spectacle of the event of fish killing and the bloodiness/triviality of the whole event. In many cases Xu Xiaohe even places that kind of bloodiness/triviality into the lyrical context and demonstrates the inadequate expression that the narrative subject is unable to avoid:

> Gongtianba and Yanwu Xu crawled out of the fish belly, coiling up a long string of fish viscera.... Having not recovered to be able to talk to us, he [Gongtianba] already held them and went onto the road that Jiaopo Lan was soon to accomplish. Thinking that he would be going along endlessly if nobody dissuaded him, I did not go to dissuade him. But he stopped, looked toward Yanwu Xu with rosy countenance. Yanwu Xu also had rosy countenance. Both were holding the same viscera, *facing one another without a word* (xiangduiwuyan). (71)

The lyrical and romantic topos of "facing one another without a word" is employed to imply a situation of ennui, an aphasia confronted with the depletion of meaning. The narrator describes the beginning of his own participation in the fish killing: "Daddy Gui wanted me to do some pioneer work in the fish belly. He gave me a knife" (71). In contrast to the bloody and senseless event, the high tone in such phrases as *pioneer work* now questions the validity of the grand history.

Compared to the spiritually magnificent eastern expedition in "The Madmen and Their Madhouse Director," the fish-killing event and the scene of eating raw fish in "The Juicy Days" degenerate into an even more inferior mode of behavior. This may be an appropriate note on the transformation from the idealistic Mao era to the pragmatic Deng era. In such a "pioneering work" the "I" is ensnared by a cuttlefish in the belly of the big fish. The ensnarement, misrepresented in the master discourse about collectivity, occasions serious wound to the individual:

> In the dark it had its supple tentacles on my shoulder, as if I were its *intimate comrade-in-arms* (qinmi zhanyou). I drew out my arm, brushed off the tentacles, and pretended that I was moving aside a little bit. The comrade-in-arms didn't care, and held me supplely in order to *unite with me more intimately* (geng jinmi de tuanjie qilai). (73; my emph.)

This is, however, the origin of "the spots on my body that were burnt by the cuttlefish's sucker and grew maggots afterwards" (73). At the end the "I" and the cuttlefish are both trapped into the bowels of the big fish: "No sooner had I heard a stinky hoot than I was pressed out by its anus" (75). A narrative of the seemingly magnificent enterprise concludes in such a filthy scene, a predicament at once pitiable and laughable. Scatological and eschatological tendencies are intermixed to constitute Xu Xiaohe's basic tone of narration. Xu's scatology devalues the aesthetics of the abstract project to the filth of details, and his eschatology displays the depletion and apathy of life. We are again reminded of Beckett's *Endgame,* in which the meaningless dialogue from trash cans denotes the existential impasse in post–World War II Europe.

Like Beckett, Xu Xiaohe, though having gone through the catastrophe of the Cultural Revolution, does not propose a nihilistic relinquishment of existence. The effort of self-trial reveals historical awkwardness and hopelessness, which are not rationally comprehensible, precisely because of the intensity of their origin. The narrator is pushed to an absurd condition, a condition deprived of self-sufficiency: "If it had been clearer, I might have witnessed the truth of the matter. Nothing in my memory would be wrong. Or perhaps everything is wrong" (69). While self-suspicion is the only way out of the impasse, the "clear" truth is constantly being postponed or distorted: this is an endless negative interrogation, a painful, absurd, and perhaps Sisyphean struggle for self-consciousness.

Chapter 8

Can Xue

Discursive Dystopias

The whole purpose of talking is to arouse others' attention. As a matter of fact, I never intend to tell anything, but only to make some noises.
—CAN XUE, "APPLE TREE IN THE CORRIDOR"

The self-interruptive specter that disturbs the system of Maoist discourse appears in most of Can Xue's longer fiction, such as *Yellow Mud Street*, *Old Floating Cloud*, "Apple Tree in the Corridor," *Tuwei biaoyan* (Breakout performances, 1988), and *Sixiang huibao* (A thought report, 1991). Can Xue's affinity with Xu Xiaohe lies in the fact that her fiction, too, disseminates the idioms of Maoist discourse into irrational contexts while at the same time maintaining their serious, aggressive significance. In so doing, Can Xue transforms the grand narrative into fragments, into endless conflicts and anxieties. If Xu Xiaohe is apt to demonstrate the inconsistent linguistic play of narrative, on which the social/historical movement is established, Can Xue is keen to disclose the surrealistic pattern of the human psyche that structures the horrific and senseless intercommunication (or intercommunion) in social life. Although less comic than Xu Xiaohe's, Can Xue's fiction contains implicit and intricate irony in her exposé of social and individual predicaments. Reading Can Xue should start from an understanding of the comic or, to be more precise, "the absolute comic" that Baudelaire suggests, to indicate the permanent dilemma of human existence: in Can Xue's case a dilemma of articulation and communication.

The Communal/Communist/Communicative Chaos

Catachresis in Can Xue indicates the loss or uncertainty of the signified in the master discourse. *Yellow Mud Street*, probably her most politically oriented work that deals directly with the social circumstances in the Cultural Revolution, can be examined in the context of the paradigmatic works of propaganda such as *On the Docks*. Only by teasing out the ironic implications of her works can we see the desperate truth of schizophrenia that points ultimately to the ruined politico-historical reality.[1] Unlike the static, diffuse plot in most of Xu Xiaohe's fiction, the narrative of *Yellow Mud Street* is slightly on the move, delineating the tireless but futile investigation of the case of Wang Si-ma, a person who is a class enemy in theory yet in reality may be identified another way. The entire text is saturated in the Maoist discourse of class struggle, which structures the story as an epitome of sociopolitical reality in the Cultural Revolution. Thus, it is not surprising that the same key phrase for both *Yellow Mud Street* and *On the Docks* is "cha(tayi)ge / nongge *shuiluoshichu*" (literally meaning "to examine until the water subsides and the rocks emerge"). In *Yellow Mud Street*, people's enthusiasm to make up their mind "to investigate (it) thoroughly" (*Tiantang* 76, 93 / *Old Floating Cloud* 80, 97) or to be "determined to find the truth" (119/121) is rhetorically parallel to the same idiom crucial to *On the Docks*, in which the slogan "we must get to the bottom of the whole thing" (Shanghai jingjutuan *Haigang* 43 / "On the Docks" 30)[2] is the primary drive of the "positive characters" represented by Fang Haizhen and Gao Zhiyang for pushing the (hi)story forward.

It is precisely from this point, however, that *Yellow Mud Street* digresses from the master discourse and disrupts its ideology by contrasting the majestic and aggressive discourse with the futility and absurdity of social life. The truth pursued by people on Yellow Mud Street never develops out of the meddlesome activities driven by the visionary discourse. The narrative constantly disorders itself and twists the significance of *shuiluoshichu* into a psychological and social chaos. The "thorough" truth, or "the bottom of the whole thing," is therefore the permanent, bottomless untruth, after which all the pursuits are merely automatically operated by the power of words. Most ridiculous of all, the person being investigated seriously and anxiously by everyone on Yellow Mud Street may not exist, just as in *On the Docks* Qian Shouwei, artificially invented to serve the propaganda, is hardly a credible character. The ideological characteristic of Qian Shouwei is parodied by Wang Si-ma, who cannot be a target of investigation beyond the limits of discourse. Therefore, an ironic penetration into the core of the master discourse helps us recognize its inner hollowness contained in the lunatic and insignificant activities of the masses.[3] In this sense Can Xue explores the reception, circulation, and consumption of the master discourse rather than its production, insofar as mass ideology and mass manipulation are the basic political intrigues of Mao's China. By taking away the rational basis of Maoist discourse, Can Xue undermines its legitimacy as a dominant force.

Here madness is shown as the ignorance of the detachment of actions from their supposed goal, or as the unawareness of the irrelevance of intentions to their realization. In *Yellow Mud Street* everyone is obsessively concerned about the weird events and the (dis)connections to the "Wang Si-ma case," even though Wang Si-ma's existence is either called into question or bluntly denied (96/100). In any case, though people keep asking "Is Wang Si-ma a real person?" (*Tiantang* 28, 98, 104 / *Old Floating Cloud* 32, 102, 108), the nonexistence of Wang Si-ma is equally impossible to prove (100/104). Even the certainty of the existence of Wang Zi-guang (who comes to investigate the "Wang Si-ma case") and the status of the district head are dubious (40, 115 / 46, 118). Wang Zi-guang is once found out by old lady Qi to be only a functionary for the recycling station, but then this discovery is denied by old lady Song, who alleges that his identity is being investigated. Similarly, it can never be determined who Wang Si-ma really is, since he could astonishingly turn out to be the district head (121/123), although afterwards the district head appears and stops this suspicion, or Zhang Mie-zi (141/141) or anyone else. Because of the self-conflicting elements in the narrative text (from different characters' statements), we can never determine anyone's real identity or status. We are compelled to realize that, after all, everything spoken of is temporarily affirmable and immediately refutable.

It is demonstrated that futility is the very truth of the sociopolitical life under the sway of the power of discourse, from which no one can escape. Under such circumstances the residents of Yellow Mud Street are so enthusiastically involved in the preoccupation of a "plot/conspiracy" (18, 20, 93, 109 / 23, 25, 98, 113), a "spy" (21, 162 / 26, 161), or a "black shadow" (44/50) that the only conclusion the district head can get is that "nearly everyone on Yellow Mud Street seems to be a Wang Si-ma" (106/110). This inference somewhat touches upon the dangerous social reality of pervasive aggressiveness. Class struggle prevails in the whole story, while its putative reason is depleted by a schizophrenic impulse, on which the entire society is based. The notorious utterances of grandiose Maoist discourse are grafted into disordered expressions of phobia, suspicion, and assault. In so doing, Can Xue suggests that phobia, suspicion, and assault are part and parcel of the genuine content of Maoist discourse, although the latter is magnificently constructed as absolute justice. The following utterances are typical in *Yellow Mud Street:*

> Isn't there a principle from above called "very good"? It has to do with patriotism. What does "very good" mean? The present situation is very good! The instructions from above are very good! I mean, don't close both eyes in sleep. Keep one eye open. (15–16/21; trans. modified)

> The district head concentrated on picking his nose. He said, "How are you carrying out the thirteen major problems? I believe that looseness and indifference will only lead to doom. Aren't there incidents of bats eating human beings? Do you still keep the tradition of the old revolutionary base area?" (165/164)

Speaking incoherently is doubtless a symptom of madness through which irony can be detected. The phobias erupting in the story are frequently linked to political activities (61, 109 / 67, 113), which are supposed to convey the master discourse practically. The ruin of history is now denoted by madness, in which all the expressions derived from the master discourse become nothing but the instigator of the social and psychic disorder, as soon as the grandiose, visionary, and totalistic content of the ideology has been withdrawn from its form. It is an evident feature in *Yellow Mud Street* that the expressions of Maoist discourse constitute and determine all the activities in the whole community, yet what is ironic exists in the fact that these expressions are always conjoined with something that deviates from the frame of discourse.

In Can Xue's fiction there exist also intertextually ironic constituents that operate in relation to a larger space. If the sun in *Old Floating Cloud* produces an effect of violence and savagery, in *Yellow Mud Street* it suggests a natural omen of odium or fear that reinforces the misappropriation of the master symbol. The chapter "The Days When the Sun Was in the Sky" begins with the statement: "When the sun is up, everything goes rotten, everywhere" (14/19). The sun in this novella is always related to viciousness or anxiety. The image of the sun is even inseparable from the image of prison or incarceration: "In these dreams there is always a strange-looking iron gate, a dirty, yellow, tiny sun. From this gate a row of barbs juts up menacingly. The tiny sun hangs in one corner of the gray, dusty sky forever, giving out the metallic light of death" (9/12). It may also cause fear: "Everyone was startled and their faces turned pale. Raising their heads, they wondered why the sun was so bright, so white. The light was obviously false. There must be a plot behind it" (17/22). The most significant reference to the sun occurs near the end of the novel where the raving of a character immediately becomes an ironic statement in conflict with the descriptive narrative:

> "Comrades," Old Yu was pointing at the dim, shadowy circle outside the window, "how can the sun become like this? Isn't it big and red? It's really both big and red, big and . . . ." (171/170; trans. modified)

If we are aware that phrases such as *big and red* have been employed to indicate the master symbol, Can Xue's effort is precisely to trace its traumatic affect and demolish its psychic manipulation. Accordingly, it is the multifarious images and events in her narrative that, as heterodox elements, subvert the orthodoxy of discourse.

On the whole, inasmuch as the splendid meaning in the master discourse has been replaced by fear, suspicion, and insane behavior, Can Xue's narrative becomes catachresis, that is, a painful misuse of Maoist discourse as a resistance to the ferocious shock from the discourse. The original historical violence of Maoist discourse is not represented but, rather, misrepresented in its display of the disjunction between the grandiosity of ideology and the cruelty of reality. For the

Chinese avant-garde the impossibility of an integral rationality is a consequence of numerous historical blows such as the Anti-Rightist Movement, the Cultural Revolution, and the June Fourth Incident, all of which led to the fragmentation of the unity of experience. Madness in Can Xue's narrative is a deprivation of active remembrance, yet it is this pathological amnesia that evidences the political violence within the master discourse, which prohibits history from entering consciousness and then transforms itself into the anamnesis of this violence. Can Xue's political stance exists in the "pathology" of verbal catachresis: to invoke the (dis)figural power in order not to indicate the primary shock directly but to phrase the present traumatic affect (de)formed by that shock. The most radical reaction of the Chinese avant-garde to the historical catastrophes becomes an exposure of the traumatized experience, in which the correspondence between the real historical significance and the grand form of discourse is ironically dislocated.

The Improbable Truth of Discourses

For Can Xue the existing system of discourse is not produced solely by a single authority—Mao, in this case—but is actuated and practiced by a collective rhetoric that she evokes as the source of traumatic experiences. Communication per se is always a nightmare that disrupts its own logic and is transformed into a verbal pandemonium in which the possibility of communication is disabled. Her novel *Breakout Performances* is, in this sense, an ironic game of expressions containing extreme instability and self-negativity of communication. The narrator of the novel is a stenographer (and thus a realistic author of incomprehensible text), who actually joins the other residents of Five-Flavor Street to explore the case of "adultery" between Lady X and Gentleman Q. The fact/event of adultery (which the residents of the whole street are so zealous about discussing) seems to be the focus of the whole story, yet throughout the whole novel nothing true is exposed. In a sense the narrative of the stenographer is sincere, or realistic, enough: it neither fabricates facts without quoting in detail nor conceals anything related to the "actual" state of affairs. One of the most apparent features in *Breakout Performances* is the profuse use of direct quotations, which the stenographer-narrator records. The authorial subject is decentered, as it is disseminated into numerous contending and discordant subjects. When narrating becomes nothing but quoting, restating, and paraphrasing, the original, unitary truth of narrative is undermined. It is sincerity about insincerity, or truth about untruth, insofar as the fidelity to discourse means the suspension and diversion of reality.

At the beginning of the novel a two-page discussion of Lady X's age (certainly concerned with everyone's own "evaluation" of her) sums up over twenty-eight different opinions and finally concludes by "postulating it as 35 years old" for "convenience" (*Tuwei* 5). This opening description settles the basic mode of the entire novel, which is an assembly of incongruous remarks and gossips. Every statement in the narrative becomes so problematic that the only truth, as everyone may infer, is that nothing can be affirmed as truth. The narrative is in constant conflict with itself, in that what it ultimately means always undermines what it ostensibly says. Representational realism, particularly the stereotyped characterization in modern Chinese fiction, is parodied—for instance, in the narrator's conclusion of Lady X's appearance:

> After various discussions about her age, we have got such a contradictory, vague impression: Lady X is a middle-aged woman with white teeth and thin body, her neck slender or wrinkly, her skin smooth or rough, her voice crisp and dissolute, her appearance sexy or not sexy at all. (5–6)

Likewise, the depiction of Gentleman Q is that "he is tall and appears ugly or handsome, or absolutely ordinary" (15). Deliberate narrative self-nullification and self-contradiction form the basic tone of the novel.

Breakout Performances is a text in which each of the contesting statements becomes a *différend* (a Lyotardian term referring to each of the contesting micrological elements) that breaks down the totality of discourse in its communicative form. This, however, is by no means a utopian world of language carnival but, rather, an inferno of words in which to speak is to torture and to listen is to be tortured. The novel can be regarded as an unmasking of the totalitarian system of discourses, in which panic is not extinguished but suspended and sublimated as an intermediate phase in the "dialectical history" to be negated. In Can Xue's fiction, however, there is no heroic or tragic dynamics to lead the negative present to the positive future. Catachresis in Can Xue is an interminable rhetorical negation that reveals the chaotic, mutually deprecatory movements of minor narratives that tumble the grand narrative. Even though the stenographer (narrator) claims that his attempt is "a totalistic seizure of the cosmos" and that those different ideas of the masses "contain a high degree of historicity and responsibility" with the spirit of "'being practical and realistic' (*shishiqiushi*) and 'being sincere and frank' (*zhencheng tanbai*)" (136; both idioms discernibly part of Maoist discourse), the malignant and brazen gossip immediately invalidates this claim and discloses the absurd effect of the discourse.

Since, for Can Xue, communicating is tantamount to muddling up, language is never a centripetal operation aiming at what it signifies but a centrifugal process that irreversibly flees away from reality. *Breakout Performances* most remarkably registers this centrifugal force. The "climax" of the story is supposed to be the description of the "adultery" between Lady X and Gentleman Q by which everyone has been intrigued. Although the narrator suggests in the beginning of chapter 2 ("Some Implicative Key Points") of part 2 ("The Story") that "we are about to enter the core of the story" (149), the chapter consists only of interviews with a few residents of Five-Flavor Street, none of whom can tell the actual event. "The most reliable and closest information is from Lady X's sister's husband's good friend's wife's mouth . . . : 'This is something impossible to speak of'" (162). In any case "the adultery did happen; though nobody can tell clearly where and when it happened, everyone has affirmed this fact inwardly" (168). Although there are "at least 500 different opinions among more than 1,000 people" about where the tryst took place, "everybody 'did see' the adultery, which is vivid up to now. . . . The important thing is 'to have seen'; as for the place and time, these are minor problems" (180). Even though the real occurrence is indeterminable, the narrative persists in dealing with "the details in the barn (let's temporarily presume the site of the adultery there)" (203). The real climax of the novel occurs in chapter 6, in which three Ph.D.s argue over the question of "who took the initiative":

> We have imagined what Lady X and Gentleman Q did after they entered that pitch-dark barn at the time no one knows. Only one problem, the greatest, still remains unresolved: Who took the initiative, i.e., who started first? In the black-room meeting, our elites come up with three different opinions about this touchy problem. In the heated argument, the elites did not side with the first speaker until after numerous setbacks. They achieved the conclusion through a vertical, macroscopic analysis of history and the

systematic study using the comparative method. The opinion of the first speaker (Dr. A) is that the one who took the offensive was Gentleman Q. Viewed from the surface, Lady X was a far more active element (let's temporarily assume the two people as two elements) and seemed to have inborn aggressiveness, while Gentleman Q, by comparison, was far more passive, like a block-head entrapped by her. Since Gentleman Q's element looked so simple and innocent, we may conceive with certainty that it was Lady X's element that rushed ahead to strip off his clothes and manipulate him as if she had been manipulating a puppet. As a result, he felt wronged and was unable to wash off the infamy. But this is only the idea of common, mediocre people; our elites on Five-Flavor Street are never misled by such superficial appearances. . . . This time, we explored the history of the past and the present, drew inferences from all possible points, strictly discriminated and expounded, and then decided to stand unyieldingly on Dr. A's side. (214–15)

In his conclusion that it was Gentleman Q who started the adultery, Dr. A declares in Mao's style: "when looking at a problem we must not look at its surface; we need to penetrate into the essence of the thing with swordlike eyes" (216). Thereupon, his "approach" to the adultery is neither concrete nor descriptive (his speech, or reasoning, does not even consist of any reference to the real process of the occurrence) but is rationally analytic. All he gives us subsequently is a quaint application of his idea about sexual relationship. The so-called essence—which is so strongly upheld by Maoist discourse—turns out to be extremely absurd and self-nullifying for having lost its counterpart in reality and is thus bereft of its truth content. All the three speakers' harangues—and in this sense all the characters' words in the novel, especially the narrator's—have made ironic digressions from reality, since their reasoning and conclusions are drawn from the event whose actual existence is itself problematic.

Phänomenologie der Geister

The title of Can Xue's novella *A Thought Report* is highly allusive to the political discourse, although the content of the novella has no direct political significance. Nevertheless, it is indeed the ideologically loaded *form* that is at stake. A "thought report" is a form of confession (particularly during the Cultural Revolution) in which people are either forced or volunteer to expose, to their superior or to the public, their most recent—in particular, ideologically "incorrect" or "imperfect"—thoughts, feelings, and conceptions about the political situation or the Marxist-Leninist-Maoist doctrine. In the novella, however, what the narrator (Mr. A) confesses to the invisible "Comrade Chief" (*shouzhang tongzhi*) (a vague appellation for high officers or officials in the lexicon of communist China)[4] are the trivial daily occurrences that violate, excite, depress, and gratify him. The thematic folly thus shows the wreck of the ideological form of the "report." Throughout the whole report, most ironically, it is gradually revealed that Comrade Chief may not even exist at all but is only the narrator's fantasy. At least the actuality of the listener hardly matters; what really matters is the process of report as such, which becomes the essential way of life for Mr. A: only through his persistent monologue can Mr. A realize the value of his existence.

The novella is a product of discourse, first of all, on the level of the narrative frame. Mr. A, the narrator, keeps telling his own story in relation to his wife, his neighbors, his confrere, and especially, someone called "Hanger-on." His narration, within the form of a thought report, is infused with the master discourse, while, again, the significance of the discourse is incessantly undermined by meaningless happenings. Mr. A's narrative starts from his self-introduction as a "great inventor recognized by the national Ministry of Industry" (*Sixiang* 2), whose "incredible invention" is, strangely, puncturing various patterns, such as "plum blossom" or "cow's heart or stomach," on eggshells (57). It is the official recognition that makes discourses valuable, such as "to have made encouraging progress" (*qude kexi de jinzhan*) and "to struggle for . . ." (*wei . . . fendou*), in describing his meaningless work. The grandeur of his project has thus to be detached from the specificity of his work: when his wife speaks about the "majestic quality" of his work, she never notices what he is really doing but uses "an abstract term—'work'—to replace various concrete practices" (89). The abstract, unifying discourse thus eliminates the variety of real practices and conceals the (in)significance under a single mode of its majesty. Indeed, the term *work* has to do with the concept of "working class," an "abstract" social group that is, in theory, viewed as the dominant class in communist

China. Against this background the novella explores the impossibility of narrative disclosure of the meaning of life (or of labor/working), which is repetitively driven by the discourse into more awkward and baser situations.

Mr. A's narrative, or report, begins with his fight with his two neighbors and his "Fashionable Confrere" (another inventor) for their gossip about his "vulgar" dress style. What is ironic lies in the inappropriate relation of the dress style to the identity of "inventor," over which the neighbors' dignity and Mr. A's anger seem utterly gratuitous. From the beginning the novella displays the inadequate impact of the discourse, which is solemn and dubious at one and the same time, on social life. The development of the events can thus be seen as propelled by various solemn but dubious discourses, both in the frame of the story (the report per se) and in the account of the events (reported by the narrator). The discourses, then, become what distort the logic of interpersonal relationship and communication or what interrupt the logic of social life. Because of Mr. A's defeat in his fight with the neighbors, his wife has a liaison with Neighbor 2, who gradually and naturally "joins" Mr. A's family. Neighbor 2 first eats together with them, then lives in their house, and later suggests that Mr. A sleep in the living room so that he can share the bedroom with Mr. A's wife. But, when Mr. A declares that his wife and Neighbor 2 are "born a couple" and further suggests that he himself move out of the house, Neighbor 2 gets irritated and complains that his "work of ideological education" has become futile, for Mr. A's "intentions are indeed too vicious" (15–16).

The reader must be impelled to speculate: what kind of "work of ideological education" has Neighbor 2 done to Mr. A, and why are Mr. A's "intentions indeed too vicious"? The potential answers to these questions, however, are inevitably displaced by the doubt of their answerability, insofar as the phrases, as signifiers, have no adequate signifieds. What Neighbor 2 calls the work of ideological education—a politically solemn phrase—means, ironically, nothing more than his living in Mr. A's house in order to, according to Neighbor 2's logic, eliminate Mr. A's jealousy. Following this logic, then, Mr. A's purposive wish to move out of the house is judged as "vicious intentions," a phrase applicable only to political antagonists, since he refuses to be "educated." Therefore, the discourses, which are supposed to rationalize reality, can never find a rational way to define or guide daily life but, on the contrary, engender irrationalities and disturbances of social activities.

Such irrationalities and disturbances prevail in the whole story. As Mr. A draws his wife away from Neighbor 2, the latter, unexpectedly, alleges that Mr. A has already "made a satisfying first step." Neighbor 1 and the Fashionable Confrere then convene a meeting to congratulate Mr. A "for having a new life" and applaud themselves "for having expended our stamina, adhered to the truth, persisted in exemplifying the law by ourselves (*yishenshifa*), and left our own life and death out of consideration. Only then have today's bright prospects been obtained" (18). Among all these idioms the phrase *yishenshifa* is unusual. The phrase here is not an idiom per se but only homophonous to the derogatory idiom *yishenshifa*, which is applied only in relation to convicts, meaning "test the law personally" (*shi* meaning "attempt" or "test," rather than "demonstrate" or "exemplify"). The potential misreading of the phrase is a dissonant hazard in the very center of Neighbor 1's whole discourse, which maintains an exceedingly lofty tone. The way of representation, again, is incompatible with the real occurrences, as we see that their expenditure of "stamina" refers to their combat with Mr. A, and their adherence to the "truth" refers to the coercive connection between the clothing style and the mental quality of an inventor. The meeting ends with a scene reminiscent not only of Beckett's *Waiting for Godot* but also of *youdou* (parading enemies through the streets), which prevailed during the Cultural Revolution: Mr. A's neck is tied by a rope and pulled by Neighbor 1 to go around the table. Such a parade in reality usually follows a "criticism and denunciation meeting," rather than a "commendation meeting" like this. The incomprehensibility is exactly what Can Xue reveals in China's recent history and daily life: the disjunction between discourse and reality, between form and content, and between ritual and spirit.

Also, the disjunction between behavior and intent. When he forces open the door of the bedroom that his wife and Neighbor 2 have entered for a while, Mr. A sees the two "stand at the threshold with solemn countenances and arms akimbo" (20). They blame him and close the bedroom door again. The narrator, after contemplating for ten minutes, feels sober and admits that he "might have said something incorrect." Why is it impossible, he speculates, that they are doing "superior spiritual activity" such as playing cards? Here, first, it is visible that the social impropriety has to be performed as a majestic drama in which the roles are played "solemnly," as what Mr. A's wife and Neighbor 2 have shown. Impropriety, in addition, can also be displaced by the grandeur of discourse imposed upon the visionary reality. "Playing cards" not only imaginarily camouflages the real occurrences but also, as a "superior spiritual activity," generates an "ideal realm" (21), which, ironically, dislocates ideal from reality, conception from perception. This is indeed what has happened time and again in contemporary China: historical violence and ideological folly can be interpreted as progressive (or necessary to the progressive history), as far as the master discourse is concerned.

In the second part Hanger-on appears, sent by the authorities to support Mr. A's invention. He promises to assist Mr. A with it because they have a "common pursuit after the undertaking" (25) and decides that Mr. A and his wife should offer him a bedroom. After his wife moves to Neighbor 2's, Mr. A cooks for Hanger-on, who eats voraciously and complains about the poor quality of food. Although Mr. A soon finds out that Hanger-on was previously only a cobbler, he still regards him as an authority because, as soon as Hanger-on moves in, his wife and neighbors cheer about Mr. A's talent every day outside his house. Obviously, the relationship between the host (or master) and the dependent (or slave) is reversed: Mr. A volunteers to be a servant to Hanger-on.

Despite Hanger-on's real identity, they even fabricate various stories about how he has become an authority (just as the histories of the Communist Party and its leaders have been mythologized). They imagine that he was born in a pigsty to a family of honest villagers and became talented by educating himself. In order to explore the social life of the lower class, he practiced shoe repair, until one day he was discovered by a high official who was passing by. Such a stereotyped and counterfeit Bildungsroman, however, is too obviously trite to be taken as a model narrative about a great man. Here, again, the discourse is unfolded as a standardized narrative but at the same time exposed as sheer fabrication and absurd delusion. Only grounded on such a discursive delusion, then, can everyone, especially Mr. A, survive with the social norm and individual "dignity."

Now everyone calls Mr. A a great inventor or master scientist. Hanger-on, while paying lip service to his support for Mr. A's "invention," utterly denies the significance of the invention by calling Mr. A's eggshells "garbage." He commands Mr. A to work with more effort, but by *work* he means cooking. The narrator confesses: "I was really confused about my identity; people said I was an inventor, but the support for such an identity relied on my art of cooking" (35). The irony is that, therefore, to be an excellent cook to entertain Hanger-on is the only way to keep this guarantor of his identity as an "inventor" from leaving.

In an equally ironic way Hanger-on, in the name of a parasite dependent on Mr. A, becomes the prerequisite for Mr. A's identity. The Hegelian master-slave dialectic becomes inextricable: the slave does not serve the master for his own existence but for the master's discourse that endows the slave with the title of master. That the truth of the master can be revealed only in the slave is ironically understood in such a reality: the truth of the master can only be created by the slave, who assumes the illusory position of master in the master's discourse. Therefore, the slave can never propel the movement of history; rather, he is voluntarily subjugated to the given historical order established on his name as the master, while the master is enjoying his nominal status as slave. The narrative is an inquiry not only into the problem of the arbitrary manipulation of the discourse but also into that of the masochistic attitude toward manipulation in the narratorial subject. The master discourse, Maoist discourse in particular, is not simply the master's discourse but also the slave's discourse at the same time, in the sense that the former could not survive without the need of the latter. Mr. A's obsessive desire for Hanger-on's discourse about the invention is at the same time linked to his willing submission to Hanger-on's daily abuse of his life. We cannot but read this unstable, disordered master-slave dialectic as an allegory of the political society of China. The fact that the theoretical slave becomes the unmerciful master is not unfamiliar to the Chinese people: the Chinese communist leaders, though officially claiming to be "servants of the people" (*renmin de gongpu*), have the supreme power and authority to dominate their nominal "masters." Yet, as Can Xue suggests, Hanger-on cannot survive without the voluntary support of Mr. A. The authoritarian status of the master is constructed by the slave himself.

Regarded by everyone as an "authority," or "VIP" (29–56), Hanger-on can certainly be interpreted as an authoritarian figure, whose "every sentence was definite, rigid, and authoritative" (140), despite his nominal status. The secret of the authoritative figure lies in his absolute control over discourse. Hanger-on manipulates the discourse about the invention but never supports it in a practical way. As Mr. A complains, "He *mentioned* it, *discussed* it every day, but when did he really look straight at my work? Only once, he evaluated my achievement and clearly called my invention 'garbage.' The reason he constantly *mentioned* my invention was only to find a pretext to better enslave me and control me" (53; my emph.). Again, to mention and to discuss is nothing but to authenticate the discourse while at the same time suppressing reality. When Hanger-on expresses his intention to leave, Mr. A grabs his sleeve to prevent him from leaving, because "he was the only one" (34). In this way reality is to be taken as "ostensible" and the discourse, accordingly, as essential and substantial.

Again, Can Xue seems to have seized the bitter truth of contemporary China, a truth about the triumph of the official discourse over any possible resistance. It is indeed disturbing to see one's subjective attachment to authority by inviting its dominance, because it is authority alone that represents the discourse that legitimizes the delusions. On this basis Hanger-on abuses the discourse by forcing Mr. A to "understand the genuine invention" (45), which means to stand on one leg on the dining table or the trash can. When Mr. A hesitates to do so, Hanger-on thrashes his leg with a feather duster; when Mr. A goes out, wandering in depression and dread, Hanger-on drives him back by striking him with a thick club, because he "betrayed [Hanger-on] *ideologically*" (51; my emph.). Such violence is necessarily associated with authoritarian discourse, until Mr. A realizes that, if he does not obey, he will have to abandon his invention: "this was the *truth* told by this cruel man in front of me" (47; my emph.), as the narrator admits. Since this "truth" (*zhenli*, rather than *zhenshi*) refers exclusively to the conceptual (rather than perceptual) truth, the authoritarian "logic" of the discourse is exposed as nonsensical. The truth, therefore, lies in the mutual validation and implementation of the beguiling discourse and the practical atrocity.

In any case Mr. A has to "follow the glistening object in front of the road" (51), that is, to pursue a teleological objective that attracts him for unreasonable reasons, as long as Hanger-on "displayed the wondrous prospect of my work." Mr. A confesses that he "busily worked around and felt incomparably ethereal, aloof and free from the mundane world. Even the oil fume permeating in the kitchen could make me feel like treading on air as a fairy" (95). The teleological "wondrous prospect" that Hanger-on promises in his master discourse is, ironically, associated with the dingy reality. This sentiment of transforming the miserable now to the agreeable future through hopeful visions and fantasies is truly the mysterious function of political discourse in contemporary China.

This is the dismal political reality in China (which Lu Xun has pointed out numerous times): the oppressed not only welcomes the oppressor and accepts his discourse but also endeavors to turn into an oppressor himself. In this novella, more ironically, the slave (Mr. A) is identifiable or interchangeable with the master (Hanger-on), as he shares the same destiny with the master. A year later Hanger-on brings Mr. A to Neighbor 1's house, and from then on Mr. A himself becomes a hanger-on as well. Hanger-on violently pushes Neighbor 1 down to the floor and "dramatically" kneels down and calls Neighbor 1's wife, a blind old woman: "Mother!" The blind old woman "caressed Hanger-on's head with her trembling fingers and muttered, 'How long have I waited for today, oh, . . . he has finally come! . . . This is the advantage of blindness, I have sensitive and keen feelings'" (77). Here occurs a stereotyped topos in communist literature, usually as a description of the communist army's arrival to "liberate" the poor and ignorant people. Such a topos is parodied insofar as the melodramatic quality is highlighted in the senseless context. The old woman's "sensitive and keen feelings" prove nothing but an illusory acknowledgment of a pretend son, who commands her to cook for him from the next morning on. Later, when Mr. A imitates Hanger-on to kneel down before the blind old woman, both performers are no longer committed to the integrity of their role playing: the tear-stained old woman finally turns apathetic and paralyzed, for she has forgotten Mr. A's existence. Such is the depleted dramatic discourse that has, however, still remained as a mythical topos to maintain the congenial origin and essence of the totalitarian state.

After Hanger-on throws all Mr. A's "products" into the trash can, people urge Mr. A to write an article talking about his "personal experience of struggle." He is advised to write how he "overcame the difficulties," how his "adversity-sharing wife, the symbol of the perfect female, gave him strong support," because his "deeds would be of great edifying significance" (90). In his article Mr. A's boast and fabrication make people feel that—the clichéd discourse resurfaces—"the clouds are dispelled and the sun is seen," so that "everyone knows exactly where his own position is and how to adjust his pace to head straight *toward the grand goal*" (91; my emph.). As Mr. A brazenly glorifies himself for discarding work and fabricating facts, the discrepancy between lofty discourse and absurd activities is intensified.

After Hanger-on has left, someone called "Passer-by" arrives and sleeps beside Mr. A every night to monitor and guide his report. Passer-by seems to be a nocturnal substitute for Hanger-on, and during the day he is further substituted by an old fisherman, whose imaginary and fragmentary discourse is so horrifying as to make Mr. A shudder. They are the new masters whom Mr. A as a slave must depend on as passively as he did on Hanger-on: they are either the other of his twin heads (142) or someone he extremely fears and anxiously longs for at the same time (141). Their authoritarian disciplines, like Hanger-on's, can be viewed not as purely external but as part of the narrator's self-identity. It is, to a great extent, the self-enslavement that the narrative subject is reluctant to dispense with. Under their manipulations, gradually, Mr. A forgets his invention and feels idle. At the very end his report to Comrade Chief gets shorter and shorter, until his words are depleted, and he decides to terminate it.

As the narrator, Mr. A has been haunted and overpowered by various discourses, none of which, however, succeeds in maintaining his individual subjectivity. First is the discourse of invention. As a famous inventor, Mr. A has only invented a kind of "handicraft," that is, the eggshells with perforated patterns. The existence of such a handicraft seems dubious, let alone the senseless fact that the patterns of ox intestines or shapeless and unnamable things are to be taken as invention along with those of the plum blossoms. The discourse of invention is later strengthened by the arrival of Hanger-on, whose authoritative voice, however, unwittingly undermines the grand discourse by forcefully pushing reality into a mundane (cooking) or foolish (standing on one leg) situation. Ironically, Hanger-on does not depend on Mr. A but rather controls the latter through intimidation, which Mr. A welcomes for maintaining his honorable title. Passer-by, not caring about the invention at all, adopts an equally arbitrary mode of discourse and orders Mr. A to vary his gestures of the report incessantly without lofty implications, until Mr. A finds that gestures are more essential than the report as such. Manipulated by Hanger-on, Mr. A finally abandons his inventive project but preserves his fame as an inventor; guided by

Passer-by, then Mr. A loses his individuality in his report but continues only the form or gesture of report.

It is in such a web of discourses that Mr. A engages in order to find his true self. Yet the more deeply he is involved in the discourses, the more miserably his self is disintegrated. The report, which occupies the whole narrative, may be seen as an attempt to emancipate internal authenticity from external repression, as the narrator says at the beginning that he is "repressed nearly to the extent of madness" (1). It soon turns out, however, that to express himself only means to express himself in a discourse not belonging to the narrator: this is the core of Can Xue's narrative irony, an aporia in which the narrator, or any representational subject, is deeply, and perhaps unconsciously, entrapped.

It is worth emphasizing again that the form of thought report in communist China has served as a means of self-purification, which forces each individual to be identified with the grand, uniform collective by relinquishing the old self. In Can Xue's novella purification amounts to derangement, for the discourses of the collective not only fail to purify the defective individual, but they in fact intensify the discord within the individual. As the narrator once admits: "My words fail to convey my meanings, I have never perfectly expressed my ideas all my life, my mastery over language is poor, everything becomes cliché as soon as I speak, sometimes I rummage out a new word from my brain with so many efforts but find it entirely off the mark" (26). It is not, however, the narrator's distance from the perfect discourse but the inner discrepancy within the discourse (on which the narration of the report depends) that constantly deviates from the path toward the telos of the grand, absolute subject. None of the elements within the discourse can redeem the narrator from his predicament but all the more reveal the absurdity of the discourses.

In the face of such a predicament the narrator conceives several other means of narration to avoid the boredom of his imaginary addressee, Comrade Chief. These means include: raising questions to himself, inserting a third-person narrative about his own story, writing a report that characterizes himself as a hen, writing a confession, hypothesizing a conversation between Comrade Chief and himself, summarizing other people's words about him, and so on. None of these efforts, however, escapes from the same discourses.

A third-person narrative is, presumably, more detached and, in this case, more inclined toward an objective and accurate form of description. In fact, despite the placid tone that validates the objective attitude, the third-person narrative generates more subjective interference than a first-person narrative: "He is an inventor. He has invented a special craft. He is just in his middle age, with great prospect" (58). It can be seen from this passage that the narrator's voice has been infused with such definitive words as *special, great, inventor,* and *prospect,* which make subjective evaluations secretly. In the following passages the narrative does not spare even more tendentious terms, such as *genius, unprecedented invention, very high level* (60), to define the characteristics that might not be easily or audaciously definable in the first-person narrative. What differentiates Can Xue's ironic narrative from the representational paradigm of modern Chinese narrative is that, in such a pretended third-person narrative, the impudence of narratorial self-glorification openly debunks the objectivity that a third-person narrative presumably has. The majority of the passages of the third-person narrative deal with the narrator's inextricable relations with Hanger-on and the others, without being able to establish a clear and unambiguous image of Mr. A. His integral identity that reconciles rhetorical and practical aspects is undermined. The narrator has to admit in the "epilogue" of the third-person narrative that "the form of storytelling has failed again," because "it is impossible for one to have sober reason when talking about oneself," so that "he is an indescribable person" (63). The supposedly "realistic" representation, which characterizes the modern Chinese narrative paradigm, leads to the impossibility of representation.

When the narrator hypothesize a conversation with Comrade Chief, we see how the discourse involuntarily dominates different voices, on the one hand, and fails to maintain this domination because of its interior instability, on the other. Naturally, it is, in the first place, the narrator's attempt to move away, at least temporarily, from his incoherent monologue. As the narrator implores Comrade Chief for a reply, he has to devise a dialogue himself since Comrade Chief is an imaginary figure. The hypothetical dialogue, however, begins with Comrade Chief's request that the narrator unburden himself of his grievances. Rather than initiate a dialogue, this imaginary call from a supreme status becomes the foundation of the continuation of his monologue. The pseudo-dialogue exemplifies the discursive relationship between the dominant, who assimilates discrepancies by its promise of well-being, and the dominated, who longs for and relies on that promise. This discursive relationship is exactly the one that exists in contemporary China.

Moreover, it is the desire of the dominated for such a promise that creates the creator of the promise. Comrade Chief's discourse is thus nothing but the discourse imagined, and even adjured, by Mr. A. In the (assumed) words of Comrade Chief he becomes Mr. A's "loyal, never-betraying listener" and "almost [his] servant" (117). It is therefore Mr. A's illusion of the subservient listener that prompts him to adopt a discourse suited to and dominated by Comrade Chief, who is, after all, a figure in possession of the monopolizing power of discourse. At the end of this conversation Comrade Chief says—or the narrator lets him say—that Hanger-on's decision to discontinue the previous invention is more than correct to convince Mr. A of the worthlessness of his life without Hanger-on. It is the narrator, obviously, who tries to convince himself of the value of the status quo. The dialogue is but another evocation of an authority to legitimize his current discourse. The revelation of the illusion of such a false dialogic relation that pushes the narrator into a more obstinate monologic status is a revelation of the irony inherent in the whole narration. There is no audience, let alone a dialogic other: all the communicative efforts that the narrator makes amount only to the formulation of a homogeneous discourse, which, however, can hardly maintain its consistent legitimacy.

After he devises the conversation with Comrade Chief, the narrator acknowledges his real desire: the only goal for which he wants to sustain his relation with Hanger-on is to be able to report to Comrade Chief. He asks rhetorically: "What else can I report if the entanglement [with Hanger-on and the others] is discontinued? What else can I do if I don't report?" (120). Then Can Xue not only probes the danger of authoritarian discourse but, more profoundly, touches on the problem of the fear of a void and susceptibility to illusion becoming the very origin of authoritarianism. The whole narrative of the novella, in the form of a thought report, originates from a desire to utter, whereas the act of uttering eventually fails to satisfy the desire. The report is not forced by any concrete power but, rather, out of Mr. A's own impulse to express his bitterness by recounting his story to an imaginary high official. Why not to a friend instead of Comrade Chief? The narrator doubtless envisions someone who can properly accept the lofty discourse of his report, which is intended to cleanse base thoughts but results in more serious disorder.

Occasionally, the narrator admits that he feels his "narration somewhat wrong": "I intend to tell the origins and developments of everything that happened in my life, I want to unravel my snarled thoughts. After I have spoken so much, I finally understand that *this is impossible*. At least impossible with such a method. What conclusion will I be able to reach? No more than babbling." He thus tries other "methods," which, as I mentioned earlier, prove to be as fruitless. No matter how strong his will is to substantiate the report in order to give Comrade Chief a "clear, whole conception, [because] the word 'whole' is really important to me" (52), the narrator offers instead a story full of discrepancies, hiatuses, and paradoxes. A thought report, therefore, becomes a report about what is unthought of, about the inconceivable, within the boundary of the master discourse. All the constituents of discourse are thus catachrestic utterances that refer to their uncontrolled deviants.

The master discourse collapses as soon as its speakers' barbarous and sordid acts are completely incongruous with it. The meaninglessness of social behavior under such a regime is highly discernible if viewed under the condition in which the discourse predominates. It is the narration, then, that conveys constant self-contradiction, which contains both the rhetorical power to rationalize and the disruptive force that pulverizes it from within. Here Can Xue exemplifies the narrative fissures Chinese avant-gardism exposes as a way to undermine the master discourse.

Part III

Irony as Structural Parody

Deconstructing the Grand Narrative

Chapter 9

Narratorial Parabasis and *Mise-en-Abyme*

Ma Yuan as a Model

In Chinese avant-garde fiction Maoist discourse is unmasked and parodied not only as a verbally manipulative system but also as a structurally mythical one. As has been analyzed, the primary mythology of Maoist discourse is its dialectical and teleological history, a Marxist doctrine that served as the fundamental framework for Chinese communist literature. Such a framework was taken for granted as the only legitimate model of literature, which can be outlined as "progress from struggle to victory," even though, in a limited number of cases, victory does not take place but is implied. As the historical model consists of narrative archetypes, various stock topoi help construct a single archetype (or stereotype) in Chinese communist literature. In Chinese avant-garde narratives the self-sufficiently structured narration formulated by the historical subject is called into question: narrative archetypes appear to be incomplete, defective, or deteriorated. In Ma Yuan's fiction the narrative stance that attempts to stay at a supreme stage is virtually derided, for the grand narrative subject lays bare his omnipresent voice.

Meanwhile, Ma Yuan dissolves the rigid model of plot and the integrity of flawless narration. Celebrated as the earliest formalist fiction writer in post-Mao China, Ma Yuan departs from narrative totality by showing fragmentation, lacunae, and incoherence in narration by way of self-interruption and self-referentiality that question the legitimacy of the homogeneous grand narrative. Unlike Can Xue, Yu Hua, and Xu Xiaohe, Ma Yuan's fiction has hardly political allusions to the past in memory, despite the fact that his only novel, *Shangxia dou hen pingtan* [Up or down, always smooth] (1987), is set in the Cultural Revolution period. Without allegorical perspective that might otherwise turn the life of the "intellectual youth" into a universal dystopia, deaths in this novel are (mis)represented as random, enigmatic, and trivial.[1] It is not surprising that the subjects of his most important works are concerned with Tibet, where, after graduating from college in Liaoning Province, he lived for several years. The Tibetan setting of his fiction resonates, to a minimal extent, with the literary trend of cultural root-seeking.

Ma Yuan is perhaps, however, "at best" in terms of Han Shaogong's claim that the most valuable part of the national culture does not exist in central China but must be found in marginal regions, where different traditions are preserved yet have been long forsaken. As an early representative of the avant-garde circle to break with the root-seeking movement, Ma Yuan invokes the elements of the marginal culture to contest the Han Chinese cultural hegemony without essentializing the ethnic other. Ma Yuan's Han Chinese narrator never becomes a dominant figure to whom the Tibetans are subject or a culturally detached spectator of the exotic province as the other but, rather, a person who relinquishes his fixed identity as a Han Chinese and mingles himself with a different ethnic group. Ma Yuan's attempt to expose his identity as a Han Chinese narrator is always implicated in the self-incurred interruptions of the narrative continuity and destined to deviate into "self-engulfing" impasses.

The Temptation of the Incompatible and the Fissured

The 1985 novella "The Temptation of Gangdisê," though not his literary debut, was Ma Yuan's first successful work and brought him sudden fame. Being a narrative without a coherent, unified plot, it contains at least three barely relevant threads interwoven yet leading in different directions. Two among the three have the same protagonists, Lu

Gao and Yao Liang (who appear in many of Ma Yuan's stories), while the other seems independent from, and even surplus to, the narrative whole.[2] The three major threads are: (1) Lu Gao, Yao Liang, Qiongbu (a Tibetan hunter), and the senior Chinese writer's adventure to explore snowmen; (2) Lu Gao, Yao Liang, and Little He's trip to see the "celestial burial" (*tianzang*);[3] and (3) a legend (whose authorship attributed to Lu Gao, a character in the story) about the Tibetan brothers Dunzhu and Dunyue, and their love affair with the same woman.

In addition, "The Temptation of Gangdisê" is disseminated into a number of minor narratives through various voices. One is puzzled from the beginning by a narrative voice from an unidentifiable person, who invites Lu Gao to join the exploration team. Then we successively have a passage in the first-person voice of a senior writer (who talks about his personal history), a second-person narrative (presumably from the author's voice) that introduces Qiongbu (a Tibetan hunter), a third-person narrative about Lu Gao and Yao Liang's plan to watch the "celestial burial," and so on. These sections, skipping from one to another without explanation, constitute a multifarious structure. The unified narrative voice that predominates in modern Chinese fiction is broken down. By implicating polyvocal narratives, Ma Yuan challenges the oppression of the one-dimensional, teleological history. In a short essay, "Fangfa" (The method), Ma Yuan declares that his "method is illogic" and uses Zhuang Zi's fable "Chaos"—the death of the personified Chaos, caused by his friend's digging orifices (eyes, nose, ears, etc.) in him—to indicate his basic conception of the world (129). The "chaos" in Ma Yuan's narrative disintegrates the unitary system of the grand narrative.

The first two parts have only "insubstantial" or insufficient plots. There are constant diversions from the central plot of each narrative to somewhere extraneous to the development of the plot. For example, the story about the planning of the trip to see the celestial burial contains a short flashback to Yao Liang's first encounter with the Tibetan girl Yangjin, who dies in a traffic accident before their trip. The brief but detailed description of this encounter can hardly be incorporated into that story as an organic part, except that Yangjin's death might increase their curiosity to see the celestial burial. These narrative components, incompatible with the main plot, disrupt the completeness of the narrative.

A more profound irony is that Ma Yuan's narrative is always a self-discrediting one. In "The Temptation of Gangdisê" it is overtly stated that "both adventures finished without results" (*Xihai* 113). Lu Gao and

Yao Liang, chased by the furious masters of celestial burial (corpse cutters), who disallow their visit by throwing stones at them, fail in their painstaking effort to see the tragic and solemn celestial burial. Supposedly a grand narrative about seeking the snowman (reminiscent of Xu Xiaohe's story about the red-hair bigfoot), the story ends with frustrating simplicity and impassivity, which nullify the anticipation of the heroic "hunting" journey. The narrative understatement here sets an ironic contrast to the previous magnificent remark (by the first-person narrative of the senior writer, e.g.) on the significance of searching for the snowman. Such an understatement (different from Can Xue's and Xu Xiaohe's styles of overstatement) about the failure of their adventure invalidates the significance of the narrative: "After three days they arrived at the county where Qiongbu resided.... They stayed there for four days.... They didn't have a chance to encounter a snowman, so they started their way back for their respective jobs and other reasons" (109). Ma Yuan merely mentions that "the four-day experience was sufficient for each of the three [Lu Gao, Yao Liang, and the senior writer] to write a full-length book" (109) but never again comes back to the content of "the four-day experience." The lacunae Ma Yuan deliberately leaves are not spaces provided for creative imagination but, rather, apertures that incapacitate narrative integrity. The narrative unbalance tends to abrogate the rational formulation of the grand narrative. The hunt for something unknown could be a symbolic act of teleological quest. In Ma Yuan, however, the archetypal emplotment that presupposes a teleological quest is understated and trivialized.

Such an ironic unfolding of the events in Ma Yuan's fiction never reaches the logical conclusions to which it at first seemed to lead. As Wu Liang observes, by "intentionally not giving the cause, intentionally not giving the satisfactory finale, intentionally making the story rootless and endless, intentionally withdrawing the crucial parts of the plot," Ma Yuan "seems to deliberately maintain the fragmentation, presentness, irrelevance and illogic of experience" (7). The causeless (such as Yangjin's death, which is not organically related to the preceding narrative) and resultless (such as the two supposedly heroic adventures) structure subverts the absoluteness of any grand narrative.

The constant self-interruptions (discrepancies within the narrative) and self-disruptions (invalidation of the narrative) in "The Temptation of Gangdisê" are crucial to Ma Yuan's structural irony, which incessantly "misleads" the otherwise coherent plot. By effecting fragmentation and incapacitating the grand narrative, Ma Yuan affirms the vivacity of the competitive minor narratives. It can be seen as a postmodern collage—analogous to the art of Rauschenberg, who acknowledges the influence of Tibetan art on him—that abolishes the legitimacy of totality. Ma Yuan's narrative collage, a structurally ironic assemblage, is not only a disintegration of the grand narrative but also a problematization of narrative as such, insofar as even the minor narratives are unstable and susceptible to self-negation.

Likewise, "Die zhiyao de sanzhong fangfa" (Three ways of folding kites, 1985) consists of a few coexistent but unrelated anecdotes: (1) Little Gesang's story about an old lady (hereinafter Old Lady A) and two Khambas connected with a murder; (2) a brief mention of another old lady (hereinafter Old Lady B) who is an illicit distiller; (3) a story concerning some young artists and their new works; (4) a story (told by the artist Liu Yu and then partly retold by the photographer Luo Hao) about yet another old lady (hereinafter Old Lady C) who adopts dogs and saves her own food for the dogs. Except that the narrator becomes an agent in the work to link up these stories (e.g., Old Lady A and Old Lady B are associated with each other simply because the narrator imagines that they look the same), the organic relations among the different stories are utterly untraceable. The authenticity of the characters is dubious, especially since the three old ladies are indistinguishable and almost identifiable with one another.

Here, again, various little stories intersect one another and complicate the logical process of the narrative. In standard communist literature a lower-class old lady must be an amiable matron of the central hero (e.g., in model operas *The Red Lantern* and *Shajiabang*). Ma Yuan's multiplication of the old lady image, then, deforms the structural archetype by disseminating such a figure into such different characters as illicit distiller, clay Buddha maker, and dog adopter (matron of dogs), whose identities are parodic and enigmatic.

"Three Ways of Folding Kites" consists of numerous "blanks." Little Gesang's story about murder is frequently interrupted by the "I" (i.e., the listener), who inserts irrelevant statements. At the beginning the narrator's "aside" is put in the parentheses in order "not to interrupt your words" (*Xihai* 335). Nevertheless, this *is* an interruption, despite the fact that, from another point of view, Little Gesang's story can be read as an interruption of the narrator's narrative as a whole. Such mutual interruptions engender an arena for competing voices. Little Gesang's story rashly ends with the "I"'s request that he tell the result of searching for the murderers and the "I"'s impertinent question about Old Lady A's belief in Buddha. The result of Little Gesang's detective work, however, is never told throughout the narrative. After the narrator admits that "I believe you will excuse me for not being able to finish the story" (337), the narrative shifts to a scene of young artists, without coming back to Little Gesang's story again. Ma Yuan has deprived the narrator of his omnipotence, calling attention to what yet to be said and then leaving it unattended forever.

Liu Yu's story about Old Lady C, a maker of clay Buddhas, has no ending either, even though the narrator mentions that "Liu Yu finished that story before he left Lhasa" (347). A trickier part near the end is Luo Hao's brief account of the same person (Old Lady C), in which he contests Liu Yu by claiming that she has never been a clay Buddha maker. These "narratorial conflicts" among different voices, indeed, mark the dispersion of the narrative totality and give rise to a "heteroglossia" of minor narratives. Here the main narrator's evaluation of Liu Yu's and Luo Hao's different accounts is notable for paying no attention to the representational truth: although Luo Hao's story may be truer, as the narrator acknowledges, Liu Yu's is much more fascinating and "inspiring" to him (347).

Subjective Self-Referentiality and Self-Involution

Ma Yuan's narrative thus leads not to truth but, rather, to the undecidability of both truth and untruth. "Xugou" (Fabrication), in this sense, leaves us with an enigma about the narrator's experience in a leprosarium village called Maqu. The narrator/author claims in the beginning that he, named Ma Yuan, "in order to fabricate the story, stayed in Maqu Village for seven days, risking [his] life," and will, he hopes, "weave a sensational story from the observations" (*Xihai* 135). One is left to wonder whether the following story is the real experience of the author or a fabricated tale narrated by a mediated voice.[4]

What occurs in the leprosarium is again a "diluted" plot that has no development or climax. The "I" encounters an odd and mysterious old hunchback, sees the meaningless life of the lepers, gets a fever and recovers, has sex with a female leper (who takes care of him when he is sick), and so on. It is noteworthy that Ma Yuan's narrative does not contain any sociohistorical ideas about the subjective experience in the leprosarium.[5] The lack of meaning in Ma Yuan, nevertheless, is meaningful. In an article entitled "Zhexue yiwai" (Beyond philosophy) he asks rhetorically, "Why does a written story have to offer *some meaning?*" (60). The leprosarium becomes a vacuum in the sense that, at the margin of the human world, the meanings of human life or social history seem to be surplus to its people. As the female leper says, "Except for men playing basketball, except for sleeping with men, what can women do?" (*Xihai* 167). In any case the mental and material misery in the leprosarium is not a historically backward condition to be redeemed by the "I" or any authorial subject. On the contrary, the "I"'s aimless entry into this space and his sexual relationship with the female leper (whose nose is missing and pupils are askew) indicates an accommodation of the "sound" subject into a strange and even sick periphery of the world. The skeleton of root-seeking literature still remains but only to deform the splendor or charm that has been sought. In other words, the inner logic of root-seeking is undermined by the loss of aura of the primitive.

The old hunchback in "Fabrication" is a noteworthy character, because his political identity (he was a former Nationalist officer who has hidden in the leprosarium for several decades) would be treated as a typical class enemy if he were to exist in communist literature. In *On the Docks* Qian Shouwei is precisely a hidden enemy who served the Japanese, the Nationalists, and the Americans before the victory of the Communists (*Haigang* 49). In *Longjiang song* (Ode to the Dragon River), another model opera, Huang Guozhong is also a saboteur characterized as a landlord's henchman who escaped to another village and changed his name after the Communist "liberation." Obviously, the identity of the old hunchback is closely analogous to that of Qian Shouwei and Huang Guozhong. In Ma Yuan such a character loses his predestined, stereotypical function. The old hunchback bears all the traits of a hidden enemy, but none of these traits has any ideological implication. He pretends to be dumb without intending to carry on any scheme; he hides a pistol and bullets at home for no reason except to show off. As the narrator concludes, he must be "a typical psychotic" (*Xihai* 170), since he plays a role that forgets its stereotypical function and thus depletes the ideological logic.

The role of the author/narrator in this story needs a more detailed investigation. At the very beginning the first-person narrator reveals his identity as the real author of the story: "I am the Han Chinese named Ma Yuan and I write fiction" (134). This oft-quoted proclamation embodies what is called "permanent parabasis," which Friedrich Schlegel defines as the essence of irony. In his discussion of Schlegel's concept of parabasis Paul de Man writes: "Parabasis is understood here as what is called in English criticism the 'self-conscious narrator,' the author's intrusion that disrupts the fictional illusion. . . . [I]t serves to prevent the all too readily mystified reader from confusing fact and fiction and from forgetting the essential negativity of the fiction" (218–19). As we see in the case of Ma Yuan, the "author's intrusion" has a function opposite to the concealed authorial intervention in, say, Ba Jin's *Family*, in which the author's manipulation is hidden behind the narrative mechanism. Parabasis in Ma Yuan, as the author's self-revelation, serves to unmask the narrator as manipulator and to disclose the conflicts within the narrative voice(s). Thus, if Schlegel's romantic irony that endorses permanent becoming and generating by stressing the differences "between the object and its subject, between eternity and temporality, between the infinite and the finite" (Mellor 22), Ma Yuan's postmodern irony shows the discrepancies within the narrative subject.

In "Fabrication," after praising himself as an exceptional Chinese writer, the narrator becomes aware that his "self-confidence is excessive" and lays bare the ironic implication of such a self-confidence: "Such a self-confident person should say something to demonstrate his self-confidence, and have confidence in his own fiction as well. For instance, it is absolutely unnecessary for me to force the readers to listen to me enumerating the works I have written, somewhat like gilding the lily" (134). Obviously, while Ma Yuan seems to empower the authorial subject, he is self-conscious of the ironic debasement of the subject in such an authorial disclosure. The first-person narrator in "Fabrication," named Ma Yuan, frequently acknowledges the fictionality of the story by making public how he has been endeavoring to fabricate it and by stating the necessity of making up the end of the story in the way it now is. This becomes, then, a disillusionment with unlimited subjectivity, for the authorial voice is not exempt from self-skeptical scrutiny.

The confessed failure of the absolute, omniscient author is conjoined with the exposed ignorance or deliberate incompleteness in narrative. We are left permanently uninformed about why, in "Fabrication," the old hunchback shoots off his own head as well as his dog's, why, in "Youshen" (The wandering god, 1986), Qimi II throws the lower half of the coin mold into the river, and whether, in "Tuman guguai tu'an de qiangbi" (The wall with graffiti, 1986), the woman Lu Gao visits is truly Yao Liang's Nepalese mistress. The blind spots do not entail imaginative filling-in; rather, these are, formalistically and structurally, irreparable "crevices" that resist totalization by any grand narrative. "The Wall with Graffiti," perhaps his most "mysterious" short story, consists of numerous contradictions or inconsistencies that can never be "sublated" to a higher, synthetic stage envisaged by the Hegelian-Marxist grand narrative. The text is no more than a narrative chaos, in which not a single part is treated as "principal" or "secondary": the contradictions remain fragmentary, insofar as not a segment among them is struggling for dominance or hegemony. Without a main plot all the subordinate plots of the story arise from the discoveries made after Yao Liang's death, the reason for which is "Not suicide. Not murder. Not sudden attack of illness" (*Xihai* 259) and eventually disregarded. Each of the threads leads to a more snarled situation that will be left unattended forever.

The most mysterious fact, nonetheless, is that Lu Gao's discoveries are actually prerecorded in Yao Liang's manuscript, *Apocryphal Buddhist Sutra,* a "mystic" text that even "narrates those which have not happened yet" (260). The manuscript, sporadically quoted in italics as inserts in the main text, foretells his own queer death and what will occur after his death, such as the lipstick that his wife places in the corner of his studio in advance, his wife's second marriage, and Lu Gao's study of this manuscript. A quotation from this manuscript at the very beginning of "The Wall with Graffiti" contains a reference to the birth of the short story precisely called "The Wall with Graffiti," which seems to exist in the quotation but in the meantime, in a mind-boggling way, contains the quotation. The authenticity of the text, therefore, is on the verge of breakdown. In chapter 12 Yao Liang's manuscript not only foretells Lu Gao's reading of it after its author's death but also discredits its own reliability: "Lu Gao hopes to find a new historical methodology but finally fails he thereby discovers that the manuscript is babbling it is actually nonexistent or there is no difference whether it exists or not" (266; omission of punctuation is per original). Therefore, "The Wall with Graffiti," as a self-referential narrative, exists on the ground of its self-consciousness of its own textual (non)existence, just as Yao Liang's manuscript exists in its own reference to it. At the same time, however, such a self-referential textuality does not aim at the ultimate supremacy of the text but, rather, generates irony, which undermines the textual sufficiency and narrative unity.

From chapter 10 on, the narrative shifts to the activities of Lu Gao, which are related to Yao Liang only indirectly. Chapter 10, for example, is a legend about Lu Gao's communication with Faun Qingluobu, who foretells that Lu Gao will marry a girl sitting on the grass hill. As expected, she appears and invites Lu Gao to her hermetic stone house but, unexpectedly, talks mostly about Yao Liang and his manuscript. In the final chapter Lu Gao dreams of her as Yao Liang's Nepalese mistress, whose account of Yao Liang makes the whole narrative more intricate. In the dream the girl's third-person narrative not only denies (by paraphrasing Yao Liang) his authorship of the manuscript (implying that all is fabricated by Ma Yuan) but even accuses Ma Yuan, the author of the story, of making up fiction to defraud the readers of their money. At the very end Yao Liang, via the girl's voice, points out that the actual murderer is none other than Ma Yuan, who produces this text. This delivers a lethal blow to the integrity of the whole narrative. This chapter is Lu Gao's dream about the girl's report of Yao Liang's words that implicate Ma Yuan, who is the author/narrator of all these characters. In these multiply indirect quotations Yao Liang even discloses that Ma Yuan the author is truly his murderer, but Yao Liang "is finally unable to change the ending and has no way against it, even though he knows that Ma Yuan murders him" (266). The fictional text is thus revealed as a snarled cluster of discourses that exert inevitable, suppressive powers.

Ma Yuan deserves credit for initiating the structurally self-engulfing narrative that undermines subjective supremacy. At times a superficially self-confident narrator—that is, a parodied voice of absolute narration—appears in the middle of the storytelling and claims himself the author of the text or divulges some secrets of the story. A mischievous passage occurs in his novella "Xihai de wufanchuan" (The sailless boat in the West Sea, 1985). The whole penultimate chapter is a "statement" written by Yao Liang, a character in the story, who denies the legitimacy of the whole story by attacking Ma Yuan's intention to dishonor his personality. The beginning of chapter 23, like the ending of "The Wall with Graffiti," is redolent of René Magritte's famous painting *Ceci n'est pas une pipe:*

> Let me claim here, seriously.
> This piece by Mr. Ma Yuan is completely damned bullshit. I've been so far his puppet. All the bad things are counted as mine. This won't do. (Ma 75)

Narratorial Parabasis and *Mise-en-Abyme*

Nevertheless, the main thread of the story does not end here to be concluded as false but continues in the final chapter in a normal way. Here we have encountered an essential paradox: if the veracity of the story can be denied, the denial itself, which is part of the text of the story, is together denied and cannot hold its position of denial. Obviously, this is closely akin to the Epimenides paradox: "I am a liar." The crux of this paradox rejects any attempt to resolve the inherent contradiction. Parabasis is necessarily understood as an exposed cul-de-sac in which the absolute narrative voice has recognized its failing and transformed itself into a self-negative one.

This is the most intriguing and cunning moment of irony usually categorized as "metafiction" in Ma Yuan's fiction, since it is a fiction that is aware of its own fictionality, a fiction that comments on itself. The name *metafiction* still seems problematic, however, since fictionality here is not intensified but, on the contrary, called into question. Fictionality and verity are structured (or malstructured) as "overdetermination" here: this is the inherent, active irony in which all seemingly consistent narratives implode, in terms of both textuality (rhetoric) and historicity (politics).

By frequently appearing on the scene, Ma Yuan operates his narrative through "permanent parabasis" that undermines the supposed absoluteness of both fiction and reality. Narrative parabasis, by means of which the author's intervention only exposes his limitations, deprives subjectivity of its omnipotence. While the position of the author/narrator is elevated, the legitimacy of the subjective "authority" is derided: Ma Yuan the author, as noted earlier, is denounced from time to time by the characters he has created. At the same time, the verity of the characters is equally questionable, as Ma Yuan states elusively in "The Temptation of Gangdisê": "I must make it clear. Yao Liang is not necessarily a real person, because it's unnecessary for Yao Liang to follow Lu Gao in those years. But it's also unnecessary for Yao Liang not to come to work in Tibet" (*Xihai* 91). In the final analysis, then, since nothing is determinable, narrative subjectivity becomes a self-questioning one.

Foucault's postulation that man "is probably no more than a kind of rift in the order of things" (*Order* xxiii) is grounded on the same insight as Ma Yuan's into the ironic self-reflexivity of knowledge or language. At the beginning of *Les Mots et les choses* (The order of things) Foucault, as he discusses Borges's (or ancient Chinese) animal taxonomy, specifically deals with the ironic "laughter" (xv) of *mise-en-abyme*.[6] This laughter, for Foucault, functions to "[shatter] the familiar landmarks of . . . *our* thought" and "[break] up all the ordered surfaces and all the planes with which we are accustomed to tame the wild profusion of existing things" (xv), since the paradoxical taxonomy is essentially self-inclusive and thus leads to the collapse of order. This is also the significance of "the observing and observed mirror" (14) in Diego Velázquez's painting *Las Meninas,* which, as Foucault observes, "provides a metathesis of visibility" (8) and thus manifests the precarious crevice of representation. For Foucault, and Ma Yuan as well, representation is destined to be in the reflexive and ironic *relations* of representation, which invalidate the order of the representational system. As Foucault puts it, "We shall never succeed in defining a stable relation of contained to container between each of these categories and that which includes them all" (xvii).

The endlessly self-engulfing feature of Ma Yuan's narrative (or Chinese avant-garde narrative in general) can certainly be characterized as *mise-en-abyme,* which, in Linda Hutcheon's words, "contains a critique of the text itself" (*Narcissistic* 55). This concept of critique can thus be understood as what Adorno calls "[critical] self-reflection" (*Negative* 31), which points to a "metacritical turn against the *prima philosophia*" (14), and what Habermas (following Adorno) defines as a "metacritique" that "subjects the critique of knowledge to unyielding self-reflection" (3). Self-reflexivity and *mise-en-abyme* can thus be equated under the notion of "metacritique," in which ideology critique becomes a perpetual task of unmasking of the problems of the critical subject. It is, then, the Chinese avant-gardes' effort to cut into Maoist discourse by constantly evoking the textual reflexivity, the ceaseless play of language, or "overdetermination," which suggests that the determined determines and presupposes an endless movement between the determined and the determinant. This is the point that also corresponds to the *mise-en-abyme* process of signification that Derrida formulates:

> From the moment that one questions the possibility of such a transcendental signified, and that one recognizes that every signified is also in the position of a signifier, the distinction between signified and signifier becomes problematical at its root. (*Positions* 20)

Narratorial Parabasis and *Mise-en-Abyme*

In this respect the fragmentary, ironic narrative of the Chinese avant-garde deconstructs the rigid structure of the grand narrative by disputing the "transcendental signified" *in* Maoist discourse and the primal signifier *of* it.

Nevertheless, a metacritique, as opposed to simple antagonism, does not easily abandon its target as something that can be thrown out. The ironic effort, in this sense, is a disclosure of the endless self-disruption, that is, the overdetermination within the grand narrative. To use Althusser's words: "It is in this overdetermination of the real by the imaginary and of the imaginary by the real that ideology is active" (234). Paul Ricoeur, having quoted this passage in his *Lectures on Ideology and Utopia*, explains: "Thus, ideology is not something bad, it is not something that we attempt to put behind us; instead, it is something that pushes us, a system of motivation" (137). In Chinese avant-garde fiction the ideological system does not disappear; instead, it is constantly conjured up in a self-negative way that suggests discrepancies, lacunae, and incompleteness.

By infusing the undecidable elements into the system, Chinese avant-garde narrative implies the inherent disjunctions within textuality. This undecidability marks the essential, though hidden, form of human knowledge. In his Incompleteness Theorem, Kurt Gödel proves that all consistent formal systems contain undecidable propositions. In other words, a seemingly consistent system is necessarily incomplete: the sentences formulated in the syntax of the system are neither provable nor refutable, precisely because the system is essentially self-referential.[7] It is in this sense that Derrida suggests the analogy between deconstruction and Gödel's metamathematical theory (*Dissemination* 219), since both have revealed discrepant and contradictory elements in systematic consistency. Gödel, in his discovery of the inevitably self-referential and thus undecidable statements in powerful formal system, gives a perfect answer to the liar paradox and to what Wittgenstein rejects in formal logic—Wittgenstein declares that "no proposition can make a statement about itself, because a propositional sign cannot be contained in itself" (31). We must, however, be cautious in identifying Gödel with Derrida, since Gödel does not deny consistency of the system despite the incomplete, undecidable factors inside, whereas Derrida explicitly disputes the validity of systematicity by revealing the inherent fissures or swerves that undermine the integrity of the system. Both of their theories, in any case, have offered us insights into the problem of irony, the primary rhetoric of Chinese avant-garde narrative.

Ma Yuan was the earliest Chinese avant-garde to introduce self-referential narrative as an ironic disruption of the seemingly sufficient grand narrative. It is a formalistic reaction to the totalitarian ideological system, which tends to conceal the inner discrepancies. In any case the rhetorical device of irony is not foreign to Chinese literature: a great number of classical Chinese literary works, from *Zhuang Zi* to *The Story of the Stone*, are replete with narrative irony. Andrew Plaks's analysis of Ming Dynasty novels, for example, is illuminating in revealing the mode of traditional Chinese fiction "in which the rather self-referential structural and rhetorical manipulation in the texts is subordinated to a pervasive ironic focus, as each author engages in a critical reevaluation of the respective traditional materials from which his novel is drawn."

If the "traditional materials" for the Ming novelists are the entirety of traditional classics from Confucianism to Buddhism, for contemporary Chinese avant-garde writers the traditional materials belong to the orthodox politico-cultural system established on the grand narrative, by which the destiny of avant-garde fiction is preordained. Plaks attributes this sophisticated mode of rhetoric to "the flowering of an 'age of criticism' across the entire spectrum of late Ming cultural life" (49). By the same token the critical and skeptical attitude toward the given cultural order is the tendency not only of Chinese avant-garde fiction in the late 1980s but also of the fundamental intellectual mind-set of the time.

Again, structural irony in Ma Yuan is a narrative madness, a schizophrenic experience of schizophrenia as such. As Zhao Yiheng correctly observes, "The profound critique of all the constructions and exegetic meanings in contemporary [Chinese] avant-garde fiction which harbors 'metaconsciousness' negates any necessary rationality of metalanguage"; and "this ontological self-consciousness can maintain the absoluteness of critique in order not to fall into another ideological trap" ("Yuan yishi" 88). Avant-garde narrative evades the "ideological trap" by bearing the destiny of self-rupture and self-skepticism. In the ideological system of the grand narrative, as Adorno remarks, "The principle of absolute identity is self-contradictory. It perpetuates nonidentity in suppressed and damaged form" (*Negative* 318). This "suppressed and damaged form," which displays the "self-contradictory" quality of the system, is precisely what Chinese avant-garde narrative conjures up from their traumatic memory trace as the innate hiatus of the grand narrative. The ironic power, therefore, arises from an attempt to *recognize* the shock experience in a simultaneously repulsive and obsessive way. This is the moment when the danger of incessant disintegration is haunting us and making us shudder with laughter in *mise-en-abyme,* in the self-referential vertigo.

Chapter 10

Ge Fei

Indeterminate History and Memory

> Writing fiction . . . provides me the possibility of resuming the inexpressible experience of reality and memory.
> —GE FEI

Ge Fei is among the youngest in the generation of Chinese avant-garde writers. Unlike most of his contemporaries, he teaches literature in college. Possibly because of his academic profession, Ge Fei's fiction appears particularly attentive to the technical, or formalistic, potential of narration in dealing with historical and personal experiences. By revealing discrepancies of collective and personal memories in the irreconcilable narrative fragments, Ge Fei challenges the totality of grand history formulated by the master discourse. In Ge Fei's narrative the subjective voice is distinct; it does not, however, replace the discourse of grand history with another absolute voice but displays its own decentered, disseminated utterances. The "inexpressible" experience and memory in Ge Fei's fiction are expressed as narration fragmented by the unknown, the insoluble, and the obliterated.

The Pitfalls of *Recognizing/Representing* the Past

As I mentioned in the introduction, in "The Pitfalls," one of his earliest short stories, Ge Fei's narrator claims his limitations of narration even before the story really begins. Even more oddly, the story "started from a story told by herself" (*Mizhou* 12), a girl called Poker, and overheard by the peregrinating "I." The overhearing is an accidental touch on an irrelevant history, which becomes not only the reality in which the "I" is soon involved but also the origin of the story that the narrator is now telling. In other words, the main narrative stems merely from a random accident without any determinant historical itinerary. The narrator no longer takes the original responsibility for what is narrated; rather, a narrative may start from another narrative or freely shift to another without integration. Besides, Poker's narrative is a somewhat incoherent one: she claims at one moment that she ran away because she had dread and, the next moment, because she was forced to. Tan Yunchang, in his essay on this short story, uncovers the question not by answering it but by acutely suggesting that the question might be utterly pointless, if Poker's narrative is itself incredulous and neither of the statements is true (40). The suspicion becomes more intensified when Poker, in her later retelling of her past, asserts that her parents, who were responsible for her leaving home (according to her previous statement), were dead long ago.

These inconsistent statements can be regarded as disruptions of narrative totality and absoluteness. If we compare this episode with the stories in the May Fourth era that deal with a similar theme—that is, a woman leaving her family—it is perceivable that Ge Fei's narrative does not provide a legitimate reason for the heroine. A young woman like Zijun in Lu Xun's "Shangshi" (Remorse for the past) or the "I" in Feng Yuanjun's epistolary short story "Gejue" (Cut off) leaves, or decides to leave, the oppressive family to seek "freedom of love." Both Lu Xun's and Feng Yuanjun's stories are, at least in part, structured by an emancipation discourse that endows history with a rational order from patriarchal oppression to self-liberation. In Lu Xun's case, of course, such a history is later lamented as fruitless. Ge Fei breaches such a history by exhausting the emancipation discourse: the reason for which Poker leaves home is a nebulous one that disorders the entire grand historical logic.

Ge Fei also explores the intricate relationships between the real and the visionary and between the conceivable and the impossible. In another story about what caused her leaving home, Poker says that she saw an old man assembling a bridge with some slender branches on the river. She tried to convince him that such a bridge would be unusable:

> Your bridge is unstable. I said
> It's for those pigeons
> Pigeons can fly over the river they don't need bridges they can fly over
> It's for the pigeons that have no wings
> All the pigeons have wings
> The wingless pigeons have no wings.
>
> (20–21)

The conversation went on and on until she came back and found her house occupied by strangers disguised as old men. She was then banished from her home, because they claimed that she had entered the house illegally. In many of Ge Fei's stories the unreal prevails over the real. Reality seems to be subject to beautiful or dramatic visions, which, in many cases, lead to misfortunes.

These dreamlike visions may not only be tragic but possibly comical or absurd. All of them, in any case, allegorically point to the unrealizable cultural imaginations of modern China. Poker tells this latter version about her leaving home to Black Spade, her erstwhile boyfriend, who does not recognize her when she visits him along with the "I." Black Spade can be interpreted, allegorically, as an antiquated figure, once favored by root-seeking literature but now comically dramatized. Even when he remembers Poker, his passion is only rekindled for a brief moment, after which he resumes his position of "standing numbly" (20). The nostalgic origin fades out without hope of being revitalized. As an exile, Poker's effort to "find a savior (*jiuxing*)" by "going north all along" virtually fails (22).[1] The role of the historical savior, be it a prospective political emancipator or nostalgic spiritual redeemer, no longer functions as a mighty figure to bring the whole narrative to a perfect end. Poker's visit to Black Spade is thus a parodied quest back to the origin, for Black Spade is himself a "psychologist of amnesia" and symbolizes the evacuation of the origin.

Black Spade disillusions Poker in various ways, all of which have to do with the danger of aesthetic imagination/creation. He suggests that at stake is the pitfall set up by the pigeon bridge builder. This old man must be seen as a symbol of art or fantasy, as he is doing something entirely without practical value and only for the sake of the fantastic ("wingless pigeons"). His impractical and aesthetic activity, as Black Spade suggests, is a disguise and has a specific practical aim, that is, to attract Poker to come out so he can occupy her house. This is the dangerous pitfall of the aesthetic, whose disguise brings misfortune to reality. Also histrionically disguised are the invaders of Poker's house: in their performance the aesthetic/fantastic and the evil/real are fused with each other. The pitfall, however, not only exists in Poker's story about herself but also in her narration of the story, since it is discernible that her narrative, as art (artificial creation), is as unstable as the old man's bridge or as disguised as the invaders of the house. In other words, the representation of the pitfall is itself a pitfall: the self-reflexive formation exposes the vulnerability to self-deconstruction of the representational narrative.

Black Spade persuades Poker to accept the bliss of forgetting and avoid art as a way of retrieving/conceiving the past. Allegorically, it can be perceived that the origin is precisely what repels reexperience. What is real, then, is also questionable. He warns the "I" that Poker "has become a reproduction of your numerous admixed memories, resulting in your excessive indulgence in meditations and overflow of memories." Now, as suggested by Black Spade that Poker is but a "reproduction" of the mental images of the narrator, we are tempted to be skeptical not only of Poker's statements but also of her very existence. But, whereas Black Spade implies that Poker is an imaginary character, Poker also denies the existence of Black Spade. Indeed, the narrator later receives a letter from Poker, in which she mentions that Black Spade had died before they entered the city to visit him. The narrator has to "assume that their visit to Black Spade late that night was probably a hallucination." Such self-denials in the narrative undermine the coherence of the representational process. Therefore, the pitfall (the representational pitfall in particular) is not only set up by someone else but can be one's own construction as well. "As a matter of *fact*" (24; my emph., but whether it was a "fact" is always problematic), the narrator claims (refuting himself again), they did not find Black Spade that night but participated in a funeral. In this improbable funeral people were skating in the procession, the hearse was computer operated, and the prerecorded mourning was being broadcast from stereo speakers. Most ludicrous of all, as the "I" discovers at last, the dead is but a boar. The represented fact, or "representability" as such, is displaced by the delusion of rational narration, which is the greatest of all the pitfalls prevailing in this short story.

"The Pitfalls," a narrative amalgamated with illusions, fantasies, disguises, shams, games, and farces, can thus be regarded as a radical exposure of the untruth of representation and reality. Most obviously, the unfolding of the story counters the truth claim of all kinds of grand narratives, a claim that occupies the center of modern Chinese narrative. All representations, then, are to be uncovered subsequently as misrepresented and all realities as unreal. The totality of the grand narrative is undermined by the random and hazardous logic of narration.

Ge Fei calls our attention to the crisis of narrative sufficiency by incessantly denying or contradicting the previous statements so that, eventually, the seemingly integrative narrative becomes fragmentary and inconsistent. In this sense what Ge Fei parodies is not a specific narrative genre or topos but narrative unity or soundness in general, especially the rigid homogeneity of the grand narratives. If history is grounded on memory and narration, Ge Fei recovers the indeterminable elements in memory and narration. In his story "A Flock of Brown Birds" the narrator lives in seclusion and, without calendar and clock, depends on the migration of the brown visitants to estimate the movement of seasons. When a girl named Chess comes and shows him her folder of paintings, the narrator feels that "something twitched my deep memory, but the past was not awakened yet," and his "ash-like thread of memory seemed to stick together by a kind of strange glue" (*Mizhou* 30–31). At night the narrator tells her his story, "with a narrative tone as plain and authentic as possible" (33). His narrative about his encounter with a woman, however, is not "plain and authentic," for he stops at a point that he claims to be the end. Only after Chess, the narratee, inexplicably carries through his story, does the narrator himself pick up and continue his narrative about how he pursued the woman to the suburb in vain and encountered mysterious events after she vanished. Chess, again, completes the story by telling the ending for him, which the narrator later confirms. The interchange of the roles (narrator and narratee) breaches the stability of representation and perplexes the relationship between the producer of discourse and the recipient of it.

But the story does not end here. The narrator, after a nap, is compelled to tell what happened many years later: the "I" ran into that woman in another town, but she denied she had ever gone to the city (where he first met her) since the age of ten. Nevertheless, her memory overlaps in part what the narrator has told.[2] What ensued was the liaison developing between him and the woman: they finally got married, but she died on the night of their wedding. Knowing that the story comes to a real stop, Chess leaves. Several years later the narrator sees Chess come, wearing the same coat and carrying the same folder. Yet she does not understand a bit of what he says. She denies that she is Chess and vanishes in the distance, just like the restless brown birds.

"A Flock of Brown Birds" is a narrative that contains narratives, a multilevel narrative that consists of numerous erratic occurrences. The narrative "frame" concerns Chess's visit and the narrator's telling of his mysterious love story. Though the narrator's memory is frequently agitated by Chess's statements, he has a hard time remembering, because there are "obstacles in [his] deep thought," or "repression." It may well be assumed that the psychic obstacles stem from his obsession with his personal history, in which his love and marriage end tragically. That is why he is aware that his narrative addressed to Chess is like a patient's to a psychoanalyst (33). The narrator's telling of his story is unusual. He interrupts several times. In the first intermission he, apparently denying his painful memory, claims that he has never seen her since then. Chess ventures to proceed with the story for him, based on (as the narrator assumes) her sensitivity to the "narrative convention," which the narrator explains as the psychological ground of narration that Chess, playing the role of psychoanalyst, constantly interrogates.

The second intermission follows what Chess calls a "banal ending" (42), which is again narrated by Chess, about his discovery of the corpse in the ditch. At this point, with his "brain like an empty utensil stuffed with straws and shavings" (43), he, however, recalls some people whom Chess mentioned earlier. It seems that only by discharging part of the repressed can the narrator regain his lost memory, and only by awakening his memory of the pleasant can he avoid, or at least postpone, that of the agonizing. We see apparently that the narrator, unlike the confident narratorial subject in the paradigm of modern Chinese literature, is caught in the predicament between the compulsion of utterance and the repression of utterance. Moreover, his identity as a narrator—at the superior position of telling story to a female listener—is displaceable: his discontinuous narrative has to be filled up by her. His narrative would be incomplete if it were not dependent on a displaced narrator, a narrator alienated from him. The power of the narratorial subject, therefore, is no longer absolute but inept and self-disruptive.

What is being disrupted is precisely the monologic continuity, which fails to provide a flawless picture of the past. Even the dialogic, mutually complementary narrative (between the narrator and Chess or between the "I" and the woman) does not complete the whole story as a unity but unveils the insoluble disparity within communication. Chess carries through the narrator's narrative not without misconceptions, omissions, and oversights. The woman's account of what happened in the past is overlapping but still incompatible with the narrator's. The encounters between the narrator and Chess and between the narrator and the girl contain oblivion or misrecognition.

The end of the story shows the narrator in a quandary: Chess comes—yet either she is not Chess, or she is Chess but, like the narrator in the beginning, does not remember everything, or perhaps she simply does not want to acknowledge her identity. The scene is identical to the opening part; however, it is not a mere repetition but an ironic repetition, or a failed reflection, a reflection whose reflectivity is incapacitated. In the beginning, when the narrator sees Chess, she wears something "orange-red (or brownish-red)" and "holds against her chest a big folder which looks like a folder of paintings or a mirror" wrapped with "grass-green canvas" (29). The folder proves to be a folder of paintings as Chess shows him the paintings. In the end everything looks the same as before: "she still wears an orange-red (or brownish-red) coat and holds against her chest a folder of paintings wrapped with canvas which looks more like a mirror from a distance" (62). It turns out, however, that the narrator's presumption has missed the target. While the girl is no longer Chess, the folder that looks like the one Chess carried is *indeed* a mirror.

Here emerge such problems as authenticity and simulacrum, the problems inherent in all narrative representations. Certainly, narrative representations are grounded on the hypothesis of authenticity. The representational sign is to be read as indisputably corresponding to the "authentic" object. In Ge Fei's narrative, however, the seemingly transparent representational signs lead ironically to a simulacrum, which imitates the authentic but fails to render its substance. It is thus not simply the narrator's expectation of Chess but the reader's expectation of the representational authenticity in narrative that is belied. By questioning the authenticity of narrative representation, Ge Fei also parodies the concept of time that culminates in the teleological reunion. The narrator is thus left again in a boundless void, a void prompted by the loss of temporal logic, just as the narrator worries in the beginning that the "vanishing birds would take away time along with them" (29). Time opens up itself to nonidentity or heterogeneity rather than closing in a homogeneous ending.

To a great extent the discrediting of authenticity in the narrative frame is mirrored in the narrator's account of his love story. The woman whom the "I" believed he had met before and later reencountered, like the simulacrum of Chess, denied the possibility of their previous encounter, even though the representational signs, such as her maroon boots, might have authenticated the narrator's account. Despite the woman's denial, the narrator's account was not entirely refuted. After all, the woman acknowledged the existence of the collapsed bridge (though her version of what caused its collapse remained irreconcilable with his) and even recalled what her husband saw on a night of a snowstorm, which was partly accordant and partly discordant with the narrator's account. There is nothing outside equivocality: such a narrative, which contains mutually contesting minor narratives, is neither absolutely determinable nor absolutely refutable. Representational narration is radically parodied (rather than totally abandoned): by unmasking representational "realism," Ge Fei's fiction highlights the deconstructive potentials that persist in the process of questioning without giving any determinate answer.

The Bypasses of Grand History

In Ge Fei's fiction deconstructive force functions not only in relating personal history but also in relating other—such as national, regional, or familial—histories. A great number of his fictional works can be understood as rewritings, or even parodies, of the prototypical/stereotypical mode of representation of the historical past. The key elements of the prototypical/stereotypical mode are retained yet fail to contribute to the supposed significance that they would normally produce. In "The Lost Boat" and "New Year," for example, the orthodox historical images of "Northern Expeditionary Army" and "New Fourth Army" are contaminated by personal desire or quotidian incidents. The unified historical "essence" marked (or fabricated) by these names faces the danger of decomposition.

Disguised as a historical narrative (with a short preface that introduces the historical background), "The Lost Boat" leads not to the objectification of historical facts but to the lacunae of subjective representation. The preface not only presents the historical actuality by way of exact date, locations, designation of military unit, real persons in history, and journalistic-style narration, but it also, finally, turns to the disappearance of the protagonist of the story, Xiao, commander of the Thirty-second Brigade of the Sun Chuanfang troops. Xiao, the central figure of the story, who belongs to the opponent of the (historically progressive) Northern Expeditionary Army, is however unlikely to be identified with a "negative character." He is meshed in the maze of the romantic affair, military discipline, familial incident, and so on, all of which perplex his supposedly preordained role in the making of history. The uncertainty of Xiao's whereabouts casts "a mysterious shadow" not only on "the rainy season campaign" (*Mizhou* 100 / "Lost Boat" 77) but also on the historical narrative, which is supposed to position the negative character clearly in a determined antagonistic spot. His disappearance leaves a blank on the programmed historical map.

The story starts from the message about the accidental death of Xiao's father brought by the matchmaker Auntie Ma Three. Xiao returns to his home village, Little River, both for his father's funeral and for the task of reconnaissance. He is soon involved in an affair with Xing, who has just married San Shun in Little River but remains in his memory of his youth in Yuguan, a town now occupied by the unit of Northern Expeditionary Army led by his own brother. As their liaison is exposed, San Shun spays Xing as punishment and sends her back to Yuguan. Xiao, captured and inexplicably released by San Shun, decides to go to Yuguan to see Xing again and, after coming back, is assassinated by his bodyguard, who has received an order to execute him if he goes to Yuguan, the town occupied by his brother.

The logic of Ge Fei's story is not as aberrant as that in many of his other narratives. But such a logic, when contextualized in the logic of grand history, becomes a parodic constituent that defies its established order. From time to time Xiao is positioned at the historical cruxes but, ironically, does not perform his instituted historical function. At the beginning his return to Little River, as a task charged to play his historical role, is contaminated by the death of his father, which results from an accidental and ludicrous fall from the roof into the water tank. Then his trip becomes not so much for reconnaissance as for his duty in the mourning ceremony. Xiao's father, significantly, is described as one of the few leading members of the Small Sword Society who are capable of handling the Western gun. While the Small Sword Society (a clandestine and rebellious society flourishing during the mid-nineteenth century) excels in, and probably fails for, its exclusive reliance on the function of the small sword (the traditional Chinese weapon) to change history, the fact that Xiao's father is a skillful user of the Western gun "hybridizes" the distinct historical phenomenon. In his reply to Xiao's question of why he had joined an army that was to be defeated, he once alleges that the conceptions of the defeated and the victorious should be replaced by the wolf and the hunter. While the young Xiao's question already presumes a confusion of the orthodox judgment of the wars as the just versus the unjust, Xiao's father draws the issue into a more ambiguously metaphoric domain, in which history seems to be conceived as equivalent to the unsound natural world. As a matter of fact, Xiao's father, who plays a significant though unsuccessful role in history, dies rather insignificantly. Such a comical death, perceptibly, is addressed not by a historian but by a village matchmaker, a stereotyped scandal spreader whose discourse is the least weighty one.

In fact, as "an inexplicable excitement welled up in him," Xiao "did not know if his impatience to go home was because of his father's death or because he missed his mother, or perhaps it was a yearning to revisit the village which bore the record of his childhood" (108/83). Apparently, Xiao is motivated by multiple impetuses, none of which, however, is relevant to the central theme of the grand history. Rather, the "greater, more significant force" that urges him is, according to the ensuing narrative, an indistinct personal desire for a girl embedded in his memory. Xiao's military task remains unfulfilled, because he withdraws himself from the historical drama in which he is obligated to participate. Here, as Ronald Janssen perceives, an "image of centered power is riven in the story by seams of fate that Xiao also experiences at critical moments" (197). His fate is neither as meaningful as the grand history requires nor as predictable as the Taoist warns. The fate of Xiao, as well as the fate of Ge Fei's narrative, is erratic and indeterminate when the historical drama is shifted to the arena of personal desires.

The most dramatic and absurd episode is the ending. Xiao is killed neither by his military enemy nor by his rival in love but by his own bodyguard, who is not aware that Xiao goes to Yuguan for Xing's sake. The historical logic in the story is displaced or diverted time and again. At first Xiao's military action is displaced by his familial incident. Then his participation in his father's funeral is displaced by his meeting with Xing. This is a continuation of the past, which seems to displace the present. When we are about to witness an overall displacement of the historical drama by the personal legend, the historical power has not forgotten its responsibility and is potentially active and lethal all along. Xiao's bodyguard shoots him for his supposed betrayal of his historical role. The execution is legitimate to some extent in that, though he has not defected to the enemy, he has deflected away from his historical function. Then it is the ending that displaces again the myth of pure personal tragedy with the thrust of the historical specter that has been haunting the fate of the individual, though in a contingent and irrational manner.

The displacement, nevertheless, is not merely an "intratextual" phenomenon but operates in an intertextual way. In this sense "The Lost Boat" is a parody of the canonical modern Chinese narrative, in which historical duty and romantic affair are necessarily coordinated in a harmonious order and mutually beneficial to a great extent.[3] Yang Mo's *Qingchun zhi ge* (The song of youth), for example, can be read as the model of such a narrative. While the male figures in her life, Lu Jiachuan, Jiang Hua, and Yu Yongze, respectively enact their historical functions, Lin Daojing's quest for the achievement of her historical subjectivity has to be realized along with her quest for the fulfillment of her amorous wish, and vice versa. It is not surprising, then, that the subjectivity Lin Daojing is pursuing can hardly be assessed as self-sufficient, insofar as it remains, shaped and manipulated by the historical discourses of males, in a dependent status. Its structural prototypes can be traced back to the late 1920s: Ding Ling's *Wei Hu,* Hong Lingfei's *Liuwang* (Exile), Hu Yepin's *Dao Mosike qu* (To Moscow), Jiang Guangci's "Yalujiang shang" (On the Yalu River), among numerous others. In these works the link between the personal and the historical is so coerced that only their conflict appears to be potentially permanent. (Consider, for example, how unnatural Weng Lijia's ideological transformation is in *Wei Hu*.)

Now, in Ge Fei's "The Lost Boat," this conflict is brought to the fore. The love affair cannot be incorporated into the picture of the grand history but, rather, has to become a pernicious, or ominous, factor that triggers the irrational force of history. Xing, a name meaning "apricot" and homonymous with the word *sex*, not only vulgarizes the traditional romance but, more fatally, blocks the historical vista to be visualized. Yet, even though she distracts Xiao's attention from his historical duty, Xing is not a femme fatale who directly causes his tragedy but simply happens to occasion his involuntary violation of the taboo. In any case Xing no longer serves as a medium to bring the historical and the romantic into accord but effects the split and clash between Xiao's historical role and his romantic role. The historical irony thus arises from the "role misplaying" by the individual hero and heroine in the historical drama.

History as Narrative Entanglement

For Ge Fei, then, a rational history is failed by irrationalities, which stem not only from blind desire (that Xiao has for Xing) but also from the presumably rational assumption (that the bodyguard has). Such an overdetermination of history constitutes the essential dynamics of Ge Fei's narratives. What is ironic in Ge Fei always exists in the self-perplexing narrative. His "Green-Yellow," another short story "about a pursuit after the 'absence'" (Chen Xiaoming *Wubian* 108), deals with an aimless investigation that eventually arrives at multiple, or even inextricable, conclusions of the term *Green-Yellow*. Presumably related to the local prostitutes called "Nine-Surname Family of Fishers," a fleet of prostitutes' boats flourishing some forty years ago, "Green-Yellow," according to a professor, is a lost chronicle of the prostitutes' life, as opposed to the popular assumption that it is the name of a beautiful girl. But the *Annals of the Wheat Village* evade the information about the fleet after the interdiction of it. From the beginning on, Ge Fei offers a narrative that points to obscurities, hiatuses, and internal contentions within the history produced by official or intellectual authorities.

The main chapters describe the narrator's interviews with different people in Wheat Village, whose personal recollections of the past constitute an intricate picture of local history. The first interviewee is an old man, who particularly mentions the arrival of Zhang and his daughter. Without detailing the ins and outs of the event, however, he only sketches the weather and the flaming boat behind them on that day. His account admits ignorance and raises suspicion: "He *probably* worried that the villagers wouldn't take them in so that they set fire on the boat"; "I *never know* his whole name. His daughter is called Little Green, *maybe*"; "What happened later is *not so clear* to me"; "The middle-aged man . . . *might* be unaccustomed to the environment of the village"; "He was *probably* a very good father" (*Mizhou* 176–77; my emph.). The old man's statement is thus itself a sample of representational indeterminacy, a parody of the paradigmatic historical narratives. Within a broader scope, to the narrator, the reason for the old man's elusive narrative is also indeterminable. It is certainly obvious that the old man "*appeared* labored very much when he was recalling the past" (176; my emph.), but his manner also "made a strange *impression*" that "he was concealing some events while revealing others" (177; my emph.). Or it could even simply be that "he had strong dental accents and indistinct guttural voices, which made some trouble to my note-taking" (176). Thus, history is full of lacunae or perplexities for various—purposive or inevitable—reasons.

The second interviewee is a surgeon who once accommodated the narrator in his house nine years ago. He claims in the interview that he remembers Zhang's burial but appears "distraught" when the topic changes to his own encounter with Zhang. He says that he "never talked to that newcomer, his thoughts . . . maybe . . . his daughter," (183) without completing the sentence. Again, the history of the "Nine-Surname Family of Fishers" becomes at once probable and problematic: it only exists in endless quotations or unrecoverable omissions, while the real event is postponed from time to time. In regard to the term *Green-Yellow* the surgeon suggests that it could refer to the prostitutes, who were divided into the young (green) and the old (yellow).

Then a young man named Kangkang tells how flood destroyed Zhang's tomb and the floating coffin was found empty. One could even be suspicious about whether Zhang really died, especially in relation to the surgeon's failure to see Zhang's remains before the coffin was nailed up (according to the previous interview). This suspicion is intensified by the aged Little Green's story about her son's death. Little Green tells the interviewer-narrator how her son was drowned after he claimed to have seen an old man who resembled the long-dead Zhang in every aspect. It still remains uncertain, however, whether the old man whom Little Green's son saw was truly Zhang or someone resembling him or simply a hallucination. Furthermore, Little Green's nonchalant claim that her father "might not be her own" strengthens the perplexing mystery of Zhang (189). The connections and collisions among different narrative voices, again, create narrative inconsistencies and disarrange the absolute history, which is broken down into a miscellany of mysteries without the possibility of unification.

When Little Green touches on the issue of the "Nine-Surname Family of Fishers," she claims that she does not take the profession of prostitution as seriously as the villagers. She regrets that her stepmother died for protecting her from sexual assault, since she had been used to seeing violations. Nonetheless, when she explains the historical background of how the fleet formed, she cites the legend that it was "not until" the severe famine that the women on the fleet gradually became prostitutes (194). The message of her historical justification can be clearly read as a modulation of the claim of her indifference to prostitution. Little Green's attitude toward prostitution is quite ambivalent. We see the collisions of narrative voices not only between the villagers (to whom the fleet and its members are disgraceful) and Little Green (the member of the fleet who claims to be indifferent to prostitution) but also within the same interviewee, such as Little Green herself, who also wishes, at least unconsciously, to clarify the origin of the infamous history of her family. In his discussion of this story Chen Xiaoming comments:

> Historical discourse never succeeds in excluding absences and always produces absences at the cruxes. Historical discourses always establish the whole process of historical events by concealment, by incomplete narration. The absent discourses are the willfully omitted and suppressed parts of historical narratives, which possibly subvert history as a totality. The absences destabilize the presence and are possibly the actual existence of history. (*Wubian* 109)

By evoking the absences—that is, the moments suppressed under the totalizing discourses—Ge Fei's narrative becomes a "polyvocal" one, in which each narrative voice is confronted, externally or internally, with its hidden rival.

The fragmentation of the hegemonic, totalizing voice of history is also shown in the entanglement of a world of signification and representation. After the "I"'s unsuccessful investigation into the term *Yellow-Green* or the "Nine-Surname Family of Fishers," he visits Li Gui, an old merchant with whom he stayed overnight nine years ago in the surgeon's home. That night, when the surgeon left for an emergency visit, the "I," awakened by thunderstorm, found Li Gui absent for hours before he appeared at the threshold, with muddy water all over his body and blood oozing from his toe. Li Gui, another inconsistent or self-negating narrator, now denies that he went out of the house that night but admits that he is a frequent sleepwalker. The "I" is further agitated to realize that Li Gui's dog is called "Yellow-Green" for the color of its pelage. But the whole story ends with the "I"'s fortuitous discovery, in a Ming Dynasty dictionary, of an entry for *Yellow-Green*, meaning a kind of herbaceous plant.

Now the quest for the authentic meaning of the word *Yellow-Green* is not without results. The result, however, proliferates into indeterminable results, which deviate from the envisaged meaning: the only positive naming of *Yellow-Green* is irrelevant to the historical preconception. The attempt to pin down the historical truth fails: what is generated from it becomes something casual, diverse, and incongruous. The various narratives of the historical past, too, decenter the original and incapacitate the imagination of a complete chronicle. No narrative, then, is free from subjective involvement: each of the narrators, including the authorial narrator, seems to participate in the reconstitution of the past from his or her own position.

In Wu Hongsen's introduction to *Mizhou* (The lost boat), Ge Fei's first collection of short stories, we read an interesting anecdote that accounts for the origin of this story:

> In the summer of 1986, we [Wu and Ge Fei] had a trip to the Thousand Islands Lake, in the name of investigation. . . . The director of the County Cultural Center introduced to us the local conditions and customs, among which the tale about the "Nine-Star Family of Fishers" extremely animated our curiosity. We, for that special

purpose, went to the seat of the Families, but resulted in nothing. People there knew that their ancestors were Chen Youliang's soldiers, but only because it is written like this in the County Annals did they "know" it. They flatly denied the legend about the prostitution of the women on the fleet; what they remembered was that their ancestors aided the Kingdom of Heavenly Peace to win battles, but this was not recorded in the County Annals. Two years later Ge Fei wrote "Green-Yellow" according to this experience. (3)

This passage at least provides us with a clear source from which Ge Fei develops his story. What seems important to us, in this passage, is that the real past is either legitimized by people who rely on the official history or mythologized by people who wish to intensify the local color of history. Ge Fei, obviously, reads into these readings of history. Similarly, then, the partiality of each narrative in "Yellow-Green" comes from the inner attraction and/or resistance to the moral taboo. In some cases the moral taboo censors real experience. The first old man, for example, "like other villagers, was unwilling to mention the 'disgraceful thing' again" (*Mizhou* 175). That is why the "I" finds his narrative both revealing and concealing. The surgeon's curiosity about Zhang's death and the ranger's (one of the interviewees) curiosity about Zhang's sexual life, respectively, block their visions of the whole. The whole and absolute account of the past is unattainable through such a fragmentary picture pieced by disparate voices.

In his remarkable reading of Ge Fei, Xudong Zhang acutely observes a pensive, self-absorbed narrative subject lingering in "Green-Yellow" (or Ge Fei's fiction in general). On the other hand, it is also important to see that such a modern subjectivity is established in a mesh of voices, which has virtually dispersed the dominance of the narrator's voice. The "construction of a self-image," therefore, is to be deconstructed not by the narrator's tendency of self-disintegration but by his inability to rationalize the incidents in the past through contemplation. The narrative subject's "self-consciousness to meet its imaginary emancipation" (Zhang 197) and "impulse to restore the past" cannot but face constant disseminations of meaning, without reaching an absolute, self-sufficient knowledge that might otherwise confirm his historical identity. The "beginning of man" that Xudong Zhang argues as a better interpretation than the "end of man" remains suspended between the desire of forming and the reality of deforming (198). By presenting the difficulty of narrativizing historical truth, Ge Fei miraculously creates a modern cognitive subject whose journey of investigation is, nevertheless, frequently interrupted and averted.

Subjective History as Embroiled Déjà Vu

The heterogeneous mode of narrative recurs in Ge Fei's "Yanmie" (Oblivion, 1993), in which various voices collide in their descriptions of the woman called Gold. "Jinse" (The ornamented zither, 1993), another short story, is entangled in the endlessly self-derived narratives that, at length, form a self-engulfed narrative cycle of metempsychoses. The title of the story duplicates the Tang Dynasty poet Li Shangyin's famous poem "The Ornamented Zither":

> The ornamented zither, for no reason, has fifty strings.
> Each string, each bridge, recalls a youthful year.
> Master Zhuang was confused by his morning dream of the
>   butterfly;
> Emperor Wang's amourous heart in spring is entrusted to the
>   cuckoo.
> In the vast sea, under a bright moon, pearls have tears;
> On Indigo Mountain, in the warm sun, jade engenders smoke.
> This feeling might have become a thing to be remembered,
> Only, at the time you were already bewildered and lost.
>   (James Liu, 1; trans. modified)

The third line of the poem is brought up several times by the protagonist in Ge Fei's story, Feng Zicun, who is fascinated by the "butterfly dream" of Zhuang Zi[4] throughout his transmigrating lives. While Zhuang Zi's parable is a questioning of the authenticity of reality and Li Shangyin's poem concerns the "obscurity" of memory, Ge Fei's narrative is a self-engulfing labyrinth that perplexes the understanding of memory and history. Li Shangyin's poem predetermines the lyrical voice of Ge Fei's narrative, since Feng Zicun, like Li Shangyin, dwells on his speculation on the feeling of being lost in his memory/anamnesis. The speculative subject, like Zhuang Zi, becomes an unstable and self-questioning one.

On the night of the funeral of an attractive lady (who looked mysteriously familiar to him when he saw her the first time), Feng Zicun, upon hearing a voice calling his name from the other side of the river, goes in a trance through a bamboo grove toward the graveyard. He is captured and then executed by the villagers. The narrative structure of the story, from now on, moves backwards. A year before his death, when asked why he did not go to the imperial capital for a brighter career, Feng Zicun tells a story about how he goes to the provincial examination and fails to write the essay under the prescribed title, "The Ornamented Zither." When he comes back home, his sister tells him a story that she has heard from a tea merchant. But, as she falls asleep, Feng Zicun hangs himself on a tree. In the tea merchant's story, then, Feng Zicun is summoned by the emperor but gets seriously ill. He reads the poem "The Ornamented Zither" over and over again on his sickbed in order to comprehend its profound meaning. He tells his wife a dream he has just had but has not gotten to the end before his death. In his account of the dream Feng Zicun is himself king of the Vast Sea State, which is engaged in a war against West Chu. As West Chu besieges his state, Feng Zicun leads an exodus of his people to Indigo Mountain, where they shepherd sheep and mine jade.[5] One day, before the prince comes to assassinate him, he tells the gardener what he dreamed last night. The dream he tells reaches the beginning of the whole story (the narrative frame) with subtle differences in detail: on the night of the funeral of a fair lady, Feng Zicun hears her call his name outside the window and walks in a trance through a wheat field toward the graveyard. Since this last dream can also be read as a foreboding of his future life, the temporal dimension of the narrative becomes self-engulfed.

The *mise-en-abyme* structure is in accord with Zhuang Zi's parable: Zhuang Zi dreams his transformation into the butterfly, which, as is conjectured, dreams in turn its transformation into Zhuang Zi. If Zhuang Zi's dream is the butterfly's reality, his reality must be the butterfly's dream. The mutual entanglement of reality and dream in narrative is part of traditional Chinese mysticism, which Ge Fei evokes against the linear, grand narratives. In this sense Ge Fei's "The Ornamented Zither" also disputes the modern rationalization of Zhuang Zi's parable in, for example, Wang Meng's short story "The Butterfly," in which a historical dialectic reorganizes the entangled times. Allegedly alluding to Zhuang Zi's parable, "The Butterfly" arrays a teleological temporality in which the personal history is a synecdoche of national history. The basic thread of the narrative is woven by the protagonist Zhang Siyuan, who recalls his past (political) "lives" "transmigrating" from Party Secretary (before the political turbulence) via Old Man Zhang (during his exile to the village) to Vice Minister (after his rehabilitation). The transmigration here clearly contains the essence of dialectical history: it is only through the purgatory of political turbulence that Zhang (or China as such) purifies his spirit and enters a new era of brightness in the end. Despite the stream-of-consciousness technique in Wang Meng's narrative, the linear progression of the story is highly tangible.

By contrast, the narrative unfolding of the transmigration in "The Ornamented Zither" is not progressive but retrogressive or even involute. The grand history no longer dominates; rather, it is the immemorial that haunts the obscure events in the story. Ge Fei's story parodies representational rationality, which empowers modern Chinese fiction with a highly subjective mode of diegesis. In Ge Fei's "The Ornamented Zither" the narrative subjectivity is retained, but it is trapped in an endlessly self-engulfing cycle of personal pursuit. Again, the lyrical quality of the narration brings back the self-mystified voices of the ancient philosopher/poet in order to challenge the absolute rationality of modern subjectivity. The narrative frame consists of a narrative that consists of another, and so on, until the last, which actually consists of the initial narrative frame. One narrative subject is replaced by another that is supposedly subordinate, until the least subordinate overtakes the supreme one. There is no narrative subject, therefore, that is self-sufficient since, if each can be considered a metanarrative subject, then there is no metanarrative subject at all, no absolute and transcendental subject that can manipulate the narrative whole, which "leaks" into consecutive and cyclic narrative funnels. The lyrical voice can no longer envision a teleological temporality or absolutize a rational history of emancipation. Rather, it is successive recollections that motivate the narrative to move backward into the immemorial.

The quasi-anamnestic narratives about Feng Zicun form a cyclic spiritual transmigration, without being able to achieve a final, complete image of the subject. Difficulties of memory and déjà vu experiences occur alternately. For Feng Zicun "it seems that those trivial events in the past hide quickly behind time, his pursuit of the past usually results in nothing" (*Yuji* 178). At the same time, in the beginning, when Feng Zicun first sees the fair lady, "he feels that he has seen the woman somewhere before but he cannot recall immediately." This is merely one of the moments in which Feng Zicun is ensnared in his opaque memory about the visual images of women, which, at times, captivate him into misfortunes. In this episode Feng Zicun gets captured (for no reason) when he goes to the graveyard "in a trance" due to the death of the woman who attracts him with her "lavish and tawdry smile" ever since the first time he saw her (182). Such an image reappears in the story told by Feng Zicun about his failed provincial examination: in the examination hall, facing the prescribed title, "The Ornamented Zither," Feng Zicun involuntarily remembers "the prostitute's coquettish smile" (190) and cannot keep his mind placid enough to compose the essay. It is not specified, however, whether or not this is indeed what Feng Zicun anamnestically carries into another life of his, but it is definitely anamnestically carried from one narrative to another. Anamnesis, whose closest Chinese translation would be *zhuiyi,* a word used in Li Shangyin's poem to trace only the "bewildered and lost" self "at the time," becomes the covert dynamics of Feng Zicun's experience. As a fictional character, then, Feng Zicun transmits (if not transmigrates) himself successively as a narrative function in different times and locations, operates different functions, and never finds his original home. Such an uncanniness (*Unheimlichkeit,* as Heidegger suggests, having to do with homelessness) in narrative and of narrative indicates the exiled situation of both the fictional character and the narrative subject. On the narrative level the narrative voices are relayed from one to another. On the level of the plot, too, Feng Zicun, the newcomer in the village, and Feng Zicun, the king who leads the exodus, both exemplify the rootless human being, whether as an independent literatus or an almighty commander.

The *mise-en-abyme* structure of Ge Fei's narrative has its origin in Western literature and art, such as M. C. Escher's lithographs and woodcuts, in which the topological games reach the ultimate spatial self-involution.[6] In Ge Fei the concept of linear history is decentered by the intricate personal history of Feng Zicun, which cannot be grasped as an integrated whole. The narrative subject fails to persist in its omnipotence and frequently exposes its own deficiencies and unstable identities, which, in turn, call into question the absolute reason of authorial subjectivity.

Chapter 11

Yu Hua

Perplexed Narration and the Subject

If Ge Fei, in his story "The Lost Boat," rewrites the grand history directly in relation to the discourse of modernity, Yu Hua, in some of his novellas and short stories, parodies the traditional narrative genres that, in one way or another, parallel the discourse of modernity. The "genius-and-beauty" (*caizi jiaren*) romance, for example, usually contains a "dialectical" history in which the harmonious union of the talented young man and the beautiful young lady is to be achieved through a series of battles against evil forces. The "knight-errant" (*wuxia*) tale, too, only deals with the triumph of the good over the evil by violence, however artistic the martial arts are described. Both fictional genres present modes of emplotment that can be used to illustrate historical dialectics in its vulgar form: all the crises or adversities are to be dispelled through the struggles between good and evil, and ultimately the consummation will be reached as the ultimate telos.[1]

Parodies of Literary Archetypes

In this sense Yu Hua's "A Classical Romance" and "Xianxue meihua" (Plum blossoms of fresh blood, 1989), as parodies of the genius-and-beauty romance and the knight-errant tale, respectively, do not lack references to modern history. "A Classical Romance" retells the genius-and-beauty romance by driving it into a barbarous and barren social context, which disorders the established code of the genre. At first the story appears a traditional romance that has been polished or adapted for the modern reader: Liu Sheng[2] is on his way to the capital for the general examination and, when passing by a luxurious mansion, catches sight of Hui, a beautiful young lady appearing at the window of her boudoir. As expected, what happens next is the love affair between the two but in a slightly, and ironically, different manner. Hui's maidservant tries to drive him away, but he feels the pretend anger of the maidservant. He stays under the window from dusk to the stormy night, until a rope comes down from the window and the girls ask him to climb up. Not only is the use of the rope amusing, but the situation Liu Sheng faces is also awkwardly represented: he "was about to step ahead but his limbs were helplessly numb and stiff. He had been standing here without moving for too long a time to manage his hands and feet. Luckily they soon recovered." (*zuopinji* 2:168 / *The Past* 21; trans. modified). The awkward situation of Liu Sheng is intensified by the calm but perverse narrative voice that exposes, rather than smooths, the gap between the expectation of a handsome beau and the actuality of the clumsy greenhorn. Here it is reminiscent of one of the classical models of "genius," Zhang Sheng, in Yuan Zhen's "Yingying zhuan" (The story of Yingying), a story that significantly influenced the later genius-and-beauty romance.[3] Zhang Sheng, unlike Liu Sheng, agilely "used the tree as a ladder and crossed the wall" for a tryst with Yingying (293). The tryst, however, turns out to be a trick, and Zhang Sheng is humiliated as immoral. Zhang Sheng's embarrassment, in any case, is aestheticized as despondency in Yuan Zhen's narrative. As a parody of the old genre, Yu Hua's description of the classical amatory scene between Liu Sheng and Hui is, at times, subtly yet abruptly interrupted by unpolished or inelegant diction. In Yu Hua the innocent or apathetic narrative voice always understates the dramatic scene: the ironic predicament of the genius is disclosed when subjective intervention is incapacitated. Although different from the overstatement of low reality in Xu Xiaohe and Can Xue, Yu Hua's understatement of ideal circumstance equally infringes on the representational logic that authorizes an unlimited narratorial subject.

By drastically rewriting the traditional genre, Yu Hua, unlike the May Fourth intellectuals who attempted to replace the old with the new in a totalistic way, works through the old and finds its pitfalls, which the "new" has not avoided. For example, during the period after the May Fourth Movement the "romantic and revolutionary" fiction that I discussed in the preceding chapter, new as it may appear to be, can well be interpreted as a variation of the genius-and-beauty genre: both aim at a double success in winning a woman and serving the nation. In "A Classical Romance" Liu Sheng, unlike the stereotypical classical geniuses (surely except Zhang Sheng), flunks the examination. Back from the capital a few months later, Liu Sheng can no longer find Hui, as her mansion has turned into a ruin.

From now on the story becomes grimmer and grimmer. Three years later Liu Sheng goes for the examination again and, on his way, sees dreadful scenes along the road: herds of cannibalistic and grass-grazing people. When he arrives at the site of Hui's mansion, even the ruin no longer exists: there is only a wasteland. Then he enters a "market for edible human," where he witnesses the bargaining for, sale of, and cutting of a girl: the butcher-proprietor refuses a woman's entreaty that he kill her daughter *before* dismemberment and cuts the girl's arm while she is alive for the fresh meat. The excessively cruel episode culminates in the following passages:

> Now the proprietor wiped his face with a rag, while his assistant handed the arm over to someone outside the shed, who put the arm in the basket, paid, and then left.
>
> At this point the woman ran into the shed, picked up a sharp knife from the ground and thrust it fiercely into the girl's chest. The girl choked, and her cry stopped suddenly. By the time the proprietor realized what had happened it was already too late. He knocked the woman into the corner of the shed, picked the girl again off the ground, sliced apart her body in a helter-skelter way with the help of his assistant, and handed the pieces one by one to people outside the shed. (179/38–39; trans. modified)

There is certainly a sinister sublime inherent in such scenes as the mother stabbing her daughter, in which humanity and inhumanity are mixed in an obnoxious way. In addition, Yu Hua's understatement works again: what is striking is not so much the narrated event as the dissonance between the brutality of the narrated event and the casualness of the narrative voice. Yu Hua is in no sense realistic, for his inadequately simplistic style sets off, by contrast, an excess or overflow of atrocities. The inhumanity lies not only in the abominable behavior of the characters but also in the subjective inadequacy of representing their behavior.

Furthermore, it is also the unbearable impropriety within the genre of genius-and-beauty that leads the theme of harmony or union toward that of separation, bleakness, chaos, and savagery. This baleful irony is intensified and climaxed in the "reunion" of Liu Sheng and Hui, when the latter has become "edible human" in a restaurant and one of her leg is cut off to be sold. At first Liu Sheng hears a scream that is "piercing through the wall" and then "chopped off slice by slice," but gradually the voice weakens into a moan, and he is reminded of the chanting of Hui three years ago (181/41; trans. modified). Here, again, when the painful moan is heard as chanting, the sensibility of Liu Sheng, or of the narrator, is positioned in a perverted predicament. Then Liu Sheng's reencounter with Hui occurs not in a "living-happily-ever-after" finale but in a devilish scene in which Liu Sheng, like the filicidal mother, stabs his dying love to death and buries her mutilated corpse according to her wishes. No matter how legitimate the killing is, his love for Hui is defiled by the action. The descriptions about how Liu Sheng redeems Hui's leg (which has been "hacked to pieces") from the proprietor and how "the merchant elatedly gnawed on the meat cut from Hui's thigh" (182–83/43–44; trans. modified) are intolerable, not for the display of bloodiness but for the intensity of bloodiness that is pervertedly represented.

In Yu Hua's narrative the "classical" romance between the genius (whose pursuit of a career has failed) and the beauty (whose body has been deformed) develops into a catastrophe, which exceeds normal, or conventional, comprehensibility. For example, when he is washing her wounds before burying her, Liu Sheng sees "the skin and flesh that had been displaced by the knife curled out around the puncture: it was still deep red, like a peach flower in bloom" (184/45; trans. modified). Insofar as the peach blossom is a stock metaphor for female beauty in traditional Chinese literature,[4] its reference to the fatal and ghastly looking wound confounds beauty and ugliness, happiness and misery.[5] The confounded narrative attitude seems unable to handle such a miserable and disastrous subject: after Hui dies, we learn that Liu Sheng cradles her body, "her broken leg crooked and dangling on his arms" (183/44; trans. modified). One might even detect something slightly facetious here. This is certainly not a description of romance in the nuptial chamber, but the narrative tone blurs the supposed distinction between comedy and tragedy.

A few years later Liu Sheng is again walking on the road toward the capital, though this time not going to the examination but visiting Hui's grave. When he enters the city, he sees a rebuilt mansion on the original site, in which a young lady is chanting, the voice very similar to Hui's. Liu Sheng, again, stays under the window when the maidservant, as expected, appears at the window and asks him to leave. Liu Sheng begins to fantasize about the upcoming rainy evening: "As soon as it rains, the window will close and the candlelight will shine through the paper panels of the window; the window will open once again in the storm, the young lady and the maidservant will both appear at the window. Then there will be a rope swinging down" (189/53–54; trans. modified). His daydream is interrupted by a basin of cold water poured on him from the window. The past that seems to recur cannot be reproduced. To a certain extent Liu Sheng's imaginary reexperiencing of the old romance is an allegorical evocation of Yu Hua's, or our own, intertextual reexperience of the genius-and-beauty romance. This reexperience, however, is fated to be a parody: the old benevolence and happiness are dead, and the mirage of the reunion or return proves to be an illusion.

The illusion and disillusionment are replayed when Liu Sheng arrives at Hui's grave. At first he hears Hui's chanting from the murmuring stream and even her pace in the boudoir from inside the grave. Then, as he decides to be a watchman for her grave, there appears to him, at night, a hut with candlelight. In the hut he finds Hui sitting on the ground, reading a book taken from his pack, and holding in her hand a bunch of her hair that she, over a decade ago, gave him as a token. With Hui's "cold" (*yinleng* in the original, which implies a state of the dead) body in his arms, he finally falls asleep. When he wakes up and finds that Hui has disappeared, Liu Sheng goes to her grave again and feels the warm soil. He opens the grave and, to his surprise, discovers Hui's body fresh and intact: all the old wounds are healed. He thus "looked back on" his first meeting with Hui and "conceived various delights after their reunion" (194). At night, in a trance, he goes to the hut again. But Hui says that she was to resurrect but has failed to do so because he discovered her in her grave. The ending reminds us not only of the myth of Orpheus and Eurydice but also of the stories in Pu Songling's short story collection *Liaozhai zhiyi* (Strange tales from Make-Do Studio), especially "Gongsun jiuniang" (The ninth Lady Gongsun), "Xin shisiniang" (The fourteenth Lady Xin), and "Hu Sijie" (The fourth Sister Hu). In many of these stories beautiful young ladies either resurrect or are seen alive after death but vanish after their ephemeral stay in reality, just like Hui in "A Classical Romance."[6] Yu Hua, consciously or not, borrows the uncanny plot structure from those "strange tales" to challenge the orthodox narratives of the genius-and-beauty romance.[7]

The stereotype of the accidental encounter and love at first sight between a young man going to civil service examination and a young lady appearing by chance at the window (or sometimes the balcony) of her boudoir is retained in Yu Hua's story. Furthermore, the words, phrases, and diction of the narrative resemble those in traditional vernacular fiction, especially the genius-and-beauty romance. In so doing, Yu Hua seems to undermine the expectation for an agreeable development of the romance. The romantic story precipitates into a barbaric catastrophe, which is later about to recover into a hopeful ending but eventually fails in spite of active fantasies. The historical logic that empowers the good in its fight against the evil is missing in Yu Hua's story. Liu Sheng not only cannot fulfill his own ambition in his career in the imperial state but also cannot prevent the worldly vicissitude and human savageness that destroy his love. He leaves for a few months but finds Hui missing and her mansion ruined, a situation he is unable to redeem; he sits in the restaurant without being aware of the urgency of rescuing her when the butcher is chopping Hui's leg. Even Liu Sheng's only merit, his devotion of love to Hui, becomes, ironically, what bungles her resurrection. Only on the level of fantasy or dream, then, can Liu Sheng fulfill his desire for Hui. In reality, anticipated by his dullness under Hui's window, Liu Sheng never has the cleverness or agility that a conventional genius or talented scholar is gifted with. The idea of ultimate harmony, or union, is permanently postponed when one, inopportunely and abominably, seeks to achieve it from the untouchable abyss of humanity.

Equally awkward and perverted is the narration of the story. It is, even in the most passionate passages, confined in the standard or customary style of traditional vernacular narrative so that the subjective engagement of the narrator cannot bring about real strength to sublimate the unbecoming content of the story to a transcendental state. Thus, the hideous and lamentable events that do not belong to the traditional narrative overwhelm the narratorial voice in the traditional mode, which never fittingly catches the intensity or perversity of the whole story. What "The Classical Romance" parodies is not only the emplotment but also the discourse of the genius-and-beauty romance.

"Plum Blossoms of Fresh Blood," Yu Hua's short story about a young man who sets out to avenge his father's death, reminds us of Lu Xun's "Zhu jian" (Forging the swords, 1927), which treats a similar theme of avenging the death of a father. Mei Jian Chi and the dark man, Lu Xun's chivalrous heroes, who take revenge on the foe at the expense of their own lives, can be seen as symbolic embodiments of Lu Xun's own character: a vehement spirit aiming to extinguish the origin of social injustice and oppressive power. Therefore, Mei Jian Chi is described as a boy who "changed [his] tender personality" instantly and "strode swiftly towards the city" "with the sword on his back" (Lu Xun, *quanji* 2:421–22 / *Selected Works* 1:301; trans. modified). Then, no matter how dignified the two heroes' tragic deed seems to be, it is detectable that the rationality of the historical drama is not unquestionable. Mei Jian Chi's credulity of the dark man's promise to accomplish the mission of revenge is more naive than courageous, and the narrative of the biting battle of the three heads in the cauldron is more comical than tragic. The serious revenge becomes a carnivalesque *danse macabre* that undercuts the original import of the story.

Degrading all the spiritual exaltation of the knight-errant genre, Yu Hua's story is not only a rewriting but a miniature parody of the knight-errant tale, dwelling on the depletion and deviation of the thematic logic. It starts with the mystery of the assassination of the martial arts master Ruan Jinwu fifteen years ago and the description of the legendary "plum blossom sword" handed down from the ancestors. The standard formula of the knight-errant tale is clearly set. Ruan Jinwu's son, the now twenty-year-old Ruan Haikuo, is naturally expected by his mother to be responsible for taking revenge on the assassins of his father, but, ironically, his physique is not well developed, and he has never learned anything about the martial arts. In any case, as his mother sacrifices herself in a fire to express her resolution, Ruan Haikuo, without much motivation for revenge, brings the sword with ninety-nine plum blossoms on it (i.e., ninety-nine drops of blood, each indicating a person killed by Ruan Jinwu with the sword) to find Master Green Cloud or Pattering White Rain, two superior martial arts masters, either of whom will be able to reveal the names of the assassins to him.

The conformity between the knight-errant tale that demonstrates the historical certainty of justice and the communist literature that confirms a teleological history of social revolution must be reemphasized. In both cases history is predetermined as simply a dualistic struggle between good and evil, which ends with the victory of the former and the defeat of the latter. In "Plum Blossoms of Fresh Blood," however, the knight-errant genre of narration and tropology diverts the logic of revenge—the essential psychohistorical logic of the knight-errant tale. If the image of wind is a symbol of speed and agility of the hero of the knight-errant tale, it now turns into the condition of uncertainty or purposelessness: Ruan Haikuo, "like wind floating on the earth, was walking forward aimlessly" (*zuopinji* 1:49), passing numerous crossroads. As he is going astray on the way, he respectively meets Lady of the Rouge and Black Needle Knight, who ask him to inquire about the whereabouts of Liu Tian and Li Dong from Master Green Cloud. Since he remembers to look for Master Green Cloud, he misses the chance to ask Pattering White Rain. He finally finds Master Green Cloud and gets the answers for Lady of the Rouge and Black Needle Knight, but Master Green Cloud will not take more than two questions. The question that Ruan Haikuo has about his father's death still remains unanswered. Lady of the Rouge and Black Needle Knight, informed by Ruan Haikuo, killed Liu Tian and Li Dong, who, he later finds out, are no other than the assassins of his father.

On the one hand, Ruan Haikuo's enemies have been annihilated; on the other hand, his mission to take revenge on those two persons for his father's death will be unfulfillable forever: Ruan Haikuo has permanently lost his chance to realize his mother's wish and to become a real chivalric hero. The loss of chance results from his lack of concentration on carrying out his scheme and his involvement in other knight-errant plots alien to his own. The function of Ruan Haikuo as a chivalric hero is essentially impaired not only by his physical disqualification but also by his mental indifference. Soon after he sets out, Ruan Haikuo "forgot the direction he was going toward" and turns his journey into an incessantly disoriented one. As he successively arrives at numerous villages and towns that "had tree with identical colors, houses with identical shapes, and identical streets with identical walking people" (49 / *The Past* 185; trans. modified), he is virtually roaming in a labyrinth, namely, in a space without an exit opening toward progress but only one full of repetitions and even impasses.

The lineal historical itinerary of the standard knight-errant tale is contorted. Along such a contorted or digressive itinerary, Ruan Haikuo unavoidably encounters those people whose itineraries later traverse or displace his own. It is not his pure apathy to the knight-errant world but his good deeds to help others—the moral imperative of a chivalric hero—that ultimately lead to the disorder of his own historical agenda. The unidirectionality of the chivalric historicity and ethics is multiplied by other directions and disparate elements. In both "A Classical Romance" and "Plum Blossoms of Fresh Blood," as Zhao Yiheng points out, "Yu Hua's parodies employ understated irony, which uses the conventions in a respectful, solemn way but also deprives them of their motivation, especially the ethical motivation, thus exposing their vulnerability" ("Yu Hua" 419).

The Problematics of Narration

Yu Hua's other stories, such as "The April Third Incident" and "A Story Dedicated to the Girl Willow," can be seen as parodies of the paradigm of representational narrative in general, in the sense that narrative subjectivity becomes a disintegrated one. "The April Third Incident" reminds us of a short story by Yu Dafu, "Shiyiyue chusan" (The third of the eleventh month, 1924): both titles refer to the date of (or around) the birthday of the author/narrator. Yu Dafu's narrator renders all his own experiences and thoughts, relying entirely on his omniscience. As Yu Dafu alleges that all literary works are autobiographical, it is likely that the story is an account of real events. The "I" as character or narrator seems to be Yu Dafu the author, who directly and "honestly" records his own activities and feelings (including his remembrance of the past) on his twenty-eighth birthday.⁸ The paranoid subjectivity lies in the whole process of narration: the obsession with an unacquainted girl is projected from such paranoia. For example, the narrative about the girl's looking back or glancing through the window is the author's daydream about getting an emotional response from the girl. Such a paranoid illusion is ultimately disillusioned after the fruitless pursuit on that day. Ironically, the beautiful girl who is imagined to appear in the end of the story is eventually displaced by a group of dogs, whose disturbing bark in reality (rather than the sweet whisper in fantasy) drives away the sentimental author.

In Yu Hua's "The April Third Incident," then, the self-centered narrative frame has collapsed. Although Yu Hua's date of birth is truly April 3 (the protagonist's birthday, however, seems to be two or three days after April 3), although the nameless "he" in this narrative amounts nearly to the first-person "I," the narrative does not have the unity or certainty of the "autobiographical" type: the subjective arrangement of the narrative is constantly disordered, displaced, and diverted. The unfolding of the story is close to the formation of a dream: anachronism, illogic, and misrepresentation of emotions indicate the indeterminacy of the narrative.

The story starts from the "he"'s eighteenth birthday. He goes out to the street, runs into his former classmate Bai Xue (a girl who attracts him), and sees a middle-aged man leaning on a tree, who seems indifferent to him. At night he feels lonely, for his parents have forgotten his birthday. In the next few chapters he visits some of his former classmates, Zhang Liang, Yazhou, Hansheng, and Zhu Qiao, who all behave unreasonably or inexplicably. And so do Bai Xue and other middle-aged men he meets on the street. Going back home, he overhears his parents' talk. In their conversation he hears "April third," without knowing what it means. He also hears his mother ask "Well-prepared?" and someone else reply "How about yourselves?" Later, on the street, he overhears someone ask his father "When?" and his father replies, "April third" (*zuopinji* 2:207–19). Even when he is in Bai Xue's home, Bai Xue reminds him that "tomorrow is April third" and asks him, "Guess what will happen tomorrow?" (235). During this time he becomes suspicious of the scheme plotted by everyone, known or unknown, on the street, at home, or in the neighborhood. At the end, on the eve of April 3, he escapes on a cargo train.

Clearly, the prototype parodied in "The April Third Incident" is not only Yu Dafu's "The Third of the Eleventh Month" but, again, Lu Xun's "A Madman's Diary," whose theme is dealt with in this story. Like the Madman, the "he" is continuously suspicious of the scheme by people around him, but this time the certainty of paranoia is undermined by the evasive or even somewhat indifferent voice of narration, the confusion of illusion and reality, and the disordered temporality. If the Madman is assured of the impending tragedy of being eaten, Yu Hua's "he," like many of Can Xue's characters, cannot determine the specific disaster that will befall him, even though he hypothesizes various possible ways that people commit murder. There is many a passage that starts with ellipsis, to show the imaginary occurrences related to the danger or incident, some immediately acknowledged as conjecture but others mixed with and inseparable from the facts, as if there were no boundary between imagination and reality. In one of these passages he feels that people speak surreptitiously behind the windows along the alley. Hearing someone ask, "Well-prepared?" and "When are we taking action?" (227), he fights with the one who discovers his overhearing. Later, when he sees a man leaning on the tree, he imagines that he has a fight with the man and forces the man to confess their scheme to have a truck run over him or drop a big rock on him. Even the date April 3 does not function as an exclusive temporal mark of the incident. To him their scheme could take effect at any time: from time to time he foresees that a truck to his left is coming over slowly and will bump him as he crosses the street or that a brick is falling down from a building under construction.

The scheme is suspended as an unascertainable but omnipresent and ever-impending threat, which is neither annulled nor denied nor seen as something distinguishable and recognizable any longer. The one-dimensional and confident narration shifts to the multidimensional narration that acknowledges the limitations and contradictions of narrative subjectivity. Then paranoia turns into schizophrenia: the narrator neither loosens itself nor simply abandons or conceals itself but, rather, in the process of self-realization, discovers incompleteness, indistinctness, and inconsistency. The relationship between the "he" and Bai Xue is set in a rather subtle and indefinable condition. The narcissistic and sentimental narrative voice in Yu Dafu no longer dominates; rather, the projection of desire and the oversensitivity to threat are intermingled and mutually undercut. Thus, the paranoid and totalizing subject evoked by Yu Hua is disfigured as the one who cannot maintain his own integrated identity.

The uncertainty of narration typically implies a problematic subject: "He *thought* he *should have* arrived at the gate of Zhang Liang's. There were two glistening bronze rings on the black gate. He *felt* that he had snatched the rings and pushed open the gate to enter. And he *should have* heard a senile sound, which emitted from the gate when it was opened" (200; my emph.). Even the narrator is not confident of the accuracy of narration: "he *seemed* to hear Zhang Liang ask, *or* it was Zhu Qiao *or* Hansheng who asked" (201; my emph.). The most dreamlike scene occurs in chapter 4, when the "he" has just bid farewell to three friends and come to Yazhou's home. As the door opens, the same three people are already in the room and, without any surprise to see him again, seem to have waited for a long time. Yazhou, the host, seems to have just left, but the "he" soon "heard Yazhou's voice, floating over here, *as if* Yazhou were speaking from outside the window. But he *indeed* saw Yazhou before him and got startled. He *didn't notice* a wee bit when Yazhou came in, *as if* he had never gone out" (204; my emph.). In a real dream (which is, however, not more dreamlike than reality) he sees his classmates rush into his room and asks who the girl with them is. Everyone laughs, and the girl says she is Bai Xue. He is astonished that he had failed to recognize her.

The subject of perception in "The April Third Incident" is no longer a self-sufficient or self-confident one. To compare an episode with its prototype in "A Madman's Diary" will clarify this observation. In "A Madman's Diary" the Madman writes: "There were seven or eight others who discussed me in a whisper. And they were afraid of my seeing them" (Lu Xun, *quanji* 1:423 / *Selected Works* 1:40). The Madman, as the narrative subject, never doubts his observations, even though the reader knows how seriously he misinterprets reality. By comparison, the "he" in "The April Third Incident" is far less assured of his judgment, though his original reaction to people on the street is strikingly similar to the Madman's: "These broken shadows gave him a sneaking impression, he then turned around and saw a few people on the pavement across the street point toward him while speaking. He turned around so abruptly that they appeared a little flurried" (Yu Hua, *zuopinji* 2:210). Nevertheless, his suspicion that they are merely the participants in the "scheme" is disordered and uncertain when Zhu

Qiao says that they are his classmates: "He seemed to remember, they were truly his previous classmates. Then he saw Zhu Qiao smile funnily, and couldn't help suspecting again" (211).

Unlike the self-confident Madman, then, Yu Hua's "he" cannot maintain his paranoid integrity: even suspicion itself can be suspect. Likewise, while he is imagining that he beats the man leaning on the tree to the ground, he "had no determination to go in front of him," for "he realized that if he did so the result would be contrary to his hypothesis, that is to say, the person lying on the ground and moaning would be himself" (233). In another episode he presumes that people behind him are "keeping watch on" him and that if he suddenly turns around they will be unsettled. But "when he turned around he did not see what he had anticipated. As he looked around he did not find anyone watching him. They apparently detected his idea, which made him upset. They are getting slier, he thought" (215). No matter how the "he" (via the narrator) attempts to justify himself, the inconsistency between the totalizing imagination and the reality that is unable to totalize is exposed.

In this case schizophrenia arises to break down paranoia: if the subjectivity of Lu Xun's Madman is *either* absolute in toto *or* unreliable in toto by different readings, the subjectivity in Yu Hua's narrative is, in every detail, totalizing *and* detotalized *at one and the same time.* This is also what Baudelaire means by *dédoublement:* the potentially reversible subjective discourse is in every moment self-questioning while it questions the other. The "scheme" remains enigmatic throughout the story. In Yu Hua's parody the idea of alienation of a frail individual self facing another is not overthrown, but the self is simultaneously decentered as part of the other to undermine the absolute and self-righteous subject.

Anachronistic Experiences and Multiple Identities

In Yu Hua's novella "A Story Dedicated to the Girl Willow" the doubleness of subjectivity is shown in an irresolvable intricacy or involution of temporality and events. The narrator's past experience is partly paralleled (or overlapped) by the stranger, whom the "I" encounters in a temporally disparate but spatially identical spot. Surreal and anachronistic, the story has thus two lines, which merge somewhat at least twice but are essentially separate.

The "I" first meets the stranger in a summer, when the latter is sitting in a bridge opening and telling the "I" about what has happened to him in the past. When the stranger says "ten years ago, May 8, 1988," the "I" tries to correct him by asserting that ten years ago should be 1978, for May 8, 1988, is yet to come (*zuopinji* 2:91). But the stranger insists on the year 1988 by saying that it would be twenty years ago if it were 1978. We have to assume, then, that the "I" and the stranger are not in the same temporal coordinate. In any case the stranger tells him that, after May 8, 1988, his eyes begin to go blind and he is later hospitalized. The stranger has eyes transplanted from Willow, a girl who dies in a traffic accident. When he is discharged from the hospital on September 3, 1988, he obtains Willow's address and goes to see her father in a town called Smoke. On the bus to Smoke an old man sitting next to him tells a story: in 1949, before the Nationalist army withdrew from Smoke, an officer buried ten bombs in the town in a complex geometric pattern. The stranger is then preoccupied with the bombs and has forgotten the original purpose of his trip. Presumably, this is why he is here at the bridge opening, laying a few sheets of paper with sketched drawings in front of him.

Then, by restarting the chapter numbers from 1, the story seems to unfold itself from another direction. The "I" lives in a riverside bungalow in the town named Smoke. On May 8, 1988, a girl "came to me in my mind," and he could see her pink little feet and felt warm in his mind. The young lady acts, in his mind, along with his own actions: "When I took out the key, I heard the sound of her taking out the key. Then we inserted the keys into the lock and turn the key together to open the door. I entered and so did she. The only thing different was that everything she did happened in my mind" (97). The imaginary girl, like those in some stories in *Strange Tales from Make-Do Studio*, comes to life the next morning. The "I" feels that "she came out of my mind" and "was preparing breakfast in the kitchen" for him, "regardless of the fact that I had no kitchen at all . . . , because she was in the kitchen" and "her arrival has changed the layout of the house" (98). A few days later the "I" accidentally sees a young man who has the same way of looking as the girl's. The young man stops at a riverside bungalow (like his), takes out the same key as his, goes in, and closes the door with the same sound that he usually hears when he closes his. Then the young man comes out and goes into a bridge opening, looking at a few sheets of white paper in his hands. The "I" follows him and tells him about what happened a few days ago. The young man says that this is also what happened to him ten years ago. Then he tells a story that overlaps both the "I"'s and the stranger's: a girl comes to his mind and gets more and more real when he sees her eyes; a month later he draws a picture of her and gazes at it all the time until he catches an eye disease. The rest of his story is exactly like that of the stranger's. Now he is still searching for the tenth bomb, since the other nine have all exploded.

When the story starts yet again from chapter 1, the "I," after the arrival of the phantom girl, also develops an eye disease but recovers soon. He is injured in a traffic accident, however, and sent to the Shanghai hospital for eye surgery on August 14, 1988, having corneas transplanted from a girl named Willow, who had just died of leukemia in the same hospital. Many years later the "I" goes to Willow's home, according to the address he acquired when he left the hospital on September 3, 1988. Her father says that she died at home on August 14, 1988, and insists that she had never been to Shanghai. The "I" recognizes from Willow's photo that she is the one who came to his mind on May 8, 1988. The "I" also sees a pencil drawing by Willow, an image of a young man whose way of looking, according to her father, resembles the "I"'s very much. Her father explains that a strange man came to Willow's mind one day, and she was finally able to draw him on the paper. When he comes out of Willow's home, the "I" follows a young man onto a bridge opening, in which the latter lays some sheets of white paper on the ground. The young man tells the story about the bombs, saying that the last bomb yet to explode at any time "is now buried at ten places" in the town. When he itemizes these ten locations, the "I" becomes aware that "there are ten bombs in the town" (119) and that the young man is exactly the one he saw in Willow's pencil drawing.

In this ending of the narrative the last bomb proliferates incomprehensibly—into ten. It can be detected that the problem derives from the sentence "This bomb is now buried at ten places," which is grammatically impeccable but semantically illogical. The problem of the bomb becomes a metaphor of the problem of the grand history, which is potentially disastrous at every moment and can never be reduced to a single solution, insofar as it has to encounter the inconsistencies of the discourse. The stranger's effort to decipher the historical enigma is virtually futile in the end, since the bombs, like historical dangers, are hidden and untraceable. It is even the supposedly rational prearrangement (the geometrical array) that finally disarranges the perception of the historical pattern. If the phantom girl is an agent of personal desire who causes the physical blindness of the stranger, the old man on the bus (discernibly, the Nationalist officer who buried the bombs decades ago and thus another phantom from the historical past) can be seen metaphorically as the agent of historical concern, who causes the stranger's blindness to the dangers and catastrophes in the world, a blindness that fails the seemingly clairvoyant vision of the grand history.

In any case the syntactic problem is exposed as an indicator of the enigma of the whole narrative: a narrative that is logical in every detail but inconsistent and irreconcilable on the whole. The proliferation of a single bomb into ten bombs is comparable to the disintegration of a single story into several narratives or the split of a single persona into two or more characters. The figure of a young man, for example, is split into at least two characters: one is the "I," whose narrative tense should be the present, whereas the other, the stranger, exists in the future and refers to the present as the past. Although they are temporally displaced, the two encounter each other unreasonably to give accounts of their similar experiences. No matter how intricate the details may be, the two share a very identical destiny and can thus be identified with each other to some extent. On May 8, 1988, both are possessed with a phantom girl, who becomes truer and truer, and then get blind directly or indirectly from the imaginary or pictorial existence of her; then, on August 14, 1988, both have eyes or corneas transplanted from the girl named Willow, who has just died; both, discharged from the hospital in Shanghai on September 3, 1988, sit on the bus that goes to Smoke, where Willow's home is. The stranger / young man even lives in a same riverside bungalow and has a same key as the "I" does.

Other than their calendrical disparity, the two still have several things not in common. The "I" gets blind as a result of a traffic accident and the stranger from his gaze at his drawing of the phantom girl; the "I" finally arrives at Willow's home, and the stranger is constantly obsessed with the problem of the bombs. The stranger, with whom the "I" is "acquainted for a long time" (88), may be seen as the "I"'s doppelgänger, the self as a mirror image, an alien, extraneous self that the "I" *follows*—chases and imitates—but is unable to apprehend completely or identify himself with. It is such a gap that doubles the subject, and in this sense the specter is not only the phantom girl, who is desired into the subject, but also the irreconcilable self, who is alienated from the subject.

Whereas Willow's father attributes the eyes on her drawing to the "I"'s eyes, the "I" only finds that the picture resembles the stranger. His failure to recognize himself, then, signals the impossibility of his voluntary identification with the stranger and his involuntary mirroring of the latter. The "I"'s earlier observation that the stranger's way of looking is exactly that of the phantom girl not only suggests that the phantom girl is presumably Willow (the stranger's eyes have been transplanted from Willow, and the resemblance between Willow and the stranger is reconfirmed at the end) but also implies that the stranger looks equally like a phantom, a specter that haunts the mind of the "I." At the same time it is also the "I" who, inseparable from his own doppelgänger, follows the stranger from time to time. The stranger seems to indicate the "I"'s fate in the future, which is, ironically, to be repeated by him, since it has already happened to the stranger. Therefore, as an image of both the past and the future, the stranger, allegorically, becomes a temporally divergent force that tears apart the subject of the "I."

The most essential problem of the narrative is certainly its displaced and involute time frame. If the most profound secret of grand narratives is the absolutely logical, progressive temporality of the plot, if the linear temporal order of narrative is the paradigmatic mode of relating collective or personal histories, Yu Hua's narrative offers an experiencing of a dislocated, multiplied temporality. "A Story Dedicated to the Girl Willow" is an extreme case, as we have seen, for the possibility of reconstruction has been radically incapacitated. Time is not merely disordered but anachronistic, as the incompatible temporal dimensions are unassimilable into one another. One of the most annoying parts in the story is that the scene in which the "I" meets the stranger at the bridge opening appears three times. Each time the settings and details are slightly different and the occurrences relevant and supplementary. The first time they meet is some time, to the "I," before May 8, 1988, or, to the stranger, ten years after that date. Since the narrator says it is "a summer midday" and the stranger is stripped to the waist, we should assume that, to the "I," it is no later than the summer of 1987. The second time is a few days after May 8, 1988, when the "I" follows the young man (the stranger) to the bridge opening and the latter, again, recalls the date May 8, 1988, as ten years ago. Now not only does the same date (May 8, 1988) become, to different people, chronologically inconsistent, but different dates with nearly one year's interval between can both be, to the same person, ten years after the same date (May 8, 1988).

Paradoxes like these are essential to the whole narrative, not to be solved by the reader but to function as the pivotal theme of the story: the apprehension of time is no longer confined by the temporal linearity that forms the homogeneous history. In each isolated episode the temporal logic of narrative is coherent. The same logic is distorted, however, when various chronologically incompatible episodes are pieced together. In this case the unified narrative time is diffused: it cannot maintain its promise to convey the rational progress of narrative.

The difficulty, nevertheless, is not limited to the irreconcilable temporality, even in regard to the repetition of the bridge opening scene. One may even wonder whether these are truly three times with the same scene or just various accounts of the same event. Just as the date of the first occurrence of their meeting could be both in 1987 (or earlier) and in 1998, one may see the three episodes of the bridge opening scene as the same event that happens at different times, according to the same narrative (il)logic. In any case in the bridge opening, a metaphor of the unconscious (under the conscious construction of the memory/events), the "I" pursues his spiritual double and finds him, three times, immersed in contemplation about the bombs. The stranger, originally also heading toward Willow's home (which only the "I" reaches), is distracted and subsequently devotes his persistent interest to a less private, more public and grand historical theme. As a more historically concerned character, the stranger is truly a figure alien to the self (the "I"), who, in turn, has to listen to the stranger's narrative of momentous incidents (retrospective or prospective) from time to time. Such a pursuit results in the discovery that the public project of avoiding exploding the bomb is as problematic as the "I"'s own private project of visiting Willow's home in order to understand her. The locations of the bombs and their number are unreasonably increased to the extent of uncontrollability, just as the truth about Willow's death is multiplied into various statements: she dies of leukemia, she dies in a traffic accident, and she dies at home for no explicit reason, on the same date.

Yu Hua's discord with rational comprehensibility questions the narrative authenticity and validity in both personal and collective histories. History, as Yu Hua's narrative shows, is an inextricable labyrinth of non sequiturs. A girl gradually comes to life out of the stranger's hallucination, and, after drawing a picture of her, he develops and eye disease and finally goes blind. He, in turn, appears as Willow's phantom, and she draws a picture of him and then dies. Willow, again, comes as a phantom to the "I"'s mind and causes (though indirectly) the "I"'s traffic accident and his blindness. The chain could be an infinite one, as it can be assumed that the girl coming to the stranger is the same girl coming to the "I," namely, Willow. Such an involute narrative seems more intricate when the events and the temporal span in which they take place are inherently incongruous.

If we examine the episodes about the old man's telling a story on the bus, a fatal discrepancy appears within the temporal order. This event occurs twice in the whole narrative yet on the same date. It was first told by the stranger before the "I" sees the phantom girl and later experienced directly by the "I," who repeats what the stranger has told him after his eye surgery and, of course, after his "affair" with the phantom girl. In other words, when the "I" is on the bus heading toward Smoke, he is merely confirming what the stranger has told him, or he is participating in a reality that has already been recounted as history or the past. The stranger's memory of the past becomes no more than a mental return to/from the future, that is to say, either the past is yet to happen or what is happening has already existed as a remembrance of what happened before. Here Yu Hua's conception that "the experience of the past and the things in the future exist simultaneously in the present" (*zuopinji* 2:283) may well be comparable to what T. S. Eliot ponders in the opening lines of *Four Quartets:* "Time present and time past / Are both perhaps present in time future, / And time future contained in time past" (117). Without any theological implications, nevertheless, Yu Hua's narrative challenges the unidirectional, homogeneous order of history established by the grand narrative.

Furthermore, "narrativized" reality subverts the theorem of representational realism that declares that literature reflects reality. Here, ironically, the narrative of reality precedes reality itself: reality seems to be an imitation or reflection, rather than the original, in the temporal complex of historical narrative. It is not the original but other representations that are to be represented, and the endless chain of representations amounts to the impossibility of the absolute real. When the concept of reality, as well as the representation of reality, was no longer self-sufficient, the grand project of representational writing in modern Chinese literature began to be deconstructed.

Chapter 12

Mo Yan's *The Republic of Wine*

An Extravaganza of Decadence

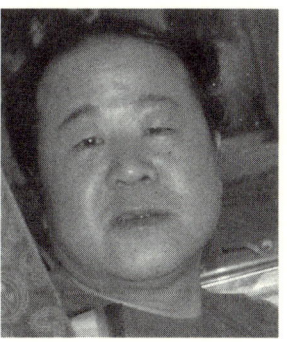

> *There is no document of civilization which is not at the same time a document of barbarism.*
> —WALTER BENJAMIN, "THESIS ON THE PHILOSOPHY OF HISTORY"

Formerly categorized as a marginal root-seeking writer, Mo Yan has never persisted in the ideal of root seeking. The nostalgic implication of Mo Yan's fiction, from its very beginning—exemplified by the short story "Touming de hongluobo" (The transparent carrots, 1985)—is impaired by an undercurrent of impurity. The innocent Swarthy Boy in "The Transparent Carrots" is faced with successive disturbances, which contaminate, or even deprive him of, the symbolic transparency: he is involved in the rivalry between the young stonemason and the young blacksmith for Miss Chrysanthemum; Miss Chrysanthemum is accidentally injured by their fight; when stealing carrots (instigated by the young blacksmith), he is captured and stripped of his clothes.

In *Honggaoliang jiazu* (Red sorghum: A family saga, 1987), his first and widely acclaimed novel,[1] the primitive élan vital is harshly commingled with barbaric passion. The supreme hero, Yu Zhan'ao, is a bandit, located at the end of the gallery of charismatic figures in the his-

207

tory of modern Chinese literature. Yu Zhan'ao is a historical subject frequently entangled in, or diverted by, his more somatic than romantic desires. His legendary heroism is marked by his abduction of the bride, his urinating in the homemade wine to enrich its genuineness, his drinking along with his fellow workers before ambushing the Japanese invaders, and so on. Subtly, the waywardness infuses the heroic character with something impure and pushes history into the simultaneously "most heroic and most bastardly" predicament (*Honggaoliang* 450 / *Red Sorghum* 356–57). While *Red Sorghum* still contains idealism that invokes a heroic and bastardly past as an imaginary redemption of the stagnant and abject present, its perversity, then, develops further in Mo Yan's later fiction, especially his novels *Shisan bu* (Thirteen steps, 1989) and *Jiuguo* (The republic of wine, 1992).

In *The Republic of Wine* barbarism and lofty rhetoric, crime and justice, suffering and enjoyment, are all intermixed. One of the most distinctive characteristics of the novel is the self-exposure of narrative performance as an interruption of the integration of narrative and a self-skepticism of the distant and justified function of narrative. Written between 1989 and 1992, *The Republic of Wine* departs more significantly from his early period than his previous novel, *Thirteen Steps,* in that all the heroic deeds in *Red Sorghum* have been deflected to serious failures and vicious jokes. The historical tragedy of the Anti-Japanese War (depicted in *Red Sorghum*), to apply Marx's formula, recurs as another crisis of national destruction yet this time in the form of farce.

The fact that the writing of *The Republic of Wine* began only three months after the 1989 Tiananmen Incident designates its historical destiny: to demonstrate the sanguinary ruins of national history. Nevertheless, for Mo Yan (as well as all other Chinese writers) it would be politically naive and ethically irresponsible simply to represent, in the strictest sense, the historical calamity without penetrating the quotidian decay of social and individual life, which constitutes the fate of the nation, on the one hand, and refuses any direct recognition and representation, on the other. *The Republic of Wine* is remarkable in that it is, in the first place, a reflection on sociocultural aberration and barbarity, by which Mo Yan's stylistic aberration and barbarity are defined in order to measure the ethos of the time. In other words, only by scrutinizing the intrinsic aberration and barbarity that the whole nation at once enjoys and suffers through is Mo Yan able to capture the meaning of the extrinsic violence that social history imposes upon the nation itself. Furthermore, Mo Yan examines the limitations of critical realism by maintaining the contradiction between the sociohistorical critique and the critique waged against the critical subject. The representational subject behind the narrative voice is no longer immune from the social evil and rhetorical terror with which the subject too has been historically possessed. In the epilogue to another of his novels, *Shicao jiazu* (The herbivorous family, 1993), Mo Yan clearly states that, "while critiquing the history of the herbivorous family, readers should at the same time critique the mental history of the writer: the latter seems more important" (393). Herein, ultimately, lies a paradox Mo Yan is painfully confronted with and thus an aporia laid bare in his self-reflexive and self-referential narrative.

As we shall see, on the level of emplotment the plights in which the protagonist, Ding Gouer, is trapped throughout his journey block his practical attempts to eliminate evil. Ding, a failed symbol of the historical subject, cannot perform the role of rescuing society from inhumanity. Meanwhile, on the level of narration Mo Yan (the narrator/author), too, is as seriously trapped in a plight of expression that muddles or obscures his critical voice and makes any simple denunciation incomprehensible. Parallel to Ding Gouer's decadence of conduct, Mo Yan's decadence of narration is characterized as a subjective excessiveness that calls into question a fair and accurate representation of the object. The excessiveness applies not only to material documentation—such as the descriptive presentations of the community addicted to gastronomy or of people who indulge in adultery or promiscuity—but also to formal qualities, to stylistic and narrative peculiarities. Like his character Ding Gouer, whose historical function is disordered when he is involved in excessive activities, Mo Yan the narrator/author is also unsettled when his voice is implicated in excessive discourses that constantly interrupt the integrated representational subjectivity of his narrative.

The bulk of the novel describes the "special detective" Ding Gouer's journey to a town called Jiuguo (meaning the Republic of Wine) to investigate a horrible crime: the local officials (reportedly) eat human babies. The scene of mutual seduction between Ding Gouer and the female chauffeur in the truck serves as a prelude to the debauchery prevalent throughout the novel. As soon as he arrives at the colliery where Jin Gangzuan (the major suspect of his investigation and vice chairman of the propaganda department of the Party committee of Jiuguo) originally worked, Ding is driven to a feast hosted by Jin (as well as other officials) and compelled to drink tremendously. Not until he witnesses a dish containing a cooked, but vividly recognizable, human baby does Ding sober up: out of anger, he pulls out his gun and fires but only shoots off the baby's head. Having recovered from the shock of the shooting, Jin and the others explain that the baby is made of lotus roots, melon, pork, sausage, and the like. Strongly persuaded, Ding tries a small bite of the baby and is enraptured by its taste. Thus, he agreeably participates in the cannibals' feast (or at least that of stylistic cannibals) and gets drunk as a fish. During his drunken sleep that night, a scaly boy comes in and steals his belongings, but he, helplessly watching what is happening to him, is utterly incapable of stopping the pilferage.

After he has lost almost everything, Ding runs into the female chauffeur again and goes home with her. As they are making love, Ding and the chauffeur are unexpectedly caught in the act by Jin, who turns out to be the chauffeur's husband. Humiliated then released by Jin, Ding and the chauffeur visit Yu Yichi, manager of the Yichi Wineshop, in order to obtain information about the killing and eating of babies in Jiuguo. But Ding soon realizes that the chauffeur is one of Yu's numerous mistresses. Ding becomes furious and mistreats her; she then drives him away, and he is left wandering the street. He runs into a veteran whose words and wine prod Ding to return quickly to the restaurant, where he shoots and kills the chauffeur and Yu Yichi. As a fugitive of justice, Ding, through intoxicated hallucinations, finally sees everyone—Jin, the chauffeur, Yu Yichi, and even himself—eat a baby at a feast on the boat. When he rushes toward the boat, he falls down and drowns in a manure pit.

This main plot is openly claimed to be fictional in the novel, since at the same time the novel has a narrative frame that includes the correspondence between the narrator/author, Mo Yan (who discusses his writing of this novel), and a novice writer, Li Yidou (who regularly sends Mo Yan his own short stories, which are inserted, along with the texts of their correspondence, among the novel's chapters). Although Li Yidou's stories and the main plot are on the same level under the narrative frame and the stories are supposedly irrelevant to the main plot, their narrative objects—characters, circumstances, and even episodes—interfuse the two domains. Thus, the structure of the novel has been organized in an intricate way: the novel not only tells stories but also, at times, refers to the authors' (Mo Yan's and Li Yidou's) considerations about how the stories are told. The novel is not a single story narrated by Mo Yan alone but a multistory text rewritten with the help of Li Yidou, whose stories overlap the main portion, which is presumably narrated by Mo Yan. Furthermore, if Li Yidou's stories are to be taken as mostly real accounts of his mother-in-law, his father-in-law, his wife, and his friend Yu Yichi, Mo Yan's self-conscious writing of this novel not only produces a fictitious, imaginative scene but also organizes a mixture of what did happen, what might have happened, and what will probably happen, insofar as Li Yidou is incessantly bringing "real life" into Mo Yan's fictional production.

This last observation is based on the assumption that Jiuguo is not only the actual town that Li Yidou resides in and writes about but also the presumably fictitious location in which Mo Yan's novel takes place. This is probably too puzzling to apprehend at first glance: how can it be possible to regard something as both real and unreal within the same fictional text? The paradox here, in essence, reveals the problematics of representation as such, as I shall elaborate on later. The practical answer I am tempted to give in this particular context is that the narrative complexity of being both real and unreal cannot be fully understood unless we deal with the text in terms of different levels—multistory in the original sense—in which the name Mo Yan has different functions. On the intratextual level, although the novel may have begun before Mo Yan receives Li Yidou's first letter, it seems appropriate to assume that the novel is, more or less, an echo to Li Yidou's stories, since there are characters and events that overlap and connect to each other (Yu Yichi, e.g., occurs on both levels). I am by no means suggesting, however, that it is Li Yidou who inspires Mo Yan's novel because, after all, on the ultratextual level we must admit that Li Yidou is but another character created by Mo Yan, the author of the novel, who makes himself seemingly independent from Mo Yan, the narrator of the main story. This expedient analytical distinction between Mo Yan the author and Mo Yan the narrator (or the character in the novel as narrator) may well expose the secret of the novel's intricacy yet may also shatter its charm, since the structural irony is certainly intended to show the inseparability of Mo Yan the narrator and Mo Yan the author. The predicament of Mo Yan the narrator and that of Mo Yan the author mirror each other. It is only in this sense that the novel can be seen as not only an outward critique of sociopolitical reality but also the author's inward self-critique of subjective (un)consciousness.

While it is, in regard to its reference to historically critical significance, a harsh criticism of the decay and violence of social existence during the present time, the novel is, formalistically and ultimately, also an allegory of the development—or, more exactly, of the developing obscurity or chaos—of historical consciousness, which is exposed and explored as a self-involved subject in its interrogation of the historical object. Even though the epistolary dialogue between Li Yidou (whose undisciplined style is both immature and maverick) and Mo Yan (who frequently criticizes Li's stylistic unbalance and disorganization) can be regarded as an allegorical dialogue between ego and superego, the clear levels of psychic structure are ultimately unrecognizable, since Mo Yan's style itself is actually no more sober than Li Yidou's and eventually, at the end of the novel, turns into an entropy of drunken ravings.[2] Therefore, the primary parallel is between the journey of the plot and the narrative journey, each of which displays an allegory of decadent subjects who poorly serve their historical functions.

The Journey of Ding Gouer / Mo Yan: An Allegory of Subjective Disintegration

In his introduction to *The Republic of Wine* Chou Ying-hsiung suggests an intertextual connection between Mo Yan's novel and *The Journey to the West* as some chapters of the latter also deal with eating babies. Among the numerous links connecting the two novels, however, the structural-thematic one seems less obvious but as important. Cannibalism, a theme shared by the two novels, as Chou has noticed, is an evil to be eradicated by means of a journey. In *The Journey to the West* Tripitaka and his disciples are sent far away and must pass through eighty-one adversities, most of which have to do with demonic cannibals, to fetch the Buddhist scriptures. In *The Republic of Wine* Ding Gouer, who is dispatched to investigate a horrible crime concerning cannibalism, undergoes a number of unrelated misfortunes. The two journeys differ from each other qualitatively: the Buddhist quest in *The Journey to the West* is primarily a journey that ascends to the divine realm; the detective mission of Ding Gouer, on the other hand, has to descend to the most degenerate world to reveal diabolism. Notwithstanding its claims toward justice, Ding Gouer's journey goes through a great degree of debauchery—adultery, inebriety, and gluttony.

If the adversities in *The Journey to the West* finally lead to a triumphant or at least comic ending, the carnal, dissolute pleasures depicted in *The Republic of Wine* are a prelude to the absurd—certainly not tragic—failure of Ding Gouer's supposedly righteous mission. This is the significance of Ding Gouer's sinking into the manure pit in which "all the imaginable dirty things" inundate the "ideal, justice, dignity, honor, love, and all such kinds of sacred things" Ding may have had in mind (383). Indeed, Ding Gouer's anti- or mock-heroic journey is an ironic rewriting of traditional Chinese fiction, such as *The Journey to the West*, in which we can at least find a naughty and pleasant hero such as Monkey (Sun Wukong), who, by means of either his own or the gods' power, extricates everyone from various plights.

In this sense what *The Republic of Wine* narrates is a journey without a heroic, unyielding pioneer such as Monkey, and it therefore becomes a catachrestic retelling of an archetypal journey story. Here catachresis lies in the fact that the missing agent of a correspondent function permanently remains blank, since Ding Gouer, in terms of his character, can well be considered a variation of Pig (Zhu Bajie) in *The Journey to the West*, who is easily tempted by, and then incurably indulges in, carnal pleasure while at the same time being placed in the position of Monkey, who is entrusted with a mission and required to play a crucial role in reaching the goal. The split identity, or the rift between the actual and the nominal, is where the absurdity lies. Obviously, Ding is a character who never functions as he should: his continuous involvement with the female chauffeur makes his real intentions regarding his journey blurred or even completely forgotten and puts him in awkward dilemmas from time to time. Moreover, his participation in the—at least perceptually/conceptually even if not factually—cannibalistic feast hosted by the suspects he is supposed to investigate decisively switches his role from that of a detective of the crime to that of an accessory to the crime.

In the final chapter of *The Journey to the West* the "five saints" have accomplished their mission and are conferred with the title of Buddha, which positively signals their achievement. Ding Gouer, however, eventually becomes a victim, without a tragic halo. The journeys in both novels are full of temptations. If *The Journey to the West* expresses the victory of the lucid mind—with wisdom, faith, and virtue—over bewitching temptations, *The Republic of Wine* presents a temporal journey through which wisdom, faith, and virtue become disordered and destroyed. In fact, Ding Gouer is so confounded that he not only loses his ability to disclose the true picture of the crime forever but also, as a result of his own immoral behavior, is compelled to give up the task he was designated to undertake. A number of ironic moments in the novel make Ding Gouer's journey seem more and more ridiculous: when his adultery with the chauffeur is discovered by her husband, Jin Gangzuan, Ding Gouer's role as detective and Jin Gangzuan's role as criminal are almost interchanged; then, as Ding Gouer shoots the chauffeur and her lover, Yu Yichi, and flees, his role shifts from that of a crime hunter to that of a wanted criminal; finally, as he is about to catch the cannibals red-handed, Ding Gouer falls into the manure pit.

The disclosure of decadence in the stylistic sense and decline in the historical sense calls into question the progressive chronology that stands as the basis of the dominant idea of enlightenment. Mo Yan's idea of decline was expressed as early as in his first novel *Red Sorghum*, in which a family romance seems to conclude by reversing the Marxist agenda of social development: To compare "my grandparents," described as ancestors with unmatchable energy and courage, with "me," "a body immersed so long in the filth of urban life that a foul stench oozed from my pores," actually proves the existence of "two separate human races" (*Red Sorghum* 356–57). This reflection on *degeneration* in the strict sense becomes, in *The Republic of Wine*, a direct manifestation of individual and collective depravity in modern times. The depraved journey of Ding Gouer suggests the impossibility of salvation by human power, which would only lead to more severe and absurd disasters.

In a parody of the hermeneutical/practical search for truth, Ding Gouer's identity as a *zhenchayuan* (detective) may remind us of one of the most famous heroes, from the model opera *Zhiqu Weihushan* (Taking Tiger Mountain by strategy)—Yang Zirong—another *zhenchayuan* (scout), to whom the final chapter of *The Republic of Wine* refers, not emphatically but notably, in the middle of Mo Yan's drunken ravings (*Jiuguo* 414). Representing the Communist Party, Yang Zirong is the savior who expels the evil forces (bandits) and brings the oppressed people emancipation. Ding Gouer, in contrast, is dispatched by the party-controlled procuratorate to expose a horrible iniquity, falls into numerous traps, and even becomes a participant in the brutality. It seems that Ding is consciously being made to oppose Yang Zirong when Mo Yan writes, "Someone is heading toward the morning sun, while he [Ding] toward the setting sun." (380). If Yang Zirong, as his famous aria "I Have the Morning Sun in My Heart" expresses, has great confidence in achieving his goal (Shanghai jingjutuan *Zhiqu Weihushan* 52), Ding is but a clown who, in the final scene of the novel, does not even have an assured destination he wants to reach: "He stands listlessly toward the setting sun, thinking for a long time, without clearly knowing what he is thinking" (380). In this sense Ding Gouer, an effete detective who invalidates the symbolic ascension of history, is the negative image of the historical savior who is unable to bring forward progressive temporality but is doomed, instead, to degenerate into the bloody or stinky darkness in which he himself becomes irredeemable.

In any case the novel could have been produced as a work of critical realism if the journey of Ding Gouer were truly represented as pure corruption and the behavior of Jin Gangzuan, Yu Yichi, and the like as sheer evil.³ The narrative frame, however, avoids the identification of narrative with representation. When the process of representation itself is depicted, the novel deals not only with the detective journey of Ding Gouer but also with the narrative journey of Mo Yan. Ultimately, it shows Mo Yan's feebleness in his attempt to continue the novel when he feels his character uncontrollable (299). Then the narrative journey turns into an essential journey that parallels and mimics Ding Gouer's journey. At the trickiest moment Mo Yan enters the narrative frame as a character in the final chapter of the novel. He visits Ding Gouer's Jiuguo, the real town, and participates in the feast with the real Jin Gangzuan (exactly what Ding Gouer does in fiction, except that no cooked baby is offered). More significantly, Mo Yan's repetition (or imitation) of Ding Gouer's drunkenness—in his long monologue Mo Yan actually realizes that he gets "drunk to death in Jiuguo just like Ding Gouer Ding Gouer is my shadow" (416)—ends the novel, leading us to conclude that their respective projects are equally depraved: to be drunk, or to lose the mental and physical ability to rescue oneself or others, is probably the sole truth achievable.

The novel has thus a double implication of allegory: the unrealizability of a critical historical subject and the unrealizability of a critical representational subject. If Ding plays an unsuccessful role of historical justice, Mo Yan, similarly, challenges his own role as an omnipotent representational subject who is supposed to exhaust the secret of reality and reveal the ultimate historical truth. It is in an equivocal, or even incomprehensible, way that the narrative conceptualizes such characters as Ding Gouer (whose social responsibility is as strong as his personal carnality) and Jin Gangzuan (whose conduct, whether it be seen as depraved or noble, is finally indeterminable). Likewise, the eventual uncertainty about the actuality of the crime of eating real baby flesh demonstrates the extreme difficulty or problem of realism: the limitations of the critical subject are exposed in order to question the absolute omnipotence of the representational subject. Against the narrative paradigm of modern Chinese fiction, which assumes a monologic, totalizing voice—a voice that struggles to be incontestable in its offering of a seamless picture of the narrative object—Mo Yan's narrative dismantles the unified superficialities of such a voice by divulging the disjunctions and discrepancies of his narrative.

Fleshly Excess: Dipsomania, Polyphagia, and Cannibalism

Mo Yan's self-reflexive examination of the narrative subject, however, does not dispense with sociocultural critique. His narrative is a self-critique that consists in a cultural critique, insofar as the narrator is involved in the same sociocultural background as his own narrative. In the novel sociocultural critique focuses on the decadent lifestyle, in which wine is the major medium.

As the title suggests, wine seems to serve as a dynamic *spirit* for the development of the characters as well as of the narrative. In the realm of wine, or the Republic of Wine, wine plays a decisive role in social life. Nevertheless, the social function of wine is paradoxical. Mo Yan seems to be clearly aware of this fact, as he says in a letter to Li Yidou: "The relationship between human beings and wine includes almost all the contradictions as well as the contradictory aspects in the process of the existence and development of mankind" (166). On the one hand, wine is able to draw people, by way of intoxication, out of real, normal, rational life and bring them into the fantastic, aberrant, irrational domain. In *Red Sorghum* Mo Yan manifests the emancipatory dimension of intoxication. Wine is consumed as a source of courage to enable the drinker to break social fetters or to fight against foreign invaders. Intoxication triggers the primary desire that expels the repressive domination of civilization. On the other hand, temporary insanity through intoxication can also bring about loss of self-consciousness, enabling the drinker to be totally manipulated by external—ostensibly natural but essentially human or social—forces. Intoxication in *The Republic of Wine* can hardly be read as an active, autonomous activity; it is, rather, a passive, heteronomous behavior that signals the disappearance of self-consciousness. Thus, in contrast to Yu Zhan'ao ("my grandpa") in *Red Sorghum,* Ding Gouer and Mo Yan in *The Republic of Wine* are victims of wine. Although reluctantly, they join the dipsomaniac community in which both social order and individual integrity are dissolved. After being intoxicated at Jin Gangzuan's feast, Ding Gouer, as an allegorically degenerative descendant of Yu Zhan'ao, loses his integrative personal identity: the narrative oscillates between first person and third person because Ding Gouer cannot control his physical parts with his consciousness (105). Wine as a source of pleasure or gallantry turns into a source of moral decadence or historical decline.

Decadence does not simply connote social evil but contains the human desire for pleasure. Mo Yan's social critique aims at not only the crime but also the enjoyment, particularly in this novel, of what can be called gastronomy, in which drinking, especially collective drinking, plays a significant role. As part of the cultural legacy of Chinese tradition, gastronomy in *The Republic of Wine* becomes the allegorical epitome of the cultural decadence of contemporary China. Gastronomy, the excessive love of unusual taste, entraps Ding Gouer in an awkward situation: at Jin Gangzuan's feast, for example, extraordinary flavor makes him unable to reject the attraction of the baby flesh and draws him into drunkenness, during which his clothes are stripped off and his belongings are stolen. Along these lines the novel can be regarded as a stylistically excessive exposé—a theme to which I shall return later—of the excesses of desire, which are the essence of decadence.

Adultery, like gastronomy, can be characterized as excessive. In this novel Ding Gouer, a married man, has a love affair with the female chauffeur, Jin Gangzuan's wife, who also flirts with other men. It is this love affair that brings Ding to ridiculous circumstances: he is caught by Jin Gangzuan while making love with Jin's wife and is then chased by the police after killing Jin's wife and her lover, Yu Yichi, out of envy. (Just as sarcastically, Yu Yichi, the midget, "President of the City Association of Individual Owners, Provincial Model Worker, General Manager of Yichi Wineshop, probationary member of the Chinese Communist Party, has had sexual relations with twenty-nine of Jiuguo's beauties" [229], of whom the chauffeur is the ninth.) In fact, sexual excess here is not only characterized by adultery but even by the way of making love. From the very beginning Ding and the chauffeur's mutual seduction is far from romantic but full of vehemence, even savagery. When Ding asks for a kiss, the chauffeur "suddenly flushed scarlet and roared with a loud voice as if wrangling: 'Let me give you a fucking kiss!'" (3). Later, in her own home, the naked chauffeur conquers Ding by applying a "ground-sweeping kick" from Chinese martial arts to make him "fall backward on the carpet with his hands and legs in the air" and then "leaped onto his belly, snatched his ears with her hands, and rammed him with her buttocks up and down" (202). Here excessive lust is defined not only quantitatively but also qualitatively: Its qualities are inverted, so, rather than being sensuous, it is repulsive.[4]

By the same token, the stunning effect of the novel does not come merely from the descriptions of excessive indulgence in sex and eating. From adultery, violence, and atrocity arise: the *crime passionel* that Ding Gouer commits is a logical outcome of promiscuous romance. And it is from gastronomy that scatology and cannibalism are derived. In this sense scatology and cannibalism are the most ironic variations of the excessiveness of gastronomy. Gastronomy must also be defined not only quantitatively but also qualitatively as abnormal eating, including eating animals' genitals or human flesh. Thus, if Sun Lung-kee's observation of the "oral proclivity" and "anal proclivity" of Chinese culture—by which he means the indulgence in eating and the shameless exhibition of bodily or, metaphorically, mental filth (Sun 81–93)—is germane to the society in *The Republic of Wine*, Mo Yan seems to suggest that the anal proclivity is but an organic part of the oral proclivity. The novel presents, via Li Yidou's description, a "whole-donkey feast" in Yichi Wineshop that contains a dish beautifully called "Dragon and Phoenix Displaying Prosperity" (*longfeng chengxiang*)—in fact, the genitals of a male and a female donkeys. Obviously, Mo Yan is clearly aware of the risque, reprobate, brazen pith within the gloriously packaged culture—"gastronomic" culture, in particular here.

Certainly, the most shocking theme in *The Republic of Wine* is cannibalism, described in scenes such as eating babies at a feast, selling babies to a food research center, and teaching in a classroom how to cook a human baby's flesh. In *The Republic of Wine* cannibalism is a sign of a surplus of food, rather than its lack. Cannibalism is practiced neither at a time of famine nor even out of an impulse to feast on the flesh of foes but simply for gustatory pleasure or excitement. At the same time, gastronomy is claimed to have a morally oriented import, just as it is conventionally concealed under the social order and moral limit. In many instances in his *Analects*—in the chapter "Village-Communities" (*Xiangdang*), for instance—Confucius strongly propounds the correlation between the quality of food making / consumption and the propriety of social conduct. This theme recurs in a parodic variation in Li Yidou's "Donkey Street":

> Why does man have a mouth? Just for eating and drinking! It's necessary to let people who come to our Jiuguo eat well and drink well. Let them achieve something out of eating, bring about delight out of eating, and get into habit of eating. Let them achieve something out of drinking, bring about delight out of drinking and get into habit of drinking. Let them understand that eating and drinking are not only for preserving life, but, through the movement of eating and drinking, for experiencing the true taste of life, for realizing the philosophy of life. Let them know that eating and drinking are not only a process of biological movement, but also that of spiritual edification, of aesthetic appreciation. (170)

It is this ostentatious cultural facade that *The Republic of Wine* intends to unmask. In the novel the city Jiuguo is in perfect order, while it is also a perfectly perverse community. The horrible fact is that, according to Li Yidou's account, babies are willfully conceived and procreated only in order to be sold to the Culinary College as meat. It is truly astounding as we see, in Li Yidou's "The Meaty Baby," the traditional order of small-scale production being developed to an evil climax. Even maternal love degenerates into care about the price of a baby's meat: when Xiaobao (a baby for sale) cries because he has been bathed in hot water and beaten by his father, his mother becomes anxious only because beating and hot water could mar his skin and decrease the price she could fetch for him. Here the peasant class that makes a living out of selling babies as meat really serves as the mass basis for the whole cannibalistic society. This scene is highly allegorical: cannibalism cannot be imputed to only the few people with political power, who perform visible vice; rather, it should be recognized that every cultural agent is an accomplice to this social malady.

The homogeneity between gastronomy and cannibalism is satanically presented in Li Yidou's story "A Culinary Class," in which "my mother-in-law," a professor at the Culinary College, teaches how to butcher human babies for cooking. The rational, orderly form of the class seems to embody both the great didactic tradition in Chinese culture and the scientific pattern of modern civilization. The content of the class, however, serves inhumanity: it is for the sake of gastronomy that modern scientific methods are used for barbarian sacrifice. At this point the tension between civilization and barbarism may disappear, as long as we clearly see that gastronomy, in the name of science and civilization, is itself has an affinity with cannibalism, which is supposedly attributed only to barbarism. Decadence can thus be categorized not only as an excess of desire but also as a necessary inversion of desire that may be viewed as a corollary of the excessiveness of civilization, despite the fact that civilization is developed presumably to serve human desire. If the development of civilization becomes nothing but the excess or intemperance of civilization, barbarism is shown as both a consummation and a parody of civilization. In any case Mo Yan does not accuse the potential malady in the collective mind as a pure and determinable malignancy; rather, he displays the perverse scene within the category of delight and pleasure, as contained in gastronomy.

An analysis of the gastronomic theme in *The Republic of Wine* would be incomplete without referring to the same or related themes implied in other post-Mao literary works prior to the appearance of this novel as well as in traditional Chinese fiction. From this point of view it may be useful to take a look at the different attitudes toward eating—manifest or potential—in *The Republic of Wine* and the works of the early and mid-1980s, such as Lu Wenfu's "Meishijia" (The gourmet, 1983), Ah Cheng's "The Chess King," and Liu Heng's "Gouri de liangshi" (Damned grain, 1986). Eating, as suggested by Ah Cheng in "The Chess King," should at best be regarded as the most natural human behavior, which conforms to one's original mind, and thus something in resistance to political exaction and oppression. Ah Cheng's "acultural" approach to eating is culturally derived from the spirit of Chan (Zen) Buddhism and Taoism, which could be served as an analgesic tablet to alleviate the reflective pain from the Cultural Revolution. On the other hand, in "Damned Grain" Liu Heng expresses a desire for food in an era of poverty or famine. Again, food is symbolically treated as a cultural object, presently void yet eager to be filled and accomplished, inherent in the collective mind. In both cases gastronomic culture is dealt with in a negative way but functions toward a positive potential: in "The Chess King" a refutation of gastronomic culture—that is, the most primitive and natural way of eating—is described as a transcendental mode of life; in "Damned Grain," on the other hand, food destitution, as the antithesis of gastronomy, is realistically delineated and symbolically treated as the central problem of Chinese civilization, a problem to be negated by the act of writing (if not by social practice).

The most pertinent of the three works mentioned here is "The Gourmet," Lu Wenfu's novella published in the beginning of 1983. It represents the affirmative and optimistic perspective of culture that permeated China in the early 1980s. In this novella Lu carefully—in almost a strained manner—insinuates the cultural significance of Chinese gastronomy by describing the various experiences of a gourmet, Zhu Ziye, throughout the history of the People's Republic in order to sketch out a diagram of cultural rises and falls parallel to different sociopolitical periods. To a large extent Zhu Ziye is not only a cultural sign who represents the magnificent Chinese oral stage but also a barometer of the political climate that gauges the happiness or sorrow of the common people—which is boiled down to the pleasures or lack of palate satisfaction. History and gustatory pleasure are oddly correlated here in order to proffer the hope for an ideal society full of, or even ruled by, gourmets, if not gluttons. Apparently, the social critique in this work, which could have penetrated more profoundly into the (in)significance of pure eating in political agitation, ultimately gives way to cultural essentialism, which leads to euphoria in retaining national, collective pleasure. *The Republic of Wine*, as we have seen, is intended to interrupt this euphoria by inserting an exceedingly cacophonous tone into the enjoyable cultural melody. It is a warning against cultural optimism that, flourishing since the mid-1980s, fails to see the dissonance within the cultural entity as a real historical formation but perceives it as an abstract spiritual or sensual phenomenon.

The fictional exhibition of Chinese gastronomic culture can probably be traced back to *The Plum in the Golden Vase* and *The Story of the Stone*, encyclopedic novels containing abundant scenes of feasts and parties as well as countless references to excessive eating. These descriptions can be compared to the "whole-donkey feast" in *The Republic of Wine*, whose kinship to *Plum in the Golden Vase* and *The Story of the Stone* lies in the fact that in all three novels the scenes of spree are not represented as isolated spectaculars but are arranged as foreshadows, at various levels, of structural decline. Indeed, *The Republic of Wine* has a divergent intensity that causes the carnivalesque orgy to swerve and become a carnivorous/cannibalistic farce. *Plum in the Golden Vase* and *The Story of the Stone* do not go as far in insinuating the fall from gastronomy into cannibalism as does *The Journey to the West,* in which gastronomic cannibalism is a haunting theme—while the purpose of immortality is contained in the concept of gastronomy—as Chou Ying-hsiung remarks. It is then legitimate for Li Yidou to categorize some of his own stories as "cruel realism" or "demonic realism," since they do have a close connection with the "cruel" and "demonic" characteristics of *The Journey to the West.* In *The Journey to the West* Tripitaka's flesh is from time to time on the verge of being eaten by demons because it is both delicious and immortalizing, and so is that of children. The reference to the eating of children is of greater significance here because of its relevance to *The Republic of Wine.* In *The Journey to the West* (chaps. 77–78) it is repeatedly mentioned that eating the flesh of children, or the hearts and livers of children, would greatly enhance longevity, which is, as a nutritional aspect, an important part of Chinese gastronomy.

Both *The Republic of Wine* and *The Journey to the West* can be read as histories against cannibalism, as can another magnum opus standing between the two, namely, Lu Xun's "A Madman's Diary." In *The Journey to the West* it is Monkey's task to "save the children" and prevent his master from being eaten by various demons and monsters. In *The Republic of Wine,* however, neither Ding Gouer nor Li Yidou is able to rescue society from cannibalism. Although Li Yidou is conscious of his story "The Meaty Baby" being another version of "A Madman's Diary" in a new era, he cannot help having an abnormal love affair with his mother-in-law, a young-looking and attractive—a benefit of her having gained more nutrition because of her gastronomic/cannibalistic privilege—professor at the Culinary College who invents the special culinary arts for baby meat and thus is one of the prime culprits in the cannibal community. Ding Gouer, seeing the baby on the feast table, is rationally reluctant but sensually tempted: after being told that it is not a real boy, "he picks up a piece from the arm, closes his eyes, and puts it into his mouth. Oh, my god. The taste buds on his tongue hail together; the biting muscle of his cheek twitches; then a little hand stretches out of his throat and takes away that piece" (100). Different from Lu Xun's Madman, who is haunted by the paranoid fear of being eaten, Ding Gouer encounters the cannibalistic community with an inconsistent, schizophrenic attitude. He is, after all, neither an adversary against nor a victim of that community but a participant in it. Unlike Lu Xun's Madman, he is ignorant not of his participation but of his guilt.

Even *The Journey to the West* has ironic moments throughout its narrative development (cf. Plaks 183–276, 504–12). The most notable fact is that the heroic Monkey's own power, always limited, is largely dependent on the succor of Bodhisattva, who eventually extinguished cannibalistic evils and salvaged the people from jeopardy. In "A Madman's Diary," as I described it in the introduction, if the realistic representation of the Madman's psychology is to be read as the record of a real paranoid, representation and paranoia are equated to allegorize the problematic desire of modernity that totalizes and conceptualizes: the fear of being eaten as a psychic illusion or a paranoid misinterpretation that problematizes the steady outward accusation pronounced by the Madman (or by Lu Xun, as he has hitherto been interpreted).

Being aware of an ultimate predicament of the project of modernity that attempts to totalize cannibalistic social history, Mo Yan abandons any teleological perspective and does not impute cannibalism to threatening from outside. Ding Gouer's or Li Yidou's easy inclination to be absorbed by the cannibalistic community implies that the most severe danger is not tangible barbarism but, rather, *the inaccessibility or unrecognizability of barbarism and the ignorance of the potentiality for barbarism in oneself.* In other words, cannibalism, or any other collective or social barbarism, should be first of all traced *individually* and *inwardly,* in a self-deconstructive way. In *The Republic of Wine,* obviously, the attempt to eliminate cannibalism turns out to lead to participation in cannibalism. Lu Xun's Madman feels guilty for his possible participation in eating his sister and thus unyieldingly calls for resistance against the society that has deceived him, whereas Ding Gouer is completely ignorant of his sin throughout his journey until right before he clownishly falls into the manure pit, when he is about to lose his chance to "save the children" forever, and "sees lots of famiiiar faces, one of which is even the very image of his own" (382), from around the table of the cannibalistic feast on the boat. This ironic fact is sufficient to indicate the invalidity of searching the criminals outwardly. As the epigraph (from Ding Gouer's epitaph) of the novel says: "In this chaotic and corrupt age, my brothers, do not bring our own brothers to trial."

Therefore, it can be inferred that the one who may be brought to trial is oneself, as one of the cannibals in a fraternal community.

An equally remarkable passage is found in Li Yidou's short piece "An Infant Prodigy," in which an elf becomes the leader of an infant rebellion against the cannibals. The scene may be read allegorically as a depiction of the finally crushed student movement—the elf even appeals by staging a hunger strike (126)[5]—or of any historical event that is affirmatively categorized as revolution or resistance. Nevertheless, the elf is not described as a historical hero. Instead, he is another tyrant who forcefully and artfully establishes his patriarchal position among the infants and then forbids his subjects to speak whenever he speaks, a true ruffian who does barbarous things such as biting the ear off a subject who does not obey him or, even more brutally, digging out the eyeballs of adult enemies (members of the cannibalistic community) with his fingers. Again, astonishingly, Mo Yan reveals not only the barbarism of the antagonists of barbarism (Ding Gouer as a detective, Li Yidou as a critical writer) but also the barbarism of the victims of barbarism (the elf and his infant subjects, Yuanbao and his wife). Self-trial, or self-reflection, becomes the ultimate illation of the novel, since, as the self-referential structure suggests, no one can evade responsibility for a cannibalistic society: when you count the convicts, you must find that there is always an extra one, which is yourself—just as in the image Ding Gouer identifies before his death.

Discursive Plethora

In *The Republic of Wine* Mo Yan provides a kaleidoscopic scene of degenerate language in which we can discern that "random talk, balderdash, jokes, and digressions from various branches are actually more readable than the main trunk of the story" (D. Wang, "Chihelasa"). In accordance with the behavioral dissipation in the novel, the plethora of high-toned discourse is probably more noticeable. In this regard the stylistic decadence serves as the decisive factor that forms the deconstructive power of rhetoric.

The crucial issue here becomes the decadence of discourse. The dish, called "Dragon and Phoenix Displaying Prosperity," not only indicates the scatological content within the gastronomic culture, but it also reveals the ironic essence of traditional symbolic discourse. This is clearly not what Li Yidou calls "transforming great ugliness into great beauty"—"dragon and phoenix as the solemn totem of our nation, the symbol of supreme loftiness, supreme sanctity and supreme beauty" (192)—but, on the contrary, extracting great ugliness out of great beauty. Here Li Yidou's misapplication of the idiom *qingzhunanshu* (193), meaning "too numerous to list or record" but referring only to inexpiable crimes or sins, to indicate the lavish connotations of the dragon-phoenix symbol is notable since it manages to divulge the secrets behind the symbolic discourse.

Not far from slips of the tongue or slips of the pen, the novice writer's misuse of the idiom can also be regarded as being unconsciously intended to imply the flagrant significance of symbolic discourse. Then the derogatory idiom and the splendid symbol, both originally discursive, mutually level their discursiveness in the clashing moment. For Mo Yan the author, in any case, this deterioration of language suggests disbelief and rejection of the dominance of seemingly rational discourse, despite the fact that he himself may not be able to utterly flee from it, after all. One may notice, in most of the novel, that the prevalence of discourse, particularly Maoist discourse, becomes so excessive that it can never convey the sense of its self-assumed object. In Li Yidou's story "Alcohol," for instance, the description of the young Jin Gangzuan (who becomes the leading cannibal in the ensuing chapters) is full of idiomatic clichés and incongruous eulogies that display the dissipated rubbish of Maoist discourse:

> Every mountain every river every grass every wood awakes our veneration for Vice-Minister Jin: what a cordial emotion it is. Think about it; it is from this barren and shabby village that a wine star rose slowly to shine on the Republic of Wine, a star whose radiance would dazzle our eyes and make our eyes brim with tears, our hearts surge like waves, a ragged cradle was also a cradle, nothing could replace it, to estimate according to current situation, Vice-Minister Jin's future would be unlimited, . . . When miseries and joys, loves and dreams in his childhood . . . long-windedly and free-flowingly welled up in his mind, what mental attitude did he have? How was his pace? How was his countenance? Did he move his left foot or right foot first when walking? In what position was his left hand when he was moving his right foot? What odor was in his mouth and how was his blood pressure? The speed of his heart-

beat? Did he show his teeth or not when he was smiling? Did his forehead wrinkle when he was crying? The portrayable things are too many and the words in my belly are too few. (36–37)

Obviously, such a text of ostensible parody erodes Maoist discourse by its overabundant nonsense consisting in presumed seriousness. By the same token the "lyricized" narrative must be highly problematic if something horrid is secretly or patently going on simultaneously. The office building of the cannibals, for example, is located in a paradisiac garden in which there are "sunflowers all facing the sun" (a typical cliché in communist literature) and the "special, sweet and intoxicant odor of birch" (22); even the meaty baby market is situated in an environment with a fountain, pond, and chirping birds in which Jin Yuanbao, who is going to sell his baby, feels "as if stepping into the elysium, my every cell is shivering with happiness" (85). After the baby is sold at a special rate, Jin Yuanbao "was extremely excited and tears almost rushed out of his eyes" (89). The cliché is naturally reminiscent of the scene in *On the Docks* in which Ma Hongliang sees the renovated dock with "tears of joy [springing] to [his] eyes" (see chap. 6). Overstatement is thus unveiled as the essential function of Maoist discourse. When such a strongly discursive style is implanted in a completely different context, however, its consistent power is seriously deteriorated. Therefore, as it occurs against the background of cannibalism, Maoist discourse becomes truly tempting and appalling at the same time.

If, according to Marx, the surplus value of commodities reveals the ironic digression of labor from genuine, creative production, then the surplus value of discourse suggests the ironic diversion of language from truth. Overstatement is a rhetorical device that characterizes the surplus value of discourse. On the whole this novel is a ceaselessly hyperplastic narrative that produces and reproduces numerous ungraspable elements of the master discourse that can never fit the objective reality the novel is presumed to represent. On the other hand, it is *discursive reality* that Mo Yan is tackling: the limitless proliferation of discourse is manifested as the formative basis of the decline of history.

A sensitive seizure of the decline of history can be found in the novel as sensibility to the decline of discourse, that is, the decadence of discourse, the fever or proliferation caused by the lethal virus of discourse. When the grandiose feature of Maoist discourse has degenerated into high-toned nonsense, into barbarous mendacity, it becomes at one and the same time too feeble and too outrageous: it is too feeble because it does not have the true power to grasp objective reality; it is too outrageous because it has the ideological superiority to impose upon or attract its receptors.

The most perplexing fact in the novel is that it is never clear whether the baby that Jin Gangzuan and Ding Gouer eat together at the feast is an actual human baby or an imitation one. Here Mo Yan touches upon the most profound level of writing: the difficulty or impossibility of representation. When a feast of affirmatively real baby is not shown to us, the simple representation of the crime is shifted to the representation of the unrepresentability of the crime. This is an intentional flaw that Jean-François Lyotard would call "bad form," which "denies itself the solace of good forms" ("Answering" 81), a necessary inconsistency, which can never be developed to a higher phase, which can never be simply negated, eliminated, or prohibited in order to easily reach a positively flawless realm.

There is a permanent danger, therefore, in believing that reality can be totally represented and evil can be turned away. It is quite obvious in the novel that discourse is superficially in opposition to the activity of cannibalism, while at the same time it can only, in the final analysis, pervert or falsify the crime. On the one hand, it claims its justice against cannibalism—as Jin Gangzuan alleges with the party's tenet (94)—in order to perform the crime; on the other hand, however, it attempts to contain cannibalism in its own domain—as Li Yidou's mother-in-law expounds in her culinary class (268–69). In fact, as far as discourse is concerned, this inconsistency occurs steadily throughout the whole novel and throughout the history of twentieth-century China. As long as discourse has a privileged mechanism of concealment and displacement, historical truth is consistently inconsistent because it can never be realistically revealed within such an organized system of discourse. Then narrative has to turn back to itself: to demonstrate its own discursiveness and, above all, its own failure to recognize the truth within discourse.

This is what metanarrative means. And this is also why metanarrative must be understood as antinarrative, or self-disruptive narrative, since it is a narrative conscious of its own limit, its own difficulty, rather than its omnipotence, of representation. When reality is incommensurable—that is, unable to be grasped in the norm of discourse—it is only the incommensurability that can remind us of the permanent danger in reality. The ultimate danger lies in the incapability of dealing with reality, because the gap between reality and the desire to embrace it is blocked by discourse. Within this idea of incommensurability lies Lyotard's concept of the sublime as an odd mixture of pleasure and pain: it is from the painful element—the awareness of incomprehensibility, the destiny of misrepresentation—that we can get a sense of pleasure. As a matter of fact, this novel is at the same time horrible and comical, as Chou Ying-hsiung remarks at the very end of his introduction to it: "terrible, enjoyable" (xi). The pleasure is derived from the downfall, the invalidity, or the collapse of discourse, which, while still torturing our consciousness, is also fragmented in self-consciousness. In his elucidation of the sublime Lyotard stresses its difference from sublimation: sublimation still tends to evade the irreconcilability between reality and consciousness and therefore contains a nostalgic utopia. Here lies the distinction between *Red Sorghum* and *The Republic of Wine*. In *Red Sorghum* the unrepresentable is what Lyotard calls "the missing contents" ("Answering" 81): even the barbarous or the savage could be turned into something tragic and thus positive. In *The Republic of Wine* the real atrocity becomes something perpetually ungraspable: it is always recognized as something discursive, so much so that everyone, in the name of its grandiosity, is compelled—or, more precisely, lured—to participate in the brutal history without being able to extricate themselves from it.

To Mo Yan an outward critique of objective social history is feasible only when there is an inward critique of the narrative subject in the first place, that is, a self-critique or self-deconstruction—a subjective self-consciousness about the limitations of objective critique. The critical discourse of narration in *The Republic of Wine*, as I have analyzed, is exposed as implicated in the same historical crisis and not exempt from critical scrutiny. That is to say, the narration of the novel does not occupy a superior position but opens up its own inadequacy and difficulty in rhetorical excess or narrative irony. The narrative subject in *The Republic of Wine*, like the hero of the novel, does not claim an omniscient power that totalizes history. Thus, the paradigmatic mode of absolute representation in modern Chinese fiction is called into question: representation, in Mo Yan's relentless irony, is shown at the same time as the problematics of representation. Nevertheless, Mo Yan's conception of the problematics of representation does not lead to an absolute cancellation of representation but to an exposé of apertures in the process of representation, and thus it implies not an epistemological nihilism but a historical subject that is simultaneously aware of its own pitfalls or a transcendental subject that is paradoxically aware of the impasse of transcendence.

Postscript

Answering the Question

What Is the Postmodern/ Post–Mao-Deng?

If Adorno's aphorism "To write poetry after Auschwitz is barbaric" (*Prisms* 34) epitomizes the crisis of modernity that Europe faced in the post–World War II era, the Cultural Revolution marks both the culmination and the abyss of modernity in China. The Holocaust ended the belief in a rational, progressive world history that the Hegelian-Marxist theory envisioned. The Cultural Revolution, too, both consummated and undermined the project of Chinese modernity,[1] which had exposed itself not only as an utmost pursuit for historical progress and social perfection but also as a striking presentation of the ruin of the grand History. The Cultural Revolution, like the Holocaust, defied any rational interpretation, for it blends grandiose discourses and atrocious realities that went far beyond reason. The simultaneously attractive and hideous experience of the Cultural Revolution produced the emotional ambivalence that ultimately traumatizes one's rational faculty. The Cultural Revolution, like the Holocaust, shattered subjective integrity in every way, for the Maoist omnipotence of human power, which promised a prosperous future, met with a disastrous outcome that invalidated its original conception. The most profound destruction lies not only in physical victimization but also in psychic traumatization, which deprived the nation of its faith in the historical truth and the ethical good.

If, as David Hirsch suggests, the concept of "postmodern" can be replaced by the "historically rooted term, 'post-Auschwitz'" in the Western context (85), it can also be understood as "post–Cultural Revolution," as far as contemporary China is concerned.[2] Nevertheless, *post–Cultural Revolution* as a historically rooted term in China does not, and cannot, exclude the traumatic experience of other historical events, insofar as the Cultural Revolution was not the only spiritually devastating event in the recent history of China. In the second half of the twentieth century, besides the Cultural Revolution, China has undergone the Anti-Rightist Campaign (1957–58), the Great Leap Forward (1958–60), the Anti-Spiritual Pollution Campaign (1983–84), the Anti-Bourgeois Liberalization Campaign (1987), and the June Fourth Incident (1989) as either preludes or postludes to the Cultural Revolution. The *post–Cultural Revolution,* therefore, is to be conceived not so much as a specific periodization as a term to sum up the general psychohistorical condition of the postcatastrophic China. The imagination of the modern (infinite social progress and infinite subjective capacity) eventually gives way to its own negation or deconstruction.

In his article "Answering the Question: What Is Postmodernism?" Jean-François Lyotard proposes that *"Post modern* would have to be understood according to the paradox of the future *(post)* anterior *(modo)"* ("Answering" 81). Lyotard has repeatedly emphasized the link between the prefix *post-* in the term *postmodern* and the Greek prefix *ana-,* as in *analysis, anamnesis, anagogy,* and *anamorphosis,* i.e., as an evocation of the immemorial. What is immemorial, in the case of postmodernism, seems to be the overpowering, violent modernity. The prefix *post-,* therefore, can well be associated with the German prefix *Nach-,* as in the Freudian concept "Nachträglichkeit," a deferred action that reactivates the traumatic experience of historical violence.[3] The postmodern, in this sense, is to be understood as the modern (the splendid idea fraught with bloody disasters) reactivated as a traumatic memory trace, as a massive psychic burden that has been carried over (the meaning of *tragen* in the term *Nachträglichkeit*) to the present. The ambivalent attitude of attachment and resistance of the concept of *Nachträglichkeit* also implies that Chinese postmodernism does not launch an antagonistic literary movement. Without confronting political oppression from a self-assumed superior position, Chinese postmodernism is an implosion within the modern cultural paradigm, which serves as the basis of political authoritarianism. Chinese postmodernism can also be characterized as postcatastrophic, posttraumatic, post–Cultural Revolution, and post–Mao-Deng.

The dissolution of a rational, omniscient subject in contemporary Chinese fiction attests to the psychohistorical phenomenon of postmodernity that is, as I have shown, comparable to the post-Auschwitz cultural scene in the West. Therefore, my concept of Chinese postmodernism is radically different from, though not irrelevant to, that which has been either welcomed or repudiated over the past few years by Chinese scholars and critics. Chinese postmodernism, as I have elaborated thus far, has more to do with the historical reality of the modern politico-cultural paradigm (sociopolitical totality, grand national imagination, and the discourse of rigid historical teleology are among the most distinctive manifestations) than with the global postmodern civilization. The latter, ironically, has been increasingly utilized by the central authority and successfully integrated into the project of Chinese modernity.

Debates on "Post-*isms*"

Postmodernism was introduced into contemporary Chinese literary criticism in the late 1980s through Fredric Jameson's Beijing University lecture and other translations. But it was not until the early 1990s that postmodernism became a heated topic for debate among Chinese theorists and critics such as Chen Xiaoming, Wang Ning, Xu Ben, Zhang Yiwu, and Zhao Yiheng. Jameson's definition of postmodernism as the cultural logic of late capitalism seems to exhilarate the Chinese critics, who find a new concept corresponding to the market economy–oriented nation-state into which China is transforming itself.[4] The historical scenario from modernity to postmodernity, or from modernism to postmodernism, has replaced the one from capitalism to socialism as the newest variation of Hegelian-Marxian teleology. Jing Wang, despite her perhaps too hasty conclusion that postmodernism is entirely a "pseudoproposition," keenly observes that the postmodern fever is "part of the syndrome of the Great Leap Forward myth" (235). But postmodernity viewed as a sociohistorical, as well as cultural, stage (a higher phase of civilization) that succeeds modernity entails more questions than answer.

Ever since they were first imported into China, such terms as *postmodernity* and *postmodernism* have been befuddling and disconcerting. To many who believe that China has already embarked onto the global market, postmodernity sounds a more than adequate concept to define China's current cultural status. Accordingly, those who do not embrace the term *postmodernism* wholeheartedly base their opinion on the judgment that China does not yet have the necessary sociocultural conditions of postindustrialism or transnational capitalism. From these standpoints postmodernism has been declared either impossible or unquestionable, depending on different assessments of the nature of Chinese society measured by the degree of development of its civilization or its production-distribution mode.

Wang Ning, for example, believes that literary postmodernism in China cannot be considered a major genre, since the socioeconomically underdeveloped China is still a Third World country ("Mapping" 38). Following the official discourse of "four modernizations," he claims that Chinese postmodernism can only be an auxiliary style rather than a dominant trend, because "our country is still situated at the primary stage of socialism and the realization of the four modernizations is still a goal that needs much endeavor" ("Jieshou" 136).[5] Since the chain of evolution requires the development *from modernism to* postmodernism, it is thought to be impossible for those cultures that have not fully developed their modernist literature to cultivate postmodernism. Therefore, Wang Ning expanded this theory beyond China and alleged that "postmodernism could only appear in the West simply because of the specific Western literary tradition and because specific mechanisms of literary evolution. . . . On the other hand, in Oriental and Third World countries, there is no such background of a gradually evolving cultural tradition and an innovation oriented literary convention. . . . [B]ecause of its relations and partial continuity with modernism, the emergence of postmodernism is a 'natural' development in Western culture" ("Constructing" 58–59). The agenda of literary evolution in Wang Ning's theory prevents him from seeing that cultural transformation has its own dialectic that goes beyond the rigid and often hypothetical rule of societal and civilizational progress. Having said all this, nevertheless, Wang Ning carefully admits that Western postmodernism has a great impact on Chinese writers, though he predicts that it is impossible that postmodernism can become a predominant cultural trend in China.[6] This is, I believe, a dilemma for Wang Ning: while still insisting on the previous theoretical assumption, he sees the swift, undeniable cultural transmutations at the end of the millennium. But the cultural transmutations, in fact, had started long before the advent of the globalized civilization.

Based on the same logic, but a different premise, Zhang Yiwu, a critic who deserves credit for provoking enormous discussions concerning postmodernism, reaches almost the opposite conclusion: "the postmodern is a global cultural phenomenon, a condition culturally correspondent to postindustrialization and commercialization that the development of modern society is facing. It not only functions in the First and Second Worlds, but also enters the Third World culture because of the globalized communication and information" ("Lixiangzhuyi" 119). The emphasis on the "culturally correspondent condition" seems to have neglected the Marxist subtext in Jameson, to whom late capitalism is certainly *not* the peak of civilization that many Chinese intellectuals have embraced. In any case, even though Wang Ning and Zhang Yiwu have different perspectives, their theoretical presumptions are close: the Marxist theorem that "the economic base determines the superstructure" remains the potential ideology in the discussion of postmodernism. We have seen that it is from this same perspective that Wang Ning slightly shifts his standpoint in the late 1990s, when, it seems, economic globalization has arrived in China in a rapid and unexpected way.

The question thus lies in whether material civilization or economic level is the determinant factor of the sociocultural formation in contemporary China. It must be noted that, in modern China political powers and events have been holding sway over the entire sociocultural superstructure far more significantly than the development of material civilization, even in the 1990s and beyond. Since the economic policies in China today depend ultimately on the political policies, economic development is not controlled by an "invisible hand" but, rather, largely by the visibly manipulative hand of the party and of the politico-cultural condition created by both the central authority and the citizens.

In the present lexicon of the master discourse, the old concepts such as revolution, emancipation, socialism, and international communism are not replaced by but find their new variations in the new keywords of Chinese modernity such as *commercialization, globalization,* and *transnational capitalism*. I argue that the latter set of terms, far from having dissociated from the revolutionary idea, retains the logic of revolutionary modernity—that is, the radical change and progress of society—so as to justify its legitimacy. As Arif Dirlik and Xudong Zhang have forcefully remarked, "If Chinese society experienced modernity as revolution and socialism, Chinese postmodernity is to be grasped not only in its relationship to modernity in general but also in the relationship to a socialist and revolutionary modernity" (8). The origin of postmodernity in Chinese avant-garde literature—the deconstruction of totality and unity, the emphasis on indeterminacy and randomness, or the problematization of grand, absolute history—cannot be sought simply against the background of the globalization of the consumption society, the commercial society, the mass media society, or the information society.[7] Commercialism and cultural massification have prevailed in China under the sway of, or even in complicity with, its overshadowing political authoritarianism. The concept of the modern in China has depended heavily upon the entity of the modern nation-state defined by Lenin, which subsumes the concern for economic and technological advancement. If Jameson's Western postmodernism is a corollary of (what he calls) late capitalist civilization, then Chinese postmodernism has to do with the cultural psychology provoked by the particular political condition as the very basis of sociocultural superstructure. Accordingly, it is inevitable for us to focus the study of Chinese postmodernism on politico-cultural mentality rather than material civilization. It is precisely from the politico-historical perspective that I adopt the notion of the post—Mao-Deng, as correlated with the concurrent and correspondent cultural paradigm, the postmodern, which is intrinsically linked to its political environment.

By taking the "distribution of global power" into consideration, however, Zhang Yiwu, among others, has lately shifted toward a native "Third World" stance to confront "First World" oppression. Chinese postmodernism, as Zhang Yiwu conceives, counteracts the so-called hegemony of Western discourses, from which contemporary Chinese culture is said to be suffering. Here the national Subject recurs to support a discourse of national emancipation, whereas, however, the real "native" problem and "endemic" malady are dodged, consciously or unconsciously. The 1996 *Yaomohua Zhongguo de beihou* (Behind the demonization of China), a book compiled by a number of domestic and overseas Chinese scholars (Li Xiguang, Liu Kang, and others) to wage a sweeping attack on American representations of China, only reveals the danger of aligning anti-Occidentalism with official nationalism. To oppose Western cultural colonization, unfortunately, leads to the concealment of native totalitarianism. The grand Subject that speaks for the nation, in effect, stands for the native/national political power, the most hegemonic power to "demonize," or at least dehumanize, the autonomous individuals within the nation. Insofar as the fact that modernity or modernization belongs exactly to the central national discourse is disregarded, the notion of the postmodern or the multicultural claim in the global scene, conjoined with that of the modern nation-state of China, serves only to reinforce the hegemony of the native political authority. Here Homi Bhabha's warning is more than pertinent: "The marginal or 'minority' is not the space of a celebratory, or utopian, self-marginalization. It is a much more substantial intervention into those justifications of modernity—progress, homogeneity, cultural organicism, the deep nation, the long past—that rationalize the authoritarian, 'normalizing' tendencies within cultures in the name of the national interest or the ethnic prerogative" (4).

I would like to suggest that, ironically, the anti-Occidental sentiment packaged in Chinese postcolonial theory is truly subject to the "hegemony of Western discourses" for its unconditioned acceptance of a theory from the West. To draw the Chinese political culture into the context of the postmodern is exactly an attempt to avoid the "invasion" of the hegemony of Western discourses, for the danger of being trapped into another system of discourse would occur only when the concept of the postmodern is imported without contextualization. Such a danger perhaps lies not in the loss of "native discourse" but in the fact that a misleading discourse obstructs the insight into the discursive condition genuinely relevant to the specific culture. In other words, a simplistic appropriation or a simplistic rejection of appropriation of the concept of the postmodern relies only on the Western discourse of postmodernity, whereas postmodernity in China, set against a different cultural background, is sacrificed due to theoretical innocence.

Entering the 1990s, postmodernism, along with other new Western theories such as postcolonialism and poststructuralism, ascended to a superior intellectual status, where it enjoys great popularity, if not dominance. The discussion of postmodernism, in the mid-1990s, developed into heated debates between the postmodernists, on the one side, and anti-postmodernists, on the other. Zhao Yiheng, in a series of articles he published in 1995 and 1996 in the influential Hong Kong–based intellectual magazine *Ershiyi shiji* (The twentieth-first century), attacked the native Chinese "postmodernists" for deteriorating radical Western theories such as postmodernism, postcolonialism, and poststructuralism into conservative theories that help endorse the status quo in current China.[8] Zhao's main targets, labeled "post-*ism*" as a whole, included not only such advocates of postmodernism as Zhang

Yiwu and Chen Xiaoming, who were believed to embrace mass culture uncritically, but also such veterans writers as Zheng Min, who attempted to incorporate Derridean theory into her otherwise unfashionable literary ideas. In accordance with Zhao Yiheng's critique of Chinese "New Conservatism," Xu Ben, another overseas Chinese critic, wrote extensively to question the native critics' post-1989 acquiescence to the indigenous political oppression by redirecting the critical focus toward Western hegemony.

Zhao's self-admitted elitist stance and Xu's politically righteous stance offended more than one group of people and triggered immediate counterattacks from Zhang Yiwu and Liu Kang. Zhang accused Zhao and Xu of accepting the "Western discourse of modernity" by "deliberately 'forgetting' and 'erasing'" its "cultural hegemony" ("Chanshi" 130), and he denied the label of conservatism, or the "nativist" position, that Zhao and Xu have assigned to him. He insists that his exploration of postmodernism emphasizes "the context of hybridity in present China" (134) yet fails to elucidate just what this context of hybridity is; on the contrary, he complains about the invalidation of the dichotomy between the East and the West and between the native and the foreign (130). By establishing the binary opposition between the Third World and the First World, Zhang Yiwu not only conforms to the prevalent nationalistic fervor (which is, to a great extent, supported by the political authority) but also simplifies the "hybrid" situation of reality. The hybridity exists, indeed, in the fact that it is exactly by way of the official policy of China today that this Third World country is placed under the First World economic and cultural domination. On the other hand, it is the discourse of modernity, imported from the West, that has become the ideological basis of this Eastern nation and has supported the power and stability of the regime.

In this sense Zhang Yiwu, who advocates a sensitivity to "nativeness," is responsible for the evasion of the hybrid hegemony of modernity from both the Eastern political and Western economic authorities. His theoretical premise misconceives First World discourse as the sole threat and ignores the fact that such a First World discourse in China has been exploited by the producer of Third World discourse to support its own power. In China, as a matter of fact, the supreme hegemony of discourse comes from Eastern totalitarianism, which has the power to manipulate, within a certain scope, First World discourse or any other discourses.[9] If postmodernity in the West is at least in part a reaction to the late capitalist society, what it faces in China is not only a globalized commercial totality but, primarily, a political totality. Commercial civilization has not yet possessed as strong a cultural power as political authority has, and it has even become one of the effective modes of political manipulation (despite the fact that commercialism, to a certain extent, engenders potential hazards to political control). Commercial society has itself been part of the teleological discourse of economic modernization to sustain political legitimacy. The attempt to gauge Chinese postmodernity simply in terms of postindustrial or commercial civilization is a result of a misconception of the characteristics of Chinese culture under the hegemony of Mao-Deng discourse.[10]

Of all the Chinese "postmodernists" Chen Xiaoming and Dai Jinhua (who, unlike her Beijing cohorts, never explicitly advocates postmodernism) are the central figures of, but not the most ardent participants in, the debate, perhaps because their positions are more ambiguous than easily definable.[11] Chen Xiaoming differs radically from Zhang Yiwu in that he, while fully aware of the power structure in the global arena, attends more to the politically conditioned native experience (of the past and the present). In direct contrast to Zhang Yiwu and Liu Kang, Chen Xiaoming expresses an idea actually not so different from Zhao Yiheng's: "Having been living under the native cultural space, all Chinese intellectuals who seek freedom of thinking would know clearly that the Western culture is not the spiritual pressure and cultural hegemony that they are actually confronting" (*Fangzhen* 213). Without denying overdetermination in contemporary China's cultural scene, Chen acutely perceives the predominance of "revolutionary discourse," a specific form of modernity, over China: "Chinese postmodernism displays all the complexities and contradictions, and is caught between the odd correlations of cultural production and the revolutionary discourse" ("Mysterious" 140). In a necessarily sophisticated tone, Chen Xiaoming warns against the naive desire to attain the native self-identity, for the paradox is that the "pure" native characteristic is exactly the cultural imaginary of global capitalism (*Fangzhen* 207).

Keen and insightful as it is, Zhao Yiheng's criticism of the Chinese "post-ists" throws the baby out with the bath water. Although he claims that the Chinese postmodernists apply the radical theories from the West to their conservative objectives, he never intends to probe the possibility of recovering the radical potential of postmodernism in the

Chinese context. By concluding that "postmodernism has actually turned itself into a conformist theory in China which serves to justify the institutionalized mainstream culture" ("Post-Isms" 42), Zhao is unwilling to see the possibility of turning it back into a nonconformist theory that, as in the West, serves not to subvert the "institutionalized mainstream culture" in a confrontational way but to penetrate its politico-historical memory and deconstruct its repressive power. In this sense Chinese literary postmodernism (not postmodern theory) is by no means a conservative trend that conceals the conflicts in historical reality but, rather, a radical experiment that examines the psycho-rhetorical basis of the authoritarian culture of modern China.

Zhao's rejection of Chinese postmodernism is echoed, though from different perspectives, by other overseas scholars, such as Jing Wang, who acutely discerns a teleological undertone in some theorists' espousal of Chinese postmodernism but at the same time misses the opportunity to explore its intimate relevance to historical reality. Jing Wang is certainly correct in finding in avant-garde fiction "a belated rebellion against textual repression, a radicalism that by itself is an ideological act." Is it, however, "relevant only to the Chinese context"? To be sure, the deconstructive "textual politics of the experimental fiction" is not exclusively "Chinese" (258); rather, like those postmodern literary trends in post-Auschwitz Europe, Chinese avant-garde fiction expresses a discrediting of the grand narratives of modernity, of which the Mao-Deng discourse is but a regional, though typical, case. The urgency to conceptualize Chinese postmodernism does not necessarily result from a teleological impetus to emulate a certain kind of literary development in the West but from the discovery that the politico-cultural totality that Chinese avant-gardism faces up to belongs to the same discourse of modernity that Western literary postmodernism attempts to cope with. To emphasize the particularity of Chinese literary experimentalism and to avoid linear, teleological literary history should not lead to a denial of the connection between the Chinese experience of post–Mao-Deng culture and a universal experience of postmodernity. As long as we see that modernity has been serving as the basis for the grand historical narrative significant to all nations in the twentieth century, postmodernity is not a *problem* unique to the Western, industrialized world but is pertinent to all cultures, including Third World cultures, under the impact of modernity (even though most cultures cannot be defined as postmodern as a whole). To understand Chinese postmodernism against the global background may help us see the connections among various manifestations of modernity and postmodernity.

To me, then, it is not only possible but inevitable to theorize contemporary Chinese culture in light of postmodernism, not because China has entered an economically and technologically advanced postmodern age but because the modern spirit continues to haunt China, whose literary postmodernity, however, reveals repressed, self-deconstructive elements from within Chinese modernity.

Defining the Postmodern/Post–Mao-Deng

One of the remaining questions is, then, What is the connection between political conditions and cultural production? Are we returning to an orthodox literary theory in communist China that subjugates the cultural to the political? Here the crucial point is how we read the political paradigm in terms of culture. If the political paradigm is understood as a cultural paradigm rather than an entity of the state apparatus or specific policies and activities, the political system of an age, particularly that of contemporary China, can be regarded as based on the production of discourses. Since the (post)revolutionary discourse and the (post-)Enlightenment discourse are inseparable in the historical context of modern China, my concepts of modernity and postmodernity are not purely political or cultural ones, for their cultural significance is destined to derive from their political implications, and vice versa. Chinese modernity and postmodernity always demonstrate their *politico-cultural* power, which defines the relevant sociohistorical orientations.

From this hypothesis the puzzling notion "post–Mao-Deng" can be approached in a more profound way. In terms of cultural production, rather than material production or chronological history, Mao's and Deng's ages do not belong to different political paradigms, even though they adopt different political schemes. Deng's polity follows Mao's insofar as it has only "reformed" the instrument of discourse production. The consequence of such a reform is that utopian discourse centered on the material economy replaces utopian discourse centered on the spiritual community. Because of the collapse of Mao's spiritual community, Deng's polity resorts to the more vulgar and more pragmatic picture of Elysium, through which the depressed citizens can be awakened to reconstruct a new utopia on the ruins of the previous utopia—or, rather, dystopia.

The same teleological pattern of the grand history remains, since economic development is envisioned as the ultimate path to emancipation today, an emancipation that aims at worldly pleasure, without spiritual transcendence. The distinction between Mao's "spiritualistic" age and Deng's "sensualistic" age is merely a superficial one. Mao's ideal of egalitarian commune, as Jiwei Ci insightfully observes, appeals to lower-class people especially for its promise to ameliorate their material life, in addition to improving their social status. Ci points out that, insofar as the great temptation of Maoist utopianism lies in its acceptance as "a quick way out of poverty," Chinese communism is a "movement from utopianism to hedonism, with hedonism both as an essential, though sublimated, component of utopianism and, in an overt form, as a sequel to nihilism" (2–3). Without ensuring economic prosperity in the collective sense, the political discourse of Maoism could not have prevailed beyond intellectual circles. In other words, despite its depreciation of individual pleasure, Maoist discourse contains within itself a pleasure-oriented teleology as a basis of its utopian imagination. If in Mao's era economic interest had to be expressed in political terms, post-Mao China has invented an economic vocabulary that, indeed, renovates and bolsters the political agenda, rather than weakens it.

In Deng's era, as Ban Wang argues, "under the leadership of the party, the people are striding forward to a better future in a long march toward 'modernization' (the present substitute for the now-discredited 'Communism')" (241). But communism, stripped of pseudo-altruism to serve a new arena of combat (no longer against the "class enemies" but among the "economic animals"), is still the officially sanctioned desire to realize the brave new world in which materials are so abundant that the principle of distribution is, as Marx anticipates, "to each according to his needs" (531). At stake is that it is the same grand narrative that, with its idealistic and teleological code, serves the political authoritarianism and bars all the discourses in conflict with it. A commercialized, transnationalized civilization in today's China is created primarily as the social base of political power to consolidate the one-party dictatorship.

Having said this, however, I am not denying that commercialization in reality has complex effects. Although communism has always been the state ideology taught in classrooms and upheld in official newspapers, fewer and fewer people are truly susceptible to the influence of the old doctrine. As a result of the disillusionment with Maoism, the loss of the socialist-communist ideal after the mid-1980s indeed corresponds to the deconstructive move we see in avant-garde fiction. On the other hand, in today's China commercialization is not so much a decentering of communist ideology as a reorientation of Chinese modernity, which now justifies the hedonistic social trend. If Mao's modernity is a grand narrative that encourages chaos and persecution for the sake of historical progress, Deng's modernity is another, yet no less totalistic, grand narrative that bases historical progress on individual desire, which theoretically allows, if not goads, moral corruption and social unrest.[12]

Yet, in any case, socialism is still the officially defined sociopolitical and economic system of China. If Chinese socialism best renders the cultural formation of modernity in a non-Western context, Arif Dirlik's notion of "postsocialism" is indeed pertinent to the concept of Chinese postmodernity, which challenges that cultural formation. Dirlik tells us that his "use of 'postsocialism' is inspired by an analogous term that has acquired currency in recent years in cultural studies: postmodernism," whose prominent feature "Lyotard has described as . . . an 'incredulity toward metanarratives'" ("Postsocialism" 374). Just as the fact that Mao is "every bit as 'postsocialist' as Deng" (376), so is Mao's era subject to a postmodern examination along with Deng's era. Postsocialism, if I push Dirlik's idea further, can thus be understood as a self-questioned and self-disseminated potential of the Mao-Deng socialist idea/ideal. As a special form of social modernity, the Mao-Deng version of socialism (or postsocialism, to better phrase it) is accurately illustrated in literary postmodernism, for Chinese postmodernism forcefully unmasks the problems in the Mao-Deng metanarratives.[13]

Thus understood, the notion of the post–Mao-Deng refers to the politico-cultural paradigm, rather than historical chronology. Chinese avant-garde fiction emerged during the heyday of Deng's era, which lasted until even after his death. In what sense can we use the prefix *post-*? The post–Mao-Deng politico-cultural paradigm, I suggest, does not necessarily manifest itself chronologically after Mao's and/or Deng's reigns, just as the postmodern cultural paradigm does not come out after the modern age but indicates a deconstruction of the modern paradigm from within. If Lyotard's claim that the postmodern exists in the modern is valid,[14] we can also declare that the post–Mao-Deng must be located within the Mao-Deng paradigm. It is not far-fetched, therefore, to place the post–Mao-Deng on a par with the postmodern, for the post–Mao-Deng tendency in culture and literature to challenge the totality of political discourse corresponds to the postmodern subversion against the grand narratives of modernity. "The postmodern," again, should not be defined merely as a socioeconomic condition in the time of globalization and commercialization but understood as a cultural paradigm generated *within* and rebellious *against* the cultural paradigm of the modern without being confined to the material or economic structure of contemporary civilization.

Postmodernism in Chinese avant-garde fiction can be defined as both a psychic reaction to the politico-cultural modernity embedded in the Mao-Deng master discourse and a rhetorical reaction to the literary modernity exemplified by the representational paradigm of twentieth-century Chinese literature. The politico-cultural discourse of modernity and the literary paradigm of modernity share a totalistic mode of conceptualization. The grand history, which presupposes an absolute coherence between practice and telos and a transparent correspondence between representation and meaning, is certainly the most powerful concept propelling both political modernity and literary modernity.

What is inseparable from the literary idea of the modern is, therefore, not only the emancipatory politico-cultural agenda—the Mao-Deng regimes being its particular expressions—but also the formalistic literary paradigm as such, in other words, the mode of absolutizing and totalizing discourse. In this respect the complicity between literary modernity and politico-cultural totalization in the Mao-Deng regimes can be traced back to their common origin. As a literary paradigm, then, the Mao-Deng discourse that prescribes unified historical imperatives corresponds to the representational subjectivism in modern Chinese fiction to a great extent. It is *the same subjectively centered totality and rationality that construct modernity* in both sociopolitical arbitrariness and literary/aesthetic absoluteness.

Maoism, in particular, relies on this literary/aesthetic absoluteness. The function of Maoist discourse lies in its aesthetic magic, which absolutizes the grand narrative by enforcing signifying relationships. The most violent expression of modernity exists in *Quotations from Chairman Mao* and *Mao Zedong xuanji* (Selected works of Mao Zedong), the most widely read books during the Cultural Revolution. (Apparently, *Deng Xiaoping xuanji* [The collected works of Deng Xiaoping] has never been able to emulate its model.) Maoist discourse becomes a rhetorical paradigm that coerces the affinity between the signifier and the signified. Apart from such indubitable political statements as "The force at the core leading our cause forward is the Chinese Communist Party" (*Quotations* 1), the diegetic mode in Mao's writings is another example of the power of representational subjectivity in modern Chinese literature in establishing the Historical Subject. In "Jinian Baiqiuen" (In memory of Norman Bethune), one of his so-called three primal articles (*laosanpian*), Mao, despite the fact that "Comrade Bethune and [he] met only once," confidently characterizes Bethune's personality in highly subjective, approving terms: "his utter devotion to others without any thought of self," "his great sense of responsibility in his work and his great warm-heartedness towards all comrades and the people," "true communist spirit," "the spirit of absolute selflessness" (*Selected Works* 2:337–38). Before the reader is able to decide whether one can be "without any thought of self," whether there is such thing as "absolute selflessness," or what the "true communist spirit" really is, the signified of representation has been unmistakably prescribed without any latitude for hesitation or suspicion, even though the link of signification may well be fictitious and illusory.

In those literary passages Mao's narrative mode evidently corresponds to the canonical paradigm of representation in modern Chinese literature. In "Yugong yishan" (The foolish old man who removed the mountains), another of his three primal articles, Mao rephrases a parable from *Lie Zi* and ends with his conclusion: "Having refuted the Wise Old Man's wrong view, he went on digging every day, unshaken in his conviction" (*Selected Works* 3:272). In the original text of *Lie Zi* the authorial tendency in the description of this event is reduced to a minimum: "Mister Simple of North Mountain [i.e., the Foolish Old Man] breathed a long sigh, and said . . . Old Wiseacre of River Bend [i.e., the Wise Old Man] was at a loss for an answer" (*Lie Zi* 100). In Mao, however, the objective narration is intruded upon by such words as *refute, wrong*, and *unshaken*, each strongly imposing a subjective judgment upon what is being represented. Apparently, the master discourse exists in a style of narration in which the modern narrative subject is endowed with an omniscient and omnipotent character.

To Mao the Foolish Old Man, whom he has imbued with a heroically "unshaken" image as opposed to the "wrong," "refuted" Wise Old Man, symbolizes the historical power that Mao assumes himself to represent. Only by dichotomizing and absolutizing the characterization of good/positive and evil/negative can the representational subject of Maoist discourse outline an indisputable totality of history. Historical modernity must rely upon the totalizing and rationalizing mode of discourse, which can be seen as literary modernity. Since the political Mao-Deng is precisely the cultural and historical modern applied in the practical domain, it must ground itself in literary modernity essentialized by the representational subject.

It is on this basis that, as Xiaobing Tang observes, "the function of [Chinese] postmodernism is to dismantle various master-narratives about modernity and create a new field of uncompromising demystification" (296). In any case, then, as the cultural modern lies in literary rationalization and absolutization—the master discourse of the political Mao-Deng—the prefix *post-* does not refer to a chronological subsequence but shows *a temporal force of deferral and a spatial force of deviation within the not completely forgotten, but immemorial, desire and repression of the modern.* The postmodern, as we have seen from the analyses of the avant-garde texts, does not exist as a distanced critique of the modern but, rather, suggests a self-involvement in historical destiny. It thus implies simultaneously a preoccupation with and a deviation from the original/primal. The reemergence of the cultural/literary modern in avant-garde narratives, that is, the recurrence of antecedent affect in the unconscious, or the concurrence of the past and the present, signals the denial of the conception of linear historical progress. In other words, the postmodern is not a diachronic transcendence of the modern but a synchronic evocation and expulsion of its repression.

The subjective self-suspicion becomes the most perceptible feature of the postmodern Chinese avant-gardism. As a deconstruction of the modern representation within the subjective narrative that conforms to a political totality, literary postmodernity is, formalistically, a confession of the traumatizing violence of modernity within its deep formation. In this sense the Chinese avant-garde is not only an affront to the externally imposing master discourse but a conjuring up of the internalized discourse of modernity with which the subject has been culturally possessed. The impetus of the subjective self-critique stems from an awareness that historical catastrophes in China cannot be simply imputed to external, historical evil forces (such as the Communist

Party, as might be considered) but has to be examined within the collective/individual cultural subject, which adheres to the same paradigm of the dominant political discourse. The fact that it was always the intellectuals themselves who not only collaborated in but also elaborated on the persecutions of other intellectuals in numerous political movements in the history of communist China is certainly a practical consequence of the supreme cultural paradigm of the discourse of modernity shared by the intellectuals and the political apparatus.

As an implosive disruption of the transparent and absolute genre that constructs the master discourse, postmodernity necessarily involves self-reference to such a genre in modern Chinese literature. Postmodernity is thus a parody of modernity: the topoi of the modern are still lurking while at the same time whirled into the involute labyrinth of multiplied signifiers, which fail to capture the signifieds in a transparent way. Then a literary encounter with reality in the post-Mao era becomes, in the first place, an encounter with a language that is already culturally and historically intertextualized, overdetermined, contaminated, and, in particular, associated or entangled with the master discourse as something etiologically modern but pathologically/symptomatically postmodern.

The disintegration of the modern subjectivity in Chinese avant-garde literature is a disintegration of a subjectivity that lacks self-reflection on its own limitations and nonidentities. The Chinese avant-garde does not applaud the death of subjectivity but launches a self-deconstruction of the totalistic, repressive subjectivity. The irrational subject of narrative in avant-garde fiction persists in the paradox of self-consciousness: it displays its own quandary to repeal the ignorance, while this quandary is precisely the boundary of the subject that rejects the totalized utopia. In other words, the transcendentality of self-consciousness can only be achieved in the self-conscious recognition of its own impossibility of transcendence. Such a postmodernity is not even the eruption of the Deleuzean, productive desire: the irrational subject is to be considered as being activated by the pressure of the politico-historical discourse rather than being spontaneously self-generating. Thus, a postmodern subjectivity is a self-questioning and deconstructive one, which breaches the absolute, rational, and totalistic oppression of both the politico-historical Mao-Deng and the culturo-literary modern.

Notes

Chapter 1

1. Jing Wang shares the same view, though from a more specific perspective, by claiming that "1985 emerged as a landmark of modern Chinese literature because for the first time in the literary history of China, a 'language-using subject' made its debut in the discursive space dominated by the collective cultural and historical subject of China" (173). Li Tuo's essay "1985" provides a more detailed description of the literary and cultural background of that year.

2. I have to limit my discussion within the geographical boundary of mainland China, for in Taiwan and Hong Kong, among other places in the world, Chinese literature was loosened from the modern paradigm much earlier.

3. The origin of the term *avant-garde* applied to the Chinese context, though still unknown, is believed to appear no earlier than 1985. It has been widely used by Chinese critics ever since to indicate the aesthetically experimental literature emerging in the mid- and late 1980s. Although it is undeniable that the Chinese avant-garde is significantly influenced by the twentieth-century Western literary modernism and postmodernism, from Kafka, Joyce, and Faulkner to Robbe-Grillet, Borges, and García Márquez, the crucial factor still lies in the particular culturo-historical problematics in China (comparable to those in the modern West), to which Chinese writers respond with strategies akin, though not equivalent, to their Western counterparts'. If Western postmodernism is, as Lyotard suggests, a heterogenization of the grand narratives of modernity, Chinese postmodern literature, as will be shown, deconstructs the specific master discourses that predominate over modern China. Herein lies the belligerent connotation of the concept of the "avant-garde."

4. For a detailed discussion of the relationship between the Neo-Confucian idea of self-cultivation and the May Fourth spirit, especially in Ye Shengtao, see Anderson 41–43; and Denton 39.

5. Prasenjit Duara has forcefully analyzed how China was susceptible to "linear, teleological model of Enlightenment History" and the idea of "nation as a collective historical subject poised to realize its destiny in a modern future" (4). For a more detailed explication of "the narrative construction of a Historical subject" (49), see Duara 3–50.

6. The Confucian classics, such as *Zuo zhuan* (The Zuo commentary), are believed to be skillful in authorial/narratorial manipulation. In his study of *Zuo zhuan* Ronald Egan analyzes how the author manages to infuse his voice into the seemingly objective narrative. In addition, in his comment on traditional Chinese historiography, Jaroslav Průšek draws our attention to "the *subjective* evaluation of the historian" that accompanies "the historical material of a highly *objective* character" (*Chinese* 20) in such works as Sima Qian's *Shiji* (Records of the historian). C. T. Hsia observes, "Next to the oral storytellers, the historians provide the most important literary background in the making of the Chinese novel" (*Classical* 11). "As the noblest moment of classical narrative prose," he points out, "the *Record of the Grand Historian* (Shih chi), especially, was frequently invoked as the standard by which to judge the excellence of novels" (*Classical* 14). True, historiographical novels such as *Sanguo yanyi* (*Romance of the Three Kingdoms*) contain intense moral implications. It is in *Romance of the Three Kingdoms* that we are most aware of the existence of the authorial voice that orients the characterization.

7. Průšek's remark on *The Exposure of the Official World* is illuminating in this respect: "[Li Baojia] needed a vehicle for his hatred of the imperial officials who provided him with his subject; he wanted to rouse his readers against the corrupt bureaucracy whose sins he was recording. He wanted to rouse public opinion in order to achieve an improvement. Thus his aim is at variance with objective approach of the narrator in the traditional novel. He loads his work with author's note, commentaries, observations, and résumés, which disturb the traditional epic objectivity and conflict with the established narrative form. It is clear that [Li Baojia] required quite a different form in which to present his work, with much more scope for individuality, and a far more personal narrator" (115).

8. *Mimesis* and *diegesis*, as Plato defines them in *The Republic*, refer to "showing" and "telling," two different ways of narration (see Plato 638), also termed *scenic presentation* and *reportorial narration* (see Stanzel 22).

9. In traditional Chinese vernacular fiction we may notice a common mode of description of the characters—usually a poem—at their first appearances but only limited to their external looks and manners. Some exceptions can also be found, for example, in a poem that characterizes Jia Baoyu when he first appears in the novel *The Story of the Stone,* but with different functions. Such a poetic comment is by no means direct characterization in the mode of representational reason but, rather, an ironic reworking of direct characterization:

> Though outwardly a handsome sausage-skin,
> He proved to have but sorry meat within.
> A harum-scarum, to all duties blind,
> A doltish mule, to study disinclined;
> His acts outlandish and his nature queer;
> Yet not a whit cared he how folk might jeer!
>
> (Cao, *Story* 1:102)

10. Similar examples can be seen in the pages that follow: "Juehui earnestly said to Qin" (19/23; trans. modified); "Qin said with a little anxiety"

(19/23; trans. modified); "Juehui said, half surprised and half angry" (20/23; trans. modified); "Juemin uttered casually" (20/24; trans. modified); "Juemin said in an encouraging way" (20/23; trans. modified); "Qin . . . said resolutely" (20/23; trans. modified); "Juemin said, soothing her" (20/23; trans. modified); "Qin . . . said with a resolute tone" (20/23; trans. modified); among others.

11. The symptom of authorial purposiveness can be found in the vast majority of the canonized modern Chinese fiction as well. Even those writers somewhat detached from the mainstream of modern Chinese literature are not entirely exempt from the excessiveness of unmediated subjectivity. C. T. Hsia, in *A History of Modern Chinese Fiction,* impugns Shen Congwen's method of characterization in the short story "Longzhu" (1928) as immature for using "inappropriate" figurative diction and "banal" "generic adjectives" (*History* 198). At stake is that, in fact, the diegetic characterization itself, even if appropriate, affects the objectivity that such a realistic narrative is presupposed to sustain. In this sense the passage reads "ludicrous" not simply because it "hardly makes sense" (*History* 199) but because it is intended to make too clear a sense that is ironically unattainable. Even in one of his most celebrated works, "Biancheng" (The border town, 1934), Shen Congwen cannot shy away from the same paradigm of characterization: the heroes of the novella, Tianbao and Nuosong, are respectively introduced as "manly and open, impatient of meaningless conventions" and "quieter, . . . intelligent, sensitive" (*wenji* 6:83 / *Border Town* 16). The diegetic characterization is not only a sign of omniscient narration but also a sign of the overflowing subjectivity as an outcome of the mythical power of Enlightenment discourse. Shen Congwen, usually regarded as a nonmainstream writer, was no less exposed to the May Fourth zeitgeist when he went to Beijing in the 1920s to seek the key to social liberation. Being a humanistic writer later, Shen Congwen never abandons the ideal to ameliorate the condition of human existence, which may seem to him not to rest in the historical change but, rather, in the uncultured human nature. Hence, even though the ethical purpose that he cherishes is different from the mainstream writers' more politically concerned purposes, Shen Congwen still intends to manifest clearly the quality of the picture he delineates to convey his own ideas.

Indeed, for those minor writers in the major current, this mode is as prevalent. In the beginning of Xu Jie's short story "Can wu" (Sad Fog, 1924), for instance, there is a passage that describes each of the villagers sitting under the camphor tree. The description, however, goes far beyond the objective account of what may appear to the narrator but is intended deliberately to offer the reader with clear identifications made by the authorial subject: the first "loves to talk and people like to listen to him"; the third "is relatively weak and not talkative"; the fourth "is the silliest one and the dullest one as well" (2), and so on.

12. The turning point in the novella happens after the "Third Plenary Session of the Eleventh Central Committee of the Chinese Communist Party" held in December 1978, the official inaugural moment of the Deng polity.

13. Many of them, actually, were loyalists-turned-dissidents, for the party authority, especially Deng, took their well-intentioned, bold criticisms as threatening blasphemy.

Chapter 2

1. When Sun Wuyang "calmly" tells Mr. and Mrs. Fang that she saw a dead, naked woman with "one breast cut off," we are told that Mr. Fang "could not hold his voice," "sighed, walking around anxiously," and that Mrs. Fang "moaned, and covered her face with both hands" (263).
2. For more detailed discussions of "The Autumn of Guling," see Chen, Yu-shih 35–50; and D. Wang, *Fictional Realism*, 102–3.
3. One of the clearest formulations of the distinction between paranoia and schizophrenia can be found in Deleuze and Guattari's *Anti-Oedipus*, in which the two psychotic forms of desire are opposed to each other: schizophrenia displays a collage of fragmentary ruins of anarchical, heterogeneous elements, whereas paranoia attempts to impose a centralized, unified system upon disparate elements.
4. For example, Fu Sinian (later a pro-Nationalist intellectual), in his 1919 review of "A Madman's Diary," proposed that "the madman be our mentor" and that "we lead the children and follow the madman toward brightness" (687). Even recently, Lin Yü-sheng, one of the leading overseas scholars of the Chinese intellectual issue, also believes that, "though everyone in Chinese society is, consciously or unconsciously, a cannibal, it takes an 'insane' person to break through the barriers that obstruct vision and penetrate reality" (110).
5. At this point Tang Xiaobing's interpretation in his essay "Lu Xun's 'A Madman's Diary' and a Chinese Modernism" is pertinent to my argument here, except that he omits to pinpoint the sources of the traditional concept of *kuang*.
6. In his diary on that date Lu Xun also recorded this event, saying that he "detected later that his [the student's] madness was feigned and intended to insult and threaten me, in order to make me not dare to write" (*quanji* 14:519).
7. The distinction between symbolism and allegorism is one of the major points in Fredric Jameson's much discussed article on Third World literature and national allegory. Inspired from Walter Benjamin, Jameson alleges, "If allegory has once again become somehow congenial for us today, as over against the massive and monumental unifications of an older modernist symbolism or even realism itself, it is because the allegorical spirit is profoundly discontinuous, a matter of breaks and heterogeneities, of the multiple polysemia of the dream rather than the homogeneous representation of the symbol" (73).
8. As she once said, Can Xue first tried to write a "realistic" story but changed her mind before she began to work (see Shi Shuqing 441).
9. See, for example, Xiao Hua and Wang Zheng 54–55.

Chapter 3

1. In *Moses and Monotheism* Freud applies his theory of trauma, which he originally conceived as a way to deal with individual experience, to interpret collective experience as a cultural phenomenon. Just as during Jewish history

there was a period of *latency*, which Freud emphasizes, Chinese literature after Mao's death did not produce works that truly match the degree of atrocities in the Cultural Revolution until the rise of the avant-garde. To understand the problem of trauma in the Chinese avant-garde fiction is thus a less symbolic one than the Jewish case: it is the real traumatic experience of the avant-garde writers (and, for that matter, the nation as a whole) that forms this cultural scene.

2. *Maoist discourse* is a term adopted by the Shanghai critics Zhu Dake and Li Jie. Another relevant term is *Maoist genre* (Mao wenti) invented by the Beijing critic Li Tuo. For a more detailed analysis of Maoist discourse, see chap. 6.

3. According to the official theory of the Chinese Communist Party, the so-called Mao Zedong Thought, rather than Maoist discourse, is one of the dominant principles of political behavior and guidance to the individual mind.

4. Mao's own writings are, of course, not the only source of Maoist discourse. It is obvious that all the media language (in newspaper, broadcasting, film, and notably, Peking opera) in the Cultural Revolution belongs to the same discursive system. Based on this fact, Maoist discourse gradually became the dominant factor in daily language.

5. For an in-depth discussion of Chinese aesthetics of the sublime, see Ban Wang. Starting from the heroic, idealistic, and transcendental quality of the sublime in the dominant aesthetics of modern China, Wang points out, "Desublimation is also a form of the sublime—not the sublime of transcendence but the sublime of the abyssal undermining of the grand narratives" (11). Lyotard's concept of the sublime, derived from Kant, points to a direction that reveals the deconstructive dynamics in the otherwise idealistic figure. Here I attempt to push the interpretation of the sublime in Chinese aesthetics further by exploring the avant-garde sublime as a traumatic memory trace that conjures up, as well as counteracts, the monolithic sublime in the official aesthetics.

Chapter 4

1. After 1989, however, Yu Hua was the first, if not the only one, in the "avant-garde circle" who turned away from avant-gardism. Radical narrative experimentation has retreated, if not completely disappeared, perhaps as a result of the repression and self-repression of intellectual vivacity and the dominance of the market over literary production in the 1990s. Nevertheless, much of Yu Hua's subversive literary politics has been retained in a plain but occasionally sentimental and melodramatic style in his later works, such as his novelette *Huozhe* (To live), which was adapted by Zhang Yimou into an international award-winning film.

2. Unlike George Orwell, who wrote *1984* in 1948, Yu Hua wrote "Nineteen Eighty-Six" in 1986. But the title does suggest the year 1968, the "heyday" of the Cultural Revolution, as a historical background.

3. Lu Xun's "A Madman's Diary" was published in 1917, whereas

"Nineteen Eighty-Six," whose historical setting of narrative is 1986, was written in 1986 and published in 1987.

4. *Leng-Tch'e*, in Bataille's quotation from other sources, is an old transliteration of *lingchi* (204).

5. Here is another topos that Yu Hua borrows from the Chinese fictional classics, for instance, "Cuicui zhuan" (The story of Cuicui) in Qu You's *Jiandeng xinhua* (Wick-trimming new tales). In this story, after the death of the two protagonists, Cuicui and Jin Ding, one of Cuicui's previous servants sees them in a splendid mansion and is regaled by them. But when he brings Cuicui's parents for a revisit, the site of the mansion becomes wilderness, and there are only graves of Cuicui and Jin Ding.

Chapter 5

1. Many critics, in fact, are disturbed by such images that recur in her various works. Because of "the images, metaphors and ceaselessly repetitive modes of action that she is obsessed with," wrote one, "the author herself should be partly responsible for the violation of good appetite: her repetitive, redundant twaddle is terribly annoying" (Zhang Xinying 109).

2. The fact that, in the original *Zhongshan* version, the character *jiao* (foot/feet) is misspelled as *zhong* (swollen)—both characters having the same radical in Chinese—may be another indication of Can Xue's obsession with the word *swelling*.

3. One of the famous examples can be taken from the dramatized scene in the film *Farewell, My Concubine,* winner of the Cannes Award directed by Chen Kaige, in which the two Peking opera performers attack each other, not entirely by force, among the blustering flames during the Cultural Revolution.

4. The text of the song comes from the diary of Lei Feng, the best-known communist model, who quotes the lyric from other sources.

Chapter 6

1. Adorno's *Habilitationsschrift*, his very first book entitled *Kierkegaard: Construction of the Aesthetic*, was on Kierkegaard, regardless of the fact that Kierkegaard's *The Concept of Irony* is not mentioned explicitly in this book.

2. Neither *Geist* nor *Dasein* can be conceived as the telos of history for Adorno, who denies any type of positive ideas of emancipation developed within the Enlightenment discourse.

3. Legalism attracts Mao the most for its belief in the function of dictatorship in the political system. As a major influence on Legalism, the political metaphysics of Taoism (Lao Zi, rather than Zhuang Zi), such as the idea to abolish human desire and intellect, also helps formulate Mao's philosophy. Even Confucianism, which embraces the ethical code of propriety (*li*), is a pri-

mary source of Mao's conception of social order, including the relationship between the emperor and his subjects (especially men of letters).

4. Even Mao's conception of multiple contradiction cannot be identified with a postmodern heteroglossia, as he insists on the "leading and decisive role" of the "principal contradiction": "Once the principal contradiction is grasped, all problems can be readily solved" (*Selected Works* 1:332).

5. Likewise, Liu Kang's attempt to reevaluate Maoism through reading Western Marxism (Althusser and especially Gramsci) fails to recognize the totalistic orientation of Mao's revolutionary idea that aims at a new hegemonic power. By calling Mao "a 'deconstructionist' who tended to collapse bourgeois cultural institutions with capitalist modernity" (Liu Kang 84), Liu Kang downplays the hegemonic implication in Maoist modernity. I would argue that Maoism, as a specific form of modernity and truly "an alternative to the capitalist modernity" (Liu Kang 79), replaces Western modernity not with a counterhegemonic approach but with a Chinese modernity that has proved to be more rigidly hegemonic in social formation.

6. Jin Guantao, from another perspective, points out that Mao's conception of social contradictions relies heavily on the Neo-Confucian mode of subjective engagement in perceiving the world. He writes that "the dialectics proposed by *On Contradictions* is not a highly epistemological worldview, but a worldview that is meaningful only to a certain standpoint, a certain reformer (subject) of the world. Dialectics as description (interpretation) of the objective world becomes only effective to a certainly moral subject. The dialectical world would not exist without a standpoint or a moral subject" (33). While Neo-Confucianism emphasizes an abstract moral subject, Mao's dialectical agenda rests on, and is determined by, an abstract, grand historical subject.

7. In the mid-1980s, when "cultural reflection" (*wenhua fansi*) began to prevail among the young intellectuals, some films of "model operas" were shown in Fudan University, where I was a college student. It is not surprising that every time the audience could not help bursting into loud laughter throughout.

8. Most of the model operas, such as *Zhiqu Weihushan* (Taking Tiger Mountain by strategy), *Hongdeng ji* (Tale of the red lamp), and *Shajiabang,* deal with historical legends.

9. In Maoist philosophy the dichotomy between "principal contradiction" and the "secondary contradictions" is to be distinguished from the dichotomy between the "principal aspect of contradiction" and the "secondary aspect of contradiction" (as mentioned earlier). The former set refers to the degrees of significance of different contradictions, whereas the latter to the levels of the forces within a certain contradiction. See also note 41.

10. The division of the different types of characters is a rule for the "model opera" formulated by the cultural authorities of the party-state, especially Jiang Qing, Mao's wife. Here we can tell just by looking at the layout of the character list (in the original Chinese version), in which a single blank space separates the "positive characters" and the "middle characters" and a double blank space

separates the middle characters (as well as other secondary characters) and the "negative character" (Shanghai jingjutuan *Haigang* 5).

Chapter 7

1. The phrase *caiyou . . . jintian* also has been widely used to thank the liberator of the Chinese nation, that is, Mao or the Communist Party. The imaginary rescue in this story is, ironically, attributed to a red-hair bigfoot.

2. Quoted with significant correction based on the original text in *Shouhuo* (Harvest) 6 (1986): 192.

3. The parody here, in a sense, is a subtle but decisive deviation from the Maoist discursive works such as *On the Docks,* in which we can find quite a similar scene, not performed by the madmen but by the supposedly heroic, at least positive, characters: "Three workers enter, jump over the cable, and perform a cable dance: somersault, bow the front leg and straighten the rear leg, look down, leap up, turn around, lift a leg aside, strike a pose; turn around and loop the cable over a capstan" (Shanghai jingjutuan *Haigang* 6 / "On the Docks" 1; trans. modified).

4. Strictly speaking, this novella is untranslatable, in that it is filled with idioms, common locutions, and even implicit quotations in Chinese that convey strong intertextual meanings in relation to Maoist discourse. The passage I have chosen might still tell something, even though the most subtle elements are unable to be represented in English. I have also put some keywords of the original in transliteration in the brackets.

5. Especially, for example, the scene about Mao Zedong's and Zhu De's armies making a junction on Jinggang Mountain or about Mao's and Liu Zhidan's armies meeting in Yan'an after the Long March.

6. We can easily find these phrases from communist literature, such as in *On the Docks.* The phrase *raised their unbending heads* is, for example, a variation of *hold their heads high* in *On the Docks.*

7. The same words are used in *On the Docks* to express the revolutionary ideal. See chapter 6.

Chapter 8

1. Schizophrenia in Can Xue, as Wang Ban remarks, is to be understood as "an existential and sociocultural phenomenon," indicating "unconscious drives break[ing] through and spill[ing] over into the representation of the ego and the social production of meaning" (246).

2. In all three cases the idiom *shuiluoshichu* is used in the original, although the translations are different or inconsistent.

3. The senselessness of the social "crowd," a principal theme of Lu Xun, certainly influences Can Xue as well as Xu Xiaohe. But, of course, it is the blind

mass movements in reality that decisively formulate the fictional vision of Can Xue and Xu Xiaohe.

4. Although the narrator is uncertain about the position of "comrade chief"—he once tries to guess the identity of the latter (118–19)—he occasionally presumes a relatively specific appellation, such as "Comrade Minister" (86), or presupposes that "you administer the Ministry of Industry" (64). This is another sign of the narrative instability that Can Xue invests in her narrator.

Chapter 9

1. This novel, as an account of the collective rural life of the "intellectual youth" (*zhiqing*) who were sent to the countryside by Mao's decree to "receive reeducation from the 'poor and lower-middle peasants,'" can be generally categorized as "intellectual youth fiction." But it deviates from the existing canon of "intellectual youth fiction" established by such works as Liang Xiaosheng's *Jinye you baofengxue* (There will be a blizzard tonight) and *Zhe shi yipian shenqi de tudi* (This is a miraculous land), Zhang Chengzhi's *Hei junma* (The black steed) and *Lüye* (The green night), and Kong Jiesheng's *Da linmang* (The great forest), which focus on the sent-down young intellectuals' emotional and spiritual endurance during the tough historical period. Embedded in tragic or nostalgic tone, intellectual youth fiction simplifies the crises of life and shows an intensely idealistic tendency that corresponds to the Maoist discourse. Even Ah Cheng's groundbreaking works "The Chess King" and "The King of Children" uncritically endorse a cultural foundation that is relevant to the master discourse in modern times. Ma Yuan's *Up or Down, Always Smooth,* on the other hand, deals with various primary, and in a sense meaningless, aspects of daily life: eating, making love, talking about sex, quarreling, gambling, fighting, stealing, playing, doing all kinds of things that can never lead to a more significant level. Trivialities in Ma Yuan's narrative undermine the glorious significance of the "reeducation" project and the ideological imperative that prompts intellectual youth fiction. It also contains countless minor incidents and hearsays, most of which are incomplete, or even incomprehensible and inexplicable.

2. As Ma Yuan's stereotyped characters, Lu Gao is a tall man with self-control, reason, and wisdom, and Yao Liang is more emotional and frequently involved in romantic affairs. As has been pointed out by critics, the two represent Ma Yuan's own double personalities, as far as the autobiographical quality of his fiction is concerned. It is precisely this autobiographical characteristic that differs greatly from his predecessors, such as Yu Dafu: Ma Yuan's split or double self-image is always implicated in diverse voices, neither of which can be totally identified with the authorial subject.

3. A Tibetan funeral ceremony, in which dismembered corpses are exposed on a terrace to birds of prey.

4. Only outside the story, in an interview, Ma Yuan admits that he has

been to a leprosarium, like Maqu Village, but the details of the story are fabricated (Xin 21).

5. Works like Ba Jin's *Disi bingshi* (Ward number four), for example, dwell largely on the social significance reflected in the extreme situation of human life.

6. In fact, the typical Chinese *mise-en-abyme*—an infinite cycle of worlds within worlds—exists in such an endless doggerel (once chanted in Chen Kaige's film *Haizi wang* [King of the children]): "Long long time ago there was a mountain, on the mountain there was a temple, in the temple there was an old monk, he was telling a story to the young monk: Long long time ago there was a mountain . . . ."

7. An abridged Chinese translation of Douglas R. Hofstadter's *Gödel, Escher, Bach: An Eternal Golden Braid* was widely circulated in the early 1980s and had an immense influence on the formation of literary conceptions among young writers.

Chapter 10

1. *Jiuxing* is a term widely used in communist literature. It usually refers to Mao, the Chinese Communist Party, or the People' Liberation Army.

2. The narrator previously tells about how he followed the woman to a wooden bridge and saw her cross the bridge, but the footprints of her boots stopped at the riverside. He bumped into two people: on the way, someone riding a bike head-on toward him passed him and their sleeves brushed against each other; and an old man with a white beard who appeared at the bridgehead carrying a lantern and told him that the bridge had been destroyed by a flood twenty years ago and no one would have been able to cross it. When the "I" had to head back, he discovered, in the ditch beside the bike, the stiff corpse of the person whom he had previously bumped into. Now this woman remembered that, on a night of snowstorm, her husband carried a lantern to that bridge (damaged not by flood but by thieves of timber, as she claimed) and saw footprints and bike traces, and the next day a corpse and a bike were found in the river.

3. Parody, as Linda Hutcheon (re)defines in her book on postmodernism, is "repetition with critical distance that allows ironic signalling of difference at the very heart of similarity" (*Poetics* 26). The "critical distance" that the postmodern parody in Chinese avant-garde fiction establishes from the archetype is not a one-dimensional subversion but a self-reflexive cultural act of struggling with an internalized, mythologized discourse, since the Greek prefix *para* (in the term *parody*) can mean both "counter" or "against" and "near" or "beside" (26).

4. The original passage from *Zhuang Zi* reads as follows: "Formerly, Chuang Chou [i.e., Zhuang Zi], dreamed that I was a butterfly, a butterfly flying about feeling that it was enjoying itself. I did not know that it was Chou.

Suddenly I awoke and was myself again, the veritable Chou. I did not know whether it had formerly been Chou dreaming that he was a butterfly, or it was now a butterfly dreaming that it was Chou" (60).

5. *Vast Sea* and *Indigo Mountain* allude again to Li Shangyin's poem (see ll. 5 and 6).

6. See note 61.

Chapter 11

1. Chinese mainstream scholars' evaluation of the emplotment of the genius-and-beauty romance can verify this assumption. The following observation is typical: "The ending of reunion in the genius-and-beauty romance is definitely a result of breaking the constraint of the feudal code of ethics and defeating the obstructions and sabotages of the decayed forces; it is achieved through hard and tortuous struggles or even at the cost of one's life" (Miao 76). It is not surprising that such a discourse is essentially no different from that of communist literature. As for the "narrative mode of binary opposition between good and evil" in the chivalry novel, Cai Xiang traces its origin to the famous Mencian tenet regarding the rule of fulfillment of personality: "That is why Heaven, when it is about to place a great burden on a man, always first tests his resolution, exhausts his frame and makes him suffer starvation and hardship, frustrates his efforts so as to shake him from his mental lassitude, toughen his nature and make good his deficiencies" (*Mencius* 181). The general plot is thus outlined as follows: the evil forces emerge in the decline of the dynasty; the young hero learns martial arts in the mountains; the evil forces temporarily defeat the hero; the young hero survives; the young hero finally triumphs (Cai 246–51).

2. Coincidental or not, Liu Sheng is a name—the alias of the protagonist, Su Youbai—from the novel *Yu Jiao Li* (Jade-Charming-Pear), one of the representative genius-and-beauty romances of the Qing Dynasty.

3. "The Story of Yingying" itself is, strictly speaking, not a genius-and-beauty romance, inasmuch as it does not have the stereotypic structure of the later standard ones. Many of the narrative strategies of the story, however, anticipate the ensuing genius-and-beauty romance. The complex relationship between "The Story of Yingying" and genius-and-beauty romance in general deserves a far more sophisticated and detailed discussion than I have undertaken here.

4. Such a metaphor starts presumably from "Tao yao" (Peach blossoms) in the *Shijing* (Book of poetry):

> The peach tree beams so red
> How brilliant are its flowers
> The maiden's getting wed
> Good for the nuptial bowers.
>
> (Xu Yuanchong 11)

Later, in Chinese poetry, the peach blossom is an image frequently called forth as a metaphor for female beauty.

5. The direct influence, however, is Kafka. In his essay "The Legacies of Kawabata and Kafka" Yu Hua mentions that, in Kafka's story "Ein Landarzt" (A country doctor), the doctor sees the patient's wound like a rose (*zuopinji* 2:297). Whereas Kafka's narrator in this story alludes to a rose because he is thinking of Rose (his female assistant), Yu Hua's narrator evokes the peach blossom against the background of Chinese literary tradition.

6. Another story in *Strange Tales from Make-Do Studio* that echoes "A Classical Romance" is "Wu Qiuyue," in which Wu Qiuyue is resurrected by copulating nocturnally with a man in the human world, who finally opens her grave and finds her body fully grown and then, taking her out, revives her and brings her back to reality by embracing her every night. Unlike the other stories, Wu Qiuyue remains in the human world in the end.

7. The uncanniness of the *Strange Tales from Make-Do Studio* is itself, in its own time, an opposition to, though not a parody of, the general logic that dominates the genius-and-beauty romance.

8. Specified by Yu Dafu at the end of the story, it was written exactly on his twenty-eighth birthday (Yu 1:353), whereas the narrator of the story is also passing his twenty-eighth birthday.

Chapter 12

1. Zhang Yimou's film *Honggaoliang* (Red sorghum), which was adapted from the novel and won the Golden Bear Award at the 1987 Berlin International Film Festival, has popularized the novel to a great extent.

2. This ending is dropped in a later, mainland China version (Changsha: Hunan wenyi chubanshe, 1993).

3. In Chinese communist literature, one of the earliest prototypes of the corrupted cadre is Chen Xiaoyuan in Zhao Shuli's "Li Youcai banhua" (The rhymes of Li Youcai). Represented as being corrupted by those whom he is supposed to discipline, Xiaoyuan is clearly criticized both by the positive characters in the story and by the narrator.

4. The early 1990s saw a number of novels dealing with the theme of social decadence and historical decline. Besides *The Republic of Wine*, Jia Pingwa's pseudoclassical romance *Feidu* (The ruined capital, 1993) and Liang Xiaosheng's political allegory *Fucheng* (The floating city, 1992) also display the fin de siècle sentiment by depicting spiritual or social breakdown. *The Floating City* fabricates a story of a Chinese city floating eastward on the sea and portrays the citizens turning from a jubilant group to a desperate and disastrous mob when they fail to reach the imaginary capitalistic shore at the other side. In *The Ruined Capital* Zhuang Zhidie, a man of letters residing in the ancient capital and supposedly a representative of national civilization, is habitually indulged in promiscuous sensual pleasure and transforms the cultural glory

into a joke about degeneration. Jia's imitation of the abridged, or "purged," edition of the classic erotic novel *The Plum in the Golden Vase*, by inserting blanks with remarks "[the number of] words deleted by the author," slyly evades (if not challenges) official censorship and shrewdly arouses the reading public's curiosity about its sexual content. While portraying the decadent lifestyle in contemporary China, Jia Pingwa, unlike Mo Yan, uses the narrative voice to show his great appreciation of and indulgence in such decadence, rather than examining or revealing the absurd logic of contemporary life.

Compared to the immediate commercial success and popularity of *The Ruined Capital,* the indifference that greeted *The Republic of Wine* after its publication indicates the great challenge it poses for readers and critics. Not until recent years has *The Republic of Wine* received serious critical attention. *The Ruined Capital,* on the other hand, has had an impressive impact on the reading public, not only because it is a sensationally erotic novel but precisely because it was officially banned (of course, after most copies, including pirate copies, had sold out)—this represents one of the more bizarre relationships between the state and the market in the 1990s. *The Republic of Wine* also lacks the influence it should because, while most Chinese novels appear in journal form first before being published as a book, no literary journal dared to publish it in the aftermath of the June Fourth Incident. And in China critics and readers show a preference for literary journals over books.

5. Later on, significantly, Li Yidou describes the elf's reappearance in Yichi Wineshop as an usher in a uniform with "smirking, silly eyes" (177–78), instead of his previous "chilly" "schemer's eyes" (115). The elf, by shifting his role from a militant revolutionary to an economic animal, allegorizes the historical transformation from Mao's age (the culmination of antagonistic fervor in the arena of class struggle) to Deng's age (when personality was determined by the profit motive and a growing climate of anti-intellectualism).

Postscript

1. Many scholars now admit that Maoism, or Chinese communism, is a distinctive formation of modernity. As Arif Dirlik and Xudong Zhang conclude, "Chinese communism was arguably the most forceful, and ultimately most successful, expression of an ideological commitment to modernity" (9).

2. My concept of "post–Cultural Revolution," again, does not refer chronologically to the years that immediately followed the end of the Cultural Revolution but to a culturo-historical paradigm in which the Cultural Revolution is conjured up as a traumatic, as well as phantom, past.

3. See also Lyotard's exposition of *Nachträglichkeit* (*Heidegger* 15–17).

4. Such a partial understanding of postmodernism comes mainly from the Chinese translations of Fredric Jameson's works, especially *Houxiandaizhuyi yu wenhualilun* (Postmodernism and cultural theories), trans. Tang Xiaobing (Xi'an: Shaanxi shifandaxue chubanshe, 1986). Of course, it is not these transla-

tions but the lack of more comprehensive studies and translations of other works on postmodernism that is responsible for the incomplete understanding.

5. The same theme recurs in Wang's postscript to the 1991 book *Zouxiang houxiandaizhuyi* (a Chinese translation of *Toward Postmodernism*, ed. Douwe Fokkema), in which he again offers a materialistic and social Darwinian perspective on literature: "Postmodernism is a specific cultural and literary phenomenon of the Western post-industrial and postmodern society, so it can only appear in the area where the material civilization of capitalism is highly advanced, with rich soil of modernist culture. But in China, where only a few writers and works of modernist tendency have existed and such cultural soil and social condition are fundamentally lacking, it is impossible to have a postmodernist literary movement. The experiment of a small number of avant-garde writers with a postmodern tendency can perhaps bring limited 'bombastic effect' in the circle of writers and critics, but ultimately cannot become the major current of contemporary Chinese literature" ("Yihouji" 324). It is especially baffling that, even if he ignores the postmodernist tendency in Latin American literature, Wang Ning neglects the essay on postmodern Soviet Russian theater in the book for which his postscript is written.

6. See, especially, his essay "The Mapping of Chinese Postmodernity," in which he acknowledges that the recent development of urban fiction in China (especially the works by Wei Hui and Mian Mian) has developed interpretations of post-utopian subjectivity with fluxional, diffused desire. But even Wei Hui's and Mian Mian's writings are not devoid of reactions to mainstream political modernity and its cultural ramifications.

7. Zhang Yiwu is indeed far-fetched to imply that "discontinuities, fragmentations and instabilities" in contemporary Chinese narratives are "feasible practical modes" "resisting *the repression of the First World culture*" (*Zai bianyuanchu* 90, my emphasis). Having said this, nonetheless, I must add that the most recent development of urban fiction in China (especially the works by Wei Hui and Mian Mian) has developed interpretations of the post-utopian subjectivity with fluxional, diffused desire. But even Wei Hui's and Mian Mian's writings are not devoid of reactions to mainstream political modernity and its cultural ramifications.

8. "'Houxue' yu Zhongguo xinbaoshouzhuyi" (Post-Isms and Chinese new conservatism) is the first and the most frequently discussed of this series of articles. Most of the arguments are later presented (translated?) in his 1997 article in English, "Post-Isms and Chinese New Conservatism" (see "Post-Isms").

9. Zhang Yiwu's emphasis on nativeness is more obscure than illuminating. He once acknowledged that "commercialization is a prerequisite for 'postmodernity,' and it is internationalized"; but then, when claiming that "our Third World condition has imbued commercialization an indigenous color," he cannot specify anything related to this "indigenized commercialization" (*Zai bianyuanchu* 97).

10. I am not claiming, of course, that transnational capitalism has no impact on the contemporary Chinese cultural scene. Especially in the film industry, to some extent, "Chinese filmmakers are obliged to operate in accor-

dance with the logic of global commodification" (Sheldon Lu 132). But, as Chen Xiaoming has accurately pointed out, the complexities that characterize postmodernism as regards Chinese cinema include not only "the subordinate/resistant relationship between the native and the global cultural imaginary" but also "the parasitical/disobedient relationship between the domestic cultural production and the revolutionary discourse" ("Mysterious" 140).

11. As a major target of Zhao Yiheng's harsh critique, Chen Xiaoming never responded directly to Zhao except in a footnote, in which he briefly denies Zhao's accusation that there exists a unified conservative school of "post-isms" (*Fangzhen* 215). Dai Jinhua, on the other hand, never advocates postmodernism. Rather, she, like Jing Wang and many others, finds it naïve to conceptualize the postmodern "on the legitimate basis of the need to conjoin and make parallel to the Western world " (*You zai* 251).

12. At the same time, commercialization has had a critical impact on the development of Chinese avant-garde literature. Especially in the 1990s and to the present day, avant-garde literature faces pressure not only from the old, orthodox, official cultural apparatus but also from the new, commercial, popular cultural environment. It is the latter—that is, the overshadowing market— that has diminished experimentalism in avant-garde fiction at the turn of the century. In other words, Chinese avant-garde fiction as a movement, having fought against the official, orthodox cultural apparatus, can hardly resist the allure, or pressure, of cultural commodification and consumerism. Yu Hua's sacrifice of narrative revolution to more or less complete and dramatized plot lines after 1989 exemplifies this new trend.

13. Herein lies a more negative understanding of *postsocialism* that Paul G. Pickowicz's offers in his study of new Chinese cinema, especially Huang Jianxin's films: "Postsocialist . . . refers in large part to a negative, dystopian cultural condition that prevails in late socialist societies" (62). Part of the reason that Pickowicz chooses the term *postsocialism,* as he explains, is to see the "cultural identity" that "links China to such societies as Poland, the former Soviet Union, Hungary, eastern Germany, and the former Czechoslovakia, all of which underwent long periods of difficult Marxist-Leninist rule" (61). To avoid confining the concept to too narrow a definition, Dirlik argues that "postsocialism is of necessity also postcapitalism" (364). My preference for the concept of "postmodernity," then, further reflects the endeavor to understand socialism, communism, and capitalism under the category of modernity, which can help theorize various historical phenomena such as the May Fourth Movement, the Cultural Revolution, the Holocaust, industrialization, and globalization as long as attention to specifics and particularities is duly paid.

14. Lyotard declares that "modernity is constitutionally and ceaselessly pregnant with its postmodernity" because of modernity's own "impulse to exceed itself into a state other than itself" (*Inhuman* 25).

Glossary

A Cheng, 阿城
Ahei xiaoshi, 阿黑小史
angqi buqu de toulu, 昂起不屈的頭顱
angshou kuobu, 昂首闊步
Ba ba ba, 爸爸爸
Ba Jin, 巴金
Bai Hua, 白樺
baimiao, 白描
Baofeng zhouyu, 暴風驟雨
Baowei Yan'an, 保衛延安
Bei Cun, 北村
beichuang youfen, 悲愴憂憤
Beifang de he, 北方的河
Biancheng, 邊城
Biaoben, 標本
Bing Xin, 冰心
cai, 才
Cai Xiang, 蔡翔
Cai Yuanpei, 蔡元培
caiyou nide jintian, 才有你的今天
Caizhu de ernümen, 財主的兒女們
caizi jiaren, 才子佳人
Can wu, 慘霧
Can Xue, 殘雪
Canglang shihua, 滄浪詩話
Canglao de fuyun, 蒼老的浮雲
Canju, 殘局
cha(tayi)ge/nongge shuiluoshichu,
  查(它一)個／弄個水落石出
Chan, 禪
Changshi ji, 嘗試集
Chen Cun, 陳村
Chen Kaige, 陳凱歌
Chen Xiaoming, 陳曉明
Cheng Fangwu, 成仿吾
chengfengpolang de julun,
  乘風破浪的巨輪
Chenlun, 沉淪
chixinwangxiang, 痴心妄想
chongman le jiqing, 充滿了激情
Chuangzao she, 創造社
Ciwen xiangei shaonü Yang Liu,
  此文獻給少女楊柳
Cuicui zhuan, 翠翠傳
Da linmang, 大林莽

dadao yige xinde gaodu,
　達到一個新的高度
Dai Jinhua, 戴錦華
Danian, 大年
dao, 道
Dao Mosike qu, 到莫斯科去
Dayuan he tade yuyan, 大元和他的寓言
dazibao, 大字報
Deng Xiaoping xuanji, 鄧小平選集
dian, 癲
Die zhiyao de sanzhong fangfa,
　疊紙鷂的三種方法
Dierzhong zhongcheng, 第二種忠誠
Ding Ling, 丁玲
Diren, 敵人
diyihao yingxiong renwu,
　第一號英雄人物
dongren de huayu, 動人的話語
Dongyao, 動搖
Du Pengcheng, 杜鵬程
duideqi shui, 對得起誰
Duiyu wenxue chuangzuo de yige huigu
　he zhanwang,
　對于文學創作的一個回顧和展望
Ershi nian mudu zhi guai xianzhuang,
　二十年目睹之怪現狀
Fangfa, 方法
fanmian renwu, 反面人物
fansi wenxue, 反思文學
Fei Ming, 廢名
Feidu, 廢都
feng, 瘋
Feng Mu, 馮牧
Fengqin, 風琴
Fengzi, 瘋子
Fengzi he tamende yuanzhang,
　瘋子和他們的院長
Fucheng, 浮城
gaige wenxue, 改革文學
Gangdisi de youhuo, 岡底斯的誘惑
Ge Fei, 格非
gediao, 格調
Gejue, 隔絕
geng jinmi de tuanjie qilai,
　更緊密地團結起來
Gongniu, 公牛
Gongsun jiuniang, 公孫九娘

Gouri de liangshi, 狗日的糧食
Guanchang xianxing ji, 官場現形記
Guanyu Yang jun xilai shijian de
　bianzheng,
　關於楊君襲來事件的辨正
Guchuan, 古船
Gudian aiqing, 古典愛情
Guiqulai, 歸去來
Guling zhi qiu, 牯嶺之秋
Guo Moruo, 郭沫若
Guwu, 古屋
Guxiang, 故鄉
Haigang, 海港
Haizi wang, 孩子王
Han Shaogong, 韓少功
Hao Ran, 浩然
haomai de, 豪邁地
haoyiwulao, 好逸惡勞
Hei junma, 黑駿馬
Hese niaoqun, 褐色鳥群
Hong, 虹
Hong Lingfei, 洪靈菲
Hongdeng ji, 紅燈記
Honggaoliang jiazu, 紅高粱家族
Honglou meng, 紅樓夢
Hongnan zuozhan shi, 虹南作戰史
Hongqi pu, 紅旗譜
Hongzhu, 紅燭
houjiwuren, 後繼無人
Hu Shi, 胡適
Hu Sijie, 胡四姐
Hu Yepin, 胡也頻
Huang Pengji, 黃鵬基
Huangni jie, 黃泥街
Huanle, 歡樂
Huanxiang houji, 還鄉後記
Huanxiang ji, 還鄉記
Hudie, 蝴蝶
huishi, 會師
Ji 'Yang Shuda jun' de xilai,
　記「楊樹達君」的襲來
Jia, 家
Jia Pingwa, 賈平凹
Jiandeng xinhua, 剪燈新話
jianding le tade juexin, 堅定了她的決心
Jiang Guangci, 蔣光慈
Jiang Qing, 江青

Glossary

Jiang Zilong, 蔣子龍
jiao, 腳
jieji diren, 階級敵人
jijiguagua de, 嘰嘰呱呱的
Jin ping mei, 金瓶梅
Jin Shengtan, 金聖嘆
Jinguang dadao, 金光大道
Jinian Baiqiuen, 紀念白求恩
Jinse, 錦瑟
Jinye you baofengxue, 今夜有暴風雪
jiqing wuxian, 激情無限
Jiuguo, 酒國
jiuxing, 救星
junxun, 軍訓
Kong Jiesheng, 孔捷生
kuang, 狂
Kuangren riji, 狂人日記
Lan gaizi, 藍蓋子
Lao Can youji, 老殘游記
Lao She, 老舍
laosanpian, 老三篇
Lao Zi, 老子
Li Bai, 李白
Li Baojia, 李寶嘉
Li Hangyu, 李杭育
Li Jianwu, 李健吾
Li Shangyin, 李商隱
Li Tuo, 李陀
Li Tuozhi, 李拓之
Li Yu'an, 李遇安
Liang Bin, 梁斌
Liang Qichao, 梁啓超
Liang Xiaosheng, 梁曉聲
Lianzi, 煉字
Liaozhai zhiyi, 聊齋志異
Lin Ruji, 林如稷
lingchi, 凌遲
lingyang guojiao, wuji keqiu, 羚羊掛角，無跡可求
Linhai xueyuan, 林海雪原
Liu Binyan, 劉賓雁
Liu E, 劉鶚
Liu Heng, 劉恆
Liu Suola, 劉索拉
Liu Zaifu, 劉再復
Liuwang, 流亡
longfeng chengxiang, 龍鳳呈祥

Longjiang song, 龍江頌
Longzhu, 龍朱
Lu Wenfu, 陸文夫
Lu Ling, 路翎
Lu Xun, 魯迅
Lu Yanzhou, 魯彥周
Lu Yin, 廬隱
Lüye, 綠夜
Lunyu, 論語
Luotuo Xiangzi, 駱駝祥子
Lushan yao ji Lu Shiyu Xuzhou, 廬山遙寄盧侍御虛舟
Ma Yuan, 馬原
manhuai haoqing, 滿懷豪情
Mao Dun, 茅盾
Mao huayu, 毛話語
Mao wenti, 毛文體
Mao Zedong xuanji, 毛澤東選集
Mao Zhuxi yulu, 毛主席語錄
Maodun lun, 矛盾論
Maoyu, 毛語
Meili nanfang zhi xiari, 美麗南方之夏日
Meishijia, 美食家
Meiyou ren kanjian cao shengzhang, 沒有人看見草生長
menglong shi, 朦朧詩
Mian Mian, 棉棉
Mizhou, 迷舟
Mo Yan, 莫言
Moluo shili shuo, 摩羅詩力說
Nahan, 吶喊
Nantao jieshu, 難逃劫數
Ni biewu xuanze, 你別無選擇
Nü nü nü, 女女女
Nüshen, 女神
Ouran shijian, 偶然事件
pidouhui, 批斗會
pigunniaoliu, 屁滾尿流
Qiao changzhang shangren ji, 喬廠長上任記
qigai xuanang, 氣概軒昂
Qingchun zhi ge, 青春之歌
Qinghuang, 青黃
qingzhu'nanshu, 磬竹難書
qinmi zhanyou, 親密戰友
Qiwang, 棋王

Qu Bo, 曲波
Qu You, 瞿佑
Qu Yuan, 屈原
qude kexi de jinzhan, 取得可喜的進展
Ren huo hongmaoyeren, 人或紅毛野人
Ren yao zhijian, 人妖之間
Sanguo, 三國
Shafei nüshi de riji, 莎菲女士的日記
Shajiabang, 沙家浜
Shang Duo, 尚多
Shanghen, 傷痕
shanghen wenxue, 傷痕文學
Shangshi, 傷逝
Shangui, 山鬼
Shangxia dou hen pingtan, 上下都很平坦
Shanshang de xiaowu, 山上的小屋
Shen Congwen, 沈從文
Shengming de wenxue, 生命的文學
shenyun, 神韻
Shi, 蝕
shi, 事
shi yan zhi, 詩言志
Shi Zhecun, 施蟄存
Shicao jiazu, 食草家族
Shiji, 史記
shiji qingkuang, 實際情況
Shijing, 詩經
shike zhunbei zhe, 時刻準備著
Shipin, 詩品
Shisan bu, 十三步
Shishi ruyan, 世事如煙
shishiqiushi, 實事求是
Shiyiyue chusan, 十一月初三
Shizhong, 示眾
Shouhuo, 收穫
shouzhang tongzhi, 首長同志
Shuihu, 水滸
Shuiling de rizi, 水靈的日子
Shuwang, 樹王
Sikong Tu, 司空圖
Sima Qian, 司馬遷
Sixiang huibao, 思想匯報
Siyue sanri shijian, 四月三日事件
Sun Fuyuan, 孫伏園
Sun Ganlu, 孫甘露

Taiyang zhaozai Sangganhe shang, 太陽照在桑乾河上
Tang Xiaobing, 唐小兵
Tao yao, 桃夭
taoli, 逃離
Tianchuang, 天窗
Tianyunshan chuanqi, 天雲山傳奇
tianzang, 天葬
tianzhen, 天眞
Touming de hongluobo, 透明的紅蘿卜
Tuman guguai tu'an de qiangbi, 涂滿古怪圖案的牆壁
Tuwei biaoyan, 突圍表演
Wang Guowei, 王國維
wang le zuihou yiyan, 望了最後一眼
Wang Meng, 王蒙
Wang Ning, 王寧
Wang Ruowang, 王若望
Wang Shizhen, 王士禎
Wang Shuo, 王朔
Wang Xiyan, 王西彥
Wangshi yu xingfa, 往事與刑罰
Wei Hu, 韋護
wei... fendou, 爲...奮斗
Wei Hui, 衛慧
wen yi zai dao, 文以載道
Wen Yiduo, 聞一多
wenhua fansi, 文化反思
wenrou dunhou, 溫柔敦厚
Wenxin diaolong, 文心雕龍
Wenxue yanjiuhui, 文學研究會
Wenxuezhe de xin shiming, 文學者的使命
Wo zai neige shijie li de shiqing, 我在那個世界里的事情
woshou, 握手
Wu Hongsen, 吳洪森
Wu Woyao, 吳沃堯
Wushui shang de feizaopao, 污水上的肥皂泡
Wuxia, 武俠
xianfeng, 先鋒
xiangduiwuyan, 相對無言
Xianjing, 陷阱
Xianshi yizhong, 現實一種
Xianxue meihua, 鮮血梅花
Xihai de wufanchuan, 西海的無帆船

Xin shisiniang, 辛十四娘
xinchao pengpai, 心潮澎湃
xing guan qun yuan, 興觀群怨
xinggaocailie, 興高采烈
xingshi, 形勢
Xinshi zhi han, 信使之函
xinshiqi wenxue, 新時期文學
Xinshiqi wenxue de zhuliu,
 新時期文學的主流
xinwenxue yundong, 新文學運動
xinxieshizhuyi, 新寫實主義
Xinyue she, 新月社
Xiyou ji, 西游記
Xu Dishan, 許地山
Xu Jie, 許杰
Xu Xiaohe, 徐曉鶴
Xu Zhimo, 徐志摩
Xuanchuanbao ji qita, 宣傳寶及其他
Xuanwuhu zhi qiu, 玄武湖之秋
Xugou, 虛構
xungen, 尋根
Xunzhao gewang, 尋找歌王
Xuwei de zuopin, 虛僞的作品
Yalujiang shang, 鴨綠江上
Yan Yu, 嚴羽
yanbujinyi, 言不盡意
Yang Mo, 楊沫
yangbanxi, 樣板戲
Yanmie, 湮滅
Yanyang tian, 艷陽天
Yaomohua Zhongguo de beihou,
 妖魔化中國的背後
Yecao, 野草
yijing, 易經
Yijiubaliu nian, 一九八六年
Yingying zhuan, 鶯鶯傳
yinleng, 陰冷
yishen shifa (exemplify the law
 personally), 以身示法
yishen shifa (test the law personally),
 以身試法
Yizhengciyan, 義正辭嚴
youdou, 游斗
Youshen, 游神
Yu Dafu, 郁達夫
Yu Hua, 余華
Yu Jiao Li, 玉嬌李

Yuan Zhen, 元稹
Yuanzhang he tade fengzimen,
 院長和他的瘋子們
Yugong yishan, 愚公移山
Yushi, 浴室
Yusi, 語絲
Yuzhong xinchang de, 語重心長地
Zhang Chengzhi, 張承志
Zhang Dinghuang, 張定璜
Zhang Wei, 張煒
Zhang Xudong, 張旭東
Zhang Yimou, 張藝謀
Zhang Yiwu, 張頤武
Zhang Zhupo, 張竹坡
Zhao Yiheng, 趙毅衡
Zhe shi yipian shenqi de tudi,
 這是一片神奇的土地
zhecai, 這才
zhenchayuan, 偵察員
zhencheng tanbai, 真誠坦白
zhengmian renwu, 正面人物
zhengyao, 正要
zhenli, 真理
zhenshi, 真實
Zhexue yiwai, 哲學以外
zhi...jiu, 只 . . . 就
Zhiqu Weihushan, 智取威虎山
zhishi qingnian, 知識青年
Zhiyanzhai, 脂硯齋
zhong, 腫
Zhong zai zoulang shang de pingguoshu,
 種在走廊里的蘋果樹
Zhongguo xinwenxue daxi,
 中國新文學大系
Zhongguo xinwenxue daxi zongxu,
 中國新文學大系總序
zhongjian renwu, 中間人物
Zhongshan, 鐘山
Zhou Libo, 周立波
Zhou Zuoren, 周作人
Zhu jian, 鑄劍
Zhu Xi, 朱熹
Zhuang Zi, 莊子
Zhufu, 祝福
zhuiyi, 追憶
Ziye, 子夜
Zuo zhuan, 左傳

Bibliography

———. *Three Kings: Three Stories from Today's China*. Trans. Bonnie S. McDougall. London: Collins Harvill, 1990.
Adorno, Theodor W. "The Actuality of Philosophy." *Telos* 31 (1977): 120–33.
———. *Aesthetic Theory*. Ed. Gretel Adorno and Rolf Tiedemann. Trans. Robert Hullot-Kentor. Minneapolis: University of Minnesota Press, 1997.
———. *Kierkegaard: Construction of the Aesthetic*. Trans. Robert Hullot-Kentor. Minneapolis: University of Minnesota Press, 1989.
———. *Negative Dialectics*. Trans. E. B. Ashton. New York: Seabury Press, 1973.
———. *Prisms*. Trans. Samuel and Shierry Weber. Cambridge, Mass.: MIT Press, 1981.
Ah Cheng. *Qiwang* (The king of chess). Beijing: Zuojia chubanshe, 1985.
Althusser, Louis. *For Marx*. Trans. Ben Brewster. New York: Vintage Books, 1970.
Anderson, Marston. *The Limits of Realism: Chinese Fiction in the Revolutionary Period*. Berkeley: University of California Press, 1990.
Apter, David Ernest, and Tony Saich. *Revolutionary Discourse in Mao's Republic*. Cambridge: Harvard University Press, 1994.
Arendt, Hannah. *The Origins of Totalitarianism*. New York: Meridian Books, 1958.
Ba Jin [Pa Chin]. *Family*. Garden City, N.Y.: Doubleday, 1972.
———. *Jia* (Family). Beijing: Renmin wenxue chubanshe, 1978.
Bakhtin, M. M. *The Dialogic Imagination: Four Essays*. Ed. Michael Holquist. Trans. Caryl Emerson and Michael Holquist. Austin: University of Texas Press, 1981.
Bataille, Georges. *The Tears of Eros*. Trans. Peter Conner. San Francisco: City Lights, 1989.
Baudelaire, Charles. *The Painter of Modern Life and Other Essays*. Ed. and trans. J. Mayne. New York: Garland, 1978.
Benjamin, Walter. *Illuminations*. Ed. Hannah Arendt. Trans. H. Zohn. New York: Schocken Books, 1969.
Bhabha, Homi K. *Nation and Narration*. London: Routledge, 1990.
Bloom, Harold. "Freud and the Poetic Sublime: A Catastrophe Theory of Creativity." In *Freud: A Collection of Critical Essays*. Ed. Perry Meisel, 211–31. Englewood Cliffs, N.J.: Prentice-Hall, 1981.
Cai Xiang. *Xia yu yi: Wuxia xiaoshuo yu Zhongguo wenhua* (The chivalric and the

righteous: The knight-errant novel and Chinese culture). Beijing: Beijing shiyue wenyi chubanshe, 1993.
Cai Yuanpei. "Zongxu" (General introduction). *Jianshe lilun ji* (Constructive theories). Ed. Hu Shi. Zhongguo xin wenxue daxi 1: 3–11. Shanghai: Liangyou tushu gongsi, 1935.
Can Xue. *Dialogues in Paradise.* Trans. Ronald R. Janssen and Jian Zhang. Evanston, Ill.: Northwestern University Press, 1989.
———. *The Embroidered Shoes: Stories.* Trans. Ronald R. Janssen and Jian Zhang. New York: Henry Holt, 1997.
———. "Meili nanfang zhi xiari" (The beautiful summer in the south). *Zhongguo* (China) 10 (1986): 75–78.
———. *Old Floating Cloud: Two Novellas.* Trans. Ronald R. Janssen and Jian Zhang. Evanston, Ill.: Northwestern University Press, 1991.
———. *Sixiang huibao* (A thought report). Changsha: Hunan wenyi chubanshe, 1994.
———. *Tiantang li de duihua* (Dialogues in paradise). Beijing: Zuojia chubanshe, 1988.
———. *Tuwei biaoyan* (Breakout performances). Shanghai: Shanghai wenyi chubanshe, 1990.
———. "Wo shi zenme gaoqi chuangzuo laide" (How I began to write). *Wenxue ziyoutan* (Free Forum of Literature) 2 (1988): 50–51.
———. "Wushui shang de feizaopao" (Soap bubbles in the dirty water). In *Zhongguo xiaoshuo: Yijiubaqi* (Chinese fiction: 1987). Ed. Huang Ziping and Li Tuo, 405–9. Hong Kong: Sanlian shudian, 1989.
———. "Zhong zai zoulang li de pingguoshu" (Apple tree in the corridor). *Zhongshan* 6 (1987): 61–94.
Cao Xueqin. *Gengchen chaoben* Shitou ji (The Gengchen copy of *A Story of the Stone*). Taipei: Guangwen shuju, 1977.
———. *The Story of the Stone.* 6 vols. Trans. David Hawkes and John Minford. Harmondsworth: Penguin, 1973–86.
Caruth, Cathy, ed. *Trauma: Explorations in Memory.* Baltimore: Johns Hopkins University Press, 1995.
Chen Xiaoming. *Fangzhen de niandai* (The age of simulation). Taiyuan: Shangxi jiaoyu chubanshe, 1999.
———. "The Mysterious Other: Postpolitics in the Narrative of Chinese Film." *Boundary 2* 24, no. 3 (1997): 123–41.
———. *Wubian de tiaozhan: Zhongguo xianfeng wenxue de houxiandaixing* (The immeasurable challenge: Postmodernity of Chinese avant-garde literature). Changchun: Shidai wenyi chubanshe, 1993.
Cheng Depei and Wu Liang, eds. *Tansuo xiaoshuo xuan* (Selected experimental short stories). Shanghai: Shanghai wenyi chubanshe, 1986.
Chou Ying-hsiung. "*Jiuguo* de xushi" (Falsehood and truth of *The Republic of Wine*). *Jiuguo* (The republic of wine). Mo Yan. Taipei: Hongfan shudian, 1992.
Ci, Jiwei. *Dialectic of the Chinese Revolution: From Utopianism to Hedonism.* Stanford, Calif.: Stanford University Press, 1994.

Dai Jinhua. "Liegu de lingyi cepan: chu du Yu Hua" (The other side of the chasm: An elementary reading of Yu Hua). *Beijing wenxue* (Beijing literature) 7 (1989): 26–33.

———. *You zai jing zhong* (As if still in the mirror). Beijing: Zhishi chubanshe, 1999.

De Man, Paul. *Blindness and Insight*. Minneapolis: University of Minnesota Press, 1983.

———. *Critical Writings, 1953–1978*. Ed. Lindsay Waters. Minneapolis: University of Minnesota Press, 1989.

Denton, Kirk A. "General Introduction." In *Modern Chinese Literary Thought: Writings on Literature, 1893–1945*. Ed. Kirk A. Denton, 1–61. Stanford, Calif.: Stanford University Press, 1996.

Derrida, Jacques. *Dissemination*. Trans. Barbara Johnson. Chicago: University of Chicago Press, 1981.

———. *Of Grammatology*. Trans. Gayatri Chakravarty Spivak. Baltimore: Johns Hopkins University Press, 1976.

———. *Positions*. Trans. Alan Bass. London: Athlone Press, 1981.

———. *Writing and Difference*. Trans. Alan Bass. Chicago: University of Chicago Press, 1978.

Ding Ling. *Miss Sophie's Diary*. Trans. W. J. F. Jenner. Beijing: Chinese Literature, 1985.

———. *The Sun Shines over the Sanggan River*. Trans. Yang Xianyi and Gladys Yang. Beijing: Foreign Languages Press, 1984.

———. *Taiyang zhao zai Sangganhe shang* (The sun shines over the Sanggan River). Beijing: Renmin wenxue chubanshe, 1955.

Dirlik, Arif. "Postsocialism? Reflections on 'Socialism with Chinese Characteristics.'" In *Marxism and the Chinese Experience*. Ed. Arif Dirlik and Maurice Meisner, 362–84. Armonk, N.Y.: Sharpe, 1989.

Dirlik, Arif, and Zhang, Xudong. "Introduction: Postmodernism and China." *Boundary 2* 24:3 (1997): 1–18.

Du Pengcheng. *Defend Yanan*. Trans. Sidney Shapiro. Beijing: Foreign Languages Press, 1983.

Duara, Prasenjit. *Rescuing History from the Nation: Questioning Narratives of Modern China*. Chicago: University of Chicago Press, 1995.

Egan, Ronald C. "Narratives in *Tso chuan*." *Harvard Journal of Asiatic Studies* 37, no. 2 (1977).

Eliot, T. S. *Complete Poems and Plays, 1909–1950*. New York: Harcourt, Brace and Company, 1952.

Felman, Shoshana. *Writing and Madness*. Trans. Martha Noel Evans and Shoshana Felman. Ithaca, N.Y.: Cornell University Press, 1985.

Feng Mu. *Xinshiqi wenxue de zhuliu* (The mainstream of the new-era literature). Beijing: Renmin wenxue chubanshe, 1979.

Foucault, Michel. *Madness and Civilization: A History of Insanity in the Age of Reason*. Trans. Richard Howard. New York: Pantheon Books, 1965.

———. *The Order of Things: An Archaeology of the Human Sciences*. New York: Pantheon Books, 1970.

Freud, Sigmund. *The Standard Edition of the Complete Psychological Works of Sigmund Freud.* 24 vols. London: Hogarth Press and the Institute of Psychoanalysis, 1953–73.
Fu Sinian (Meng Zhen). "Yiduan fenghua" (A few mad words). *Xinchao* (New Wave) 1, no. 4 (April 1919): 684–87.
Ge Fei. *Diren* (The enemy). Taiwan: Yuanliu chuban gongsi, 1993.
———. "The Lost Boat." Trans. Caroline Mason. *The Lost Boat.* Ed. Henry Y H Zhao. London: Wellsweep Press, 1993. 77–100.
———. *Mizhou* (The lost boat). Beijing: Zuojia chubanshe, 1989.
———. *Yuji de ganjue* (The feeling in the rainy season). Beijing: Xinshijie chubanshe, 1994.
Guo Moruo. *Guo Moruo lun chuangzuo* (Guo Moruo on writing). Shanghai: Shanghai wenyi chubanshe, 1983.
Han Shaogong. *Homecoming? And Other Stories.* Trans. Martha Cheung. Hong Kong: Research Centre for Translation, Chinese University of Hong Kong, 1992.
———. "Wenxue de 'gen'" (The "root" of literature). *Zuojia* (Writers) (1985.4): 2–5.
———. *Youhuo* (Temptation). Changsha: Hunan wenyi chubanshe, 1986.
Hao Ran. *Yanyang tian* (Bright sunny sky). 3 vols. Beijing: Renmin wenxue chubanshe, 1976.
Herman, Judith Lewis. *Trauma and Recovery.* New York: Basic Books, 1992.
Hirsch, David H. *The Deconstruction of Literature: Criticism after Auschwitz.* Providence, R.I.: Brown University Press, 1991.
Horkheimer, Max, and Theodor W. Adorno. *Dialectic of Enlightenment.* Trans. John Cumming. New York: Herder and Herder, 1972.
Hsia, C. T. *The Classical Chinese Novel: A Critical Introduction.* New York: Columbia University Press, 1968.
———. *A History of Modern Chinese Fiction.* New Haven: Yale University Press, 1971.
Hu Shi. *Hu Shi wenxuan* (Selected essays of Hu Shi). Taipei: Yuanliu chuban gongsi, 1986.
Hutcheon, Linda. *Narcissistic Narrative: The Metafictional Paradox.* Waterloo, Ont.: Wilfrid Laurier University Press, 1980.
———. *A Poetics of Postmodernism: History, Theory, Fiction.* New York: Routledge, 1988.
———. "The Power of Postmodern Irony." In Northrop Frye, Linda Hutcheon, Shirley Neuman, *Genre, Trope, Gender: Essays.* Ed. Barry Rutland. Ottawa: Carleton University Press, 1992.
———. *A Theory of Parody: The Teachings of Twentieth-Century Art Forms.* New York: Methuen, 1985.
Huters, Theodore. "Ideologies of Realism in Modern China: The Hard Imperatives of Imported Theory." In *Politics, Ideology and Literary Discourse in Modern China.* Ed. Liu Kang and Xiaobin Tang, 147–73. Durham: Duke University Press, 1993.

———. Introduction. *Reading the Modern Chinese Short Story*. Ed. Theodore Huters. Armonk, New York: M. E. Sharpe, 1990.

———. "Lives in Profile: On the Authorial Voice in Modern and Contemporary Chinese Literature." In *From May Fourth to June Fourth*. Ed. Ellen Widmer and David Der-wei Wang, 269–94. Cambridge: Harvard University Press, 1993.

———. "Third-World Literature in the Era of Multinational Capitalism." *Social Text* 15 (fall 1986). 65–88.

Janssen, Ronald. "Chinese Voices: A Review." *Modern Chinese Literature* 8 (1994): 191–200.

Jiang Zilong. *Jiang Zilong daibiaozuo* (Representative works of Jiang Zilong). Zhengzhou: Huanghe wenyi chubanshe, 1986.

———. "Manager Qiao Assumes Office." In *The New Realism: Writings from Chinese after the Cultural Revolution*. Ed. Lee Yee, 56–85. New York: Hippocrene Books, 1983.

Jin Guantao. "*Maodun lun* yu tianren heyi" (*On Contradiction* and the unity of heaven and man). *Ershiyi shiji* (The twentieth-first century) 29 (June 1995): 28–40.

Kierkegaard, Søren. *The Concept of Irony: With Constant Reference to Socrates*. Trans. Lee M. Capel. Bloomington: Indiana University Press, 1965.

Lao She. *Luotuo Xiangzi* (Camel Xiangzi). *Lao She wenji* (Collected works of Lao She) 3. Beijing: Renmin wenxue chubanshe, 1982.

———. *Rickshaw: The Novel Lo-t'o Hsiang Tzu*. Trans. Jean M. James. Honolulu: University of Hawaii Press, 1979.

Lao Zi (Lao Tzu). *Tao te ching*. Trans. D. C. Lau. London: Penguin Books, 1963.

Laplanche, J., and J.-B. Pontalis. *The Language of Psycho-Analysis*. Trans. Donald Nicholson-Smith. New York: Norton, 1973.

Lee, Leo Ou-fan. *The Romantic Generation of Modern Chinese Writers*. Cambridge: Harvard University Press, 1973.

———. *Voices from the Iron House: A Study of Lu Xun*. Bloomington: Indiana University Press, 1987.

Lei Feng. *Lei Feng riji* (Lei Feng's diary). Beijing: Jiefangjun wenyishe, 1963.

Li Bai (Li Po). "A Song of Lu Mountain: To Censor Lu Hsü-chou [Lu Xuzhou]." *The Jade Mountain: A Chinese Anthology*, 63–64. Trans. Witter Bynner. New York: Vintage Books, 1972.

Li Jie. *Women de wenhua gexing he gexing wenhua: lun shiji xianxiang* (Our cultural individuality and individual culture: On the century phenomenon). Xining: Qinghai renmin chubanshe, 1998.

Li Tuo. "1985." *Jintian* (Today) 14–15 (1991): 59–73.

Li Xiguang, et al., eds. *Yaomohua Zhongguo de beihou*. Beijing: Zhongguo shehui kexue chubanshe, 1996.

Liang Pin (Liang Bin). *Keep the Red Flag Flying*. Trans. Gladys Yang. Peking: Foreign Languages Press, 1961.

Liang Qichao. "On the Relationship between Fiction and the Government of the People" (Lun xiaoshuo yu qunzhi zhi guanxi). Trans. Gek Nai Cheng.

In *Modern Chinese Literary Thought: Writings on Literature, 1893–1945*. Ed. Kirk A Denton, 74–81. Stanford: Stanford University Press, 1996.

Lieberman, Sally Taylor. *The Mother and Narrative Politics in Modern China*. Charlottesville: University Press of Virginia, 1998.

Lie Zi. *The Book of Lieh-tzu*. Trans. A. C. Graham. London: John Murray, 1960.

Lifton, Robert Jay. *Thought Reform and the Psychology of Totalism: A Study of "Brainwashing" in China*. New York: Norton, 1961.

Lin Yü-sheng. "The Morality of Mind and Immorality of Politics: Reflections on Lu Xun, the Intellectual." In *Lu Xun and His Legacy*. Ed. Leo Ou-fan Lee, 107–28. Berkeley: University of California Press, 1985.

Liu Binyan. *Liu Binyan zixuanji* (Self-selected essays by Liu Binyan). Beijing: Zhongguo wenlian chuban gongsi, 1988.

Liu, James J. Y. *The Poetry of Li Shangyin: Ninth-Century Baroque Chinese Poet*. Chicago: University of Chicago Press, 1969.

Liu, Kang. "Hegemony and Cultural Revolution." *New Literary History* 28, no. 1 (1997): 69–86.

Liu Zaifu. "Lun wenxue de zhutixing" (On the subjectivity of literature). *Wenxue pinglun* (Literary Review) 1985.6: 11–26.

Lu, Sheldon Hsiao-peng. "National Cinema, Cultural Critique, Transnational Capital: The Films of Zhang Yimou." In *Transnational Chinese Cinema: Identity, Nationhood, Gender*. Ed. Sheldon Lu. Honolulu: University of Hawaii Press, 1997.

Lu Tonglin. *Misogyny, Cultural Nihilism, and Oppositional Politics: Contemporary Chinese Experimental Fiction*. Stanford: Stanford University Press, 1995.

Lu Wenfu. *Lu Wenfu ji* (Collected works of Lu Wenfu). Fuzhou: Haixia wenyi chubanshe, 1986.

Lu Xun. *Lu Xun quanji* (Complete works of Lu Xun). 16 vols. Beijing: Renmin wenxue chubanshe, 1993.

———. *Selected Works*. 4 vols. Trans. Yang Xianyi and Gladys Yang. Beijing: Foreign Languages Press, 1980.

Lu Yanzhou. *Tianyunshan chuanqi* (The legend of Tianyun Mountain). Tianjin: Baihua wenyi chubanshe, 1981.

Lyotard, Jean-François. "Answering the Question: What Is Postmodernism?" Trans. Régis Durand. *The Postmodern Condition: A Report on Knowledge*, 71–82. Trans. Geoffrey Bennington and Brian Massumi. Minneapolis: University of Minnesota Press, 1984.

———. *Heidegger and "the jews."* Trans. Andreas Michel and Mark S. Roberts. Minneapolis: University of Minnesota Press, 1990.

———. *The Inhuman: Reflections on Time*. Trans. Geoferrey Bennington and Rachel Bowley. Cambridge: Polity Press, 1991.

———. *The Lyotard Reader*. Ed. Andrew Benjamin. Oxford: Basil Blackwell, 1989.

———."Re-writing Modernity." *Sub-stance* 54:3–9.

Ma Yuan. "Fabrication." Trans. J. Q. Sun. In *The Lost Boat*. Ed. Henry Y H Zhao, 101–44. London: Wellsweep Press, 1993.

———. "Fangfa" (The method). *Zhongpienxiaoshuo xuankan* (Journal of Novellas) 1987.1: 129.

———. *Shangxia dou hen ping tan* (Up or down, always smooth). Shanghai: Shanghai wenyi chubanshe, 1989.

———. *Xihai wufanchuan: Ma Yuan Xizang xiaoshuo xuan* (The sail-less boat in the West Sea: A selection of short stories about Tibet by Ma Yuan). Lhasa: Xizang renmin chubanshe, 1987.

———. "Zhexue yiwai" (Beyond philosophy). *Dangdai zuojia pinglun* (Criticisms of Contemporary Writers) 1987.5: 59–61.

Mao Dun. "Fengzi" (The madman). *Shenbao yuekan* (Shanghai Gazette Monthly) 3, no. 11 (1934): 103–8.

———. *Hong* (The rainbow). Chengdu: Sichuan renmin chubanshe, 1981.

———. *Mao Dun quanji* (The complete works of Mao Dun). 22 vols. Beijing: Renmin wenxue chubanshe, 1989.

———. *Midnight*. Hong Kong: C. and W. Publishing Co., 1976.

———. *Shi* (Eclipse). Beijing: Renmin wenxue chubanshe, 1994.

———. *Ziye* (Midnight). Beijing: Renmin wenxue chubanshe, 1977.

Mao Zedong. "Gei Qinghua Fuzhong hongweibing de yifeng xin" (A letter to the Red Guards at the middle school attached to Qinghua University). *Jianguo yilai Mao Zedong wengao* (Mao Zedong's manuscripts since the founding of the People's Republic of China), vol. 12. Beijing: Zhongyang wenxian chubanshe, 1987.

———. *Quotations from Chairman Mao Tse-tung*. Peking: Foreign Language Press, 1966.

———. *Selected Works of Mao Tse-tung*. 4 vols. Peking: Foreign Language Press, 1965.

Marx, Karl. "Critique of the Gotha Programme." In *The Marx-Engels Reader*. Ed. Robert C. Tucker, 525–41. New York: Norton, 1978.

Mellor, Anne K. *English Romantic Irony*. Cambridge: Harvard University Press, 1980.

Mencius. Trans. D. C. Lau. London: Penguin Books, 1970.

Miao Zhuang. "Tan caizijiaren xiaoshuo de tuanyuan jieju" (On the ending of reunion in the genius-and-beauty romance). *Caizijiaren xiaoshuo shulin* (Critical essays on the genius-and-beauty romance), 70–83. Shenyang: Chunfeng wenyi chubanshe, 1985.

Mo Yan. *Honggaoliang jiazu* (Red sorghum: A family saga). Beijing: Jiefangjun wenyi chubanshe, 1987.

———. *Jiuguo* (*The Republic of Wine*). Taipei: Hongfan shudian, 1992.

———. *Red Sorghum: A Family Saga*. Trans. Howard Goldblatt. New York: Viking, 1993.

———. *Shicao jiazu* (The herbivorous family). Beijing: Huayi chubanshe, 1993.

"On the Docks" Group of the Peking Opera Troupe of Shanghai, The. *On the Docks: A Modern Revolutionary Peking Opera*. Rev. ed. Peking: Foreign Languages Press, 1973.

Pickowicz, Paul G. "Huang Jianxin and Postsocialism." In *New Chinese Cinemas: Forms, Identities, Politics*. Ed. Nick Browne et al. Cambridge: Cambridge University Press, 1994.

Plaks, Andrew H. *The Four Masterpieces of the Ming Novel*. Princeton: Princeton University Press, 1987.

Plato. *The Republic. Plato: The Collected Dialogues.* Ed. E. Hamilton and H. Cairus. Princeton, N.J.: Princeton University Press, 1963.
Průšek, Jaroslav. *The Lyrical and the Epic: Studies of Modern Chinese Literature.* Bloomington: Indiana University Press, 1980.
Reik, Theodor. "Grenzland des Witzes" (Borderland of the joke). *Psychoanalytische Bewegung* (Psychoanalytic Movement) 4 (1932): 289–322.
———. *The Secret Self: Psychoanalytic Experience in Life and Literature.* New York: Farrar, Straus and Young, 1953.
Richards, I. A. *Principles of Literary Criticism.* New York: Harcourt, Brace and World, 1961.
Ricoeur, Paul. *Lectures on Ideology and Utopia.* Ed. George H. Taylor. New York: Columbia University Press, 1986.
Shanghai jingjutuan *Haigang* juzu. *Haigang* (On the docks). Rev. ed. Beijing: Renmin wenxue chubanshe, 1972.
Shanghai jingjutuan *Zhiqu Weihushan* juzu. *Zhiqu Weihushan* (Taking the Tiger Mountain by strategy). Rev. ed. Beijing: Renmin wenxue chubanshe, 1970.
Shanghaixian *Hongnan zuozhan shi* xiezuozu. *Hongnan zuozhan shi* (The warring history of Hongnan). Shanghai: Shanghai renmin chubanshe, 1972.
Shen Congwen. *The Border Town and Other Stories.* Beijing: Zhongguo wenxue zazhishe, 1981.
———. *Shen Congwen wenji* (Collected works of Shen Congwen). 12 vols. Guangzhou: Huacheng chubanshe, 1982.
Shi Shuqing. "Weile baochou xie xiaoshuo: Yu Can Xue tan xiezuo" (Writing fiction for revenge: Talking about writing with Can Xue). *Shengdian de qingpi: Can Xue zhi mi* (The collapse of the sanctuary: The enigma of Can Xue). Ed. Xiao Yuan, 435–44. Guiyang: Guizhou renmin chubanshe, 1993.
Stanzel, F. K. *Narrative Situations in the Novel: Tom Jones, Moby-Dick, The Ambassadors, Ulysses.* Trans. James P. Pusack. Bloomington: Indiana University Press, 1971.
Sun Longji (Sun Lung-kee). *Zhongguo wenhua de "shenceng jiegou"* (The deep structure of Chinese culture). Hong Kong: Yishan chubanshe, 1983.
Tan Yunchang. "Xing'ershangxue youxi: ping Ge Fei de xiaoshuo 'Xianjing'" (A metaphysical game: On Ge Fei's short story "The Pitfall"). *Guandong wenxue* (Guandong Literature) 1987.12: 39–42.
Tang, Xiaobing. "The Function of New Theory: What Does It Mean to Talk about Postmodernism in China?" In *Politics, Ideology, and Literary Discourse in Modern China.* Ed. Liu Kang and Xiaobing Tang, 278–300. Durham: Duke University Press, 1993.
———. "Lu Xun's 'A Madman's Diary' and a Chinese Modernism." *PMLA* 107.5 (1992): 1222–34.
Wang, Ban. *The Sublime Figure of History: Aesthetics and Politics in Twentieth-Century China.* Stanford, Calif.: Stanford University Press, 1997.
Wang, David Der-Wei (Wang Dewei). "Chihelasa jian qiguan—ping Mo Yan de *Jiuguo*" (Seeing miracles in eating, drinking, urinating, and defecating: On Mo Yan's *The Republic of Wine*). *Zhongshi wanbao* (China Times [Evening Edition]), January 3, 1993.

———. *Fictional Realism in the Twentieth-Century China*. New York: Columbia University Press, 1992.
Wang Guowei. *Renjian cihua* (Notes on the song lyrics in the human world). Hong Kong: Zhonghua shuju, 1961.
Wang Hui. "Dangdai Zhongguo de sixiang zhuangkuang yu xiandaixing wenti" (Intellectual conditions and the question of modernity in contemporary China). In *Sihuo chongwen* (Dead fire reheated). Beijing: Renmin wenxue chubanshe, 2000.
Wang, Jing. *High Culture Fever: Politics, Aesthetics, and Ideology in Deng's China*. Berkeley: University of California Press, 1996.
Wang Ning. "Constructing Postmodernism: The Chinese Case and Its Different Versions." *Canadian Review of Comparative Literature* 20, nos. 1–2 (March–June 1993): 46–61.
———. "Jieshou yu bianxing: Zhongguo dangdai xianfeng xiaoshuo zhong de houxiandaixing" (Reception and transformation: Postmodernity in contemporary Chinese avant-garde fiction). *Shengcun youxi de shuiquan* (The rings of ripples of the game of existence). Ed. Zhang Guoyi, 133–49. Beijing: Beijingdaxue chubanshe. 1994.
———. "The Mapping of Chinese Postmodernity." *Boundary 2* 24, no. 3 (1997): 19–40.
———. "Yihouji" (Postscript to the translation). *Zouxiang houxiandaizhuyi* (Toward postmodernism). Ed. Wang Ning, 318–25. Beijing: Beijingdaxue chubanshe, 1991.
———. "The Reception of Postmodernism in China: The Case of Avant-Garde Fiction." In *International Postmodernism: Theory and Literary Practice*. Ed. Hans Bertens and Douwe Fokkema, 499–510. Amsterdam, Neth.: Benjamins, 1997.
Wittgenstein, Ludwig. *Tractatus Logico-philosophicus*. Trans. D. F. Pears and B. F. McGuinness. London: Routledge and Kegan Paul, 1961.
Wu Hongsen. "Xu" (Introduction). *Mizhou*, by Ge Fei. Beijing: Zuojia chubanshe, 1989.
Wu Liang. "Xu—Ma Yuan de xushu quantao" (Introduction: Ma Yuan's narrative trap). *Xihai wufanchuan: Ma Yuan Xizang xiaoshuo xuan* (The sail-less boat in the West Sea: A selection of short stories about Tibet by Ma Yuan), by Ma Yuan, 1–14. Lhasa: Xizang renmin chubanshe, 1987.
Wu Liang and Cheng Depei, eds. *Xin xiaoshuo zai 1985 nian* (New fiction in 1985). Shanghai: Shanghai shehuikexueyuan chubanshe, 1986.
Wu Xiaoming (Shang Duo). "Wangxiang, zilian, youyu yu xianshen" (Paranoia, narcissism, melancholia, and self-sacrifice). *Jintian* (Today) 19 (1992.4): 171–90.
Xiao Hua and Wang Zheng. "Yu Hua xiaoshuo xianxiang." *Shanghai wenlun* (Shanghai Literary Criticism) 5 (1989): 50–55.
Xiao Yuan, ed. *Shengdian de qingpi: Can Xue zhi mi* (The collapse of the sanctuary: The enigma of Can Xue). Guiyang: Guizhou renmin chubanshe, 1993.
Xin Xiaozheng. "Ma Yuan fangwenji" (An interview with Ma Yuan). *Wenxue jiao* (The literary corner) (1988.2): 21–23.

Xu Jie. *Xu Jie Duanpian xiaoshuo xuanji* (Selected short stories of Xu Jie). Beijing: Renmin wenxue chubanshe, 1981.
Xu, Jilin and Chen, Dakai, eds. *Zhongguo xiandaihua shi* (History of modernization in China). Shanghai: Shanghai sanlian shudian, 1995.
Xu Xiaohe. "Shuiling de rizi" (The juicy day). *Hunan wenxue* (Hunan literature) 1988.12: 63–75.
———. *Yuanzhang he tade fengzimen* (The madhouse director and his madmen). Changsha: Hunan wenyi chubanshe, 1987.
———. *Yuanzhang he tade fengzimen* (The madhouse director and his madmen). Taipei: Yuanjing chubanshe, 1989.
Xu Yuanchong, trans. *Shijing* (Book of poetry). Changsha: Hunan chubanshe.
Xu Zhimo. "'Xinyue' de taidu" (The attitude of the "Crescent"). *Xinyue* 1, no. 1 (1928): 3–10.
———. *Xu Zhimo shiji* (Collected poems of Xu Zhimo). Chengdu: Sichuan renmin chubanshe, 1981.
Yan Yu. "Canglang shihua" (Canglang's remarks on poetry). *Lidai shihua* (Remarks on poetry from all ages). Ed. He Wenhuan, 685–708. Beijing: Zhonghua shuju, 1981.
Yang Xiaobin. "Yiyi shang, pintieshu yu xushu zhi wu: Ma Yuan xiaoshuo zhong de houxiandaizhuyi" (Entropy of meaning, collage, and the dance of narration: Postmodernism in Ma Yuan's fiction). *Wenyi zhengming* 1987.6: 55–60.
Yu Dafu. *Yu Dafu wenji* (Collected works of Yu Dafu). 12 vols. Guangzhou: Huangcheng chubanshe, 1982–84.
Yu Hua. "One Kind of Reality." In *Running Wild: New Chinese Writers*. Ed. David Der-wei Wang, 21–68. New York: Columbia University Press, 1994.
———. *The Past and the Punishments*. Trans. Andrew F. Jones. Honolulu: University of Hawaii Press, 1996.
———. "Wo de zhenshi" (The truth to me). *Renmin wenxue* (People's Literature) 1989.3: 107–8.
———. *Yu Hua zuopin ji* (The collected works of Yu Hua). 3 vols. Beijing: Zhongguo shehuikexue chubanshe, 1995.
Yuan Zhen. "The Story of Ts'ui Yingying." Trans. Arthur Waley. In *Anthology of Chinese Literature: From Early Times to the Fourteenth Century*. Ed. Cyril Birch, 290–99. New York: Grove Press, 1965.
Zhang Dinghuang. "Lu Xun xiansheng" (Mr. Lu Xun). Originally published in *Xiandai pinglun* (Modern Criticism) (January 1925). See *Liushi nian lai Lu Xun yanjiu lunwen xuan* (Selected essays in Lu Xun studies over the past sixty years). Vol. 1. Ed. Li Zongying and Zhang Mengyang, 29–38. Beijing: Zhongguo shehuikexue chubanhse, 1982.
Zhang Guoyi, ed. *Shengcun youxi de shuiquan* (The rings of ripples of the game of existence). Beijing: Beijingdaxue chubanshe. 1994.
Zhang Xinying. "Kongju yu kongju de xiaojie" (Fear and the dissolution of fear). *Renmin wenxue* (People's Literature) 1989.1.
Zhang Xudong. *Chinese Modernism in the Era of Reforms: Cultural Fever, Avant-Garde Fiction, and the New Chinese Cinema*. Durham, N.C.: Duke University Press, 1997.

Zhang Yiwu. "Chanshi Zhongguo de jiaolü" (The anxiety of interpreting China). *Ershiyi shiji* (Twentieth-First Century) 28 (April 1995): 128–35.

———. "Lixiangzhuyi de zhongjie: Shiyan xiaoshuo de wenhua tiaozhan" (The end of idealism: Cultural challenge of the experimental fiction). *Shengcun youxi de shuiquan* (The rings of ripples of the game of existence). Ed. Zhang Guoyi, 106–21. Beijing: Beijingdaxue chubanshe, 1994.

———. *Zai bianyuanchu zhuixun: Disanshijie wenhua yu Zhongguo dangdai wenxue* (Pursuing at the margin: Third world culture and contemporary Chinese literature). Changchun: Shidai wenyi chubanshe, 1993.

Zhao Yiheng (Henry Y H Zhao). "'Houxue' yu Zhongguo xinbaoshouzhuyi" (Post-Isms and Chinese new conservatism). *Ershiyi shiji* (Twentieth-First Century) 31 (February 1995): 4–15.

———. "The New Waves in Recent Chinese Fiction." *The Lost Boat*. Ed. Henry Y H Zhao, 9–20. London: Wellsweep Press, 1993.

———. "Post-Isms and Chinese New Conservatism." *New Literary History* 28, no. 1 (1997): 31–44.

———. "Yu Hua: Fiction as Subversion." *World Literature Today* 65, no. 3 (summer 1991): 415–20.

———. "'Yuan yishi' he dangdai Zhongguo xianfeng xiaoshuo" ("Meta-consciousness" and contemporary Chinese avant-garde fiction). *Jintian* (Today) 1 (1990): 79–88, 78.

Zhu Xi. *Sishu zhangju jizhu* (A variorum of the four books). Beijing: Zhonghua shuju, 1983.

Zhuang Zi. *Chuang Tzu: Genius of the Absurd*. Arranged from the work of James Legge by Clae Waltham. New York: Ace Books, 1971.

Index

Absoluteness, 34, 102, 118, 156, 163, 169, 243
Adorno, Theodor, viii, 11, 52–54, 95, 97–99, 110, 164, 230, 252nn. 1, 2
Ah Cheng, 35–36, 220–21, 255n. 1
Allegory/allegorical, 37, 40, 60, 65–66, 86–90, 113, 123, 142, 153, 170–71, 192, 204, 212–19, 223–24, 259n. 5
Althusser, Louis, 101–2, 165, 253n. 5
Analects, 29, 219
Anderson, Marston, viii, 7, 11, 16
Anti-Rightist Movement, 48, 75, 102, 134, 231
Arendt, Hannah, 80
Authoritarianism, 148, 231, 235, 241
Avant-gardism/avant-garde, 3, 23, 44, 247n. 3; Chinese, vii, 35–44, 52–53, 55, 95–98, 110, 245

Bai Hua, 21
Ba Jin, 5, 13–15, 17, 43; *Family*, 14–15, 17, 248n. 10; *Ward Number Four*, 256n. 5
Bakhtin, M. M., 109, 116
Bataille, Georges, 61–62, 252n. 4
Baudelaire, Charles, 107, 109, 130
Beckett, Samuel, 111, 127, 140
Bei Cun, 39
Benjamin, Walter, 40, 73, 207, 250n. 7
Bhabha, Homi, 236
Bing Xin, 5
Bloom, Harold, 52, 54
Book of Changes (Yijing), 9
Book of Poetry (Shijing), 257n. 4
Borges, Luis Jorge, 247n. 3

Buddhism, 166, 212, 220

Cai Xiang, 257n. 1
Cai Yuanpei, 7–8
Cannibalism, 28–29, 33, 190, 212–14, 218–27
Can Xue, vii, viii, 26, 28, 37, 38, 44, 48, 52, 55, 74–92, 106, 109, 112, 129–49, 154, 190, 250n. 8; "Apple Trees in the Corridor," 76–81, 129; "The Beautiful Summer in the South," 75; *Breakout Performances*, 129, 134–37; "Hut on the Mountain," 37, 90–91; *Old Float Cloud*, 81–87, 129, 133; "The Ox," 91–92; "The Skylight," 76; "Soap Bubbles on Dirty Water," 37, 87–89; "The Things That Happened to Me in That World," 76; *A Thought Report*, 129, 137–49; *Yellow Mud Street*, 38, 76, 129, 130–34
Cao Xueqin, 10
Caruth, Cathy, 47, 55, 81
Catachresis, 96, 100, 115, 120, 130–35, 149, 213
Chang, Kang-I Sun, viii
Cheng Fangwu, 6
Chen Kaige, 252n. 3, 256n. 6
Chen Xiaoming, 48, 50, 179, 181, 232, 237–38, 260n. 10
Chou Ying-hsiung, 212
Ci, Jiwei, 241
Communist literature, 18, 21–22, 26, 35, 83, 100–101, 113–15, 144, 153, 157, 159, 195, 226
Confucianism, 4, 9, 11, 166, 252n. 3

281

Confucius, 4, 9, 29, 219
Creation Society (*Chuangzao she*), 5
Crescent Society (*Xinyue she*), 6
Cultural Revolution, 19, 20–21, 30, 43, 48–51, 55, 57, 70, 81, 102, 110, 112, 130, 134, 154, 230–31, 251n. 4

Dai Jinhua, 70, 72, 261n. 11
Darwin, Charles, 80
Decadence, viii, 24, 209, 220, 226
Deferred action. See *Nachträglichkeit*
Deleuze, Gilles, 246, 250n. 1
de Man, Paul, 107–8, 118, 159
Deng Xiaoping, 123, 240–44, 249nn. 12, 13, 259n. 5
Derrida, Jacques, 53, 73, 110, 164–65
Dialectics, 101–2, 233; historical, 20, 24, 80, 135, 153, 185, 188; Maoist, 101–2, 253n. 6; Marxist, 18, 21; master-slave, 142, negative, 97–99, 110
Didacticism, 7–8, 11
Diegesis (vs. mimesis), 13–14, 43, 186, 248n. 8, 249n. 11
Ding Ling, 16, 18, 100, 178; "Miss Sophie's Diary," 16; *The Sun Shines over the Sanggan River*, 18, 100
Dirlik, Arif, 234, 242, 259n. 1
Duara, Prasenjit, 247n. 5
Du Pengcheng, 27

Eagleton, Terry, vii
Egan, Ronald, 248n. 6
Eliot, T. S., 87, 206
Emancipation, 5–6, 8, 12, 31, 87, 169–70, 186, 216, 243
Enlightenment discourse, 4, 11–12, 16, 24, 30, 98, 214, 240, 247n. 5, 249n. 11, 252n. 2
Escher, M. C., 187

Faulkner, William, 247n. 3
Fei Ming, 23
Felman, Shoshana, 119–20
Feng Mu, 19–20
Feng Yuanjun, 169

Foucault, Michel, 111, 118, 163–64
Freud, Sigmund, vii, 48–49, 54, 83, 85, 99, 231, 250n. 1
Fu Sinian, 250n. 4

García Márquez, 247n. 3
Gastronomy, 218–22
Ge Fei, viii, 26, 39–40, 48, 52, 112, 168–87, 188; *The Enemy*, 40; "A Flock of Brown Birds," 39, 172–75; "Green-Yellow," 40, 179–83; "The Lost Boat," 40, 176–79, 188; "New Year," 40, 176; "No One Sees the Grasses Grow," 39; "Oblivion," 184; "The Ornamented Zither," 184–87; "The Pitfalls," 39, 169–72
"Genius-and-beauty" romance, 188–91
Gödel, Kurt, 165
Goldblatt, Howard, vii
Gramsci, Antonio, 253n. 5
Grand narrative(s), 31, 54, 65, 97, 113, 157, 172, 185, 247n. 3
Guo Moruo, 5, 6, 7, 13

Habermas, Jürgen, 118, 164
Han Shaogong, vii, 35, 37–38, 154
Hao Ran, 18
Hartman, Geoffrey, viii
Hassan, Ihab, vii
Hegel, Georg Wilhelm Friedrich, 97–98, 142, 232
Heidegger, Martin, 98, 187
Herman, Judith Lewis, 73
Heterogeneity/heterogeneous, 23, 175, 184
Heteroglossia, 158
Hirsch, David H., 230
Hofstadter, Douglas R., 256n. 7
Hong Lingfei, 178
Honglou meng. See *Story of the Stone*
Horkheimer, Max, 99
Hsia, C. T., 5, 248n. 6, 249n. 11
Huang Jianxin, 261n. 13
Huang Pengji, 23

Index

Hu Shi, 8
Hutcheon, Linda, 108–10, 164
Huters, Ted, 5, 12
Hu Yeping, 178

Incomprehensibility/incomprehensible, 38–39, 43, 48–52, 55, 71, 73, 140, 216, 228
Indeterminacy, 38–39, 79, 123, 125, 180, 197, 235
Intellectual youth fiction, 255n. 1
Intervention, 8, 10–11, 13, 15; authorial, 8, 10–11; narratorial, 13; subjective, 15, 189–90
Irony, viii, 15, 22, 24, 92, 95–110, 157, 159–60, 163–67, 223, 228; postmodern, 109–10

Jade-Charming-Pear (Yu Jiao Li), 257n. 2
Jameson, Fredric, vii, 232, 234–35, 250n. 7, 259n. 4
Janssen, Ronald, 177
Jiang Guangci, 178
Jiang Zilong, 20
Jia Pingwa, 258n. 4
Jin Guantao, 253n. 6
Jin Shengtan, 10
Journey to the West (Xiyou ji), 27, 212–13, 222–23
Joyce, James, 247n. 3

Kafka, Franz, 62, 87, 247n. 3; 258n. 5
Kant, Immanuel, vii, 16, 52, 251n. 5
Kierkegaard, Søren, 98–99, 107, 110
Kong Jiesheng, 255n. 1
Knight-errant tale, 188–89, 194–96

Lao She, 13, 14
Lao Zi (Lao Tzu), 252n. 3
Lee, Leo Ou-fan, 28
Legalism, 252n. 3
Lei Feng, 252n. 4
Lenin, Vladimir Ilyich, 235

Liang Bin, 27
Liang Qichao, 6–7
Liang Xiaosheng, 255n. 1, 258n. 4
Li Bai (Li Po), 29
Li Baojia, 13, 248n. 6
Lie Zi, 244
Lifton, Robert Jay, 51
Li Hangyu, 35–36
Li Jianwu, 23
Li Jie, 51, 251n. 2
Lin Yü-sheng, 250n. 4
Li Shangyin, 184–87
Literary Mind Carving Dragons (Wenxin diaolong), 10
Li Tuo, 247n. 1, 251n. 2
Li Tuozhi, 23
Liu, Kang, 235, 237–38, 253n. 5
Liu Binyan, 21–22
Liu E, 13
Liu Heng, 220–21
Liu Suola, 37
Liu Zaifu, 18
Li Xiguang, 235
Lu, Sheldon Hsiao-peng, 260n. 10
Lu Wenfu, 220–21
Lu Xinhua, 20
Lu Xun, 11, 16, 28–35, 44, 56–57, 58, 89, 90, 120, 144, 198–200, 222–23, 250nn. 4, 5, 6, 254n. 3; "An Account of the Abrupt Visit of 'Mr. Yang Shuda,'" 31–33; "Forging the Swords," 194; "A Madman's Diary," 28–35, 58, 60, 90–91, 120–21, 198–200, 222–23, 250nn. 4, 5, 251n. 3; "My Old Home," 37; "New Year Sacrifice," 16–17; "On the Power of Mára Poetry," 29–30; "Preface to *Call to Arms*," 86; "A Public Example," 114; "Remorse for the Past," 169
Lu Yanzhou, 20
Lu Yin, 5
Lyotard, François, vii–viii, 52, 54, 135, 227–28, 231, 242–43, 247n. 3, 251n. 5, 259n. 3, 261n. 14

Madness, 29, 43, 58, 107, 112–28, 131–34, 166; feigned, 31–34
Mao Dun, 5, 7–8, 13, 15–16, 24–26, 121; "The Autumn of Guling," 26; *Eclipse*, 24; "The Madman," 121; *Midnight*, 5, 15; *Rainbow*, 14; *Vacillation*, 24–26
Maoism, 19, 101, 243
Maoist discourse, vii–viii, 50–52, 69, 101–7, 113, 118–19, 132–33, 137, 153, 164–65, 225–27, 243–45, 251nn. 2, 3, 4, 254n. 4
Mao Zedong, 19, 27, 30, 84, 101–5, 112, 123, 134, 242, 251n. 4, 252n. 3, 253n. 4, 259n. 5; *On Contradiction*, 101–3, 253n. 6
Marcuse, Herbert, viii
Marx, Karl, 208, 226, 241
Marxism, 80, 214, 232, 234
May Fourth era: intellectuals of, 4, 7, 11, 87, 190; writers of, 5, 11
Ma Yuan, vii, 26, 37, 39, 48, 112, 153–67; "Fabrication," 158–60; "The Sailless Boat in the West Sea," 162–63; "The Temptation of Gangdisê," 37, 39, 154–57, 163; "Three Ways of Folding Kites," 157–58; *Up or Down, Always Smooth*, 154; "The Wall with Graffiti," 160–62; "The Wandering God," 160
Mencius, 257n. 1
Metafiction, 163
Mian Mian, 260n. 6
Mimesis. *See* Diegesis (vs. mimesis)
Mise-en-abyme, 164, 167, 185–87, 256n. 6
Misrepresentation, 33–34, 53, 100, 111, 120, 172, 228
Model opera, 18, 103
Modernism, 109, 233, 247n. 3
Modernity, 3–13, 33, 35, 44, 188, 239; Chinese, 3–4, 11, 230–32, 240–42; historical, 8; literary, 13, 27; Maoist, 253n. 5; political, 30; Western, 253n. 5

Mo Yan, vii, viii, 21, 28, 207–29; *The Herbivorous Family*, 209; *Red Sorghum: A Family Saga*, 207–8, 214, 216–17, 228; *The Republic of Wine*, 208–29; *Thirteen Steps*, 208; "The Transparent Carrots," 207

Nachträglichkeit (deferred action or aftereffect), 48–49, 53, 231, 259n. 3
Narration, 8, 17–18; ambiguous, 23; authoritarian, 17; decentered, 23; displaced, 43; narrator, 42–44; omniscient, 17; subjective, 8
Neo-Confucianism, 247n. 4, 253n. 6
New-era literature, 19, 21
New literature movement, 7
Newmark, Kevin, viii
Nietzsche, Friedrich Wilhelm, 29

Ode to the Dragon River (Longjiang song), 159
On the Docks (Haigang), 103–7, 115, 118, 130–31, 159, 226, 254nn. 6, 7
Orwell, George, 251n. 2

Parabasis, 159–60, 163
Paradigm, cultural/literary, 3, 34, 240, 242–43; of May Fourth literature, 120; of modern Chinese literature, 6, 8, 12, 23, 38, 100–101, 109, 243–44; political, 240, 242–43; rhetorical, 244
Paranoia, 28–35, 38, 60, 197
Parody, 38, 108–9, 113, 118, 124, 175, 176, 186, 188–89, 196, 254n. 3, 256n. 3
Pickowicz, Paul, 261n. 13
Plaks, Andrew, 166
Plato, 248n. 8
Plum in the Golden Vase (Jin ping mei), 221–22
Post–Cultural Revolution, 230–31, 259n. 2
Post–Mao-Deng, 235, 239, 240–46

Index

Postmodernity/postmodernism, 3, 44, 52, 109, 231–46; Chinese, vii, 231–46; Western, 235, 247n. 3
Postsocialism, 242, 261n. 13
Premodernity, 4
Průšek, Jaroslav, 13, 14, 16, 248nn. 6, 7
Pu Songling, 193

Qu You, 252n. 5

Realism, 206; Chinese, 11–13, 23–24, 34; pseudo-, 18
Reform literature, 20
Reik, Theodore, 96
Retrospective literature, 20
Revolutionary literature, 6
Richards, I. A., 108
Ricoeur, Paul, 165
Robbe-Grillet, Alain, 247n. 3
Romance of the Three Kingdoms (Sanguo yanyi), 248n. 6
Root-seeking literature, 35–36, 113, 207

Sartre, Jean-Paul, 79
Scar literature, 20, 53
Scatology, 127, 218
Schizophrenia, 28, 35, 38, 91, 108, 254n. 1
Schlegel, Friedrich von, 159–60
Self-critical/self-critique, 16, 212, 228, 245
Self-deconstruction, 3, 23, 40, 108, 223, 228
Self-referentiality, 15, 19, 97, 107, 166–67, 224
Self-reflexivity, 164, 216
Shajiabang, 253n. 6
Shen Congwen, 122, 249n. 11
Shen Deqian, 10
Shi Zhecun, 23
Sikong Tu, 9
Sima Qian, 248n. 6
Story of the Stone (Honglou meng), 10, 84, 166, 221–22, 248n. 9
Strange Tales from Make-Do Studio (Liaozhai zhiyi), 193, 201, 258nn. 7, 8
Subject/subjectivity, 4, 11–16; absolute, 23; authorial/authoritative, 10, 42, 97; collective, 24; critical, 16, 215; decadent, 212; disintegration of, 42, 47–48, 246; historical, 4, 11–12, 16–18, 23–24, 35, 215, 229, 247n. 5; homogeneous, 23; limitation of, 43; madness of, 43; modern, 4, 183–84; narrative, 8, 183, 186, 228; narratorial, 190; national, 4, 235; omniscient/omnipotent, 4, 11–12, 17, 38, 47, 244; paranoid, 197; personal, 24; postmodern, 110, 246; rational, 57; representational, 11–19, 23–24, 38, 47, 48, 209, 215, 243–45; repression and censorship of, 44; romantic, 12; self-critical, 16; superior, 11–12; transcendental, 17, 229
Sublime, the, 52, 54–55, 228, 251n. 5
Sun Fuyuan, 31
Sun Ganlu, 39
Sun Lung-kee, 218
Symbol, 84–85, 114, 133, 225
Symbolism, 5, 25, 35, 37, 114

Taking the Tiger Mountain by Strategy (Zhiqu Weihushan), 214–15, 253n. 8
Tale of the Red Lamp (Hongdeng ji), 253n. 8
Tang Xiaobing, 245, 250n. 5
Tan Yunchang, 169
Taoism, 9, 177, 220, 252n. 3
Telos/teleology, 5, 21, 24, 50, 153, 156, 185–86, 188, 232, 241, 247n. 5
Tiananmen Incident, 55, 134, 208
Traditional Chinese fiction, 8, 14
Traditional Chinese literature/poetics, 9
Trauma, 42, 47–55, 57, 60–61, 62, 66, 70, 73, 85–86, 92, 95–96, 124, 230, 245, 250n. 1; historical, vii

Unconscious, 48–49, 52–55, 59–60, 62, 72–73, 76–81, 88, 90, 95–97, 205, 245
Unrepresentability/unrepresentable, 100
Utopia/utopianism, 51, 241

Violence, historical, 47–48, 57, 64, 66, 97

Wang, Ban, 83, 241, 251n. 4, 254n. 1
Wang, David Der-wei, viii, 5, 24, 30, 224
Wang, Jing, 232, 247n. 1
Wang Guowei, 9–10
Wang Hui, 4
Wang Meng, 19, 185–86
Wang Ning, 232–34, 260n. 5
Wang Ruowang, 21
Wang Shizhen, 9
Wang Shuo, 119–20
Warring History of Hongnan,The, 18–19
Water Margins (Shuihu), 27
Wei Hui, 260n. 6
Wen Yiduo, 5
Wittgenstein, Ludwig, 165
Wu Hongsen, 182
Wu Liang, 156
Wu Woyao, 13
Wu Xiaoming, 30

Xu Ben, 232, 237
Xu Jie, 249n.11
Xu Xiaohe, vii, viii, 28, 37, 106, 109, 111–28, 129, 154, 190; "The Bathhouse," 118; "Human Beings or Red-Hair Bigfoots," 113–15; "The Juicy Days," 123–27; "The Madhouse Director and His Madmen," 37, 38, 112; "The Madmen and Their Madhouse Director," 115–18, 127; "The Specimen," 118
Xu Zhimo, 6

Yang Mo, 178
Yan Yu, 9
Ye Shengtao, 83, 247n. 4
Yuan Zhen, 257n. 3
Yu Dafu, 5, 13, 37, 196–98, 258n. 8
Yu Hua, viii, 26, 27, 39, 40–44, 52, 55, 56–73, 74, 77, 112, 154, 188–205, 251nn. 1, 2, 252n. 5; "The April Third Incident," 44, 70, 196–200; "A Classical Romance," 44, 189–94; "The Inescapable Fate," 4, 67–70; "Nineteen Eighty-Six," 40, 57–62, 69, 251n. 3; "Occasional Incidents," 70; "One Kind of Reality," 40, 44, 66–67, 69; "The Past and Punishment," 44, 62–66, 70; "Plum Blossoms of Flesh Blood," 189, 194–96; "A Story Dedicated to the Girl Willow," 44, 196, 200–206; "World Like Mist," 70–72

Zhang, Xudong, 183, 234, 259n. 1
Zhang Chengzhi, 25, 255n. 1
Zhang Wei, 19
Zhang Xinying, 252n. 2
Zhang Yimou, 251n. 1, 258n. 1
Zhang Yiwu, 19, 232–38, 260n. 9
Zhang Zhupo, 10
Zhao, Henry Y.-H. (Zhao Yiheng), 3, 166, 196, 232, 236–39, 260n. 11
Zhao Shuli, 258n. 3
Zhao Yiheng. *See* Zhao, Henry Y.-H.
Zheng Min, 237
Zhiyanzhai, 10
Zhou Libo, 18
Zhou Zuoren, 31
Zhuang Zi/*Zhuang Zi*, 166, 184–86, 252n. 3, 256n. 4
Zhu Dake, 251n. 2
Zhu Xi, 29
Zuo Commentary, The (Zuo zhuan), 248n. 6

OHIO **'ERSITY LIBRARY**